MAIL-ORDERS

THE SUNY SERIES IN
POSTMODERN CULTURE
Joseph Natoli, *Editor*

MAIL-ORDERS

The Fiction of Letters in Postmodern Culture

SUNKA SIMON

State University
of New York
Press

Published by
State University of New York Press, Albany

Printed in the United States of America

For information, address State University of New York Press,
90 State Street, Suite 700, Albany, NY 12207

Production by Susan Geraghty
Marketing by Jennifer Giovani
Cover art by the author

Library of Congress Cataloging-in-Publication Data

Simon, Sunka.
    Mail-orders : the fiction of letters in postmodern culture / Sunka Simon.
       p. cm. — (SUNY series in postmodern culture)
    Includes bibliographical references and index.
    ISBN 0-7914-5349-9 (alk. paper) — ISBN 0-7914-5350-2 (pbk. : alk. paper)
       1. Epistolary fiction—History and criticism. 2. Letters in literature. 3. Literature,
    Modern—20th century—History and criticism. I. Title. II. Series.

PN3448.E6 S49 2002
809.3′04—dc21
                                                                         2001041118

10 9 8 7 6 5 4 3 2 1

CONTENTS

Acknowledgments   *vii*

Preface and Postal Route   *ix*

1. A Briefing   1

     Mailing Women and Feminisms   5
     Epistolary Theory and Fiction: A Postmodern Poetics?   12

2. Rhapsody in Letters: Ingeborg Bachmann's *Malina*   19

     Epistolary Metonymy or the Letter as Metaphor   20
     Rhapsody and Letters   23
     Rhapsody #1–4   28

3. Chain Mail: Letters°Postcards°Travel Guides . . . ?
     Barth, Derrida, and Levi   59

        "LETTERS"   71
        "POSTCARD"   95
        "TRAVEL GUIDE"   122

4. Mass-Mailing: The Language Hazard   139

     Mail-Order Manual   148
     The Discourse of the Other   153

5. Romancing the Post:
     Peter Handke's *Short Letter, Long Farewell*   165

6. Mail-Art: *Einsteckalbum*   197

     First Insert: Nick Bantock's *Griffin and Sabine*   197
     Second Insert: Karl Schaper's "Post Office of Thanatos"   203
     Third Insert: Nicomedes Suárez-Araúz's *Amnesis Art*   206

7. Posting E-Mail   213

    Posting 1 on "the electronic word"   220
    Posting 2 on *Exegesis*   223
    Posting 3 on *The Postman*   227

P.S.   239

Notes   *243*

Selected Bibliography   *297*

Author and Title Index   *313*

Subject Index   *321*

ACKNOWLEDGMENTS

Lieber Mike! Dir danke ich für deine Liebesbriefe aus NY, Düsseldorf und Ohio, für deine Treue und Zuversicht in unsere Zukunft seit 1983. Liebe Eva and Dieter! Ich danke euch beiden für eure vielen Briefe in den Südwesten damals 1978/79 und in den Nordosten seit 1986. Für eure seelische und körperliche Unterstützung, euer Vertrauen in mein Selbstvertrauen und für die vielseitigen Anregungen aus stundenlangen intensiven Gesprächen werde ich mich hoffentlich noch lange immer wieder zu bedanken haben.

Dear Tamsin, Liliane, and Dick Macksey! I sincerely thank you for your friendship, for your influential contribution to my educational and professional development, for your invaluable critical feedback to *Mail-Orders*, your attention to detail, especially regarding style.

Dear anonymous readers and fellow critics of epistolarity! Thanks for your acumen, your fabulous suggestions, your constructive criticisms, your wit, and your time. I hope you will enjoy reading your mail a second time around.

Dear James, Joseph, Susan, Jennifer, and Katie! Thank you and SUNY Press for your editorial guidance and your continuing support of this project.

Dear Daniel Schenker, Craig Hawks, and Susan Kray! Thank you for allowing me to reprint the revised Karl Schaper section of my "Mail-Art: Posting Postmodernity" paper, which appeared in your published conference proceedings *Inner Space-Outer Space: Humanities, Technology, and the Postmodern World*, ed. Daniel Schenker, Craig Hawks, and Susan Kray (Huntsville: Southern Humanities Press, 1993), 105–119.

Dear editors! I collected the postal material that occasionally appeared in my mailbox and now appears in boxes throughout the text of *Mail-Orders* from personal observation, from the unused portion of my research, from various newspapers throughout the past ten years, from my personal mail and e-mail, from advertisement clippings sent to me by friends. As *objects trouvés*, they are vital to the understanding of mail-orders I am developing in the book, so please leave them in, even though some of them might not have a date, return address, or destination. Thanks!

PREFACE AND
POSTAL ROUTE

1. Modernist mail-orders: to secure all channels, to make the process of communication and its content fail-safe, to return to sender by default, to guarantee delivery, to obey the privacy of the post.

2. Postmodernist mail-orders: to read "displacements" as spatial and temporal dislocations that are neither absolute nor necessarily chronological, not to think of displacement as the replacement of a singular object by another singular object but rather to trace the multiplicity and multidirectionality of messages, of mediation, of envelopes, and of dislocations.

3. ───

Date: Mon, 22 January 2001 11:34:xx (EST)
From: ssimon@swarthmore.edu
To: readers@sunypress.com
Subject: Mail-Orders

───

Thesis of book: The modernist fiction of letters as one-on-one written communication whose contained messages deliver the enlightened modern subject has become its postmodern crisis, a crisis of the subject, of identity, of culture. This book investigates the miscarrying transitions between modernist and postmodernist mail-orders by reading the epistolary relay-tionships among literature, theory, film, electronic media, and the arts.

:) Sunka Simon

Notwithstanding the internationally recognized privacy of the post, letters, their writers, and their recipients continue to be affected by interceptions, exchanges, and re- as well as misdirections. In turn, letters determine our understanding of the communication process by actually and metaphorically shaping what transpires between send-off and arrival. E-mail and the Internet have but increased the proclivity of messages to disappear, to appear elsewhere, to carry software viruses, to be read by strangers, co-workers, or the e-mail system itself (as is the case in Astro Teller's 1997 novel *Exegesis*). Yet, these so-called messages, supposedly simple exchanges of information in an intranet of a company or between e-mailers in a chatroom have reattained some of traditional letters' romantic and erotic potential not despite but because of their factious waywardness.

It seems that the displacement of modernist aesthetics and its epistolarily derived subjectivity has not been absolute. The subject of letters still matters. In prefacing the state of letters and mail-orders at the beginning of the twenty-first century, I seek to locate not only the subject of mail-orders but also subjectivity. In historical epistolary criticism, this dual task was often achieved by manipulating or faking a dislocation, physically, culturally, historically, technologically, fictionally, emotionally, and/or sexually. The middle class's subjectivity was constructed aesthetically by fictionally pitting it against a corrupt aristocracy (Samuel Richardson's *Pamela*) and a "marginal subject's point of view" (a woman, a non-European, an emigrant, a worker, a prostitute). In eighteenth-century white, male-dominated European culture, an author might have taken on the role of editor, the editor the role of confidant, playing French translator of a Peruvian woman's letters.[1] Suffice it to say at this point that the enlightened middle-class subject, negotiating the broadening split of public and private spheres, mail-ordered itself via its colonial and colonized Others. In the postwar crisis of modernity, it is therefore not surprising to see a renaissance of the letter form and discussions of epistolarity (as a mode and a genre), which began in Germany and France around 1970 and in the United States a decade later, thus coinciding with the transcontinental delay of the arrival of postmodernism and poststructuralism. Here, too, academic critics have turned to epistolary fiction and "real letters" S.O.S-ing for Western culture's "lost subjectivity," for a lost sense of wonder in language. In the wake of third-wave feminism and cultural studies, epistolary critics have been searching for "ethnic authenticity" and "active respondent[s]," while hoping to elicit "dear reader"- sympathies from an audience grown weary of theory.[2]

Indeed, this preface should be my opportunity to get up close and personal with the reader. This genre-induced, playful proximity between author and reader in the preface is not much different from the fictionalized authenticity within the epistolary discourse of desire. The catchword here is "desire." What am I programmed to desire in writing this preface? Is it a second-wave feminist desire for a homogeneous community or a third-wave feminist desire to connect through recognition of racial, ethnic, class, sex, and gender differences? Or is it a humanist desire to return to a pre-postmodern condition through a nostalgic parody of intermediate immediacy? The "dear reader" gesture reminds me of a MacGyver maneuver: a voice-over monologic dialogue that introduces the speaker as a traditionally male-defined subject who assembles the chaotic pieces, including language, around him in a godlike manner, yet remains himself undivided—as narrating subject and as narrative. In the desire to initiate or bear witness to a passing of poststructuralism, posting the freshly deconstructed self as the new departure point might make the postman ring twice—to verify the address, to gather a signature, to deliver more posts, to remail male-orders.

While supposedly a straightforward introduction to the central focus of a study, the preface "has become a space for gender-specific poetological reflection."[3] It seems that the genre of the preface cannot stand apart from my consideration of contemporary mail-orders but has to be a part of it. What then is this relationship among the preface and letter-writing, the letter as genre, epistolary fiction, and mail-orders? And is it possible that in the process of describing the relationship I can also delineate what I understand under mail-orders without pretending I am on the outside? In his *Postcard*, Jacques Derrida attempts precisely this by instructing the reader in his "first" line of the untitled preface to "*Envois*": "You may read these *envois* as the preface to a book that I have not written,"[4] because any preface that would be written prior to having the body of the text in place would most likely be an introduction to a different text altogether. Derrida thus not only plays on a long-standing tradition of prefaces to "collected," that is, fictional, letters, among the most famous ones those written by Samuel Richardson and Jean-Jacques Rousseau, he also treats his letter-novel "Envoy" as part of a spatial-temporal distortion that connects these "collected" letters structurally to their prefaces.[5]

Prefaces and letters share an intense involvement in literary reflections, subjectivity, and cultural practices. Both genres depend on processes of literary legitimization. It has not been long since the question whether letters were worthy of critical attention was answered in the negative. The only legitimacy for a preface, on the other hand, is its teleological purpose, developing a trajectory for the exegesis ("the critical explanation or interpretation of a text").[6] Literary criticism and poetological reflections have long focused on cultural practices exhibited in letters from different centuries, have used letters and the epistolary mode of writing and reading as indicators of the state of individuality, of gender roles, of society, of literature in general. But inseparable from this, the very aesthetic and cultural codes these letters exhibited and to which they were exposed determined—and still determine—their "worth" as documents or fiction. Since each written letter, whenever it is read, continues to arrive anew, literary critics, while protracting the mail-order also tend to arrest the letter in midtransport, purloining it from its addressee and redirecting it to themselves. Sometimes, they describe only those letters that they, due to their ruling mail-order, can receive, sometimes only those they would have wanted or wish to receive.

A letter, real or metaphorical, is a dispatch; its very existence as a letter presupposes a detachment from its originating environment (writer, sender, place, time) but also its arrival at another time elsewhere. That is why letters to a higher degree than other genres have been considered extraliterary. As missives, letters have a physical and psychological impact upon the times, people, and places at their release, in transfer, and at their arrivals. The myth about prefaces is that they, too, can influence the reader precisely because they appear to stand apart from the main text; like Hugo von Hofmannsthal's famous "Lord Chandos Letter," they, too, have been written after the end of writing. Due to their function as quasi-autobiographies of the textual process, they help to authenticate the body of text through the author's supposedly much more perceptible because generically legitimized subjectivity. And here the circle closes. In the heyday of epistolary culture, a "discovered bag of mail" by the editor writing the preface to the supposed "collection of letters" served to authenticate fiction via fiction.

Precisely because the preface is a first and last attempt to claim the text as his own, to already sign what is supposedly still unborn with the always uncertain paternal authorial name, Derrida points out to the reader at the very beginning of his *Postcard* that his addresses have as yet to find their destinations and vice versa. In their place is either a gap, a lack, where there should be a text or another, an unfamiliar, text. And this lack of text or "other" of the text is disconcerting for a Western tradition based on the prevalence of speech over writing, of the paternal over the maternal, and on the illusion of transparency among sign, signifier, and signified. But instead of becoming that other text, the lack continuously turns out and bears the paternal name.[7] Derrida's "Envois" "accepts" these occidental premises as one would a certified letter that cannot be opened until signed for.

This certified letter functions like the blind spot of the oedipal conflict. Seeing what cannot and culturally should not be seen—the lack of the phallic signifier—has become the definitive scene of sexual identification and gender role assignment for the twentieth century. The successful repression of this knowledge, not the knowledge of what one has seen, but the knowledge that the crisis of binary thinking lies at the very foundation of subject formation, is thus written into the DNA of narratological sequencing and epistolarity. It should therefore not come as a surprise that letters—which rely on this foundational paradox to function—surface throughout modern and postmodern literature, the arts, and other media, even though they have often been proclaimed "dead on arrival" since the fin de siècle.[8] In the spirit of our own fin de siècle, letters appear as psychological baggage, providing our cynical times with a sometimes nostalgic-romantic *You've got Mail*, at other times with a nondetachable and threatening link to the past: *I (still) know what you did last summer*. Akin to Freudian "memory traces," letters act as driftwood on the cerebral ocean of the twentieth century, occasionally serving up the repressed, whether it is desired or not. At the same time, with what Nicomedes Suárez-Araúz calls "letters to amnesia,"[9] they even formulate their own antimnemonic aesthetics by arriving devoid of content in order to be able to send themselves at all. (Such a letter was delivered to the prisoner in the early 1990s short-lived sci-fi TV series *Time Trax*. As both guards and prisoner search in vain for a content—the guards assuming the letter safe to deliver precisely because of the lack of content—the prisoner turns from disappointed reader into unwitting self-sender *and* letter by licking the lips of the envelope, whereupon he vanishes from the cell without a trace.)

These bits and pieces of psychological rubble displaced to the outer fringes of the subconscious consistently produce identity and gender oscillations. While letters may construct the genders of writing and reading, they are themselves constructed by the gendering of mail-orders. Dis/locations of identity and gender assignments are the norm rather than the exception when concerning oneself with letters. After all, uncertainties surrounding an epistolary author's or character's gender and sexual identity have only ever added to and not subtracted from the literary-historical, textual-sexual fascination with the genre's possibilities, the most famous case being the mystery of authorship behind *Les Lettres Portugaises*.[10] For an analysis of the state of letters and mail-orders today, it is important to keep in mind that what you see is (not always) what you get, what you get might not be what you want but something that wants you, and that you might get something you cannot open, read, or, once opened, close. Remember to ask yourself, while you wander through the following museum of undeliverable letters, how what you find there got here and there, what speaks to you and what doesn't, what or who might be missing. Occasionally, you will come upon signposts scattered throughout the book, that urge you to remember that . . .

> mail-orders are made up of letters, playing cards, postcards, tickets, tags, legal briefs, decrees, alphabetic characters or fonts, wills or testaments, notes, manuals of instruction, the desktop pattern of your computer, guides, catalogues, interfaces, networks, search engines . . .

POSTAL ROUTE

"Thoughts meander like a restless wind inside a letter box."
—John Lennon/Paul McCartney

After an investigation into the dialogues among epistolary fiction, feminist criticisms, and modernist and postmodernist literary poetics, the
relationship between women and letters provides an intriguing fictional
beginning for the modern/postmodern debate. In the second chapter, I
therefore follow the gender/genre relays into a feminist interpretation
and rhapsodical usage of the letter form. Ingeborg Bachmann's *Malina*
(1971), prematurely buried by the male-dominated German press, experienced not only a feminist renaissance aided by Anglo-German criticism
in the 1980s, but in turn helped to define and elicit critical feminist reac-
tions to poststructuralist theory and textual practices.

Chapter 3 continues with a reading of three mail-ordered fictions:
John Barth's *LETTERS* (1979), Jacques Derrida's *The Postcard* (1980),
and Jonathan Levi's *A Guide for the Perplexed* (1991). *LETTERS* features a formalistic design that is tightly interspersed with its personae
and its plot, and Levi's novel plays havoc with the idea of orientation
and genealogy. Barth's novel conceives of itself as a highly complex
practice of signification in the process of aborting the "agency" of the
letter design. Are *LETTERS* continued or replaced by *A Guide* or *The
Postcard*? Or, are the sweeping changes in the letter's format, delivery
system, and content supplemental to each other, as the title of a recent
German publication on the correspondences between poststructuralism
and Critical Theory declares: "message-in-a-bottle *and* postcard"?[11] The
merger of epistolary fiction and theory becomes a problem of textual
genealogy, legacy, and cultural status.

With *Erwin's Bathroom or the Hazardousness of Language*
(1984), the popular German author, Hans Bemmann, addresses the
current crisis of language and literature in the shape of a science fiction
novel. It employs epistolary genre history, and the genre's connection
to gender in a partisan effort to reinvent language's revolutionary
potential. Taking my cues from the secret microfiche library in Erwin's
bathroom, Erwin's futuristic literary salon, and Albert's love letters to
Rachel, I inquire into the (post)modernity of Bemmann's mass-mailings
in chapter 4.

Derrida's and Barth's iconoclastic answers to the pessimistic
media-competitive predictions for "letters" (i.e., print culture) necessi-
tate a closer look at the presentation of language critique and genre history in Peter Handke's *Der kurze Brief zum langen Abschied* (*Short
Letter, Long Farewell*, 1972). Through the cinematic lens of *Romanc-*

ing the Stone (1984) chapter 5 follows the letter's potent transmutation into a romanticized filmic relay system.

Chapter 6 takes stock of contemporary mail-art as exhibited emphatically and idiosyncratically by Nick Bantock's *Griffin and Sabine* trilogy (1991–93), Karl Schaper's installations, and Nicomedes Suárez-Araúz's *Amnesis Art* (1973–88). I discuss the reasons why these disparate artists find their medium in the letter. Nick Bantock's expensive coffee table epistolary romances combine aspects of children book graphics with fetish-erotica, whereas Scharper insists on getting across a politics of communication. Nicomedes Suárez-Araúz, on the other hand, investigates and represents "the conceivable termination of human memory."[12]

From contemporary plastics and montages of *objects trouvés* to "Amnesis Parks" and "lost objects," it is not far to the Internet. The final chapter inspects and interprets current developments in the postmodern metaverse: epistolary fictions of, on and about the Internet, addressing both dystopian accounts of "the end of letters, that is, printed matter" and utopian visions of "the electronic wor(l)d."

In all chapters, translations into English from German literary and scholarly sources are mine unless otherwise noted.

CHAPTER 1

A Briefing

In her essay, "Carnal Knowledge," Jane Gallop collected a number of book covers featuring paintings of women writing and receiving letters, among them Terry Eagleton's *Literary Theory. An Introduction*, Elizabeth Abel's *Writing and Sexual Difference*, and Hélène Cixous' *La venue á l'écriture*.

This briefing concerns itself with the critical tradition of letters and epistolary fiction from the eighteenth century to today. It attempts to outline the connections among letters, fiction, and theory, and to differentiate among modernist, feminist, and postmodernist assumptions about epistolary discourse while also emphasizing the continuities between them. Literary criticism and theory have based their disciplinary legitimacy on a mandate to analyze, categorize, to "order" the multifarious aesthetic and stray "subjective" elements of literature so that these establish discernible patterns, which then form norms for future classifications. At conferences, in journals and books, these norms are tested in a pseudoscientific manner. Some stand up to scrutiny, others don't, depending not only on the veracity of arguments but also on the hierarchies of voices within academic circles. Until quite recently, this hierarchy almost exclusively privileged white males and their literary and aesthetic interests.[1]

With few exceptions, the critical treatment of epistolary fiction epitomizes the schizophrenic elitism inherent in modern literary criticism: In the eighteenth century, literary critics stripped the letter of most of its classical ideas of rhetoric and style. In place of classic formulas, they cultivated the aristocratic idea of aesthetic *Natürlichkeit* (naturalness) and bourgeoisified this concept in the process.[2] Simultaneous with the emergence of the concept "fiction" in literary history, naturalness was imbued with authenticity. In the process, letters, but especially letters by women, or written as women would supposedly write them, presented such a "natural origin" which could then be framed by an authorial male narrative. From the beginning, the unstable binary division between fiction and authenticity was gendered. In a double twist, akin to the powerful new scientific discourse of the two-sex model initiating modernity's *sex-gender system* (a term coined by Gayle Rubin), empirical, biological authenticity wrote the fiction of gender, while fiction became the authentic genre. Elizabeth J. MacArthur points out that "critics have traditionally believed that to be literary a text must not be authentic, and that authentic texts inevitably display a disorder incompatible with the definitions of literature." She concludes that "this treatment of genuine correspondences is based on the assumption . . . that letters are pure, undistorted reflections of life."[3] This is precisely the discourse that epistolary fiction, and especially the epistolary novel, preserved while undermining it. In imitation of the economic and sociopolitical development of the middle-class family triangle, the new literary genre, adopted from its reputed extraliterary existence, was therefore given an always present mother (natural grace and spontaneity) and an absent father (aesthetic form).[4] This "natural daughter" supported the fiction of its legitimacy in the epistolary novel.[5] By its example, the naturalized letter simultaneously thrived on and admonished against erotic love to rationalize the marriage to the paternal figure (most clearly observable in Richardson's *Pamela*, Rousseau's *Julie*, and La Roche's *Sternheim*). The letter imparted its incestuous and adulterous desire (also the desire for the transgression of its generic limits) to the modern novel, a desire that both founded and challenged the novel's status.[6] In addition to the importance of the epistolary form for the modern novel (the letter's ability to "stand in for an oral dialogue," to "speak straight from the heart" of a particular character, preserving that character's style, sentiment, and dialect, to act as agent, to retard or speed up the narrative, to serve as deus ex machina, etc.),[7] authors and scholars conducted their literary theory and philosophy as, not just in form of, epistolary correspondence, and thereby expanded their bourgeois private sphere to a literary public.[8]

For the German context, Gert Mattenklott explicates how that "longing for autarchic self-creation," which irrevocably intertwines the history of modern subjectivity with the epistolary genre, reached its high point with the Romantics and their "embracing of theory and novel," whose mixture of philosophical reflections, letters, dialogues, poems, and novellas, ruptures the narrative authority and structurally shapes the polyphony of the modernist novel.[9] For some critics, this narratological self-reflexivity exhausted the letter's special qualities as a dialogic medium. At the same time when women were finally gaining acknowledgment as authors, readers, and critics, the letter, one of the genres that had aided their arrival on the literary scene, was attested to have lost its ability to communicate and to have become just another manneristic narrative form.[10] Women's voices and their literary expressions seemed destined to be dead on arrival.

The mail-orders responsible for these genre and gender definitions mark the history of epistolary criticism and articulate themselves in the separation of the letter's "particularity of material existence in a specific historical moment" from its vehicle function for literary or theoretical contents.[11] In the wake of positivist science, nineteenth-century critics chose to edit or analyze letters for their autobiographical authenticity (if their author was important enough due to his or her canonical productions) and for their historical value. In this extreme form of criticism, the letter is reduced to supplying substantial evidence for the master narratives of literary criticism and historiography. The other extreme includes studies in which letters carry out the critic's aesthetic directions. Karl Heinz Bohrer, reacting against poststructuralist notions of subject displacement, illustrates how the critic's own expectations and assumptions about letter-writing can become those letters' only literary and theoretical merit:

> The "subject" does not disappear "in the text." Without presupposing the subject, the perusal of these letters would be boring. They are interesting as texts only because we a priori assume a concept of the subject. The impression of a new subject stems from the contradiction between our supposition and the aesthetic effect of the letters undermining our expectation.[12]

Both extremes of epistolary theory are interested not so much in the letters as in the male-defined subject who wrote the letters and the subject that constitutes itself in and through the letters. For theories based on the definition of the letter as a "direct personal expression of a subject's feelings and intentions," the questioning of male-defined subjectivity automatically results in a proportional superfluity of the epistolary genre.[13]

The insecurity about the "law of genre" also points to the larger problems and challenges for literary criticism today. The complexity of communication forms and their interaction with the epistolary form necessitates interdisciplinary cooperation and a diversity of methodological approaches.[14] The increasing literary and theoretical interest in the letter form since the late 1960s in Europe and the late 1970s in the United States,[15] can be tied to specific crosscurrent cultural movements within the postwar period. While dependent on the historical developments in each country, several general trends reveal themselves. Foremost, women's movements and feminist criticism established a line of inquiry into gender/genre connections while a general revision of "high-art" modernism reshaped generic parameters throughout art and literature. The critique of the unified subject *and* of the Eurocentered modernist fixation with the white, male, Anglo-Protestant self included long-overdue reappraisals of center/margin concepts, including the mind/body dichotomy.[16] The decentralization and delegitimization of Western grand narratives in the tow of postcolonial issues incurred a shift from *grande histoire* to social and oral history,[17] but also threatened emerging minority voices with the theoretical and political undermining of their freshly gained identity-based positions of power. Subsequently, Nancy K. Miller argues that the increased tendency toward personal criticism, in which she includes criticism written in and on the epistolary mode, is a direct reaction against the proclaimed loss of the subject, because the letter is multigeneric and can incorporate greater and more complex diversity in styles and voices. She also sees "autobiographical acts" as a reaction to the crisis of representation and as the result of the feminist call for personal "engaged" writing.[18]

At the same time, although not always synchronically, the 1968 student movement's critique of the silence or lies of adults about the Holocaust, and the debunking of aesthetic elitism and academic authority made it possible to question language as a pure medium that reliably transmits thoughts and meaning between the stable positions of sender and receiver.[19] With the help of structuralism and the psychoanalytic poststructuralist conception that "the unconscious is structured like a language,"[20] the humanities and the social sciences shifted their exclusionary focus on the analysis of empirical phenomena to include the analysis of discourses and their legitimization processes, a movement that amounted to a self-study of the disciplines and their histories.[21]

As textual criticism moved toward communication theory, semiotics, and reception theories,[22] theoretical mathematics began to separate information from meaning.[23] Chaos theory, including its diverging applications in the different disciplines, joined systems theory in reevaluating the notions of closed systems and laws of repetition.[24] Investigations of modern mass media and their relationship to conventional disciplines took (inter)disciplinary shape in film, video, TV, and culture studies, while the personal computer started to function as a multimedia center.

Even computer-generated and -delivered e-mail still "reminds us of the importance of writing as a structure."[25] What happens in between send-off and arrival, the place where Franz Kafka's infamous letter-ghosts once roamed free, has been traditionally silenced or mystified for three reasons. First, since the phase difference is uncontrollable, one could neither analyze it scientifically nor come to reliable conclusions. Second, to dwell on the letter's path would have demanded a recognition of the indeterminable fictionality of any letter and subject position. Third, it would have entailed the recognition that the postal route and mailing system not only deliver mail but also structure the letter's writing and reading moments, and determine its subjects' positions.[26] But new departures in mailing systems have increasingly forced our attention on the "in-between," whether on the activities of hackers and cyber-FBI or amazon.com's and UPS's customer service which allows one to track one's orders and their postal route to our mailbox.

MAILING WOMEN AND FEMINISMS

> Sophie la Roche's spelling mistakes were found charmingly ade-
> quate as long as they occurred in letters but as soon as these letters
> turned into a novel found "irritating" by her mentor and editor
> Christoph Martin Wieland, and Dorothea Schlegel's epistolary
> prose was considered superior to her attempts at any other literary
> form due to its "natural tone."

The modernist fascination with and repulsion by correspondences—whether between humans and primates or between chatroom users—can be explained, in part, by Bruno Latour's analysis of networks and hybridity. Following Walter Benjamin, he argues that two types of practices result in two types of modernism: "translation or mediation" and "purification."[27] Both practices depend on each other for their success. Whereas "translation" produces hybrid communicative structures (between humanistic, scientific areas, nature and culture, etc.), "purification" separates nature from culture and society. While literary critics as well as scientists and philosophers more or less effectively strive to separate letters from literature, facts from fiction, high from low culture, according to Latour, their "division is powerless to account for the multiple links, the intersecting influences, the continual negotiations" (13). As a corrective, he suggests a "nonmodern Constitution," in which the "clandestine proliferation of hybrids" is exchanged for "their regulated and commonly-agreed-upon production" (141–142).

Despite Latour's far-reaching discussion of modern and postmodern hybridity, he does not dwell on specific historical manifestations of the "nonhuman," as he calls it. While his approach helps to explain the modernist dilemma of needing yet negating the multiplication of mediators and mediation processes, one of the most striking absences from his book is an analysis of the historical configuration of Woman and women as nonhuman, noncitizen, and as delicate and "communicating vessels."[28] This is particularly disconcerting, since in the aftermath of 1989, he claims to lay the philosophical ground map for a new democratic constitution. If he wants to let in the hybrids, is Woman one of them? Is she among those writing the new constitution, is she excluded or profiting from it? Or is he going one step further and hoping to eliminate the Woman question by giving rights to the hybrids produced through her body?

Even though "Vive la Difference" feminism has been taken to task for not striking at the core of patriarchal hierarchy, epistemological sexism, and racism, women's equal rights movements have been simultaneously praised and blamed for having initiated the crisis of modernity.[29] Feminist concerns with marginality, borders, fragmentation, liminality, and identity, as some would have it, have infused theory with political practice and joined forces with postcolonial and multicultural developments. In addition, fear of worldwide atomic, bacteriological, immunological, and environmental holocaust in the 1980s combined with the anxiously encountered flux in sexual identity has brought forth a vehemently expressed rigidity when incorporating or chauvinistically rejecting "the hybrid" within. Women, symbolically and sexually seen as both the mediators and the traded objects between men in a patriarchal society, have begun to refuse their cooperation and begun to change the binary heterosexual structure on which this gendered traffic is based. Their manifold deliberations and actions have impacted the forms and functions of mediation and exchange in postindustrial and postmodern societies. Similar to the politically motivated and artistically articulated misogyny of the "roaring twenties" and "depressed thirties" (particularly visible in the German Expressionism of George Grosz and Otto Dix),[30] the crisis of modernity in postwar postcolonial societies has led to the excessive symbolic and actual abuse of women's bodies.[31] Male-dominated societies in transit from one hegemony to another or wedged in between dominant cultures have made women responsible for their loss of orientation and power. Raping Bosnian women in the Bosnian-Serbian conflict of the early 1990s, for example, became an ethno-marker, a politically charged symbolic action of not just territorial but also racial appropriation.[32] At the same time, the angst-ridden misogynism tends to revive the Freudian stereotype of the "castrating woman" or Lacan's monstrous "phallic mother" in representations of women in the mass media.[33]

Andreas Huyssen seems convinced that "the gendering of mass culture as feminine and inferior has its primary place in the late 19th century, even though the underlying dichotomy did not lose its power until quite recently."[34] He insists that due to the inclusion of women artists in high art and popular culture, the perceived "feminine threat" of mass culture is a thing of the past. His conclusions make it sound as if only men could be the target of a "feminine threat" and that only women were targeted by a masculine "obsession with gendered violence." If the "old rhetoric" were really gone, then why uphold the heterosexual assumptions of traditional reception analysis?[35] And is something only dangerous if it is perceived as a threat? How is danger constructed, assessed, and transmitted by language and mass-mailings of gender, sex, race, and class preconceptions?

The crosscurrents between feminism and a particular postmodern utopian/dystopianism have attracted critical attention ever since Craig Owens's 1983 essay "The Discourse of Others: Feminists and Postmodernism."[36] In his essay, Owens investigates the correspondence between a critique of representation and the feminist insistence on and critique of sexual difference. He evaluates the political activism of the feminist movement as a utopian potential within postmodernism. Although Owens's article was not the first scholarly product to link a critique of patriarchy with poststructuralist and postmodern theories—he himself acknowledges the work of Luce Irigaray, Hélène Cixous, and others— "the pathbreaking quality of Owens's essay was that it placed the feminist issue at the center of the debate on postmodernism."[37]

Despite Owens's careful reading of the interstices between postmodernism and feminism in the visual arts, he ends his essay by advocating a gendered awareness of difference. Owens applies the "female knowledge" of difference directly to language, to gestures and customs, and to the resistance against an "anything goes-postmodernism":

> Each term now seems to contain its opposite, and this indeterminacy brings with it an impossibility of choices. Or so it is said. The existence of feminism, with its insistence on difference, forces us to reconsider. For in our country good-bye may look just like hello, but only from a masculine position. Women have learned—perhaps they have always known—how to recognize the difference.[38]

Whereas the masculine linguistic position ignores the differences within the postmodern discourse, the feminine position brings forth and insists on its internal differences. The masculine position is above difference, whereas the feminine is difference itself. Even though Owens praises Barbara Kruger's work for her demonstration "that masculine and feminine themselves are not stable identities, but subject to ex-change," he assigns gender marks to the postmodern condition (77). If the exchange between the genders is equated with an exchange between a female feminism and a masculine postmodernism, does this exchange amount to a "mutual opportunism," as Susan Rubin Suleiman contends?

> In short, feminism brings to postmodernism the political guarantee postmodernism needs in order to feel respectable as an avant-garde practice. Postmodernism, in turn, brings feminism into a certain kind of "high theoretical" discourse on the frontiers of culture, traditionally an exclusively male domain.[39]

These complex issues threaten to lose themselves in speculations and accusations, based on the various assumptions one holds true for "gender," "feminism," "theory," and "postmodernism."

A writer who struggles with the ideological "Traffic in Women"[40] is Ingeborg Bachmann. She relies on the epistolary genre to investigate the interrelation between gender and sex, among culture, nature, and history, and specifically between women's writing and the idea of the "monstrous feminine." Bachmann's *Malina* takes on the various ideologies of mediation itself. Her text might help us come to terms with one of the absences from the feminist discourse on letters, namely, the link between the "Traffic in Women" and epistolary mediation, especially since feminist epistolary critics have interpreted "mediation" in its epistolary mode in a largely positive light. Janet Altman views it as an epistolary mediation between time and space, levels of agency and communication. Linda Kauffman takes specific interest in the intertextual mediation accomplished by letters, and Anne Bower applies all of the above for her argument of epistolary responsiveness, for self-conscious intertextual mediation.[41] The challenge for my project lies in transiently unhitching the letter form from the idea of "correspondence" as an interpersonal, interindividual, but really intraindividual, activity, and to connect it to the mediation politics of mail-orders.

In her novel, Bachmann explicitly evokes the essentialist paradigm of conventional and feminist research on the "natural" connection between women and letters, a "natural" connection between two hybrids. But as I will argue in detail below, the tensions that this connection produces figure into the structural designs of her novel. At first sight, it appears as if Bachmann goes back to a *Pamela* scenario with live-in *Briefsteller*. Her epistolary writing could also be considered reform literature much in the same vein as it was in the eighteenth century. But are the results comparable to a modernist or a nonmodernist constitution, or do they construct something quite different altogether?

Bachmann does not simply write her narrative in epistolary form for the traditional reasons; she is quite aware of the literary his-story conflating letters and women, the mediation of ideas in corporeal form and gender. A curious chain of male-dominated critique and reform spirit indeed unfolds when taking a closer look at supporters' rhetoric of a "feminine epistolarity":

> [In the eighteenth century, the women] were especially encouraged [to write letters] by those, who also represented and strove for a theoretical-programmatic improvement, a reform not only of the German language and literature but specifically of the letter and epistolary style.[42]

This relationship among women, letters, and aesthetic as well as political reform is not as neatly causal as Reinhard Nickisch would like his readers to believe. He expresses an almost naive wonder about the epistolary capacities of Luise Kulmus Gottsched: "Already in the style of her first letters to the learned friend she executed his progressive reformational linguistic ideas almost naturally."[43] This unproblematized gender/genre relationship becomes rather revealing in the case of Goethe's, Schiller's, Jean Paul's, and Hölderlin's epistolary essays and letters, which Nickisch unwittingly compares to Bettina von Arnim's and Rahel Varnhagen's epistolary texts. On the one hand, Nickisch praises the great men for their "controlled expression and complete mirror of human and intellectually outstanding personalities and their time" as well as for their "synthesis of pragmatic and essayistic form."[44] On the other hand, he agrees with Otto Heuschele that Bettina von Arnim's "art has 'completed but also exhausted itself in . . . letter writing'."[45] Nickisch criticizes those aspects of her writing which he admires in the works of her literary colleagues.[46] He also demonstrates a rhetorical tendency to personalize and sexualize women's writing in contrast to men's writing when discussing Luise Adelgunde Victorie Kulmus' letters. Throughout the paragraph, he moves from "Jungfer Kulmus" (Miss Kulmus) to "Gottschedin" (the Gottsched woman) to "Frau Gottsched" (Mrs. Gottsched) and finally "'Gehilfin' Gottscheds" (Gottsched's female assistant). This chain of proper names outlines the common fate of heroines in the eighteenth-century epistolary novel: with her writing she sacrifices her virginity, reinstates her virtue with her marriage, and henceforth ranks as her husband's loyal assistant (46).

Although Nickisch justly admonishes readers against the assumption that the letter is *the* female genre par excellence (48), his critical language nevertheless reveals a biological essentialism that reaches back to Christian Fürchtegott Gellert:

> The person, who can select the lightest, the finest and the most necessary among many products of the imagination with the help of a tender and happy impression, and who can observe a specific balance in their combination, will assuredly write good letters. For this reason one can tell oneself whence it comes that the women generally write more natural letters than the men. . . . The women care less about the organization of a letter, and because they have not given their mind an unconventional direction through the rules of art: that's why their letter becomes freer and less anxious.[47]

Ernst Brandes, although a critic less known than Gellert not necessarily less influential, wrote several tracts on the differences between the sexes and their education in the late eighteenth century. He exhibits another strain of sexual/textual criticism. Brandes separates *Schriftstellerinnen* (female authors) from *Briefeschreiberinnen* (female letter writers), public from private authorship and thus expresses the double bind of the woman writer. As soon as she goes public she loses her "natural style."

The aesthetic norms, which critics as disparate as Brandes, Gellert, and Nickisch conceptualize and publish for the purpose of imitation, are now construed to hinder the woman writer's progress:

> The awkward situation, to appear publicly, the unfamiliarity of the language, that one believes to have to articulate in writing, where chiefly the women think one should distance oneself from the good language of the common life—not uncommonly, all of the above bestows something affected onto those writings of the ladies intended for publication, or an anxious striving for a regulatory method and correctness, that hinders the free flow of delicate thoughts and makes visible the struggle of composition. This is not the case in those letters, which are only written for individuals or at the most for a circle of friends.[48]

Moving well into the 1960s, one can still find a nostalgic regret for women's lost innocence and naturalness, which is connected to their ability to read and write. James Krüss, author of the children's book *Letters To Pauline* (1968), even believes that the best letters by girls are letters dictated by them and written by someone else. He justifies the second volume's lack of correspondence and increased storytelling "for Pauline" (instead of an exchange) by stating that "in the meantime, Pauline can read and write. (That's why she no longer tells [stories] as prettily as before.)"[49]

Roland Barthes' annotated alphabetic list of *A Lover's Discourse* (1978) also suggests a close affinity between gender and epistolary position. He calls his book a structural portrait, "which offers the reader a discursive site: The site of someone speaking within himself, *amorously*, confronting the other (the loved object), who does not speak."[50] His project considers the "extreme solitude" of a lover's discourse in the Western world, but presupposes a homoerotic consensus among lovers: "Each of us can fill in this code according to his own history." He depicts a lover's discourse as an open dialogue between texts and readers, a discourse that is "offered to the reader to be made free with, to be added to, subtracted from, and passed on to others" (5). Within this "hommosexual" discourse (as Lacan would call it), the author as lover of the text argues that "only the Other could write my love story, my novel" (93). In the eighteenth century, letters, as the Other of literature, write the novel: "Only a very archaic form can accommodate the event."[51]

> Historically, the discourse of absence is carried on by the Woman. . . . It is Woman who gives shape to absence, elaborates its fiction. . . . It follows that in any man who utters the other's absence something feminine is declared: this man who waits and who suffers from his waiting is miraculously feminized. A man is not feminized because he is inverted but because he is in love.[52]

Metaphorized by Barthes, a lover's discourse is always "feminine." The transgendering male author loves his text like a woman loves a man. The image of the morphological connection between the female body and a woman's text is reclaimed for women by feminist literary critics like Hélène Cixous. Cixous reinterprets Freud's definition of woman as a deficit, as no-man, into a positively elusive economy of women's writing. When Cixous writes (of) *écriture feminine* and *jouissance*, she describes the resulting "feminine text" in hybridized epistolary terms:

> A feminine text cannot not be more than subversive: if it writes itself it is in volcanic heaving of the old "real" property crust. In ceaseless displacement. . . . In the Selfsame Empire, where will the displacement's person find somewhere to lose herself, to write her not-taking-place, her permanent availability. . . . But has there ever been any elsewhere, is there any? While it is not yet "here," it is there by now—in this other place that disrupts social order, where desire makes fiction exist.[53]

Luce Irigaray also investigates the sexual and symbolic dichotomy inherent in Freud's psychoanalysis, in which Woman comes to stand as "the Other." Irigaray herself attempts to resist the dominant theoretical discourse through the structure of her writing style.[54] Rachel Blau DuPlessis views the letter as one of these possible narrative strategies of feminist resistance:

> Something I call an emotional texture, a structural expression of mutuality. Writers know their text as a form of intimacy, of personal contact, whether conversations with the reader or with the self. Letters, journals, voices are sources for this element, see "no reason why one should not write as one speaks, familiarly, colloquially," expressing the porousness and nonhierarchic stances of intimate conversation in both structure and function.[55]

This resistance, however, conjures Barthes' adjectives describing a feminized lover's discourse: "No logic links the figures, determines their contiguity: . . . they stir, collide, subside, return, vanish with no more order than the flight of mosquitoes."[56] In a similar vein, Jane Marcus,[57] Sara Lennox,[58] and Patricia Meyer Spacks try to arrive at the positive essence of sexual difference and the means for its expression: "Female correspondence, their letters suggest, supplies means of evasive self-definition, and the sex of women letter writers informs their use of the epistolary form."[59]

The specific relationship of women to epistolary fiction reappears in the larger context of the debate about the existence of a feminine aesthetic in the 1970s.[60] Two questions dominate this discussion: Did and do women have "a literature of their own" and if they do, how is it possible to subvert the patriarchal discourse to express the female voice?[61]

And, would the result be the end, a reform or a reproduction of patriarchy? In the 1970s and 1980s, the literary community, in concert with the publishing houses, began to supply the growing demand for "women's literature" by creating new paperback series.[62] This trend resulted in the publication and critical analysis of numerous anthologies of diaries, autobiographies,[63] and of new epistolary fiction.[64]

Poststructuralist feminist critics started to investigate these "necessary essentialisms" for their implicit phallocentric inscriptions of the "Feminine" and "universal womanhood."[65] They were in turn criticized for their hegemonic assumptions about white middle-class womanhood and their perceived lack of political engagement and subservience to the "male discourse of theory."[66] The debate about the political stance of feminisms and feminist criticisms began another rereading of the gender/genre relation, which continues today.[67] These "(ex)tensions of feminist criticism," to borrow a term from Elizabeth Meese, also included the critical investigation of the relationship between feminism and postmodernism.[68]

EPISTOLARY THEORY AND FICTION:
A POSTMODERN POETICS?

> Sigrid Weigel subsumes a study of the correspondences between Poststructuralism and Critical Theory under the title *Message-in-a-bottle and Postcard*, while Diane Elam addresses postmodern romance in letter form.

Molly Hite began investigating postmodern feminist fiction as "another side of the story," a story which "is not in any absolute sense unimaginable or inconceivable (or outside the symbolic order in Lacanian terms)." She views "female-created violations of convention or tradition as deliberate experiments." This leads her to ask: "Given such discursive practices, under what conditions and using what strategies are we most likely to discern them?"[69] She further discusses the notable absence of women writers in lists of postmodernist authors and some scholars' underlying assumptions about women's "natural" and "realist" writing style that portray women writers as occupied with "other" things than formal experimentation (16–17).

Hite insists that women's narrative strategies can neither be reduced to a postmodernism that resists closure and metaphorizes women's supposed undefineability nor to a postmodernism that overturns any kind of "culturally constructed oppositions" (16). She would rather "*re-*cente[r] the value structure of the narrative" than allow feminism to be enveloped by what she perceives as a phallocentric "postmodernism" (2,

16–17). How difficult this project proves to be surfaces in the end, when Molly Hite has to return to the positivist use of metaphors like "eluding" and "overflowing" to express what contemporary feminist narratives might look like (18).

Patricia Waugh similarly seeks a feminist difference within the discourse of postmodernism but also realizes that this discourse of difference has affected the literature she analyzes. Discussing contemporary Anglo-American fiction by women, she argues that most of them "show less concern with 'splitting' and disintegration than with merging and connection."[70] While Waugh's and Hite's arguments posit that generic and thematic narrative practices are gender-dependent, that is, dependent on a network of sociohistorical developments, they also illustrate the dilemma of subscribing to a feminist criticism that posits the existence of a community, an origin, and a goal. This idea of community has been justifiably attacked by ethnic and lesbian feminists who emphasize the differences within and between women. To simply exchange the dominant notion of subject as "Western, bourgeois, white, heterosexual, and male" and literary values for another "universal" concept of the universal female subject and "her" writing technique constitutes an act of oppression in itself. Difference is voiced as an ever-growing list of attributes as each group and individual announces its special circumstances, characteristics, problems, and needs. On the one hand, this new discourse of plurality and polyphony underscores "the shift from an epistemological account of identity to one which locates the problematic within practices of signification."[71] On the other hand, it cannot help but be involved in the dual project of "translating" and "purifying," as Bruno Latour demonstrates. This shift and its indebtedness to the modern constitution, in my opinion, aptly describes the signifying practices of postmodernism, both for the constitution of the discourse of feminist versatility in the first place, and for the scholarly and literary activities it produces.

It is precisely the confrontation of an idea of "agency" with a practice of signification that the letter form carries out in contemporary fiction and theory. The query into agency and practices of signification is not only a query into the role of women writers, readers, and heroines in literature, but also into the role of fiction as gender and gender as fiction. In which way is gender an agent or a part of the practices of signification in contemporary epistolary fiction? If contemporary epistolary fiction writes a postmodern poetics, what role does gender play in its construction and execution? For the purpose of this study, I believe that it is indispensable for feminist scholarship to analyze that aspect of postmodernism *as* a discourse, as *one* discourse among others.[72] An analysis in this manner needs to pay attention to the discrepancies within that discourse and its individual packaging.[73] If feminists treat both feminist and phallic discourses each as a single body, as a totalizing, unifying contraption, "we" re-cloak what "we" wish to disrobe.[74] The very concept of gender, race, and sex as social constructs is a postmodern phenomenon, and part of my research should show that postmodern fictions of gender and genre enter into a dialogue with eighteenth- and nineteenth-century configurations of gender and genre. Instead of harmonizing the interrelations among authors, characters, critics, and readers, the texts and myself, I hope that readers will engage their own fictions of letters in the practices of interception and rerouting.[75]

Throughout the following chapters, I will analyze some of the most striking occurrences and conundrums of the epistolary manner sketched above. At the same time, my project is deeply involved in uncovering the connections between the renaissance of the letter form and what Linda Hutcheon terms "a postmodern problematics."[76] Although recent contributions to epistolary theory deal with the history of the letter from antiquity to the twentieth century, and come to tentative conclusions about its function and future in contemporary Western societies, further research of the letter form at the beginning of the twenty-first century is essential. Most monographic studies direct their attention to the literary history of the letter form, to its general traits as a device in literature, or to its nonliterary status. Since the development of the social and cultural importance of the letter is closely interwoven with the rise of the middle class, and with it the rise of a literary public, many studies focus exclusively on the eighteenth century. There is a discernible lack of literary research into the specific usages of the letter and the design of mail-orders in contemporary society, culture and literature. A growing amount of research on electronic communication, stemming largely from interdisciplinary interests based in America's English, communication, and sociology departments, as well as a vast number of newspaper series devoted to the issue of Internet and e-mail survival skills, attest to the anxious fascination with the all enveloping changes in interpersonal and cyborgian communication. The reasons for this, in my view dangerous, oversight and disinterest on the part of the traditional disciplines lie in the assumptions about the generic possibilities and limits of the epistolary genre, and not, as some critics assume, in the lack of correspondences and publications.[77]

With the advance of mechanically handled mail, mail-order business transactions, computerized banking, electronic mail via fax, satellite, or computer, it is understandable that literary scholars find it difficult to sort out their letters.[78] What is often stated as the essential coordinate system of epistolary correspondence, namely, the temporal and geographical distance of sender and addressee and the resulting time lapse of arrival and response appears outmoded when compared to the increasing pace of information transmission via computers and satellites. A comparison like this equates computer, telephone, and letter as media that facilitate the flow of communication but does not take into account the narrative strategies, functions, and specific communicative logic of each individual medium that determine and hinder its creation, transmission, and reception.[79] In addition to the ensuing changes in reading and writing habits, the sheer mass of material makes an empirical study of the form and functions of epistolary communication in the postwar era next to impossible.[80] As I argue in detail below, it is highly doubtful that the notion of an "authentic" letter, of "private" correspondence, and the letter's historical function as "evidence" can still serve as the premise for an analysis of the intersections between a postmodern poetics and fictions of the letter circulating among literature, literary theory, film, electronic media, and the arts.

To sum up, two of the most obvious traits shared by epistolarity and postmodernism are their interdisciplinary and intercultural characters. Letters do not stop at political, geographical, cultural, linguistic, or sexual borders. Their intersubjectivity and intertextuality, their transgression or subversion of borders, is precisely what is at stake here. The desire to unsettle and sidestep sedentary and totalitarian power structures through mobile linguistic (dis)connections by juxtaposing themes, styles, and interpretations is probably the most common element of many postmodern theories and literary works.[81] While I am concerned with the textuality of the epistolary relay system in particular, I also inquire whether postmodernist writers ignore their own conspicuous use of these "forces that escape coding, scramble the codes, and flee in all directions."[82] The interrelation between postmodern theories of multiplicity, indeterminacy, and epistolary fiction exposes the dilemma within postmodernism. On the one hand, postmodernist narratives and theories hybridize disciplines and genres and resist totalizing closures in reading and writing (like symbolism or the separation of form and content). On the other hand, they create a "carrier" for these desires, they transform the carrier of meaning and transparency—of substance—into a vehicle of vehicles, of flows of desires: a body without organs.[83] This is precisely what Katherine Hayles notes about Michel Serres' theory of language as informational equivocation based on the second law of thermodynamics:

> [H]e points out that fighting against entropic decay is the openness of all living systems—their ability to take in sunlight, food, information. Since this flow sustains life, he proposes that we regard ourselves not as stable bodies through which constantly changing streams of matter and energy flow but as stable flows encased within constantly changing bodies.[84]

Serres' proposition neither acknowledges this purely vehicular mediation as a "conduit metaphor" for communication in general ("meanings are objects that are placed into containers; these containers are sent to others, who open the containers and take out the objects")[85] nor as an allegory of postmodern discourse. I am using the term "allegory" here, because there is no one absolute synthetic "symbol" in postmodern discourse. It is precisely the disintegration and dissemination of the letter and letters, along with the symbolic order, which "carries" postmodern discourse, a carrier imparting its instability and indeterminacy upon the very structure that determines its path. Epistolary practices seem to encompass the conflicting desires, positions, and self-enforced taboos of the postmodern condition all too perfectly.[86]

Depending on each user's critical heritage and focus, the multifaceted term "postmodernism" indicates an epoch or a period supplanting modernism, an aesthetic style, a poetics, a trend in French philosophy and poststructuralist theory, a transavant-gardism, the crisis of modernism and its transcendence by self-reflection, a postindustrialist consumer culture, and a paradigm shift in the natural sciences.[87] Ingeborg Hoesterey treats this "Babylonian quality" of postmodernism as "being concretized in the dialogical space where the different discourses meet, clash, or exist in a modus vivendi."[88] Postmodernism is subjected to its own postmodernism in Hoesterey's and Hutcheon's focus on the "significant overlap of theory with aesthetic practice . . . , a flexible conceptual structure which could at once constitute and contain postmodern culture and our discourses both about it and adjacent to it."[89] This aspect of postmodernism is precisely what enables Hutcheon to call it a "poetics," a theory and its own vehicle, something that contains and exceeds itself, which is always already doubled and disseminated—like the letter.

In this light, restricting my study of contemporary mail-orders to a single period, one country, one type of letters, one author, one discipline, one gender, or one theoretical approach would be counterproductive, even impossible. While my selection is based on my dialogues with feminist and poststructural criticisms, I also attempt to disrupt the poststructuralist tendency of concentrating solely on texts which, due to their prominence in ideological and literary criticisms, indicate a profitable deconstruction.[90] As a result, the different works correspond without corresponding. Their assembly into linear order on paper stems from an archeological digging into the "letters to amnesia."[91] I hope to expose some of the gummed-up connections along with whatever cultural, psychological barriers created them in the first place. Therefore, my inquiries into the different epistolary texts are themselves guided by Jacques Derrida's question in "Borderlines": "How can one text, assuming its unity, give or present another to be read, without touching it, without saying anything about it, practically without referring to it?"[92] Or, put in another way, sometimes there are so many overlapping correspondences that one cannot deal with all of them without turning one chapter into a glossary. This might help to explain that some readers may encounter delays in the introduction and analysis of key concepts in the next chapter. A certain epistolary chagrin may develop as different readers' interests and priorities assert themselves against my own. I would hope that readers insert their own dis/connections at any time using mine as a jumping or sounding board. While I concentrate on specific concepts for each chapter, such as rhapsody for chapter 2 and intertextuality for chapter 3, I rework them as new intertextual couplings announce themselves in subsequent chapters. For readers unsympathetic to my anachronistic snail-mail style, I would suggest the index as a way to "get there from here."

The question of correspondences points to the process of fictionalization. While obvious correspondences may elicit a "Duh!" from interested readers, they also court the reader's desire to be confirmed (in their education, their expertise, their personal interests). Especially in the hype-prone America at the beginning of the twenty-first century, less obvious correspondences have to be packaged attractively in order to entice readers to skip over their initial hesitant impatience. Whereas in the first case, the fiction of correspondence hides itself, it seems obvious in the second. The roles have switched. A deconstructive practice, which is created by and in turn reads textual indeterminacies or inconsistencies, Alan Kennedy argues, can interpolate any text without reducing itself to a methodology or a theoretical decoder of literary texts.[93] Since I am writing this as the star of deconstruction is rapidly waning, I have to be more suspicious of the process of invisible master key fabrications. But residing in "Poststructuralism's Wake," to purloin the title of Michael Phillipson's book, also gives me more incentive to combine its best aspects with interdisciplinary approaches suggested by feminist, cultural, and postcolonial studies.

In looking beyond the strictly literary and disciplinary boundaries, my own project sets out "to situate the letter in its relationship to and as a part of literary works at the center of literary scholarship and to upset seemingly self-evident assumptions about it."[94] The discussion of mass culture products alongside "arrived" classics is first of all motivated by the specific epistolary economy of desires, second by the reception history of the letter form as a "trivial" and "feminized" genre, and third by a critique of dominant discursive networks. Although I criticize and revise the modernist rhetoric of generic limitations, my criticism cannot but rely on and include those very assumptions.[95] Yet while contemporary fictions "propose the rules that underwrite their genesis at the same time as they produce the fiction that is discovered within the rules of the game," a postmodern poetics fictionalizes those rules and thereby strives to resist them.[96]

The contradictory reconfigurations of the literary theoretical discourse not only take aim at the "verifiably historical and referential," they also include an "intimate complicity between theory and practice."[97] Within the framework of a book, which combines great creative freedom with rigid technological and economic limitations, the investigation of "a theory of literature or recent literature as theory" presupposes a metadiscourse of control that the theme itself tries to undermine. In order to avoid an illusory metanarrative position, I experiment with an alternative to the conventional *Briefsteller*.[98] Instead of writing either a literary history or a normative poetics of the epistolary device in the postwar era, I want to examine the paradoxical usage of the letter form as a reliable vehicle at a time that radically questions language's ability to provide and maintain stable meanings, and in which the technological bases of writing and communicating are drastically changing. In close readings of specific texts, I attempt an inner- and intertextual dialogue between postmodern and epistolary narrative strategies. A certain parodist "miming" of the individual texts is unavoidable in tracing a structural referent like the letter, which by means of its generic law continuously shifts its contextual positions.[99] While I analyze the intersections among epistolary theory, literature, film, electronic media, art, and their fictions of letters in six case studies, my own writing thus deliberately partakes in the structural creation of the intersections among them.[100]

CHAPTER 2

Rhapsody in Letters:
Ingeborg Bachmann's Malina

"... how vehemently this 'I' ..."—
"... *verschreibt* itself ... could one say it that way?"—
"*Verschreiben*—that is a lovely word."[1]

Ingeborg Bachmann's *Malina* is not, conventionally speaking, an epistolary novel. Rather, the author employs the epistolary form as one of
many expressions in the novel.[2] Within the medley of genres that constitutes the narrative rhythm in *Malina*, the letter form gains particular
structural importance through its multileveled dislocation of the reading
and writing subject, and its disjointing of the narrative movement. In the
epistolary interchanges that write against yet produce the novel as text,
gender constructions are mirrored by genre transformations and narratological categorizations.[3] While remaining in the grid of the novel,
Malina sounds out this genre's innate instability. As the novel develops,
it also presses the female voice into its service.[4] Bachmann investigates,
records, and transcribes the genre's conspiracy with a female writer's
muted discourse in a different key. I argue that *Malina* composes an
epistolary rhapsody of the female voice.

Malina, which was published in 1971, draws out the gender-determined generic "types of death" *(Todesarten)* of its female protagonist.[5]
Christine Kanz contends that Bachmann's novel-trilogy "is called *[To-
desarten]* because all female protagonists are presented 'in their dying
and their demise' (KA 2, 18) and because they die in different ways
after a journey through dream, illness and madness."[6] *Malina* is composed of three chapters and an overture: "Happy with Ivan," "The
Third Man," "Of last Things."[7] In the overture, the nameless female
protagonist and narrating subject—simply referred to as "Ich"—sets up
the list of characters as for a play or a police report. She mentions
Malina (her male counterpart and potential murderer), Ivan (her lover),
his two children, and herself. Her prologue summarizes and foreshadows the plot and its themes, including the musical theme from Schönberg's "Pierrot lunaire" (op. 21).

On the plot level, the narrator protagonist, who is a female author, a nameless "I (ich)," lives in a modern Vienna whose topography is overlaid and inundated with remembrances of its rise to and fall from power. One of these personified reminders of Austria's history as empire, in the role of the military antiquarian and historian Malina, cohabits her apartment. She experiences an intense love affair with Ivan, a divorced Hungarian father of two children who lives across the street. After his sexual desire abates, he distances himself relatively quickly, and she experiences a severe depression accompanied by alcohol, pills, and nightmares. Malina cares for her in a mixture of warden and therapist, and attempts to trigger her repressed memories of past abuses and separations. At the end, after connecting her current pain and inability to counter its force to childhood trauma and general gender-determined suffering, narrative disruption and fragmentation increase. She repeatedly attempts and fails to write her will and finally disappears into a crack in the wall while Malina destroys the last things of importance to her. He denies her existence, the existence of (a) Woman, to a telephone caller, who might well be Ivan.

In the novel, epistolary situations develop into novellas, and into novel narratives. While these situations propel the narratives along their general triadic procession, each letter scenario adheres to its generic code: the necessary split between writing and reading, between sender and addressee, between places and times. Each epistolary moment shares conflicting movements, antagonistic roles, and transmits this tension to the narrative positions it stimulates. This subnarrative strand parallels the thematic countergestures of end and beginning: The end of the novel marks Malina's beginning. Aesthetic and political reform are mail-ordered through women's lives.

EPISTOLARY METONYMY OR
THE LETTER AS METAPHOR

Malina represents itself as an ambiguous melodrama of feminine endings. The epistolary form functions as a testament to the protagonist's demise and her (non) existence. Bachmann's novel deals with the Holocaust and links its psychological effects, the working through of traumatic residue, to gendered memory and subject formation in postwar Austria. Taking her key from fellow Austrian Schönberg, Bachmann employs music to facilitate the horror of that which cannot be said, cannot be represented. The combination of this seemingly disparate material in the text leads to the rewriting of modernist classics, to the experimentation with genres, and the literary reaction to an opening and closing of emancipatory space for women (as experienced most dramatically at the end of World War I, in the Nazi-era, and after World War II).

The second and third chapters of *Malina* rewrite Arnold Schönberg's "Erwartung" ("Expectation") and Arthur Schnitzler's "Die Toten schweigen" ("The Dead are silent"), in which the solitary female voices rapidly span the emotional field of intense longing to absolute terror, as they find their lovers dead on the edge of town. Hybridizing singing with speaking, Schönberg's musical scenario of an inner monologue and Schnitzler's dissolving narrative construct the female unconscious as rhapsody. Left alone to deal with the death of their lovers and their certain punishment by society, these women become survivors, and ironically enough, mourners of the decaying superstructure whose rules they have already transgressed via adultery and the longing for more in life than their "female destiny" as wives and mothers. But in both representations, these women, so desperate to reintegrate themselves into male-dominated "normalcy" after their lovers' deaths, are shown governed by their guilt-ridden *Angst*, which finally, with epistolary delay, "speaks itself," or more correctly, "speaks them."

In Schnitzler and Schönberg, the moment of uttering the female voice also betrays that voice to the mail-order. And at this point, male-dominated narrative control resumes. Bachmann, on the other hand, seeks out the potential of these moments to disturb the mail-order from within. While Schnitzler's and Schönberg's narratives break off at the point of reintegration, Bachmann wants to reshape feminine endings and the modernist narratological structure they are based on. Bachmann recognizes and represents the intellectual, desiring, misfit woman's continuously experienced psychological and social trauma. Losing a lover here converts into losing the desire to desire, but where male authors have for generations thrived on the creative energy of unrequited love, a scorned woman traditionally has had little dignity, and her creativity exhausted itself with the loss of a heterosexual direction for her desire.

For many Bachmann scholars, Julia Kristeva's work has been crucial in understanding Bachmann's complex relationships of desire, creativity, and terror. Kristeva´s critical reading of Freud's theory of the death drive leads her to investigate a "poetry that is not a form of murder" (72). Kristeva discusses the practices of sacrifice and sacral rites, of which only the representation that mimes sacrifice "tends to dissolve the logical order."[8] She links this movement specifically to the Dionysian festivals. Kristeva´s topographical choice of words—she likens the division between semiotic chora and the symbolic to a "border" and a "frontier" that can only be crossed by a "signifying path"—almost literally describes the final scene of *Malina*, in which the female narrator, after her operatic ecstasy, mimetically sacrifices herself for the novel-child-man *Malina* and retreats, imitating the hiding of the letters she had previously stuffed into crevices in the desk, into the vaginal fold of the symbolic wall, "from which nothing can ever be heard again" ("aus der nie mehr etwas laut werden kann," 356).[9] In the original German, "laut werden" explicitly links sound to knowledge and meaning. Kristeva describes the mimetic crossing in form of a combination of verbal, physiognomic, and vocal signs as the signifying movement as such, whereas the result, neither positive nor negative, is an erasure of meaning. While Bachmann's narrator's singing and the novel's musical score oscillate among analytic serenity, Tristan and Isolde´s passionate duets, and symbolic violence,[10] two questions have yet to be answered satisfactorily: Do the gendered voices in *Malina* sustain a structural, not simply reader-oriented, cacophony that refuses to unite even posthumously, under the sole authority and subjectivity of the male protagonists? Does the letter form aid in leaving a trace of otherness, of nonhegemonic subjectivity without recourse to an extraliterary position?

In her study of epistolary dynamics in the seventeenth and eighteenth centuries, Elizabeth MacArthur argues that the letter does not simply deviate from the literary norm.[11] She suggests the term "extravagant" to describe the tendency of epistolary fiction to resist the subordination of its metonymic flow to metaphoric teleology. Can the inclusion of epistolary fiction, situated among and against other narrative forms, similarly be viewed as a resistance to metaphor? In "Theses towards a Feminine Aesthetic" (1984), Renate Lachmann develops the idea of metonymic writing as a poetic and semiotic concept that links the constitution of the subject to its specific generic expression. Barbara Lersch locates Lachmann's idea of metonymy in this exchange of subject and text, which also reminds us of Kristeva´s crossing of the symbolic.[12] Two observations connect this description of "metonymic writing" to the epistolary form and the female voice.

First, the subject of a text, of a letter, of addressee and sender, constitutes itself between writing and reading "as the proper/essential product of the work of the text."[13] The letter form is built on an intersubjective exchange, therefore letter and subject already enter a metonymic situation in that the text becomes the subject in the hands of the other. Second, I have already mentioned the metonymic shift between literature and the letter, between language and the letter that seems to be at work in much of experimental contemporary fiction.[14] In poststructuralist and postmodernist discourse, Woman and letter are defined and function like a medium that refuses to mediate, a metaphor for the metonymic process of undecidability.[15] In this chapter, I want to suggest, without limiting Bachmann's writing to differential theories or metaphoric metonymy, that her narrative rhapsodic techniques with the help of and in spite of mail-ordered epistolary fiction provides a commentary as well as a basis for poststructurally inspired critical discourse.

RHAPSODY AND LETTERS

The rhapsodic aspect of contemporary epistolary fiction's narrative strategies in combination with my own reading practice offers a concept which unites and separates, which performs itself as it (re)defines itself. A rhapsody insistently refers to its simulation of other generic devices while it engenders a genre of its own. In this section, I want to problematize the relationship between rhapsody and epistolarity, among women authors, feminist narrative, and critical strategies.

The introduction of the rhapsodic element, of an "extravagant effusion" as the rhapsody was known in the seventeenth century,[16] into contemporary fiction, and its introduction into this chapter compels me to pursue an excursion, to wander (Latin: *extravagari*) from the path without actually leaving it. By refusing to participate in the veiling procedure (not to hide but to reflect on the process and direction of reading, interpretation, and writing) many courageous feminist artists and scholars forsake the safety blanket along with the blinders. Their writing draws attention to the contradictions involved in the dominant ideology, which may leave readers confused as to the destination of their arguments, a conflict which is often solved by stating that "they don't know what they are saying" or that there is no visible destination for them within "the" system.[17]

On the one hand, doing feminist theory implies a negotiation with the mail-order, acknowledging its contradictory aspirations and limitations as Bachmann did when she decided to write in the novelistic mode. On the other hand, to use political and musical metaphors, like the concepts of "border-crossing" and rhapsody, as an analogy for literary dynamics is to enter a *tertium comparationis*, a metaphysical realm, in which language's products suddenly seem describable and fathomable. Barbara Naumann, who studies Friedrich Schlegel's genre-poetics in relation to his reflections on music, justifiably admonishes the eager comparatist against this tendency when dealing with music and musicality in literature.[18] Her essay not only underscores my point about veiling procedures but it also provides me with a transition toward the discussion of epistolarity and rhapsody whose connection takes its Romantic roots in Schlegel's poetics.[19]

Naumann defends her own comparison of Schlegel's poetics and reflections on music with his idea of music as an "undefinable signifier," an understanding that lets him view music as "the expression of Idealism" (78). She continues that the affinity of musicality to Schlegel's Progressive Universal Poetry lies at "the point at which the thematic indeterminacy turns into the definition-signal of music and of eternal reflection, i.e. at which the two different media are made commensurable through their indeterminacy" (79).[20] Indeterminacy ensures the comparability of music and *Poesie*. Both media, music and poetry, have to lose their generic specificity in order to interact, even interphase with each other. Both critics, Naumann and Schlegel, have to create a mail-order clearinghouse that (con)fuses the distribution of generic characteristics and protects their generic integrity just the same. Friedrich Schlegel's "intensive relation of the musical to the *reflexive* and 'sentimental' gesture of modern art" concerns me here in particular because he explicates it by and through the novel (80): "The inner form of the novel is mathematical, rhetorical, musical. The potentializing, progressing, irrational, furthermore the rhetorical figures. With music it understands itself by itself."[21] At the center of Schlegel's idea of the novel, at the core of the novel and the innermost form of novels ("die innerste Form des Romans") lies a dialectic chain. Schlegel's triangular chain places Progressive Poetry between the poles of continually multiplying rational mathematics and irrational music. He depicts *Poesie* as the product of logic and the constituent of irrationality, which is in turn *potenziert* by logic leading to *Progression* and the *Irrationale* ad infinitum.

One should not misconstrue "progressive *Poesie*" as the synthetic link between rational and irrational. In the rhetorical figure of Schlegel's own discourse and on the syntactic level of the chain itself, the "rhetorical figures" combine aspects of "poetics," logic, and irrationality to enter a place simultaneously within and apart from synthetic resolution. In Schlegel's clever verbal construct, adjectives repeat themselves as concepts only to again break down into their characteristics. This movement between the poles neither harmonizes the violent antagonism nor prevents understanding. It describes the flow of the "innermost form of the novel" along the self-understanding sensualized intellectual dynamics, the hypertactical and yet paratactical score, of a musical composition. "The innermost form of the novel" is the dialogue between self and other, between subjectivity and objectivity, between logic and madness, in short the novel is intersubjective, intertextual at its core. In 1797, two years prior to *Lucinde*, he claims that there is as yet no genre that would be able to contain this difference, remain a fragment, and be an essential part of the sciences.[22]

A rhapsody was defined as a "recitation of parts of an epic poem" in ancient Greece. The Latin term *rhapsodia* was first applied to a book of Homer by Cornelius Nepus.²³ The "*Iliad* consists of a number of rhapsodies recited or written down in a sequel."²⁴ Etymologically, it forms a Greek compound of *rháptein* (to stitch) and *oîdé* (ode, song). In the sixteenth century rhapsody literally meant "miscellany, medley." The seventeenth century labeled it an "extravagant effusion." In the eighteenth century, "rhapsody" referred to a piece in one movement based on popular, national and folk melodies. Since then, "the rhapsody had no regular form and was not confined to any particular medium."²⁵ Its style is usually characterized as "passionate, nostalgic, improvisatory."²⁶ Franz Liszt's Hungarian rhapsodies, for example, "are characterized by remarkable changes of mood, supposed to be typical of the Slav temperament, moods which range from deep gloom to joyful excitement."²⁷ The characterization of Liszt's rhapsodies is especially relevant in connection with Bachmann's *Malina*, because it specifically deals with the Slavic influence in Vienna, and its narrative fragments feature such "changes of mood."

The applications and changing meanings of the term "rhapsody" demonstrate a certain resilience against normative categorizations. The term most often refers to a style rather than a genre of itself, a limitation that it shares with certain definitions of postmodernism. The notion of applying the term "rhapsodic" to a textual construct is already woven into "rhapsody's" linguistic design and its historical usage. Interestingly, *rhapsoidiá* (rhapsody) and *rhapsoidos* (rhapsodist) are both feminine nouns. Friedrich Schlegel, for example, believes Caroline Schlegel-Schelling's letters to contain "one great philosophical rhapsody,"²⁸ yet he disapproves of Caroline's rhapsodic fragments. While complimenting Caroline on her "natural" talent in letter-writing, he claims that the fragmentary philosophical form, including the rhapsody, is the "natural" expression for himself and his male colleagues.²⁹ Christa Bürger, countering Schlegel with a feminist reading, interprets Caroline Schlegel-Schelling's letters themselves as "luciferic rhapsodies." Bürger defines the writing style of Romantic rhapsody as "a type of writing that corresponds to the philosophic style but refuses every attempt at systematization" and *Diaskeuse* as a "type of writing that consistently erases and resurrects its character as a work of art." Bürger's notion of Caroline's luciferic rhapsody is composed of anecdote, irony, paradox, parody, and portraiture. Her rhapsodic practice, she contends, belongs to an "aesthetic interstice hovering between classicism and modernism that is difficult to grasp."³⁰

Neither Caroline Schlegel nor Ingeborg Bachmann confined themselves totally to their male compatriots' assignments. But before I can investigate whether Bachmann employs certain "luciferic" tendencies against the gendered artistic self stuck between modernism and postmodernism, and whether she parodies the operatic pathos of its demise in *Malina*, it is indispensable to stay a bit longer with considerations regarding the historical relationship among rhapsody, letters, and images of femininity.

In rhapsody's meandering meanings over the centuries, one can discern its affiliation with the female gender, as well as that gender's representation in male histories. The phrase "extravagant effusion" reminds one of the German uneasiness with the more "natural" French correspondence style in the seventeenth century, and the largely positive, albeit fearful, descriptions of personal letters as "outpourings of the heart" in the eighteenth century.[31] This leads back to Elizabeth MacArthur's definition of "extravagance," which she associates "with the epistolary form and with metonymic desire." A text is said to be extravagant if it is "not incorporated into the canonic collections," remains "outside of common sense," and "strays from the path."[32] Even today, critics distrust the uncontrollable flow of female narratives, whether by a real woman author or a female protagonist. Eberhard Lämmert, one of the most influential contemporary German critics of the novel, polemicizes against Clarissa's and Pamela's extravagant combination of letter-writing and life, and instead praises Werther's almost absolutist retirement to his imagination:

> It is a commonplace that one cannot write and also act at the same time. In the case of Richardson's noble minded letter writers, one really wonders how, in their lives filled with continuous scriptomania, the bemoaned seductions could even take place. Werther's life already takes place to a much higher degree in his imagination than in the real encounters and events of his external existence.[33]

While Goethe's contemporaries depicted the sentimental novel as suffering from extravagant, effusive imagination, Lämmert, from his late-twentieth-century vantage point, attempts to lift Goethe's *Werther* beyond the physical-materialist confines of the sentimental novel into the realm of pure thought—not despite but because of its own economics of "effusive imagination." Schlegel's thoughts appear to run a similar course in his philosophical fragments. As he engrosses his mind in minute definitions of the forms our imagination can assume, one term, written down, conjures up the next. As he reads and reflects on previous writings, they construct a cyclical chain of substituted definitions of speech, letter, rhapsody, and monologue:

> Speech is from nobody to nobody, or from all to all. The letter is from somebody to somebody, very definite, (cyclic, stanza, monody, cyclic nature) / The true [rhapsody] must simultaneously be letter and absolute speech, dialogue and monologue--parallelism to thoughts as in Fichte. The true letter must be [rhetorical], and in addition sapphic, like a stanza.--The monologue is a cyclic speech.--[34]

Although equivocally adhering to his genre definitions while proclaiming them, Schlegel arrives at a self-definition of his own writing only after trespassing on other genres. The sixty-ninth fragment starts with speech, a genre that addresses itself to no one and yet to everyone. At its end, the fragment returns to speech. In the intergeneric definition, letter and monologue have been adjusted by the adjective *cyklisch*. Their cyclical nature allows for speech to address and respond to speech, for communication. The response, however, is not a restatement of the same. The monologue is now defined as cyclical speech, which catapults speech onward and backward once more.

The nonidentical "other" within the cyclical pattern of the fragment and Schlegel's definitions arises during his intergeneric wandering from speech to letter to rhapsody to letter to monologue to speech. In the middle, all genres meet in the definition of true rhapsody only to stray apart again with the letter. The letter definitions in the fragment are situated before and immediately after the consummating rhapsody, so that one could speak of an epistolary structure of Schlegel's poetics. The letter is sent, arrives in rhapsody, and is sent again to take parts of this meeting along on its journey toward another consummation.

Since "speech" has neither author nor addressee, the letter (as literal letter in writing) has to provide the specificity, the concreteness of the dialogue. The letter guarantees the possibility of speech. Even though writing is repressed into the folds and unstable meandering of the letter within the hermetically "cyclic" world of "speech," the letter ensures perfect correspondence between "speech" and "speech." Schlegel's paragraph on speech and rhapsody outlines the discourse of modernity. It also literalizes the modern mailing system of literary aesthetics and language theory. In this system, the letter is both guaranty of dialogue and dialogue's impostor.

Rhapsody, at the center of this postal universe (in Schlegel's understanding), manages to thrive on the generic tensions that sustain it. Because a rhapsody simultaneously has to be a letter, the tensions cannot resolve into harmony. In Schlegel's writerly sample of the rhapsodic discourse, the letter summons and disseminates before the quavering center can establish a unified authority over the margins. But because the letter's specialty is the incorporation and evocation of an "other," this encounter transmits itself to the margins. The set of two hyphens indicates a rupture in that they call forth a particular dialogical echo, contained in Schlegel's literary discourse: Fichte. The normative return to "monologue" and the cyclic control over "speech" cannot exterminate the parallelism of discourse. A textual rhapsody therefore is not one but polyphonous, it is never just one of the genres alone, neither monologic nor a literary *Gesamtkunstwerk*.[35]

A last glance into the program: The sequel of four epistolary rhapsodies, which I intercept in *Malina*, attunes the reader to the de/con-
struction of the female voice in literary and critical discourse. The rhapsodic element simultaneously engages me in a writing procedure that
connects and disconnects the interpretations of the novel. The first rhapsody traces the letter form's mediation of memory, in particular, the psychological history of the Third Reich and the Holocaust. Through the
letter's position at the crossroads of autobiographical writing and the
public sphere, this movement seeks to sound out the precarious
mnemonic intertextuality of gender, history, autobiography, and *belles
lettres*. The second rhapsody sets up the letter as a bridge between
sender and addressee, letters and literature, history and present, space
and time, reality and art, man and woman. The narrator and her author
explore the "androgynic" illusion of (epistolary) correspondence. This is
a romantic rhapsody in letters. The third rhapsody no longer establishes
the letter form as a reliable, impartial mediator of the illusion of immediacy and meta-gender/genre constructs. Instead it shows the letter to
participate in the writing movement's violence and pleasure; it lays open
the tensions resulting from the structural framework of epistolary
dependencies, of the gender/genre system. One could call this a modernist rhapsody in letters. In the fourth rhapsody, Bachmann decon-
structs epistolary rhapsody at an ideological intersection. Despite the
chronological movements within my score, each rhapsody interacts with
and rewrites the other just as the gendered subjects interact with their
various layers of self-understanding, their chorus of projected selves. In
a postmodern move, in which boundaries are confirmed while they are
destroyed, the female voices risk the rhapsodic play of the letter.

RHAPSODY #1

What has been bemoaned as postwar German society's "inability to
mourn" cannot be applied to Ingeborg Bachmann's works.[36] *Malina* represents a "work of mourning" by a woman born in the 1920s. Her
Trauerarbeit focuses on Germany's and Austria's Nazi past, her own
involvement as a woman in the rise of fascism and its atrocities. In the
novel, repressed personal memories come to the surface in letters never
mailed. As implied readers we witness the struggle to get these letters
written, witness their contents and their various interpretations, witness
their destruction or alteration afterwards. In the postwar era, what one
could not or would not speak about, apparently needed another outlet.
What one could or would neither publish in prose nor as autobiography
(especially by women writers in the 1950s) found its way into the fugi-

tive form of letters within fictional narratives. If a postwar German or Austrian author wanted to empathize with victims of the Holocaust and the war, a self-enforced sense of sensitivity, respect, and justice in general prohibited them from filching survivors' stories, turning terrified sensations into sensationalist narratives. Accounts of the Holocaust had to be mediated through survivors' testimonies or through another nation's attempts at portraying that part of the German and Austrian past within a fictional frame.[37] Although Bachmann does not seek to become an impostor of the victims' memories, she is intent on providing herself and her public with a viable alternative to autobiographical material. She found this alternative in already mediated letters, diaries, and dreams.

In these narrative shapes, a controversial dialogue on fascism, the Holocaust, and its multiple victims takes place. The application of the term "fascism" to "war" and the oppression of women has been justly criticized as problematic.[38] *Malina* redefines the fascist mode of *Gleichschaltung*, in which the National Socialist Party platform controls the ideological content and form of art, economy, politics, and general society, to include the experiences of the majority of women, especially women artists under an omnipotent patriarchy. The possibility of equating fascism with the oppression of women presented itself to Bachmann in the process of an ethical and psychological *Vergangenheitsbewältigung*, which focused on the terrorization and execution of minorities, among them women and girls singled out for forced sterilization, medical experiments, or euthanasia because of their childbearing potential, Jewish women singled out for their supposed "hypersexuality." Bachmann's comparison of racism, anti-Semitism, and sexism can be situated within the context of the first wave of the postwar European women's movement, still heavily indebted to Marxist theory, one of whose first goals was the establishment of a universal solidarity of the oppressed.[39] She begins to ask:

> where does fascism begin? It does not begin with the first bombs that are thrown; it does not begin with the terror, about which one can write in every newspaper. It begins in the relationship between human beings. Fascism is the first thing in the relationship between a man and a woman, and I have tried to say, in this chapter, here in this society, it is always war.[40]

The fact that Bachmann witnessed three types of fascism—Austrian fascism and the aftermath of fascism in Germany and Italy—might help to explain why fascism for her was not restricted to the German phenomenon, and why her understanding of fascism is largely, but not exclusively, rooted in psychosexual behavioral norms.

Malina appeared after Bachmann's own long publishing silence, and after the initial sociopolitical idealism of Germany's student movement had begun to turn sour.[41] Coming from Austria, which represented itself as "the first victim of Nazi aggression" in 1938, Bachmann's 1973 trip to Auschwitz in a Poland torn apart by both Nazi and Soviet occupation, must have triggered her realization that Polish and Jewish accounts of Nazi atrocities and the war were not comparable to stylized Austrian "victimization." In an allegorical essay-fragment, she admonishes herself and the reader against the counterfeit trade conducted with the word "victim." She explains that people who wished to clear their names both by claiming victim status and by association with victims carried out "one of the most terrible and thoughtless, weakest poetizations" ("eine der furchtbarsten und gedankenlosesten, schwächsten Poetisierungen"), namely, by turning the victims of the Holocaust into symbols of "fascism," thereby closing history for themselves.[42]

At the height of Marxist theories of fascism, Bachmann's psychosexual understanding of fascism and her equation of fascism with war was perceived as overly generalized and simplistic. Read through the glasses of feminist solidarity, Bachmann's application of the terms *faschistisch* and *Faschismus* to the "battle between the sexes" may have hoped to initiate a *Vergangenheitsbewältigung* for this other "dark history" through a provocative decontextualization or as an intentional distortion of the term in an attempt to prevent closure, to ensure continuing confrontation with its terror.[43] But it is also noticeable that the author claims a certain right to suffering for her artist-character, paradoxically arguing that as a postwar female artist she had to suffer doubly from the Holocaust-induced writer's block because it made all other suffering trivial by comparison, also that of being a female artist in a male-dominated profession. At the same time, she was aware of shouldering a specific responsibility as an artist to aid remembrance.

The interpersonal approach to Germany's and Austria's past is reflected in the author's understanding of her writing as an intersubjective act, an act of mediation among individuals, times, and places. But Ingeborg Bachmann's relation to the writer-reader dialogue and epistolary communication is full of tension. For her, this dialogue needs to increase that tension rather than to alleviate it for the sake of a momentary consensus. In 1959, when she discusses the role of the writer, she thinks of transmitting pain, forcing the reader to relive pain: "Therefore it cannot be the task of a writer to belie the pain, to cover up its traces, to feint it. On the contrary, he must realize it and once again make it come true, so that we can see."[44] She further describes the writer as intersubjective by nature:

The writer is directed towards a you with his entire being, towards a human being, to whom he wants to transmit his experience of the human (or of his experience of things, of the world and his time, yes, also of all of those!), but especially of the human being, that he himself or the others can be and where he and the others are most human.[45]

Her "letters of personal experience" are targeted toward the core problems of society, not to heal them but to uncover and inspect them. In this "inspection" lies the only avenue toward a perpetrator's "righteous suffering."

In the essay on "victims," quoted earlier, she relates the poetization of victims to her ambiguous role as a postwar writer, to the telling of truths. Even though the survivors, including herself, can determine the semantics of the Holocaust, they are not "in der Wahrheit" ("in the truth"). In the last paragraph, Bachmann metonymizes the metaphorized "victims." Instead of expressing "the truth," she expresses "the difficulty to express that." She literally relates the process of converting "truths" into "dead messages" ("victims" into "symbols") to the execution of minorities:

Sometimes I feel very explicitly the one truth or the other standing up, and feel how it is trampled down by other thoughts in my head or feel it wilting, because I don't know what to do with it, because it doesn't let itself be communicated, I do not know how to communicate it or because right then nothing demands this message, I cannot hook in anywhere and with anyone.[46]

Bachmann portrays the verbalization of truths as an ongoing battle among sender, message, and receiver, both internally and externally. Victimization starts with the psychological linguistic process that is intricately interwoven with political and social realities. A truth can only come forth if it can be transformed into a message, is understood by the sender and called forth by the recipient, and finally if it initiates a response in the recipient. In this complicated discursive procedure, many truths are condemned to a short shelf-life through self-censure, violent oppression, incomprehension, or denial. In the post office of the brain, these truths remain "dead letters." If they have neither come forth, nor been articulated and received as messages in their time, they have no life, they have been killed. They cannot be claimed as lost or delayed messages later, although this is strictly what the "traffic in victims" is all about. For Bachmann, there are no *Persilscheine* ("whitewash-certificates," idiom for denazification papers stating one's cleared status) for one's conscience. In Bachmann's analogy, there must not be any of these "dead letters" in postwar consciences, in postwar society: "This is precisely the reason why there must not be any victims (human victims), humans as victims, because the sacrificed/victimized human results in nothing." ("Eben deshalb darf es keine Opfer geben (Menschenopfer), Menschen als Opfer, weil der geopferte Mensch nichts ergibt").[47] As Christine Kanz notes, Bachmann wants to develop a "writing practice that also signifies a 'dramatization' of the physicality of suffering, an 'authenticity' producing victim-language, which can further express fear and terror."[48] In light of these statements, any reading of the end of *Malina* as a self-sacrificial act has to be rethought.

In a later essay for the proposed international journal *Gulliver* (1964), she questions whether letter-writing is still possible or even justifiable. In her eyes, "sacred epistolary art" ("sakrale Briefkunst") is affiliated with modernist intellectuals' idealistic nostalgia for a lost totality and immediacy voiced with cosmopolitan aloofness. Bachmann here equates "sacred epistolary art" and the "enamored adoration of the literatures, paintings, and music of others" with a belief in the primacy of aestheticism and the illusion of the unity of a "European intellect."[49] Similar to Adorno's "poetry after Auschwitz" dictum, she argues, this stylized version of a European cosmopolitan society collided with the realities and global implications of the two World Wars. In the postwar situation, for her, the coordinates of time and place as well as of the subject are no longer "stitched with golden thread into the ordinary geography of this continent" which enabled letters to become "printable," to turn into the literary and intellectual history of modernism.

> A sacred observation of the terrain and along with that a sacred epistolary art—one has been allowed to call it European—has come to an end, and there will not be much more to collect afterwards, a few telegram pieces, postcards, also a few letters. Why not letters as well? But without the fold, the significant, the "responsible," that betrays itself already by the form of address and consistent stylization. An impoverishment, one will say. Yes, but maybe one wanted to become impoverished, maybe one has become too ill-humored and too impatient in order to celebrate thoughts and feelings that one also has, or one becomes aware that it no longer does any good to talk about them when one is in the position of the wheel changer. And sometimes, one doesn't feel up to dipping the gold feather into the ink and creating eternity or, in a superior manner, to give sign from person to person between filling out the tax forms and a trip to the baker.[50]

Written seven years prior to the publication of *Malina*, this theory of modernism as an age of the epistolary production of the metaphysics of Being, of subjectivity and national identity, foreshadows Bachmann's treatment of epistolary fiction in her novel. Something remains to be collected after the end of this epistolary era: shreds of telegrams, postcards . . . and also a few letters, a different kind of letters, perhaps letters freed from their prescripted destinations within a modernist trajectory. She proclaims here what Jacques Derrida will later call "the unlimited empire of a postcardization" in his *Postcard* (104).[51]

In some ways, *Malina* is an open letter to modernist Vienna, a critique of its cultural history, the repression of Slavic, Jewish, Turkish, and Italian influences, and of its unrelenting male dominance. Bachmann admits that the novel could only have been written "in my double life," from a distance in Rome, where her writing is motivated through scraps of memories, maps, pictures, and music. In general, the writing of letters psychologically and pragmatically combines the gestures of "fetching" with "sending" and "letting go," words that Bachmann uses to describe her composition of *Malina*.[52] Yet, simultaneously, letters can no longer be written after the Holocaust precisely because they involve "letting go." Letting go in form of a disclosure, a remission system that reinstates the status quo after a period of a ritualized exhibition of remorse is not something Bachmann is willing and her character "Ich" is able to do. Instead, Derrida's epistolary postcards and Bachmann's letter-fragments in *Malina* take issue with the modernist tradition of representational-computational systems as messages of Being.[53]

RHAPSODY #2

"Einen Brief absenden heißt in Österreich einen Brief aufgeben."
("To send a letter is referred to in Austria as giving up a letter.")
—Karl Kraus, 1874–1936, "Wien"

Any reader of *Malina* confronts the severe contradictions of an unstable narrative position which in turn unhinges the reader's own pattern of understanding. Ingeborg Bachmann works with an utterly unreliable narrator, a narrator who repeatedly states that she does not wish to narrate or cannot narrate. Sometimes everything in her memory disturbs her, at other times nothing disturbs her in her past.[54] Whatever she voices at one point and time will find its direct opposite at another point and time. The narrator refuses to mediate a unified and factual reality. The borders between her dream world, her thoughts, her actions, and the narrating and narrated worlds shift and dissolve. She chooses to involve the reader in complex interrelations among pluralistic wor(l)ds within the frame of the novel as a whole, the individual chapters, the segments that comprise those chapters, the various genres employed to formulate a certain memory, and finally among paragraphs, sentences, and each subclause. For now, I want to concentrate on the way *Malina*'s epistolary situations introduce and execute this network of structural grammar and intergeneric writing.

The intricate generative grammar of the language games in *Malina* is paralleled by the novel's playfulness with title, personae, and preface. Its title is also the name of one of the male characters, the character Malina, who controls the narrative closure. Even before opening the book, the author plays on the reader's expectations and habits. The West European reader assumes the title to be the subject of the novel, a feminine subject at that. Instead, in analogy to Barth's *LETTERS*, the title writes an anagram of its various characters: Malina, Lina, Melanie, Jellinek, Lily, Marcel; or, in other words, its characters' letters can only be derived from the novel's title, which itself derives from "MAskuLIN," "ANIMAL," "ANIMA/ANIMUS," and "MAL."[55] Ingeborg Bachmann plays with the illusion of a closed, a hermetically sealed phallocentric narratological system that engulfs any "other" into its framed totality. The narrative world of *Malin-a*, however, constitutes a mimetic transcription, not a transgression of the represented worlds. What the female protagonist says about her superfluousness while retelling the Adam and Eve story provides the edge for the possibility of storytelling:

> It seems to me, then, that his calmness stems from that fact, because I am a much too unimportant and familiar I for him, as if he secreted me, a waste, a superfluous incarnation, as if I was only made from his rib and since then expendable, but also an unavoidable dark story, that accompanies his story, wants to complement it, but which he distinguishes and delimits from his clear story. As a result, only I have to clear something with him, and most of all I have to and can only clear myself before him. He has nothing to clear, no, not he.[56]

But Malina is not Malin. While the feminine and Hungarian suffix -*a* is literally secreted and distinguished from the male and racially purified body, it still defines it. If we read the title and beginning of the novel in light of Bachmann's "victim" essay discussed above, the subconscious communication system, complete with the nineteenth-century legacy of racial and sexual anxieties, plays itself out on Ich's *Gedankenbühne* (thought stage). The character Malina puts himself in control of the semantics of the narrated worlds, yet is in return engendered by the language and stories of the suppressed worlds as the title indicates. Traveling between the discourses and worlds fenced off by him for his own protection and enjoyment, he has nothing to clear, nothing to declare. But she always has to clear her itinerary with him, clear her name in front of him, and declare her excesses at the border. He is judge, priest, psychotherapist, immigration and custom's officer rolled into one.

The attempt at secretion becomes most evident in the second chapter, in which Malina interrogates Ich about her dreams. Even though Malina's seemingly disengaged questions about the identity of Ich's tor-

mentor lead to an innertextually transparent result—total war, apocalypse, castration—he cannot clear Ich's narrative from its contradictions
other than to manipulate Ich's insight according to his assumptions. For
him, everything is already clear, before as well as after her stories.[57] As
much as he distances himself from the polymorphism of Ich's daydream
and nightmare narratives, and as much as he is made to represent the
instance of power and the concept of totality itself, he simply cannot
stand outside the narratological system. But neither can she. Ingeborg
Bachmann's multiple frames indicate a philosophical proximity to
Heisenberg's "unclear relation" *(Unschärferelation)*, which Wolfgang
Welsch describes as follows:

> There is no complete transparency, not just in the totality, but already
> in the individual system. Properties like space and impulse or time and
> energy may be defined in the same system, and though they are canon-
> ically conjugated properties, their simultaneous definition reaches
> untranscendable limits. The precise focus on one makes the simultane-
> ous grasp of the other impossible.

Welsch further links Heisenberg's theory to Gödel's "incompleteness
axiom" *(Unvollständigkeitssatz):* "It states that every . . . formal system
is incomplete and that its freedom from contradictions cannot be proven
with its own means."[58]

The following quote illustrates the built-in Heisenbergian tension of
Ich's narrative, a tension that reveals itself in an emphasis on structuring
conjunctions which turn into disjunctions:

> Even when Malina is silent, it is better than being silent alone, and it
> helps me along with Ivan later, when I cannot grasp it, and when I can-
> not grasp myself, because Malina is always there for me, firm and col-
> lected, and so the realization stays with me, in the darkest hours, that
> Malina is never going to be lost to me—and even if I myself got lost![59]

On the semantic surface of the utterance, the narrative voice announces
her relief to have Malina with her at all times, even when he is silent.
Should she be lost, Malina will still be there. The end of the novel seems
to settle the ambiguity: Malina remains. The converging world of Ivan
and Ich is built on the diverging world of Ich and Malina. Malina
strengthens her in the period of mindless infatuation, in a period that
opens all emotional channels, otherwise kept under lock and key. The
interruption and continuation of the sentence at another *caesura* tells a
different story. She cannot come to grips with herself because Malina—
strong, strict, and in control—is blocking her path. Malina and Ich: the
divergingly united world of master and slave.[60]

The message one reads depends on the relay mechanism of the sub-
ordinate and coordinate clauses. This mechanism within the sentence

structure could be called the post office of language. It is here where letters are sorted and mailed, where their addresses are deciphered and distributed according to postal regulations. Due to the *Briefgeheimnis*, letters are relayed "blindly." The post office's semantics is its structure. However, letters without sufficient value are not delivered. When Ich gets into the line for postal stamps, literally "postal value signs," she is shopping to increase the value of her messages, her letters (26). While she thus attempts to manipulate the relays in favor of the female voice, the increased value enslaves her to the rhythm of the relay. Her letters are accepted into the flow of mail but caught between Ivan's and Malina's correspondence.

In addition to this postal converging/diverging world in which Ich comes into existence only to disappear, Bachmann constructs the novel out of multiple epistolary instances. On the first few pages, Ich defines "today" *(heute)* as a word only appropriate for "real" letters, suicide letters and those letters which are never sent due to their inability to communicate the specific time, place, and mood immediately to its addressee (8/9). Real letters would be the medium of immediacy but since they are letters, immediacy is an innate impossibility. However, these unfinished, torn, and silenced letters remain "real" letters, because for her as a writer, these letters send themselves beyond themselves to arrive back at the literal meaning of a word: "Today" does not mean a day full of errands to run but indeed plainly "today," the only "today." These letters create a loop in time and space.[61] They strip away the common ground of idiomatic and metaphoric language and their implied meanings, what Ludwig Wittgenstein calls "the silent agreements for the comprehension of colloquial language," to lay open the process of subject (dis)location.[62]

Ich refuses to write business letters, which conceal this dislocation behind a mask of communicability. Fräulein Jellinek, her secretary and alter ego, is eager to do business: "etwas 'erledigen'" (70). While Jellinek insists on getting something done, Ich hears her saying that she wishes to "kill or finish something off, to exhaust something, to close a matter." Ich, who just began an affair with Ivan, dreads the idea of any kind of narrative closure because it reminds her of the precariousness of her life's balance. She therefore postpones the composition of these letters to the indiscernible future. Since these letters would not depart and arrive in her definition of "today" anyway, Ich could care less about their timely *Erledigung:* "You know what, we'll just stop today and write this stuff next week. Absolutely nothing comes to my mind" ("Wissen Sie was, wir machen heute einfach Schluß und schreiben dieses Zeug nächste Woche. Mir fällt überhaupt nichts ein," 50).

This statement, although intended to classify these letters as nonletters, also describes the status of literature. They cannot be finished today, that is, in today's world, due to a lack of imagination and creativity and because their composition depends on a team of producers instead of a single author. Ich's frenzied attempts to compose some of the answer-letters independently at night are, in fact, a desperate rescue mission to reinscribe letters into literature. This can easily become a catch-22, as I will discuss in detail in movements 2 and 3. First, however, I want to trace Ich's utopian epistolary activities.

Instead of differentiating herself from the male positions within a dualistic philosophy, Ich at first tries to incorporate their positions into her generic code, and repeatedly travels back and forth between them, from Ungargasse 6 to Ungargasse 9. "In greatest fear and tremendous hurry" ("in höchster Angst und fliegender Eile"), she composes letters that leave her distraught. She sends herself across the street to modulate the harmony she craves (80 and 74). At this stage, she is most terrified by the *differance* created between send-off and arrival. With every turn of the page, these epistolary poles collapse into the selfsame, the eternity desired and feared. The numbers 6 and 9 turn into an 8 when laid on top of each other; the symbol of 8, placed on its side, is also the symbol for eternity. Ivan's telephone number demonstrates this appropriately: 72 68 93 (26). The narrator reflects on her relation to the street and the numbers in the preface:

> I will not even begin to posit untenable assertions about my street, our street, I should rather search for my inter-locking with the Ungargasse in myself, because it makes its bend only in me, up to Number 9 and Number 6, and I ought to ask myself, why I am always in its magnetic field.[63]

The bend takes place solely within her. She intertwines with the street and the curving numbers. These numbers frame and paraphrase her sense of being. They form the positive and negative poles of a magnetic field, to which she applies "the feeling of coming home" ("das Gefühl des Nachhausekommens"), even though her own magnetic directions never permit her to rest in either place. Reading *Malina* with Queer Theory, one could argue that Ich is mapping the queering of gender designations and sexual orientation within compulsive heterosexuality. As Malina and Ivan draw in and repel her (13), Ich experiences a queering of her and Viennese society's "straight mind."[64] Ich's sense of queerness, of an in-the-closet outness, expresses itself as a letter which, although obeying the postal regulations of sending and arriving, cannot deliver. Her address instructions are readdressed whenever she arrives: "[D]ates and a profession follow, twice crossed out and written over, addresses, three times crossed out and written over, and in official handwriting above, one reads: lives in Ungargasse 6, Wien III" ("[E]s folgen Daten und ein Beruf, zweimal durchgestrichen und überschrieben, Adressen, dreimal durchgestrichen, und in korrekter Schrift ist darüber zu lesen: wohnhaft Ungargasse 6, Wien III" 8). The narrating voice keeps read-dressing herself. Since the bend takes place within her and through her, she has to question herself about the validity of identity, of the metaphysical oneness of time and place, of sex and gender.

Somehow, her metaphysical notion of an attainable union between self and other, between time and place, is an anachronism in postwar Vienna. After all, at the turn of the century, Hugo von Hofmannsthal had already raised this to the central issue of modernity in the letter to Lord Chandos. But Ich distinguishes her thoughts on time from Hofmannsthal's: "[W]hen I turn into my district . . . then it is not like the being sick of time, although the time suddenly converges with the place" ("[W]enn ich *einbiege* in meinen Bezirk . . . dann ist es nicht wie mit dem Kranksein an der Zeit, *obwohl* die Zeit plötzlich mit dem Ort zusammenfällt," 13; my italics). Looking back at fin-de-siécle Vienna, Bachmann emphasizes the state of melancholia, of mourning the past and the present that resulted precisely from the increased sense of mediated immediacy, of the technological fabrication of a confluence of time and place. For Ich, this state of synchronicity only appears at the moment of *einbiegen*, of turning into her *Ungargassenland*, at the moment of return to a place named for the migrant Hungarian merchants whose routes between their lodgings, the hay market, the bars, and back to Hungary are still engraved in the dreamscape of the city. Ich's physiological and mnemonic intertwining with the *Ungargassenland* stresses that Vienna was never one with itself. Therefore, Ich's sporadic experiences of synchronicity do not elicit the Viennese disease of mourning temporality.

They do, however, bend her opposite personality poles to the authority of the semantic field with which she hopes to describe and escape her situation. The prison effect of a fixed set of words and combinations (according to Ludwig Wittgenstein's popular sentence that "the borders of my language signify the borders of my world" ["die Grenzen meiner Sprache bedeuten die Grenzen meiner Welt"]) becomes clearer in a later passage, in which Ich expresses relief at her life's stasis:[65]

> Since I can dial this number, my life finally no longer takes its course, I no longer get underneath the wheels, I get into no inescapable difficulties, no longer forward and not off the path, because I hold my breath, delay time and phone and smoke and wait.[66]

Whereas she had earlier described the moment of return as synchronicity of time and space, Ich here describes motionlessness as an avoidance of her *errands* ("mistakes" and "getting lost" in one), as a standing still of life. Again, in her attempt to portray her infatuation and romantic anticipation, the semantic field of "not taking its course" ("nimmt keinen Verlauf"), initially emphasizing Ich's self-determination, curves back to its negative pole of objectification, of motion without purpose, of the story of an absolutely obedient and automated Little Red Ridinghood, who might as well never have left her mother's house.

In the Grimm tale, Little Red Ridinghood is a messenger who does not obey the postal code. She breaks the golden rule of the sanctity of the mail. She tells the wolf what is in her basket and who its addressee is. She also strays from the path to pluck wildflowers, forgetting the time of day. Because she is hungry, she even eats a bit from the cake. The allegory about the mailman Kranewitzer in the final chapter, which Gudrun Kohn-Waechter justly considers to be the leading allegory for the entire novel's structure, has its precursor in the first chapter, when Ich meets Ivan in front of the window display of a *Türkenbund*.[67] This "bunch of turk's cap lilies" with its exotic and erotic shades of red ("seven times redder than red"), comes very close to the wildflowers that Little Red Ridinghood cannot resist (67). In the hectic modern city of Vienna, the wolf might not even have seen her, had the *Türkenbund* (here also connoting Vienna's bond to the Turks through the occupations in 1528 and 1683) not drawn her into his path and into the past. In a city that officially only recognizes this part of Vienna's history in its coffeehouse tradition and the high point of baroque architecture after 1683, Bachmann's recontextualization of the fairy tale allows one to read the Grimm text as exoticized anxiety over interracial hybridity. Consequently, her first meeting with the Hungarian Ivan reveals how fragile Austrian-Turkish-Hungarian relations still are:

> A small detail could suffocate it in its beginning, nip it in the bud, bring it to a standstill from the start, that's how sensitive are the beginning and the creation of the strongest power in the world, because the world is actually sick and it does not want the healthy power to appear.[68]

Within this statement, Ich also inverts the fairy tale's lesson. Instead of the wolf, who devours Rotkäppchen, the world's sickness chokes love and converts it into "universal prostitution," a theme that Bachmann had previously explored in her radio play "The Good God of Manhattan." Bachmann rewrites the morale of the fairy tale to ponder questions raised by women's and civil rights movements. But that is not all. The Ivan narrative parodies both the romantization of the sexually and racially "other," and rational enlightenment's belief in *Bildung* (all-inclusive humanist education). It contrasts the context's complex psychology with simplistic language. The wolf, who is only interested in her body and utters but three sentences, is idolized into Pamela Andrew's and My Fair Lady's linguistic and cultural mentor.

Ich's longing for Ivan, the wolf, is stylized into a lesson in reevaluating and relearning the body of language. Ivan's mouth, ears, and eyes have incorporated her sense of self: "Finally I even walk around in my flesh. . . . How good, also, that I have grasped in a flash, what grabbed me in the first hour, and that I therefore immediately went with Ivan without acting up, without an act" (34).[69] The language used in this paragraph combs her naive consent against its grain. Studded with passive prefixes, she is not only coerced by Ivan but also by the linguistic comprehension and expression of this deed. Without creating a fuss, putting on a show, she simply resigns herself to the expressionlessness of her own desire, a desire that has to mask itself.[70]

The ambiguous verb *anstellen* (both: to get into line, to hire, and to act up) combines this window display of the sexual-textual order with their journey to the post office. The romanticized flowers of "universal prostitution" send Ich into the wolf's arms. Whereas Ivan stands in line at the counter for *Postanweisungen* (mail-orders), Ich has to get into the line for *Postwertzeichen* (stamps). That the narrator expresses a forceful hierarchy here is striking since she did not express a need to go to the post office before she met Ivan. She simply decides to follow him on his postal route. This entails what Gudrun Kohn-Waechter so nicely describes as "sich schicken," to "send herself," to resign herself to his postal code.[71] In the post office scene, she literally is about to valorize the mail/male-order. However, when the phrase "ohne mich anzustellen" reappears in the reiterated window scene, it again discloses its mischievous connotation of not getting into line at all, of refusing to play along.

Embedded in the genre of this common fairy tale, in which the benign grandmother's bedtime story is reversed into a discourse of desire, the nameless female narrator senses her awakening desire to be the image of male desire, her inquiring language to be stifled by his self-serving teleological causality: "Aber Großmutter, warum hast Du so einen großen Mund?" "Damit ich dich besser fressen kann." ("But grandmother, why do you have such a big mouth?" "So that I can eat you better."). Ich rewrites this exchange in acquired newspeak:

Denn er ist gekommen, *um* die Konsonanten wieder fest und faßlich zu machen, *um* die Vokale wieder zu öffnen, *damit* sie voll tönen, *um* mir die Worte wieder über die Lippen kommen zu lassen, *um* die ersten zerstörten Zusammenhänge wiederherzustellen und die Probleme zu erlösen. (29; my italics)

Because he came *in order to* make the consonants firm and tangible, *in order to* open the vowels, *so that* they sound full, *in order to* let words come over my lips once more, *in order to* repair destroyed connections and to redeem the problems.

She becomes his creation, a cyborg bride that is hooked up to the telephone, her energy source. Ivan's and Ich's body language is already disembodied by the telephone, where one voice cannot be told from the other, where total correspondence signifies the end of communication.[72] In order for this modern-day Machine-Maria to (re)learn language, Ivan and Ich "have left much at rest" ("haben vieles auf sich beruhen lassen"). They left much unsaid, "because even three sentences at this spot in front of the shop window would have been too much" ("weil schon drei Sätze, an dieser Stelle vor dem Schaufenster, zuviel gewesen wären," 35). In defense of this nonverbal language lesson, she contends: "That's why it took us so long to get beyond the first nonsense sentences" ("Darum haben wir lange gebraucht, bis wir über die ersten kleinen nichtssagenden Sätze hinausgefunden haben," 35). Bachmann's delightfully sacrilegious usage of *erlösen* instead of *lösen* actually rescues the problems from a final solution. It also shows up Ich's narrative as riddled with errors and disconnections that make new connections. Rather than simply reinventing Pygmalion's Galatea or the infamous Olympia, the homuncula Ich hybridizes vowels and consonants to write the story of her creation and termination. Bachmann employs a German language trait, in that letters, as pre- and suffix characters, when attached to stems of verbs can drastically change their meaning. In the context of mail-orders and epistolary fiction, these attachments indeed become codified messages to say the unsayable, to sneak her letters around the official postal routes that classify them as mistakes and misprints, especially when the author is a woman. "The Third Man" picks up on this movement as I will discuss in a subsequent rhapsody.

Bachmann incorporates the fairy tale into her text in a *mise en abyme* of the devouring wolf's doublespeak. "Glücklich mit Ivan" tells us an ecstatic story of misdirected mail, about the violation of authorship and the privacy of the post. Before she even realizes it, Ich's generically framed and purloined memory of her encounter with Ivan has granted her the wish to write an "Inkunabel" with her own fairy tale, "Die Geheimnisse der Prinzessin von Kagran" ("The Secrets of Princess von Kagran"). The letter has arrived before she sent it. Her fairy tale has already been written in the key of the wolf. This time around, as "Die Geheimnisse der Prinzessin von Kagran," its mechanism of shifting letters, although rendering a beautiful typography that stands off from the text and is never reprinted in its entirety, simply transposes the key with a piece of chalk.[73] The *Wulf* is still a wolf, whether seven little goats or Little Red Ridinghoods are on the menu (51).[74]

The precious and original "Inkunabel" reveals itself as a reprint unworthy of its price. The "princess's secrets" are a prostituted text. The story does not merit the antique desk that Ich wanted to purchase specifically for its composition. Appropriate to the history of the letter, the desk comes from a cloister, and she could not have conceived of anything while sitting at it: "that also bothers me, and in any case I could not have written on it, because parchment and ink do not exist" ("auch das stört mich, und darauf schreiben hätte ich doch nicht können, weil es Pergament und Tinte nicht gibt," 70). She wanted to write letters *à la Portuguese* or like Madame de Tourvel, but instead has to write like a combination of Valmont and his lover: on her own naked back. Realizing the vulgarity of her story, Ich wished she "could hide in the legend of a woman who never existed" ("und verstecken könnte ich mich in der Legende einer Frau, die es nie gegeben hat," 61), but instead makes the story disappear into a portfolio: "I let the pages about the Princess of Kagran hastily disappear into a portfolio, so that Miss Jellinek doesn't see what I have written" ("Ich lasse die Blätter über die Prinzessin von Kagran rasch in einer Mappe verschwinden, damit Fräulein Jellinek nicht sieht, was ich geschrieben habe," 70).

Instead of a personal letter, the embarrassed Ich hides her apocalyptic utopia. Within the fairy tale context, one could read this scene as a parody of the particular feminist fantasy associated with the letter and the fairy tale as "female" genres. In Bachmann's work, the directing role is played by an unwilling woman, who has difficulty dictating her refusals and regrets to another woman or, in this case, the other woman in her. Even in a director's, a boss's shoes, Ich is disorderly, thereby perturbing her secretary:

> [S]he fiddles with the files, where an unbelievable chaos reigns, she now discovers letters, kilos of them, from the years 1962, 1963, 1964, 1965, 1966, she sees her attempts spoiled to come to an arrangement with me.

> [S]ie hantiert jetzt mit der Ablage, in der ein unglaubliches Durcheinander herrscht, sie entdeckt jetzt Briefe, kiloweise, aus den Jahren 1962, 1963, 1964, 1965, 1966, sie sieht ihre Bemühungen vereitelt, mit mir zu einer Ordnung zu kommen. (70–71)

Woman desperately tries to get the better of the undecided woman, who feels displaced as "director" due to her momentary sensuous involvement with Ivan. Romantic infatuation and fulfilling her duty as secretary is not a problem for Fräulein Jellinek. Pretty Fräulein Jellinek, engaged to a neurosurgeon, does not suffer from nervous disorders like her boss. Her relay system functions like clockwork. She loves to make up words for and by someone else: "she really wants to begin, she wants to try it herself" ("sie will unbedingt anfangen, sie will es selbst probieren," 50). Miss Jellinek is happy to fill in the blanks, to obey the postal code. She assigns herself to these disembodied letters and forms.

Her Womanliness thrives on creating order even in her own ghostly dislocation: "[B]ut while her secret thoughts are in the policlinic and with setting up the house, she fills out forms for me" ("[A]ber während ihre heimlichen Gedanken in der Poliklinik sind und beim Wohnungseinrichten, füllt sie für mich Formulare aus," 70).

Ich, on the other hand, believes, "that I myself have to come to an arrangement [and that] an order for this heap of papers becomes ever more unimportant" ("daß ich selber in Ordnung kommen muß und eine Ordnung für diesen Papierwust immer gleichgültiger wird," 71). As there is no "one" woman, there is no "one" order for women. The idea of "female" genres is led ad absurdum. Two "orders" parallel each other. Both Ich and Miss Jellinek are in similarly enamored phases in their lives. While the freshly engaged Miss Jellinek's idea of order is the status quo, the woman as Woman, Ich understands order at this point to consist of the struggle for a livable balance between her sensuousness and her intellect.

The black knight of Ich's fairy tale *"silently designs his and her first death"* (*"entwarf schweigsam seinen und ihren ersten Tod,"* 69). Bachmann's *Malina* admonishes against the belief of outmaneuvering the mail/male-order with essentialist fictions. The female subject, whether on her way to fuse romantically with her lover or in the search of androgynous heroism, dies along with the modern "universal" male subject.

RHAPSODY #3

Whereas up to this point, I have focused on the novel's epistolary beginnings, I would now like to turn to the letters *en route*. The act of writing and the act of sending are quite different from arriving: "In höchster Angst und fliegender Eile," Bachmann's narrating voice sends herself across streets and genres, across gender barriers and philosophical theorems. Yet she never wholly arrives on time at any destination. This is the rumor that Antoinette Altenwyl, the representative of traditional Austrian gentry and Womanhood, heard about Ich: "She is astonished that I arrived intact, one would constantly hear such strange things about me, I would arrive nowhere, in any case never on time and never in the place where one expects me" ("Sie wundert sich, daß ich heil angekommen sei, man höre dauernd solche komischen Sachen über mich, ich käme nirgendwo an, jedenfalls nie zu der Zeit und nie an dem Ort, wo man mich erwartet," 137). In the following section, I will first explore my thesis that Ingeborg Bachmann's novel offers an archeology of the female voice by executing epistolary femininity as a mediating device.

In the course of *Malina*, the epistolary prototype recurs in the form of Ich's replies to invitations, replies to requests for interviews, her business correspondence. Instead of fulfilling her part and responding with yea or nay, she composes letters on letters, on specific words and the proper names (Schönthal and Ganz) of the addresses. Ingeborg Bachmann demonstrates in these letters that Ich's very struggle to escape by redirecting her letters to the postal code binds her ever more tightly to that system. While, at first sight, these letters only interrupt the plot and create a moment of retardation, they are firmly rooted in their specific textual surroundings, their *heute*. Due to their "otherness" as semiformal letters addressed to the extranarrative world, they redirect the focus of the text to its mailing procedure, to its mediating structure. They literalize the novel as letter. In the Schönthal-Ganz letters, each of which has multiple versions, Ich addresses not a particular person but the act of "addressing" itself.

Thematically, the addressee's proper names, the letters of their names, direct Ich's letters. The addressee "Schönthal" (beautiful valley) induces her to write on "bad manners" because the "friendly facade," which is invoked by his name, has less and less to do with her. It should be a name she can identify with, because her gendered education has traded her female identity for feminine manners. Now almost all she has left are manners and mannerism (72). She believes that these manners are responsible for her being "incapable to think of those things that one ordered me to think about, about a deadline, about a project, about a date" ("unfähig, an die Dinge zu denken, die man mir zum Denken verordnet, an einen Termin, an eine Arbeit, an eine Verabredung," 72). Yet her very letters to Schönthal are a sign of her inability to resist this decree, whether on the structural or thematic level.

It is not coincidental that the first draft of the letter to Schönthal includes a variation on Malina's "death sentence" at the end of the novel: "the person, to whom you turn, whom you believe to know, whom you even invite, she does not exist" ("die Person, an die Sie sich wenden, die Sie zu kennen meinen, die Sie sogar einladen, die gibt es nicht," 71). Since she addresses the form of the address itself, the authoritative character and property of the address in her letter (which, as a mailed letter, would become the property of the addressee), she reflects the addressee back to the addressee. In her place is nothing. Her adherence to conventional manners causes her to become nothing but a reflection of the addressee. In a way, she is turning the tables on Schönthal in that she reads his name and address to stand for his reality. In Schönthal's Nürnberg Wielandstrasse address, literary and political oppression meet under the facade of congeniality.[75] Ich therefore decides to send an impersonal telegram followed by an explanatory letter:

"Impossible to come stop letter will follow" ("Kommen leider unmöglich stop Brief folgt," 72). She checkmates him in his own language game but is still bound by its rules.

The constant struggle with the postal code leaves her "mortally exhausted" ("zu Tode erschöpft") "einfach tot" ("simply dead") on the phone with Ivan, whose fatigue is caused by a night on the town (73). Language allows them to share a semantic field when their feelings derive from opposite factors, one from writing two hundred and more desperate letters to the unresponsive outside world, the other from arriving home after excessive carousing in that outside world. She waits in vain for a sentence that will secure her in the world but realizes "[t]here would have to be an insurance which is not of this world" ("[e]s müßte eine Versicherung geben, die nicht von dieser Welt ist," 73). Whereas he is satisfied with her echo, because he detects no difference, she is aware of a redundancy without overlap. Despite the repetitions "werfe hin," "werfe ab," "angelehnt," "noch einmal," "auch," "müde," "erschöpft," "Erschöpfung," which already repeat the telephone conversation and should express an increased level of intimacy, she painfully experiences her "secretion." In order to be tired *with* him, she had to cast off ("werfe ab") her own particular understanding of fatigue that now reclaims her and leaves her wide awake (74).

In her letter to Ganz, she again meditates on her addressee's name, which in this instance also indicates an entire ("ein ganzes") genre. The first drafted letter to Ganz supersedes her intention to create a new metaphysical species, a new sex: "I produce a new species, that which is willed by God comes into the world out of mine and Ivan's *union*" ("ich erzeuge ein neues Geschlecht, aus meiner und Ivans *Vereinigung* kommt das Gottgewollte in die Welt," 106; my italics). The letter answers her claim that she and Ivan can create an organic unity. They do not need a weapon delivery "for the aid and protection of ourselves" ("zur Unterstützung und Sicherung unserer Selbst") because "[t]he basis is loose and good, and what falls onto my soil thrives, I disseminate myself with words and I also disseminate Ivan" (" [d]ie Basis ist locker und gut, und was auf meinen Boden fällt, das gedeiht, ich pflanze mich fort mit den Worten und ich pflanze auch Ivan fort," 106). Within the organic realm of the selfsame—"We get along even without translator" ("Auch ohne Dolmetscher kommen wir aus")—lies absolute cautious silence—"I find out nothing about Ivan, he finds out nothing from me" ("ich erfahre nichts über Ivan, er erfährt nichts von mir").[76] Her language and her desire have already erected the fascistic glass house that she fears: *wir* ("we," 105). Her last sentences reiterate "the womb is still fertile" ("der Schoß ist fruchtbar noch"). What reads like an essentialist feminist utopia moves uncomfortably close to what Godele von der Decken in her study on the role and image of women in National Socialist Germany calls "emancipation gone astray."[77]

The list of metaphysical objects to which Ich gives birth prior to the letter rewrites the fairy tale as the aesthetic union of Dionysian and Appolonian forces: fire birds, azurrite, diving flames, jade drops ("Feuervögel, Azurrite, Tauchende Flammen, Jadetropfen," 106). These liquefied jewels dip into and create—as a metaspecies—the Ganz letter. Ich addresses this letter to the phenomenon of totality. In it, Ich states her aversion to Ganz's name, meaning "total" or "whole." She considers it an inappropriate form of address. She does not want to direct her writing to the totality which it evokes.[78] She has to call the ghost she freed with her foretold progeny by his name.

Whether she adopts a writing style of repression: Genz or Ginz, of parody: Gans, or even of ridicule "with a dialect coloration" ("mit einer dialekthaften Färbung"): Gonz, each remains but a temporary escape. Ganz's name is doubly precarious because his language consists of trite *bon mots* for every conversational situation, and "because the word 'ganz' appears every day, uttered by others, not to be avoided even by myself, finds itself in every paragraph in newspapers and in books" ("weil das Wort 'ganz' jeden Tag vorkommt, von anderen ausgesprochen, auch von mir nicht zu vermeiden, in Zeitungen und in Büchern sich in jedem Absatz findet," 107). As a genre, Ganz's stories reach a permanent form and content through the repression of their form and content. They neither change themselves nor their context. The word genre "Ganz" has entered what Walter Benjamin would call "das Gerede." Only Ich feels violated by its common exchange, its currency and because she cannot forget its mailing process as she could the various forms of "Schmidt" and "Meyer": "I should have been careful, already because of your name, with which you continue to invade my life and strain it excessively" ("Ich hätte mich vorsehen müssen, schon Ihres Namens wegen, mit dem Sie weiter in mein Leben einfallen und es strapazieren über Gebühr," 107). The postal value *(Gebühr)* for "ganz" is inflated. Every time she or someone else utters the word *ganz*, it increases the systemic powers of the modernist patriarchal mail order.

Reflecting back to the Schönthal letter, her very means of resistance, her writing styles and manners, are either produced by the enemy itself or fail to provide adequate hold. The military fashion, with which she arms herself for the encounter with Ganz appears *shortly after* she fears to see him again, and her *whole* ears cannot support the thorny earrings:

A short time ago, when I almost had to fear to see you again, shortly after the new fashion appeared, with the metal dresses, the chain-mail

shirts, the thorny fringes and the jewelry made of wire-cages, I felt
equipped for a meeting, I wouldn't even have had the ears free, because
dangling on my earlobes, I had two thorn bushels in the most beautiful gray, that hurt or slipped with each turn of the head, *because at the
earliest age one had forgotten to pierce these holes into my ears, which
otherwise in the country all little girls get drilled without mercy, in
their most tender age.*[79]

Even though she has escaped the "fashion police," which earmark little
girls for the cattle drive to the meat market, this does not provide her
with a means to protect herself against this absolute power.[80] Pierced or
not, her ears only signify within the system of *ganz,* even if she meets her
maker as a thorn-crowned martyr or armed as a cyborg Amazon.

With the second letter to Ganz, which she simply addresses to a
"Herr" ("mister"), Ich strives to withdraw from the mailing process
altogether. Ganz has used *Du* since the specific "Intermezzo," resulting from the fatal attraction between them. *Du,* especially when capi-
talized, was the epistolary form of address for friends and confidantes
until the 1998 language reform, but when abused, also stands for a
lack of respect. Ich has learned an early lesson that trusting someone
simply because he calls her *Du* leads to a slap in the face and the
"knowledge of pain" ("Erkenntnis des Schmerzes," 22). With each
Du, Ganz sadistically claims carnal knowledge of her and seeks to
reassert his mastery over her. She pleads with Ganz to stop its circulation, to withdraw her from his mailing list. For her, his continuous use
of *Du* resembles blackmail: "Thy obvious inability to sense my sensitivity for the You, to extort it from me and others, let me fear that
thou art still not conscious of blackmail, because it is 'entirely' common for thee."[81] The organic unity of Ich and Ivan, praised in the final
paragraph before the letter, begins to resemble the "Intermezzo"
between Ganz and Ich. Whereas Ich's words for fatigue stem from her
battle with the problem of the post, Ivan demands her to perfect the
postal code: "I want you here immediately!" ("Ich will dich sofort
hierhaben!," 74). Like Ganz, he is neither sensitive to her "sensitivi-
ties" nor conscious of his extortion.

Ich's attempt to withdraw from the mailing process continues in
the letter to the president. In that letter, she insists that she would
rather not receive any more letters "in Ihrem Namen und im Namen
aller" ("in your name and the name of everyone") which halfheart-
edly publicize and threaten the intimacy of epistolary communication, which she here identifies with her birth. She turns traditional
birthday greetings into the breaking of a taboo. The president's
knowledge of her birthday reveals total access to information and

"data processing" that bases its right of access on the spirit of the Enlightenment. If, in this case, the birthday card is linked to the age of total information, Ich

> cannot get around forwarding these congratulations in thought to a long deceased woman, a certain Josefine H., who is registered as midwife on my birth certificate. One should have congratulated her then, for her skill and for a smooth delivery.[82]

With this metaphor of the midwife and her birth, she and the letters become one. Ich pits the postmaster general, the president, against the female version of a mail carrier, the *Hebamme* (literally "carrying, lifting nanny"). Ich passes his congratulations on to her in her thoughts, which the mail-order cannot prevent.

What seems to be a promising beginning as a female-determined "letter" becomes later, upon entrance into the Father-Tongue, a "message that didn't quite make me happy" ("Mitteilung, die mich nicht gerade glücklich machte," 110). Upon entering male-dominated discourse, she learns that a child born on a Friday is born with "half a good luck cap" ("einer halben Glückshaube," 111). From then on, the awareness of having only "one half of a cover" ("die Hälfte einer Bedeckung") makes her increasingly introspective, autistically "absorbed." Although "one thinks, a half is better than nothing" ("eine halbe ist besser als gar keine, meint man,") what one, or in this case man says, does not convince Ich. Like the compound noun *Mitteilung*, which includes the notion of "disconnection," she writes half a letter because "[m]y letter to you cannot be a whole letter, because my gratitude for your good wishes can only come half-heartedly" ("[m]ein Brief an Sie kann kein ganzer Brief werden, auch weil mein Dank für Ihre guten Wünsche nur aus einem halben Herzen kommt," 111). This letter is not a whole letter because she does not send it, and in completing it, it would be a letter to "Ganz." The story of her birth becomes a story of castration. As she aborts the letter, she removes herself from the Freudian mailing process (like Dora removes herself from Freud's therapy). She signs off: "But these are unreasonable letters that one receives, and the letters with which one answers them are also reasonable for no one—Vienna, the . . . A Stranger" ("Es sind aber unzumutbare Briefe, die man bekommt, und die Briefe, mit denen man sie beantwortet, sind auch niemand zumutbar—Wien, den . . . Eine Unbekannte," 111).

The Schönthal-Ganz-President chain letter structurally inverts the process of *Zustellung* (distribution) from the whole to the part, from teleological totality to the origin of birth.[83] All that remains is the skeleton of the mailing system. But even the aborted fragments, the "waste" products of the process, are ordered according to epistolary aesthetics:

The torn letters are lying in the waste paper basket, artistically dispersed and mixed with crunched invitations to an exhibition, to a reception, to a lecture, mixed with empty packs of cigarettes, dusted with ashes and cigarette stubs.[84]

The throwing away of letters is a leitmotif in the novel and ties in directly with Bachmann's portrayal of the sex/gender system. The extinction of the other in the form of the female gender and the abduction of letters fall under the same authority, as one of Ich's dreams explores.

In the second chapter of *Malina*, letters first appear in Ich's dream about her semi-imprisonment in a foreign country where she neither speaks nor understands the language. She is homesick. The dream combines parts of Anne Frank's diary with the letters of fictional Fräulein von Sternheim. Ich seeks consolation through the writing of letter-fragments, one of which she hopes to send out of the house as testimony of her plight. She hides them all over the room, only to have her father extract them one by one. Her father, who she believes is trying to poison her, searches for letters in her mouth (210), and in the process, places poisoned words in her mouth. With her mouth open, she can only speak visually: "With the eyes, I tell him: I am homesick, I want to go home!" ("Mit den Augen sage ich ihm: Ich habe Heimweh, ich möchte nach Hause!," 211). Writing from a position of elsewhere, a woman's longing for home, for belonging, expresses itself as letters. Each turns into a symbol for the other in her father's discourse: "Homesick! What a beautiful homesickness, indeed! It's letters, but according to me, these will not be sent, your precious letters to your precious friends" ("Heimweh! Das ist mir ein schönes Heimweh! Briefe sind das, aber die werden mir nicht spediert, deine werten Briefe an deine werten Freunde," 211).

In light of the attempt to reinscribe letters into literature, the father figure, who stands for the institution of the arts in the age of mechanical reproduction (film/opera/ theater/ice-skating director and producer) in all of Ich's dreams, designates letter-writing as sentimental nostalgia yet cannot help but feel threatened by their ability to make connections beyond his control. Patriarchal literary norms decide both, that letters are not literature and that a woman's "homesickness" can only be expressed in feminine fictions, that is, letters. While the father figure attempts to control any type of communication, he caused her "homesickness" by imprisoning her "high above" ("hoch oben") in the master's house in the first place. At the same time, he is angry that the letters are not for him, that they "will not to be sent (to him)" ("werden mir nicht spediert").

If one takes "high above" to imply her Rapunzel-like residence in the ivory tower ("Lady Bachmann"), to which the German father figures of Group 47 advanced Bachmann somewhat against her will, they later literally punish her for writing and speaking her mind. The father's repeated command that she open her mouth is a double bind. She is enticed to speak, yet he speaks for her; she seeks to write, yet is hindered and ridiculed when she does. Despite Ich's growing awareness of this double bind, she keeps writing letters in her dreams, and in her last days.

These letters are the fragmented body of the novel *Malina*. The father-daughter scenario repeats itself at the end of the novel when Ich hides her letters and herself in the wall. The novel writes itself as epistolary antipoetics. *Malina* becomes one and all of these letters which could and should not have been sent.[85] Since these letters speak of the impossibility of "authentic" female authorship and fiction, the novel writes itself as nonfiction, its *Zustellung* (distribution) is canceled through *Zustellung* (blocking). With her own body and the body of the text, Ich delivers/blocks the crack in the wall ("stellt den Riß in der Wand zu").[86]

Read together with the next installment of the *Todesarten Projekt*, *Der Fall Franza*, and with Ich's incineration hallucinations, the "old stable wall" into whose foundation settlement crack Ich steps, mummifies her, binding her with and to her letters and notes. The reader has to be cautious not to imitate the gawking authenticity-hungry tourists in Egypt, whose behavior makes Franza so sick she has to vomit. The gothic Orientalist quality of Bachmann's image-spaces, which combine the Indian custom of *Sahti* (widow-burning) with Egyptian mummification, point to the intersection of racial and sexual discourses that transform Vienna into the Orient after all. At the same time, the third chapter of *Malina* also reveals a metaphoric compensation of comparably "insufficient" and thus "inauthenticized" Western female suffering through Orientalist imagery. Since Ich's perilous attempts at storytelling and letter-writing do not seem a matter of life and death (as was the case for Scheherezade), merely one of hysteric degree, Bachmann injects the narrative with urgency via Orientalist imagery. However, rather than deconstructing the race-sex system in this case, Bachmann actually builds on it, imbuing her d.o.a. letters with the possibility of a new hieroglyphic extraliterary afterlife. Tattooed on her body, the letters will now, she hopes, have to be read with a different eye/I. Yet, I would contend that while she has deconstructed the sex-gender system, Bachmann has replaced it with a race-sex system, in which the "Other" body, the "Other" text, becomes inhabitable and consumable by imperial mail-order.

RHAPSODY #4

"Wenn ich manche Leute zurückgrüße, so geschieht es nur,
um ihnen ihren Gruß zurückzugeben."
("When I greet some people back,
it is only in order to return their greeting to them.")
—Karl Kraus, 1874–1936, "Wien"

The female narrator in *Malina* encounters and barely survives a love affair with Ivan that comes to an abrupt end in a sidewalk scene. This particular fragment literally opens an intersection between parallel universes, between conflicting ideologies, between resistance and reintegration. It composes an intertextual letter that highlights the mailing route of the female voice in contemporary literature. *Malina* demonstrates how the debate between modernist and postmodernist factions, between essentialist feminism and poststructuralist feminism, by some surmised to lead to the "end of feminism," is itself structured by and in turn structures a literary intertext, an exciting and courageous feminist literature.

The final chapter of *Malina*, in which the sidewalk fragment is located, changes Ich's nightmares into daydreams, and the psychoanalytic dream sessions into operatic libretti, in which only Ich's voice is modulated. Malina speaks with an inquisitor's voice whereas Ich sings. Between the libretti and the interrogations, Ich narrates the various experiences and images she confronts or remembers.[87] She sticks her memories, which at this point resemble feverishly projected dream scenes, into the cracks between the operatic dialogues. This writing technique recalls Ich's letter-hiding frenzy in the second chapter and structurally foreshadows the final epistolary scene in the novel, in which Ich first hides her letters and then steps into the cracked wall herself.

But these letters and dream scenes are also novels, which code her gender-determined destiny in shifting generic forms to approximate their greatest possible chance for delivery and reception. Ich, for example, imagines her murder taking place in the famous Restaurant Sacher. It would be a genre-specific death. Almost all gangsters are allowed to eat well before they are killed, whether on death row or in Mob circles. She also imagines that another person would take her place at the same table after her death (318). Malina, as gangster boss or bad cop, tortures Ich verbally and physically to make her admit what she has seen (318). He wants her to confess that she is an accomplice, to reveal her other selves so that he gains total control over her. Ich finally "sings." After the last conversation in Italian, so to speak, she dies the stereotypical Mafia death: she steps into the wall, is thrown/throws herself into concrete, disappears. Malina, as mafioso and KGB agent in one, throws away her sunglasses and gives his boss Ivan, whose call he is awaiting, the coded message of the successful assassination (355).

Off the record and on the beaten track, genre meets mainstream fiction on the side. Contemporary culture has the sidewalk segment begin appropriately with the word *heute*, which Ich had previously classified as the time of "real letters," those that are not sent, cannot be sent "because they are from today and arrive in any today no longer" ("weil sie von heute sind und in keinem Heute mehr ankommen werden," 9).

According to Ich's epistolary poetics, the fragment writes itself as a "real letter" with regard to its position in time and place. The place is "corner Beatrixgasse-Ungargasse," an all too familiar intersection for Ich. At the beginning of the novel, Ich had always felt relief at this point (13). The intersection constitutes the border between greater Vienna and her *Ungargassenland*. Its magnetic field, constructed of the Ivan/Malina poles, has always had an immediate physiological effect on Ich in that it increased her blood pressure while it lessened her tension.

Today, however, she stands at this corner and cannot move: "I look down at my feet that I can no longer move, then around on the sidewalk and on the intersection where everything is discolored" ("Ich sehe auf meine Füße nieder, die ich nicht mehr bewegen kann, dann rundum auf das Trottoir und auf die Straßenkreuzung, wo sich alles verfärbt hat," 318–319). For some time, she is stuck between departure and arrival at the center of her route, which at the same time represents a void of power for both realms. The *trottoir* or *bordure du trottoir* is indeed a border in and of itself: the edge of the street, an interconnected band separated from the opposite side, a French word in a German-speaking context. Ich literally stands on the edge. While Ich had previously only pondered the state of mailmen's feet (257), she now looks down upon her own: "Since the Kranewitzer case, a lot in me has changed unnoticed" ("Seit dem Fall Kranewitzer hat sich in mir unmerklich vieles verändert," 255).

In the "Trottoir-Scene," Ich acts like the mailman Otto Kranewitzer, who could no longer carry out his duty and deliver mail. Ich interprets his refusal as a reaction to the "postal crisis ("postalische Krise") as a philosophical and epistemological crisis (254–255). He took the ground rule of his profession and "calling" literally for the first time: he observed the "secrecy of the mail" *(Briefgeheimnis)* by not delivering any mail. Kranewitzer realized that "the problem of the post" lies in the institutionalization of breaking the sanctity of the mail, in the "accessory character" *(Mitwisserschaft)* of the mail carriers, the complicity of the mailing system (251).[88]

When Ich declares "I cannot see that which I see" ("Ich kann es nicht sehen, was ich sehe"), she refers to the change of color in the pavement, but also to the dilemma of the postal mediator, the writer, and especially the writing woman. Like Kranewitzer, she stops to think and reflect, and is appalled by what she sees, but cannot see, because the mailing system does not permit "Thinking-Wanting-Being, no scrupulous and sublime renunciation" ("Denken-Wollen-Sein, kein skupulöses und erhabenes Entsagen," 253). It is supposed to work "under cover." Its very function relies on the dialectics of betrayal as obedience to the *Briefgeheimnis*. Implicated in this sanctification process are also the secrets of gender designations and sexual orientation, of all ideologies which, because observed by the majority, do not think of themselves as obeying a specific code, or constituting a theoretical construct.

The female narrator, confronted with "the important place" ("die wichtige Stelle"), forgets both origin and destination: "I must have gotten lost, I cannot go on, I don't know my way around here, please, do you know, where the Ungargasse is?" ("ich muß mich verlaufen haben, ich finde nicht mehr weiter, ich kenne mich hier nicht aus, bitte, wissen Sie, wo die Ungargasse ist?," 319). She sees the scene around her in time-lapse photography, where stills make the previously unnoticeable interchanges and movements visible. The sight of so much traffic through her own and other women's bodies overwhelms her. Like her nightly letters, she stops dead in her tracks, sees herself as "human waste." "I stand in a pool of blood, it is quite clearly blood" ("Ich stehe in einer Blutlache, es ist ganz deutlich Blut," 319). She stands at the scene of the crime, the murderous place of postal transfer.

The symbolism of the blood points in different directions. On the one hand, her child by Ivan—"my beautiful book" ("mein schönes Buch," 319)—ends in a miscarriage: "In the apartment, I lie down on the floor, I think of my book, it has been taken from my hands, there is no beautiful book, I can no longer write the beautiful book" ("In der Wohnung lege ich mich auf den Boden, ich denke an mein Buch, es ist mir abhanden gekommen, es gibt kein schönes Buch, ich kann das schöne Buch nicht mehr schreiben," 320). On the other hand, due to the shock of seeing what she cannot see, her menstruation sets in with a vengeance after a long anorexic phase in which she could not eat anything but scraps and leftovers (277). Her "gender trouble," to borrow Judith Butler's phrase, caused her to "eat her heart out." She consumed herself in (and as) bits and pieces.[89] In this rhapsody of letters, the utopia of writing a "schönes Buch" despite "universal prostitution" miscarries, but its violent abortion also resumes Ich's womanly cycle of exchange.[90] In this scene, Bachmann refuses and reappropriates the bodily metaphors of "production," applied to pregnancy by twentieth-century medicine, and "waste," applied to menstruation or miscarriage.[91]

At the intersection, Bachmann has "a woman with a shopping bag" ("[e]ine Frau mit einer Einkaufstasche") pass Ich and turn around to look at Ich questioningly. The *Doppelgängerin* senses Ich's dislocation, her edginess and desperation. This encounter between two very different women rewrites and underscores the necessary phase of women's solidarity. The *Doppelgängerin* empathizes with Ich because she is certain about their common map, their mutual destiny and destination: "Here you are already in the Ungargasse" ("Hier sind Sie schon in der Ungargasse," 319). With her help, Ich manages the first crossing. For the female pedestrian, Ich was already where she wanted to be, but Ich's map differs from her helper's. She has a long way to go.

Ich crosses to the *Beethovenhaus* number 5, instead of turning the bend as usual: "I am safe beside Beethoven" ("ich bin bei Beethoven in Sicherheit," 319). She stays across from Malina's even-tempered residence, number 6, without reverting to its supposed opposite of desire at Ivan's residence, number 9. She views the street like a mail carrier who has to deliver mail from the post office to her own house: "and I glance from number 5 across to an estranged house entrance, which bears the number 6" ("und ich schaue von Nummer 5 hinüber zu einem mir fremd gewordenen Haustor, auf dem die Nummer 6 steht," 319). From this uneven "blind spot" between her two crossings, from this ideal(istic) position, she can muster up the courage, the heroism, to send herself home without simply returning.[92]

It takes a lot of strength to act upon her newly won realization. She also knows that she has to cross again, that "blindness" and "music" partake in a differential structure even though they seem to stand above or even erase it: "and I glance over at the other shore, I have to get down off the sidewalk and reach the other shore" ("und ich sehe ans andere Ufer hinüber, ich muß vom Trottoir herunter und das andere Ufer erreichen," 319). Rather than the certain *zu* (to), Bachmann selects the cautious *an* (at) to indicate Ich's awareness of the liminality of the moment. Her eyes and verbal expression halt at the margin, just as they pause every few words at a comma. The second paragraph in this story-fragment is made up of liminal expressions, which, concatenated, form one long sentence. Very slowly, Ich strings together her sensations and movements so as not to jeopardize her newly acquired sense of otherness.

The retreat into the safety at Beethoven's steps cannot last: "the O-tram jingles as it drives by, . . . I wait until it has passed, and quivering with strain, I take the key out of my purse" ("der O-Wagen fährt klingelnd vorbei, . . . ich warte bis er vorbei ist, und zitternd vor Anstrengung nehme ich den Schlüssel aus der Handtasche," 319). Her ability to hear the jingle of the tram saves her life. Had she stepped across, she would have been hit. Instead of ending with feminine melodramatic flair, Ich makes full use of the structural confrontation with a familiarity suddenly estranged and with the differences within and among women. As a woman writer, Ich needs to find a means of expression equipped to deal with her task of crossing "the other" without crossing over to the male-dominated position.[93]

In accord with Sigrid Weigel's and Luce Irigaray's ideas of "crossing over" and "crossing through," these multiple crossings become an act of expressing the culturally acquired and socially dominated layers constructing and obstructing the female voice:

I *take on* the crossing; I already *draw up* a smile, so that it *arrives* at Frau Breitner, I have *reached* the other shore, I *stroll past* Frau Breitner, *for whom* my beautiful book is also *intended*, Frau Breitner *does not smile back*, but she *does greet* anyhow, and I have *reached* the house *once again*. I have seen nothing. I have come home.

ich *setze* zur Überquerung *an;* ich *setze* auch ein Lächeln schon *auf*, damit es bei Frau Breitner *ankommt*, ich habe das andere Ufer *erreicht*, ich *schlendere* an Frau Breitner *vorbei, für* die auch mein schönes Buch *sein soll*, Frau Breitner *lächelt nicht zurück*, aber sie *grüßt* immerhin, und ich habe das Haus *wieder erreicht*. Ich habe nichts gesehen. Ich bin nach Hause gekommen. (319–320; my italics).

Ich writes the crossing and herself as dual letters with the intention of "not colliding with" Frau Breitner, the *Hausmeisterin*, whose name and profession connote the opposite of the pedestrian woman's solidarity. As housewife, landlady, and master of the house, Frau Breitner represents Woman's collaboration with the male/mail-order. Ich realizes that she can pass the gate and enter the master's house only by the laws of universal prostitution. Frau Breitner guards the doorway and its mailboxes like a goalie with her name's massiveness.[94] Ich puts a smile on her face like Fräulein Jellinek would draft letters (*aufsetzen* means to "put on" as well as "to draft"). This smile follows the official postal route directly to Frau Breitner. Indeed, Frau Breitner acknowledges the receipt of this letter with a greeting.

At the same time, Ich reaches the other shore by strolling *past* Frau Breitner, by differing with her and herself. Like a professional double agent, she counterfeits the delivery. Frau Breitner does and does not receive "das schöne Buch." In this gesture of withholding by delivering, Ich observes the sanctity of the mail but leaves something behind as well: "Ich möchte das Briefgeheimnis wahren. Aber ich möchte auch etwas hinterlassen" ("I would like to observe the sanctity of mail. But I would also like to leave something behind," 345). She double-crosses the discourse of the post and her ma(i)l(e)-dominated agency. In the predetermined syntax and the genre- and gender-specific vocabulary of that discourse, she has seen nothing and has come home like Woman, the carriers of mail, should: "Ich habe nichts gesehen. Ich bin nach Hause gekommen" (320). From within the confines of the master house of language and signs, women's multiple crossings are rendered invisible and unreadable. In this historical moment of postwar Vienna, she has to deny her continuous hybridization, her double-crossing, for her own protection.[95]

As a feminist reader, I have the option of declaring Bachmann's undelivered mailings essential feminine fictions in their fragmentary character, their epistolary structure. I could conclude that she withholds herself from male novelistic discourse, that she manages to differentiate herself and her writing. But turning this argument around, she also initiates and facilitates that discourse. If I wanted peace of mind, I could find relief in the fact that my reading has engendered a place for Ich's voice, that the external and implied female reader will break the sequence of male-dominated narrative, deferred and differing from his text. But all these options rely on the postal code of insides and outsides, on clearly definable genre and gender borders and that a letter always arrives at its destination: in the name of the sender.

I have tried, instead, to emphasize that *Malina* creates epistolary intertexts that reopen the *Zustellung* ("delivery/blocking") of unresolvable differences. These intertexts constructively reconsider and literalize the problems of and within (feminist) criticism and fiction. If I shift the verb's grammar, I can also take it to imply: "sich zu etwas und zu etwas anderem zu stellen," to accept without introjecting the other. This "standing by" the other combines aspects of solidarity and respect with a sense of indeterminacy regarding one's place. One is never one or in one place alone, just as one text is never simply one with itself. Intertextual indeterminacy, as produced by the rhapsody in letters in Bachmann's novel, "makes for the kind of active and even strenuous, but disciplined commitment that, more than anything else, characterizes literary response to perceived literariness."[96]

Malina accepts the legacy of modernism and essentialism but instead of safekeeping the traces of the female voice "in his heart," Malina (ob)-literates them according to Ich's instructions: "I have to overcome myself" ("Ich muß mich überwinden," 307). She has to surmount a notion of self that is "[i]n the main point actually counterfeit. I was completely forged, one had pressed false papers into my hands, deported me hither and thither. . . . At the end I was a unique falsification" ("[i]n der Hauptsache aber eine Fälschung. Ich war ganz verfälscht, man hat mir falsche Papiere in die Hand gedrückt, hat mich deportiert dahin und dorthin. . . . Am Ende war ich eine einzige Fälschung," 313). Ich's dreams and dream analysis as well as her other narrative fragments stress her participation and subjection to this counterfeiting, to her "extradition" to the fictions of an identifiable, stable, and unified self, whether female or phallocentrically human. Malina does not understand that Ich practices what he later prescribes as a postmodern philosophy of the subject. He criticizes her for not knowing "which of your lives were former and what your life is today, you even mistake your lives for one another" ("welche deine Leben frührer waren und was dein Leben heute ist, du verwechselst sogar deine Leben"). She contends: "I have only one life" ("Ich habe nur ein Leben"). Malina seductively pleads: "Leave it to me" ("Überlaß es mir," 233). She should bequest her life to Malina, so that toward the end of the novel, he can voice his theorized version of Ich's shifting subject positions: "One should one day be able to switch back and forth between a rediscovered and a future self that cannot be the old self. Without effort, without illness, without regret" ("Man sollte aber eines Tages hin- und herwechseln können, zwischen dem wiedergefundenen Ich und einem künftigen, das nicht mehr das alte Ich sein kann. Ohne Anstrengung, ohne Krankheit, ohne Bedauern," 325–326).

Malina considers this shifting sense of self and subject to be a natural, positivist progression of mankind according to his understanding of postmodernism as the perfection of modernism. Ich, on the other side, has never had anything to lose: "I don't regret myself any longer" ("Ich bedaure mich nicht mehr," 326). Throughout the novel, her self, the "Ich-instance," is the floating signifier, constructed by and producing each textual situation. The "I's" different echoes interact in a continuous deconstructive dialogue whose indeterminacies reside in its structural composition. Even when one voice dominates, the others are present, inextinguishable and disruptive, converting "Glücklich mit Ivan" into a sadomasochistic nightmare comparable to Ich's worst misogynist memories. Bachmann sarcastically dramatizes the economy of critical discourse in *Malina*'s operatic exchanges and Ich's epistolary fragments. Within that discourse, the female protagonist is first criticized for her techniques of *Verwechseln* (mistaking something for something else) and *Verschreiben* (miswriting). The *culture industry* then inherits and uses these techniques to formulate a normative narrative theory of whose standards women's texts fall short. If the mailorder of critical discourse works for Malina, he will never have to change, never have to live his writing.

The minute Malina clears his creative space of Ich's symbolic presence so that he can "see everything," he becomes deaf to the discords, the residues of otherness in his own voice: "Malina meticulously looks around himself, he sees everything, but he doesn't hear anything anymore" ("Malina sieht genau um sich, er sieht alles, aber er hört nichts mehr," 355). The text written in his name, the (post)modernist text *Malina*, will feign and claim a pluralism and "polyphony" that he is unable to live. As the figure of the critic, Malina will edit Ich's epistolary reaction toward the crisis of the post as a feminine ending of modernism, an extravagant phenomenon, a fashionable erraticism. Whatever he creates will be a "forgery" deriving from her correspondence, an *Apokryph* of letters and fragments excluded from the canon.[97] Thus Malina can create and define a theory in which the meaning and the borders of the canon shift to allow publication of the text under the male critic's name. But *Malina*'s ending also spells out the vicious cycle of dominant signifying practices that incorporate anti-establishment movements such as feminism. With this premonition of the critical reaction to her novel and of the canonization of "women's literature," Ingeborg Bachmann transcribed her rhapsodic *Todesarten* into the larger frame of contemporary philosophical and literary discourse.[98]

CHAPTER 3

Chain Mail:
Letters°Postcards°Travel Guides . . . ?
Barth, Derrida, and Levi

What do you do, when you receive the blurry copy of a chain letter pushed anonymously under your office door or surreptitiously dropped in your mailbox after hours? In the past ten years, I have received approximately thirty versions of chain letters. The latest, claiming to originate in Venezuela but supposedly stemming from a South African missionary with the original letter now residing in New England, is quite blatant in its fortune cookie promises and threats: "You will receive good luck within four days of receiving this letter—provided you in turn send it on." I did not copy it twenty times in the time frame specified, but you are now reading parts of it. On the dust jacket or somewhere in this book, you might want to check what happened to me before you read on and decide what to do about chains. Letters and magic: a potent combination!

The metaphor of the chain abounds not only in communication theory or epistolarity but also in structuralist linguistics. It has been used by Jacques Lacan to signify a metaphor of a metaphor, "the chain of signifiers," constituting the substitution of signifiers without an external referent.[1] In 1966, at the Johns Hopkins symposium entitled "The Languages of Criticism and the Sciences of Man," Jacques Lacan addressed his understanding of the structure of the subject and the unconscious. In his talk, the subject of his talk, of language, and the subject of the unconscious, first appears as a message from the Other: "The message, our message, in all cases comes from the Other by which I understand 'from the place of the Other'" (186). Instead of basing the idea of the subject on a humanistic sense of "total personality" or a unity among mankind, he introduces the concept of "the countable unity one, two, three" (190). That which marks the one as one is the number 2, which for Lacan becomes the question of the subject. It is important to remember that "the two does not complete the one to make two, but must repeat the one to permit the one to exist" (191).

Instead of securing the subject's identity through repetition, Lacan's chainlike unity shows the subject as the product of a repetition that divides the subject. The subject therefore resides in the cracks, at the moments of marked identity which are at the same time its division: "All that is language is lent from this otherness and this is why the subject is always a fading thing that runs under the chain of signifiers. For the definition of a signifier is that it represents a subject not for another subject but for another signifier" (194).

Even though Lacan refers to the idea of the unifying unity of the human condition as a "scandalous lie" (190), he does not discuss the issue of the sex-gender system in connection with the structure of the unconscious and the subject. Since the language of letter-writing, and specifically of epistolary correspondences, has traditionally been viewed as closely imbued with the matter of subject formation, the concept of chain letters in relation to the writers' and readers' genders raises many questions.

John Barth, the author of *LETTERS* (1979), divides himself into multiple male protagonists who correspond with each other and with the epistolary novel incarnate, the only woman writer in the novel. Due to the unambiguous typecasting of Germaine Pitt Gordon Amherst as "an old time epistolary novel," the reader of *LETTERS* construes her as the allegorized subject of language, literature, and letters, and within Lacan's terminology, as the repetition of a repetition. Barth's novel is a brilliant example of epistolary cloning. His chain of letters produces Woman as a mail-ordered woman's product.[2]

A postcard, the next link in my chain letter, is usually divided into four sections: picture, address, stamp, and text. Derrida's *Postcard* also has four parts: "Envois," "To Speculate—On 'Freud'," "Le Facteur de la Vérité," and "Du Tout." "Envois" begins with a preface dated September 7, 1979, and continues with letters and postcards dated from June 3, 1977, to August 30, 1979. Like *LETTERS*, "[t]his satire of epistolary literature had to be farci, stuffed with addresses, postal codes, crypted missives, anonymous letters, all of it confided to so many modes, genres, and tones. In it I also abuse dates, signatures, titles or references, language itself" (back cover of *The Postcard*). The book design resembles the Oxford postcard of Plato and Socrates with its frontispiece and its backside text, which portrays itself as a postcard from J. D. dated November 17, 1979. As we[3] turn it around and read the dust jacket, we discover that we "were reading a somewhat retro loveletter, the last in history. But [we] have not yet received it." Will the act of reading permit us to receive it?[4] Yes and no: "its lack or excess of address prepares it to fall into all hands: a post card, an open letter in which the secret appears, but indecipherably." We have various options.

KISS SOMEONE YOU LOVE
WHEN YOU GET THIS LETTER AND MAKE MAGIC

This paper has been sent to you for luck. The original is in New England. It has been around the world nine times—the luck has been sent to you. You will receive good luck within four days of receiving this letter—provided you in turn send it on.

This is no joke. You will receive good luck in the mail. Send no money. Send copies to people you think need good luck. Don't send money, as faith has no price. DO not keep this letter. IT MUST LEAVE YOUR HANDS WITHIN 96 HOURS.

An RAF Officer received $470,000. Joe Elliot received $40,000 and lost it because he broke the chain. While in the Philippines, George Welch lost his wife 51 days after receiving the letter. He had failed to circulate the letter. However, before her death, she won $90,000 in the lottery. The money was transferred to him four days after he decided to mail the letter.

Please send (20) copies and see what happens in four days. The chain comes from Venezuela and was written by Saul Anthony DeGrow, a missionary from South Africa. Since this copy must tour the world, you must make twenty (20) copies and send them to friends and associates. After a few days you will get a surprise even if you are not superstitious.

Do note the following: Constantina Dios received the chain in 1963. He asked his secretary to make twenty (20) copies and send them out. A few days later, he won the lottery of two million dollars. Andy Dodd, an office employee received this letter. He forgot it had to leave his hands in 96 hours. He lost his job. Later, after finding the letter again, he mailed twenty (20) copies. A few days later, he got a better job. Dan Fairchild received the letter and not believing threw the letter away. Nine days later, he died.

In 1987 the letter was received by a young woman in California—it was faded and barely readable. She promised herself she would retype the letter and send it on, but she put it aside to do later. She was plagued by various problems, including expensive car repairs. The letter did not leave her hands in 96 hours. She finally retyped the letter as promised and sent it on and then got a new car.

REMEMBER—SEND NO MONEY—DO NOT IGNORE THIS.
IT WORKS!!
"WITH LOVE, ALL THINGS ARE POSSIBLE!!"
ST. JUDE

FIGURE 3.1

We can attempt a reading while the postcard passes us by or we can "pass it off." We can act as if we had read it, assuming that all postcards, and therefore all texts by Derrida, say the same. We can feign that it does not concern us. Either way, "instead of reaching [us] it divides [us] or sets [us] aside, occasionally overlooks [us]" (back cover).

While Derrida was traveling on his conference tour, buying and sending postcards of and from the legs of his journey, he might have found Levi's travel guide useful. In Jonathan Levi's *A Guide for the Perplexed* (1992),[5] three female travelers, stuck in Mariposa, Spain, cannot reach their travel agent in a time of crisis. This supposedly all-knowing and inter- or better metaconnected travel agent, Ben, also happens to be the editor of "the" travel guide, to which one of the travelers regularly contributes reviews and of *A Guide for the Perplexed*, the book we are reading. Ben seems undisturbed by the fact that *A Guide* really shows three women able to make do without him and his master text, transforming it into "A Guide for Reaching Independence from Guides." This "Guide" is also already a reedition of a previous guide. There is the mysterious "Esau Letter," a combination of Jewish cabbala, folkloric mythology, travelogue, and familiar correspondences. Similarly, the characters with which the "Esau Letter" and *A Guide* familiarize us, are not one, but always harbor another "original" somewhere else—drawing from their own resurrection of Maimonides' "epistolary epic" to his perplexed son-in-law. And after both characters and readers rejoice in the family reunion, the bringing together of a lost people, of the Jews from the Diaspora, which seems to take shape before our eyes, the very materiality and importance of the genealogical imperative, the survival of the race and its traditions, is exchanged for the notion of a tele-harmonic "textology" of literary, musical, scientific, and philosophical legacies that can only become legacies by way of dis- and reconnections.

The letters of *A Guide*, *Postcard*, and *LETTERS* form correspondences, and correspondences, in turn, develop into what the character Ambrose calls "chain-letter narratives."[6] Chains indicate captivity, a strict linearity, and the possibility of infinite progression. How does one read chain-letter narratives like *LETTERS*, *The Postcard*, *A Guide*? The opening in each link enables links to interlock and form a chain. This guarantees both the possibility of limitless extension and of closure. Therefore, a reading and writing that attempts to fill the gaps can only obstruct the production process. A theory of reading as "filling the gaps," filling those textual disconnections produced by "unexpected twists and turns," is presented by Wolfgang Iser in *The Implied Reader* (276–282). In Iser's phenomenological approach, the reader actually "links the different phases of the text together," synthesizes the indeterminacies of each reading situation. While Iser stresses that a literary text is always "on the move" and undergoes "continual modification," according to him, a successful reading should actually mediate the inconsistencies.

Computer programming code presents the reader and writer with another set of chains: for example, for the software program "Deconstruction." This self-engendering word program is based on the Markov chain concept that analyzes recurring clusters in one's prose and imitates a text in the style of several scanned-in source texts. In its "Teach Text" introduction, "Deconstruction's" writers encourage you to use a specific genre as source text: the letter. The outcome uncannily resembles the input yet doesn't make much sense, to the delight of deconstruction critics who feel that when they are reading Derrida they see old and valorized ideas, namely, their own, reconfigured and cloned by incomprehensible language games. While the grammar of the "new text" is mostly correct, the semantics are off, sometimes grotesquely so and in other places ever so subtly.

Contemporary epistolary fiction and theory challenge its readers to interrupt and expand the chain, to stretch and test its material and composition, to play with its links, and simultaneously to add our own links by contributing to the discourse. This intriguing game corresponds to a brainteaser made of metal pieces that one is supposed to dis/connect, although one's eyes hesitate to believe in the possibility of dis/connection. The solutions to these concrete puzzles adhere to an abstract pattern: the pattern of correspondence, of not trying to yank one piece away by force, but rather to have them casually interact to aid the dis/connection. But when have literary critics ever been casual on the job?

In order to read epistolary fiction, one needs time and patience because (a) it tends to be maximalist rather than minimalist and (b) one constantly has to retrace one's steps, wade through anecdotes, repetitions, digressions, specific references to other letters, stories, times, places, and persons. During this process, the reader must interact with the correspondences on multiple narratological and mnemonic levels, she or he must remember and reproduce letters as intertexts.[7]

In the nineteenth and early twentieth centuries, the reading and performing of intertextuality developed alongside the field of comparative literature. The school of French *comparatistes* and their German and Anglo-American colleagues were mainly interested in analyzing how different authors and their works influenced each other within and across national boundaries.[8] This type of comparison describes the transfer of textual legacies from author to author, or from one work to another. From a formal standpoint, if a critic is concerned with the residues of one text in another, or with the referential system between two or more works by different authors, she or he is already involved in an intertextual comparison. However, it still remains to be investigated whether the works themselves, their authors, and their critics, other than simply referring to one another, engage in an intertextual writing practice. In the following paragraphs, I outline the implications of intertextuality as such a writing practice and how that practice toys with and differs from a system of reference.

As a textual practice, the term "legacy" recalls the etymological link between the letter and the law. Throughout its long history, the letter as the Latin *brevis*, the old high German *briaf*, or the new German and English *Brief/brief* retained its affiliation to a concise legal document and to legal instructions and decrees.[9] While the letter itself is legally binding, it also binds sender to receiver through a signature or even both parties' signatures. In some instances, the letter transfers its privileges or demands onto the descendants of its bearer. In their function as written legal documents, letters constitute and contribute to legacies.

What then, is the relationship between legacy and a system of reference such as one finds in quotations? Like letters, quotations and references move from one context to another and constitute a dialogue. Unlike letters, citations derive from an original text that does not participate in the decontextualization. As copies of the original, their movement reinstates borders between the texts. While this particular intertextual mechanism begets textual progeny, it also preserves the unity of each text and ensures both the source and the host against dissemination.

References and quotations are most obvious when they appear in quotation marks, with which the host text marks their borders and their difference. The quotation marks for citations are the same as those that delimit oral utterances in writing. With quotations from another text, a written work divides itself into dialogic scenes. In drama, in letters, and in quotations, characters and authors speak for themselves yet address themselves to another person or situation. Within a narrative, quotations mark the other's voice, which is at the same time the other of the written text. Living speech enters the text. In fact, it is through an intertext that writing reverts to its other. The intertextual system of reference highlights a process by which texts seek to move beyond themselves as texts. This type of intertextuality constantly transforms "dead letters" into "living speech." While the two concepts of intertextuality, exemplified by legacy and quotation, take place as writing and in writing, they do not yet amount to intertextuality as a writing practice.

Much of contemporary fiction and theory questions the limited notion of intertextuality as a straightforward transferal (between identifiable and wholesome individual texts, characters, genres, authors, discourses, schools of thought, and periods)[10] and plays upon the labyrinth of textual demarcations. Structuralist critics began by extending the meaning of literary intertextuality to include the integration and interrelation of all texts, including "texts" heretofore not seen or read as "texts," as Jonathan Culler explains: "It is important to assert that a work's relation to other texts of a genre or to certain expectations about fictional worlds is a phenomenon of the same type . . . as its relation to the interpersonal world of ordinary discourse."[11] Structuralist intertextuality, the idea that "every text takes shape as a mosaic of citations," also leads to a replacement of intersubjectivity. A structuralist understanding of the relation between texts transforms the place of the speaking or narrating subject into another textual intersection.[12] Poststructuralist critics and postmodern writers refute any idea of a knowable and maintainable subject position, whether of writer, reader, character, or text. Those categories themselves are subjected to continuous ruptures, erasures, and overlappings in poststructuralist literature and criticism.[13] The erosion of dialectical oppositions and categories often derives from the self-conscious "recycling" of characters, themes, and structures, which Barth elaborates in *LETTERS* and Jonathan Levi presents in *A Guide for the Perplexed*.[14] Neither authors, characters, nor their experimentation with nonliterary genres can transcend the fictional worlds which they create and of which they are products. Theoretic novels like John Barth's *LETTERS*, novelistic theories like Jacques Derrida's *The Postcard*, and fictional topographies of contemporary theories like Jonathan Levi's *A Guide* thematize and structurally undermine the idea that they can transcend their textuality.[15] These works demonstrate that any transference, whether epistolary, linguistic, or psychoanalytic, cannot but remember its dismemberment. In a double gesture, a transference reinstalls in a new context what was previously decontextualized, yet the intertextual crossing is also remembered and thus threatens the coherence of its surroundings.

In a postmodern context, the problem of textual incorporation, of borders and references, not only takes place in the moment of transmission between stable texts, but in the very notion of "text." For Jacques Derrida, the text is not one with itself; it is a "differential network":

> When a text quotes and requotes, with or without quotation marks, when it is written on the brink, you start, or indeed already started, to lose your footing. You lose sight of any line of demarcation between a text and what is outside . . . a text that is henceforth no longer a finished corpus of writing, some content enclosed in a book or its margin, but a differential network, a fabric of traces referring endlessly to something other than itself, to other differential traces.[16]

According to Derrida, genres similarly partake in this differential network; intertextuality is already inscribed within the law of genre: "It is precisely a principle of contamination, a law of impurity, a parasitical economy" that determines a genre's history.[17] The epistolary genre puts the differential network, that Derrida here attests for all textual products and their categorizations, into concrete terms.

Derrida faces a great challenge in *The Postcard*: how to deconstruct a genre that, according to Paul Hernadi, performs the postmodern turn:

> There is ample evidence that the epistolary form is experiencing a renaissance in the postmodernist era when so much fiction is questioning the representative status of writing, when discursive self-consciousness is overtly challenging the novel's traditional narrativity. . . . In fact, what makes this form so intriguing to study . . . is the way in which it explicitly articulates the problematics involved in the creation, transmission, and reception of literary texts.[18]

While he is engaged in writing *The Postcard*, Derrida has to confront his own legacy: the transformation of his grammatology and of deconstruction into an authoritative authoring system for literary criticism and philosophy at the century's end.[19] Derrida satirically inverts the tradition of epistolary poetics with its "letters to a young poet," in which the older, experienced author generally seeks to bridge the generational divide in order to transmit his or her legacy to "those who will write in the future."[20] But, as Thomas Nolden argues,

> the attempt to enduringly mediate traditions becomes always crucial in literary history, when the representatives of a specific tradition no longer feel understood by the spokespeople of the following generation, when the bridges between them threaten to tumble, communication between them threatens to break off. (41)

Has the effect of Derrida's writings been the temporary swapping of authorities only to have the deconstructive alliance tumbled by the next oedipal strike? Isn't the dissemination, adulteration, and, to some vehement critics, the cloning of "pure" Derrida into Butlers, Ronells, Kauffmans, Hamachers, Weigels and Co. precisely the unavoidable point of the exercise? Why are Derrideans and anti-Derrideans alike complaining about publications "*à la Derrida*" when it was expected and accepted to write "*à la Portugaise*," "*à la Wellek*," or "*à la Iser*"? Is it because Derrida's fiercest critics are disappointed in discovering that the powerful law of inheritance, of academic legacies, has survived the "great inquisitor"? Or is it because the post-poststructuralist pods have arrived in literature departments and have contributed to some unwanted yet necessary structural and thematic shifts: literary theory, interdisciplinarity, multiculturalism, cultural studies, postcolonial studies, feminist, queer, and media studies, and so on? Is it time for post-structuralists to ask "Where do we go from here"? and become clients of Ben's travel agency in *A Guide*, to which they occasionally mail restaurant and brothel reviews in the form of letters and postcards in order to be included in the next edition of the guide, which is always published before they have sent them off? In a way, chain letters are the ultimate form of plagiarism. Derrida writes (on) the death of letter-writing in epistolary fashion while at the same time ascertaining the longevity of his own (non)concept. The question remains whether the genre allows him to get away with murder.

The letter and the postcard form a differential network due to their temporal, spatial, and intersubjective coordinates. Epistolary fiction was never considered "a finished corpus of writing." A letter differs with itself in that it is a whole yet can also be part of a correspondence cycle, a novel, or a person's (auto)biography. Letters have always infiltrated other literary and theoretical genres. The status of letters relies on the discourse of the post and the mailing system. The post dispatches whomever and whatever is involved with it, even the letter and eventually also the postcard.[21]

This quality of postal dispatch is one of the reasons why Edgar Allan Poe's "The Purloined Letter" from 1845 has attracted so much attention from contemporary critics, particularly from psychoanalytic theorists. Poe's story inverts the hermeneutic enterprise by transferring meaning from a hidden content to a visible surface and the transfer of meaning itself, and thereby transforms the letter into a postcard. "The Purloined Letter" is, in fact, purloined by the postal principle of psychoanalysis itself. The increasing popularity of the postcard and the telegram in the late nineteenth century coincides with the beginning of psychoanalytic theory, which further divides and supplements the letter.[22] Historically and socially, the postal code's (dis)connections appear to determine the language of the unconscious as well as the structure of psychoanalytic discourse.

In his *Postcard*, Derrida relates intertextuality and the contamination of genre to the postal principle and the pleasure principle in psychoanalysis and philosophy. His interdisciplinary and intertextual readings resonate with the debate about the legacy of modernism in postmodernism, a legacy that is already apparent in the questions asked by scholars and analysts. What is the legitimacy of a concept that declares itself a "post-"concept? What or who is its proper origin, its address and application? What is its time frame; when was it sent and when received? What is its content and format?[23]

These questions do not produce the desired clarification of the concept of "postmodernism" and its characteristics. Critics disagree on each issue. Why? Although I deliberately envelope them in a letter format, the questions themselves point up not only the strong ties between post-modernism and epistolarity but also the crisis of knowledge that Jean-François Lyotard describes in *The Postmodern Condition*. This connection becomes quite obvious when we compare Lyotard's rhetoric on human and atomic communication. Lyotard argues that the communication system, and here he particularly refers to a postmodern system's theory model, determines knowledge, what knowledge is, how one knows, and what one knows:

> A *self* does not amount to much, but no self is an island; each exists in a fabric of relations that is now more complex and mobile than before. Young or old, man or woman, rich or poor, a person is always located at "nodal points" of specific communication circuits, however tiny these may be. Or better: one is always located at a post through which various kinds of messages pass. No one, not even the least privileged among us, is ever entirely powerless over the messages that traverse and position him at the post of sender, addressee, or referent. . . . The atoms are placed at the crossroads of pragmatic relationships, but they are also displaced by the messages that traverse them, in perpetual motion. Each language partner, when a "move" pertaining to him is made, undergoes a "displacement," an alteration of some kind that not only affects him in his capacity of addressee and referent, but also as sender. (15–16)

While human beings are located at posts and in positions, the atoms are placed at crossroads. Information passes through the posts in the human model. The medium as agent accords human beings their position in the communication triad. In the atomic model, messages directly traverse the atoms. Atoms, once assumed to be the tiniest particles of matter, are intersected by messages that also continuously displace them and change, if not the way we think about the building blocks of the universe, at least their proportions and material combinations. Lyotard develops two different game plans here. In the human model, despite the displacement of the human agent with the medium as agent, the conventional postal code remains intact. No one is completely powerless over the messages and their displacement. In contrast, Lyotard builds his atomic model on intertextual indeterminacies. This plan does not allow for even temporarily stable positions in the communication network; every atom, and every position, is already an intersection of pragmatic relations. There is no discernible medium or agent involved; the disjunctions appear as processes of signification.

As a result of the intertextual gesture between these two scenarios, Lyotard displaces the crisis of modern knowledge into the "inner" realm of the atom and postpones the crisis' arrival on the "external" social level. It seems as if the "correlative displacement" in Lyotard's post-modern knowledge game has affected Lyotard's own analysis of its postal directions (15). Derrida arrives at a similar conclusion when he analyzes Freud's description of the postal *fort/da* scene:[24] "The scene of *fort/da*, whatever its exemplary content, is always in the process of describing in advance, as a deferred overlapping, the scene of its own description" (*The Postcard*, 321). Wolfgang Welsch delivers another example of this uncanny relation between *fort/da*, the post, and "post-" in his discussion of the etymology of the name and meanings of "post-modernism." He maintains that it is a property of postmodernism that opponents often come to identical, or more precisely, "same-sounding conclusions."[25] Faced with such paradoxes, it might be understandable,

> if one let go all hope of grasping this phenomenon and followed the rec-ommendation voiced some time ago that in the future one should simply resort to traditional word-combinations such as *post office, postman, post(al) money-order* and no longer take notice of *postmodernism*.[26]

Welsch plays devil's advocate with this "simple" retreat into the post office, which regulates the referential system of language, including the tangible order of things. One is tempted to let go of the term "post-modernism" and instead resort to traditional compounds, words that have been brought to and collected by the post office a long time ago. But before one can reclaim these words, one has to send something off: the idea to seize postmodernism as a modernist phenomenon. One can-not expect to arrive at an understanding of postmodernism with a mod-ernist set of criteria, with the hermeneutic methods that largely con-tributed to the self-understanding of modernists and modernism alike. While retreating to the post office—the institution of selection, organi-zation, and distribution—one has to recognize that knowledge is deter-mined by a postal economy, which has already been trading under-handedly with its postmodern bonds:

> That is reminiscent of a relevant corny joke that was told at an archi-tecture conference. One had just observed that several buildings of the postmodern era referred back to a prime example of early modernism, to the grand cashier's hall of Otto Wagner's 1906 Viennese Postal Sav-ings Bank. With this reference in mind, one of the participants wittily remarked, one finally had found a compact definition of "postmod-ernism": "Post-Modernism," that would obviously have to be the modernism of this post office and the tradition emanating from it.[27]

The narrator of the pun does not dwell on this "superficial joke" ("vordergründige Scherz"). Instead, Welsch seeks for a deeper meaning of the joke in the relation of modernism and postmodernism. His own memory, however, connected the language of the post office with the tradition of postmodernism. Welsch, as the mailman who disappears in the second scene (he turns into the convenient multivocal "one" and remains hidden in the passive voice), delivers *and* covers up the postal code of postmodernism. He refuses to acknowledge his own "posting" as a structural element of his discussion. He observes the sanctity of the mail and searches elsewhere for "meaning."

Welsch's two scenes almost homonymically reiterate Freud's analogy of the unconscious, the joke, and the infantile. The identical, that is, "same-sound meaning," further illustrates Lacan's and Derrida's comparison of the letter and the postal code to Freud's signification of the unconscious. Freud analyzes the joke's relation to the dream and to the unconscious in the sixth section of "The Joke and its Relation to the Unconscious" from 1905. His thesis, "that during the formation of a joke one lets go of a train of thought for one moment, which then suddenly surfaces as a joke out of the unconscious," is based on an intertextual gesture.[28] He seeks to understand more about the unconscious by comparing the dream and the joke to his own analysis of each (158). Freud distinguishes the dream from the joke using the category of their communicability. The dream is a totally asocial psychological product— "it does not have anything to communicate to another [person] . . . it can only exist in disguise." By contrast, the joke is the most social of all those psychological performances that are directed toward achieving pleasure—"It often necessitates three people and demands its completion of the mental process stimulated by it through the participation of another [person]."[29] Whereas the dream needs to hide its meaning to spare its host an unsatisfactory moment *(Unlustersparnis)*; the joke survives only when it heeds to the "condition of comprehensibility" ("Bedingung der Verständlichkeit") and its own gain of pleasure *(Lustgewinn)* (168). Nevertheless, all psychological "texts" unite in these two goals *(Unlustersparnis* and *Lustgewinn)* within the pleasure principle.

Both Welsch's ironic retreat to the post office and the thought's momentary submergence into its infantile unconscious produce a joke:

> The infantile is the source of the unconscious, the unconscious thought processes are none other than those which were produced solely and exclusively in early childhood. The thought that dips into the unconscious in order to form a joke only seeks out the old homestead of the former play with words.[30]

When setting up his joke about the post office, Welsch is already inside the postmodern "cashier's office" to cash his check from the pleasure principle. His passage performs Freud's route into the unconscious and structures the unconscious as a post office. Freud's infantile unconscious as the former home of language games as well as linguistic and psychological "displacements" reappears as Welsch's post office of the "traditional word combinations." What Welsch offers the reader as a respite from the seriousness and strangeness of postmodernism might be more postmodern than any of his "serious" passages, if only because it indicates that there is no inside or outside to the discourse of the post, not even in the unconscious.

"LETTERS"

Wreaking havoc with "traditional word combinations" but also with multimedia intertextuality, John Barth's *LETTERS* plays out the role of technology for orality and literacy, print, electronic, and visual media. *LETTERS* is composed of the correspondences of seven characters, whose place in the novel is determined by the graphic design of *LETTERS* and its *Akrostichon* subtitle: "An old time epistolary novel by seven fictitious drolls & dreamers each of which imagines himself actual," which is superimposed onto the calendar dates from March to September 1969.[31] The characters' individual letters spell out this subtitle arranged by each letter of *LETTERS*, of which the first list, marking the letter *L*, begins to count down the alphabet from *A* to *E*. Each literary subject of the novel *LETTERS*, each character, gains his/her/its material existence solely through the material presence of the written or typed alphabetical letter. Barth turns the symbolic relationship between the novel's personae and the medium upside down. In a sense, the letters become the decentered and destabilized personae of the postmodern novel. They write and read themselves, especially when we consider that Barth recycled most of his characters from his previous works.[32]

In addition to the individual letters, each epistle features a subtitle and summary of intent and purpose, for example: all letters of section 2 spell the letter *E*, one of which is the letter *Y*: Todd Andrews to the Author. *Acknowledging the latter's invitation and reviewing his life since their last communication. The "Tragic View" of things, including the Tragic View.*" The italics of each letter's subtitle not only turn each letter into another *LETTERS*, another novel, but further demonstrate Barth's awareness of a letter's material presence, its typography and topography. Yet another inclusion and indeterminacy resides within this babushka-like subtitle chain: the "Tragic View," which is a part of itself. Todd Andrews writes a total of nine letters. When read linearly, his chain spells out "BYSEVENFI." This only makes sense if one disconnects it according to one's grammatological and rhythmical code *and* connects it to Lady Amherst's and Jacob Horner's letter chains. But even then the message is cryptic: "anoldtimeepistolarynovelbysevenfictitious."

Each of its characters, both graphic letters and personas, strive to outmatch their designated time and place in writing, while their author and Author experiment with different letter and media combinations, and are, in turn, experimented upon. Even though some of the characters shun other characters, and actually never write to each other, they are connected through the chain letter of *LETTERS*. Much of A. B. Cook VI's and Jerome Bray's letters discuss revolutionary plots, assassinations, and plagiarism, with which they hope to upset and disconnect the chain of *LETTERS*. As some would have it, anarchy reigns in *LETTERS*.

As E. P. Walkiewicz expresses in quotes from the novel, "any 'formal system' that is 'powerful enough' to attain 'the capacity for self-reference' must contain 'a hole which is tailormade for itself,' which 'takes the features of the system into account and uses them against the system,' dooming it 'to incompleteness'."[33] Unfortunately, Walkiewicz does not read *LETTERS* through its textual opening and against the "seams," that "its Maker, like a Persian artisan, has woven into the design" (131). Rather, he chooses to weave over the flaws and read the novel as a return to linearity and Ambrose Mensch's stated "farewell to formalism" as a black-on-white contract with the reader that all is well again in the "Menschhaus," that is, in the house of letters (138–139). Leaving *LETTERS* with this impression reduces it to one letter: Arthur Morton King's "AMATEUR or A Cure for Cancer" story, which alludes to one of the greatest legends of all time (as in the King Arthur saga), and incorporates the legacy of realist fiction (L 149–189). Walkiewicz is not alone in trying to save the novel from its critics by reintegrating it into a hermeneutic appraisal of postmodern experimentalism.[34] He gladly picks out the characters' hints toward the "unfinished project" of modernism and underwrites Barth's program of "replenishment," which Walkiewicz takes to be fulfilled by *LETTERS*. At issue in "A Cure for Cancer" is precisely the writer's and critic's dilemma of writing against yet inside of a teleological and moribund pattern.[35]

"A Cure for Cancer" is enclosed in Ambrose Mensch's second literary love letter to both "Yours Truly" and Germaine G. Pitt Amherst. To claim that this letter, or one of the character's more accessible, plot-oriented narratives, represents all of *LETTERS* separates form from content, characters from letters, and letters from literature. Any attempt to increase the novel's accessibility, such as a plot summary, extends instead the confusion built into the language games Barth and the genre play with the reader. To speak through Jacques Derrida and Friedrich Schlegel: "Mixture is the letter, the epistle, which is not a genre but all genres, literature itself" (*The Postcard*, 48).

In the attempt to summarize a personal letter, one generalizes and condenses the content to its most action-oriented, and therefore plot-oriented lines, reducing a letter to a message. It was not simply due to the historical situation or in reverence to the artistic style at the turn of the nineteenth century that letters were read aloud to others or read alone, but rarely paraphrased. The susceptibility and resistance to linearity is a generic feature. Yet many letters consist of nothing but paraphrased narratives and utterances (like A. B. Cook VI's correspondence in *LETTERS*). *LETTERS* works to sustain this tension by creating an interconnected chain that ruptures linear plots at the moment of intersection.

Despite and because of the dangerous lure of "AMATEUR: A Cure for Cancer," I will introduce *LETTERS* through this particular link, not because it is the key story, but because it makes clear that any key to and of *LETTERS* turns into another hole, another key, which does not fit or breaks off in its lock. In the story's introductory paragraphs, Ambrose Mensch reiterates how he could neither come to terms "with conventional narrative" nor with his marriage to Marsha Blank in 1960, how he took thirty libriums and tossed the bottled story into the Choptank River on his thirtieth birthday, only to retrieve it from there one year later.[36] In the interim, this experience "liberated [him] from the library of [his] literary predecessors, for better or worse" (L 150–151). Upon receipt of the bottle and in search of reinspiration, he becomes "reenamored" with his first love Magda (his brother's girlfriend) and with the novel. Throughout this affair and on the site of Magda's and his adultery, Ambrose is building the newlyweds' future house according to his brother's "epistolary consent." Here, Barth parodies Tony Tanner's thesis that in the early-nineteenth-century novel, adultery as an "invisible, inaudible deed becomes a silence and an absence in the text that gradually spreads, effectively negating what *is* made audible and present" (*Adultery in the Novel*, 13). The deed is not only visible but it is also responsible for the Menschhaus and the story. In addition, that which spreads is not an absence but a cancerous growth resisting its amateur cure through *LETTERS*. His new work is thus a lover's struggle against the origins of the novel. Instead of stating what he found, he defers his response like the find of his own missive, the AMATEUR story, which he now, belatedly, transcribes into a letter and *LETTERS*, "again to launch this old chronicle on the tide" (L 152). The story is also not one with itself since three stories in its midst were rewritten and appended by a "certain fellow fictionist," to whom Ambrose showed it in 1962 (L 150). These parts consequently appeared in various magazines from 1963 to 1967 until they ended up in Barth's collection *Lost in the Funhouse*. In that collection, the realist plots of "Water-Message," "Ambrose His Mark," and "Lost in the Funhouse" appear somewhat interpolated when compared to the textual self-reflexivity of the companion stories.

"A Cure for Cancer's" alphabetical letters "A" to "N, O etc.," form both the title and first letter of each episode. This design is similar to, but not the same as, the design of the novel *LETTERS*. Arthur Morton King begins in the first person, shifts to the third, and ends in the first person. At the intersection between first- and third-person narrative, the older narrator cannot refrain from interspersing his comments, displacing the story for his critique of story and of the authorial subject. He changes monologue into dialogue and the dialogue with himself into an epistolary communication by addressing Germaine: *"I'm lost in the funhouse, Germaine. The I of this episode isn't I; I don't know who it is. . . . But I can't speak further of this story, this episode, these events. An end to I"* (L 168–169; Barth's italics). Whereas the older narrator is suspicious of "I" due to his temporal and local distance to himself, his critique of the unified subject, and the rerendering of the story by his author friend, John Barth, the younger narrator finds his voice during his *"lostness in the funhouse,"* which for him symbolizes the *"verbal transmutation of experience into art"* (L 168). They differ on the manner and goal of their fictions, but the amateur and that writer's older self recognize their communal attempt to *"'rescue' fiction from its St. Helena by transforming it altogether, into something full and luminous as the inside of Rosa's egg"* (L 189).

The egg depicts Lorelei on her Rhine-rock, leaning against the castle tower and combing her hair: a beautiful spectacle of the imagination, a legend, and a peril to the ships on the Rhine is now enshrined in an Easter egg. Every notion in the story "hatched from Aunt Rosa's Easter egg, that Uncle Konrad gave her in 1910. . . . Our story is *ab ovo*: nothing here but hatched from there" (L 153). The "Cure for Cancer" story writes itself as an organic text that connects all its characters with its author's personal experience and universal humanity, the "Menschhaus" (L 158). It views its aesthetization of these experiences as a "cure," a "rescue" for both the ailing human society and its own textuality. This story differs from *LETTERS* in that it does not perceive of its "cure" as part of the problem. If everything hatches from the same "egg," the same genes, the cure *of* cancer has to turn into a cure *for* cancer: St. Helena is transformed into a literary "Eiland," "the landscape in that egg" (L 153). From this perspective, the reference to St. Helena (Napoleon's second exile upon his failure to establish his reign and cure the decrepit old order with his own tyranny) hints at the irony and ambivalence of any rescue mission: although it strives to revolt, it inevitably returns to the point of departure.[37]

These narrative signs of closure and nonclosure, of inheritance, conjure up the debate on modernist closure itself. It will do little to enhance our understanding of the meaning of that debate nor the work of the text before our eyes to simply state that a text progresses ad infinitum, forms an ever progressing spiral, or that it ends. Considering critics' anxiety over a novel that refuses to be or have "a" story, it is maybe not surprising that a work like *LETTERS* can still produce such faithfully modernist readings. When the characters pledge to stop sending water-messages or to transform fiction, many readers take the characters' words for granted. This kind of interpretation takes on a cynical note in the case of Ambrose's pledge to abstain from formalist reading and writing. It is as if the old-time charm of the epistolary genre had enveloped the critics in its soothing and soothsaying magic, its "truer than life" attributes, and transformed the late-twentieth-century critics into their eighteenth-century ancestors.[38]

But *LETTERS* does not seem to leave the reader much choice. It begins in *medias res*, an epistolary technique that forces the reader to refrain from handy (re)solutions and programmatic answers. The first letter comes from a character (Lady Amherst), the alphabetical letter *A*, and the "old time epistolary novel." It is Lady Amherst's written invitation to the Author to accept an honorary doctorate from Marshyhope State University, followed by a long postscript in which she outlines the history of that institution and its faculty intrigues, including the Tower of Truth project. The Author has to wait his turn to officially begin *LETTERS*. In his final letter, he declines the doctorate but extends his own request to Lady Amherst to become a character in his new project. The novel *LETTERS* begins without official acknowledgment or title. It feigns to originate outside the literary and scientific establishment in order to revolutionize and establish its (his)story.[39] Barth thus allegorizes the history of the epistolary novel in the eighteenth century.

According to a conventional chronology, several letters from Todd Andrews, Jacob Horner, Jerome Bray, A. B. Cook, and Ambrose Mensch have already been written, reach back through history and toward the future of an unborn child. In declaring an end or beginning of letters and *LETTERS*, reader *and* writer stand on a slippery edge.[40] John Barth's opus offers a striking series to the reader of contemporary fiction. Regardless at which "end" of Barth's work the reader begins, traces will involuntarily lead outside each work's bindings to his other works. Not just the characters and themes of *Lost in the Funhouse* reappear in *LETTERS*; letters are literally mailed between the works. With the *Funhouse*, the reader follows an external chronology, the chronology of publication, to read *LETTERS* next. To begin with *LETTERS*, as I have done, picks up intertextual hints of fictive origination. But are the two readings really different from one another?

What is/was first or second, when the characters themselves reenact and struggle against the reenactment of their pasts? Is it really necessary for an understanding of *LETTERS* to read its predecessors, when the characters indulge in (re)writing their autobiographies, or when Lady Amherst summarizes all essential plot information and details for the Author's and the reader's benefit?[41] Isn't it true to its epistolary form that the reader has to rely on secondhand gossip to gather the tangents of the plot? The complaints against Barth's "indigestible classroom soufflé"[42] do not hold water against such brilliant reworking of genre-specific narratological demands.[43] Letters do not stagnate or die after arriving; they continue to establish a relay of references. Even with the knowledge of this particularity of reading letters, *LETTERS* requires patience of its readers. It dares them to get involved in a "holesome" perusal.[44]

In his foreword to the 1988 edition of *Lost in the Funhouse*, Barth casts his intertextual lure:

> The series was written and assembled between 1966 and 1968. The first Doubleday edition (1968) was prefaced by the Author's Note which follows; to subsequent editions I appended "Seven Additional Author's Notes" set here at the end (I was busy by then with a novel that pretends to have seven authors). The reader may skip all these frames and go directly to the first story . . . called "Frame-Tale." It happens to be, I believe the shortest short story in the English language (ten words); on the other hand, it's endless. (F vii, written in 1987)

Barth calls his fourteen short stories with two official forewords and one postscript an assembled series, not a collection. This choice of word already hints at the difference between the chain and its treasure case, between the postmodern concept of bricolage and the modernist notion of a unified whole. Between the foreword to the new edition, itself called "Lost in the Funhouse," and the "Author's Note" to the earlier edition, the contents form a chain. One of the titles is a "Title" itself. One of the stories repeats the title of the whole series and of the foreword ("Lost in the Funhouse"), and finds its dilemma reflected in a so-called "Echo" story, which, strangely enough, appears *before* the "Title" story (a dialogue between a "he" and a "she" on writing the story of one's life) but *after* the title story "Lost in the Funhouse."

The "Echo" in the center is framed by two "title" stories, one that repeats the name of the series and one that repeats its own function: the entire book writes itself from the inside out, forming a structural mimesis of a funhouse mirror that separates images, themes, and characters into their hundredfold, slightly warped reflections. At the same time "Echo" transcribes Echo's mythical story. In appropriating the female voice, whose essence is a babylonious refraction of the dominant male voice, echo affirms and uncenters the caller's voice at the same time.[45] The "Echo" story calls out in concentric waves; it transmits a sonar water code back to the sender. Just because the stories have a common center does not single them out as their "titles'" expositions. Each title could be placed above each story, thereby calling the functions associated with "naming," "addressing," and "signifying" into question. As the long nameless Ambrose finds out, he is not simply "his mark": "knowing well that I and my sign are neither one nor quite two" (F 34).[46]

In addition to the function of the proper name in relation to characters and motifs, the titles also refer to the process of writing and reading, thereby not only breaking down the barrier among prologues, the text, and the epilogue, but also among characters, authors, and literary genres as well. The story "Autobiography: A Self-Recorded Fiction" demonstrates this most clearly. The speaking subject mocks its name and project but nevertheless writes of its genealogy and life. But parentage is not a straightforward matter in Barth's fiction: Ambrose's mother slept with her brothers-in-law and Hector, and neglects her son most of the time, so that Aunt Rosa becomes his substitute mother (F 14–34); Marsha Blank, Ambrose's first wife, informs him at the end of the novel that Angela is not his but his brother's daughter. Germaine Pitt's son in *LETTERS* has a father who delights in role playing and shape-shifting to the point that not even she is certain of his existence as an individual.

And when "Autobiography" cynically laments, "I've a pair of dads, to match my pair of moms," the idea of aesthetic insemination, that is, influence, as a means to ensure a writer's and a text's heritage is defunct. Modern autobiography's "first" mother "was a mere passing fancy who didn't pass quickly enough," "a mere novel device, just in style, soon to become a commonplace." The epistolary novel is (just) the (French) mother of novels, *en vogue* and then used by everybody: "In either case she was mere, Mom." The father, who "found himself by himself with pointless pen" and who "went by the book," could be interpreted as normative literary criticism, biography, and history.[47] Engrossed in, used up, and deserted in his attempts to aesthetically control the merger of "reality and fiction," his masturbatory pen has become pointless (F 36). In an inversion of sex/gender positions, the mother leaves the seduction scene and disseminates the father's contribution: "What fathers can't forgive is that their offspring receive and sow broadcast their shortcomings" (F 36). The father "persistently" attempts but fails to kill his offspring. Mere Mom and pointless Dad, a curious set of parents for what is often hailed as man's unique lifework, "a thrust of subjective self into external reality."[48] This thrust takes its toll in "Life-Story," in which the injection of self into world leads to endless autofiction. As the Author instills his fiction with increasing self-awareness of its fictitiousness, one of his autoselves connives to murder him (F 116–129). The funhouse, like the movie *Tron*, in which a video-game player becomes a two-dimensional gladiator in his own murderous program, does not appear so safe anymore.[49]

In the late twentieth century, postmodern fiction, bearing a "misleading, if not false" name like autobiography, conceives of, writes about, distorts, and executes its premodernist and modernist pasts (F 35). John Barth phrased his idea of the postmodernist author accordingly in his article "The Literature of Exhaustion": "[T]he ideal postmodernist author neither merely repudiates nor merely imitates either his twentieth-century modernist parents or his nineteenth-century premodernist grandparents."[50] The family of genres and literary modes is linked to the community of writers; literary history and biography are linked to autobiography. Even though each link can be endlessly substituted, the principle of inheritance and heritage remains, but with a twist. Serialized parentage, from Don Quixote to Madame de Staël, from Mark Twain's *Prince and the Pauper* to reproductive technology and cloning, alters the imagined future distinctively. There is no "one" past and no "one" future, only different temporal and spatial loops that have begun to show their effects on interpretation and genealogy.

A child's fantasy of being adopted, of belonging to an entirely different set of circumstances, is the first attempt at revolution. This theme manipulates the Cook/Burlinghame clan in *LETTERS* and functions as their quest throughout history: not to do what the fathers set out to do, believing that their actions were but a cover-up for a truer design. By reading and interpreting their forefathers' letters and strategies with a symbolic decoder, the Cook/Burlinghames run themselves ever deeper into the mud. Here the chain takes on the ambiguous meaning of "shackling," of being chained to the past via one's parents, in turn also imprisoning one's own children. However, the self-contradictory literary attempt to leave a mark, and simultaneously to set one's words and children free, is still under way, with no end in sight. At the end of "Autobiography," the period is omitted from the chain of last words: "Nonsense, I'll mutter to the end, one word after another, string the rascals out, mad or not, heard or not, my last words will be my last words" (F 39).[51]

The foreword precedes the "Author's Note," which follows the new edition, but preceded the older edition. In this, the former beginning has already been undermined through a familiar play with prefaces and epilogues. The "Seven Additional Author's Notes" were written as post-instructions to the reader, at a time when another work *(LETTERS)* led Barth himself to reconsider and reread the *Funhouse*. They appear at the end, although, as an instruction or a blurb, they should conventionally precede the tales. The advertisement for these "Notes" in the "Foreword" will very likely prod the reader to skip to the end to be introduced to the text, skipping "Frame-Story" for another frame-story. Even though this postscript reads "Author's Notes," not "Authors' Notes," they are seven additional notes, which were initiated by the book pretending to have seven authors. As soon as readers encounter these notes about the *Funhouse* in the form of a postscript, they have unwittingly started to read *LETTERS* before actually getting to the *Funhouse*.

The later novel provides the postscript for the earlier fiction at the same time that it pretends to provide a critical introduction to the *Funhouse*. It thus not only reverses end and beginning once more, but also includes the assembled series in the epistolary exchange in *LETTERS*, illustrating the Barthian idea of a postmodernism that historically succeeds modernism. Yet through its almost obsessive rereading and reworking of modernism, it also introduces and presents a funhouse mirror's image of the modernist project to contemporary readers. While he awaits "the unwritable postscript," the lonely bard in the "Anonymiad" finally launches his "tail[tale]piece." He turns yet another possible ending into an "ironical coda" (F 200) by metaphorically connecting the "Night-Journey" of the spermatozoa at the beginning of the series to the perilous bottle-journey at the end of the book.[52] The postscript that can't yet be written appears almost magically through the medium of *LETTERS*. The "Seven Additional Author's Notes" are literally "lost" in the funhouse. By displacing the message, Barth links the sequel to the series and has the reader find a sign that imitates the mysterious message in the bottle, arriving at the shore with just an anonymous "To whom it may concern" and "Yours Truly."[53]

This barest of letters arrives in *Lost in the Funhouse* during the story "Water-Message," before it is received and "launched" in the "Anonymiad." And it arrives again and again in *LETTERS*, once when Ambrose Mensch's narrator-author, Arthur Morton King, retells the story of young Ambrose. Its format underlies Ambrose's and the Author's letters, which are in themselves interpretations and a continuation of its intriguing "fill in the blank" game (L 38–49). In addition, as I mentioned above, some of these bottle-messages are actually launched and received by their senders. All of literature comes down to this bare intersubjectivity which, in and of itself, is depicted as a commercial hoax in the age of ecstatic self-reflectivity. The *Funhouse* and *LETTERS* mass-produce bottles with messages like tourist souvenirs. Including a formalized address and a standard sign-off, they might just as well be a discarded form letter found in a wastepaper basket.

Not surprisingly, such a wastepaper basket plays a notable role within Barth's fictional world. Todd Andrews, the lawyer in *LETTERS*, keeps all his notes and fragments in a basket. He and his secretary, Polly

Lake, make form letters and shredding them their business. Based on a legal grievance, a formal form letter attests to some lack of convention. It therefore shares aspects of a fart Polly releases in the office one day. A fart often arrives before the sender is located. In Todd's case, he does not let the fart go, he keeps it filed away and even includes it on "his life's recycling" list, which he writes to his dead father. Due to Polly Lake's fart, he claims to have found the answer to the Mack versus Mack trial (L 258–259), all relating to the pattern of "praeterital stercoration" (the past manuring the future).[54] In an ironic way, Todd Andrews, who believes in a totally patterned life, an ultraparanoid perception of a deus ex machina, relies on "slips": slips of the tongue and of Polly Lake's behind.

In the same letter, he voices his skepticism of his inclination to "see patterns everywhere" (L 255) and gives two lists of "more or less correspondent events" in his life, fearing that his life is a "reenactment" (L 256). The left column consists of thirteen "early work-notes for my own memoir" and the right column of nine events since 1937 with four blanks still to be filled in. The reader, however, not yet having read this "pattern," has already established it by reading the sender's and the recipient's address: Todd Andrews writes from "Slip #2, Municipal Harbor" to his father in "Plot #1, Municipal Cemetery." The plots have already been staked out beside the blatant matching symbolism of harbor and cemetery, through which one gets the impression of a dead letter exchange (Todd in fact has a dead letter file in a Cambridge P.O.). Todd's father's suicide plot leads Todd to fictionalize his own in *The Floating Opera* and continues to control him in *LETTERS*. His "Slip #2" is but a series to the master narrative and indicates its fragmentary nature. He is in danger of becoming one of the "slips" of paper in his own wastepaper basket. As we shall see, even his testament eludes his urge to control. While waiting for the bomb to detonate in the Tower of Truth, he is forced to let the codicil slip out of the window, let it fly in the shape of a paper airplane to find its own address, preceding his exploding body parts by only seven minutes.

In his fictionalized fantasy, the letter either always already arrived and keeps arriving, or else the letter would not be written at all.[55] The motion of tossing any letter away carries with it a preconceived impression on the addressee, whether real or imagined, and it does not prevent the letter from turning up somewhere at somebody's shore just the same. One finds what the Author's additional first note terms the "emblems of the theme":

as to the serial nature of the fourteen pieces and as to the ideal media of their presentation: the regnant idea is the unpretentious one of turn-

ing as many aspects of the fiction as possible—the structure, the narrative viewpoint, the means of presentation, in some instances the process of composition and/or recitation as well as of reading and listening—into dramatically relevant emblems of the theme. (F 202)

The ideal media of presentation has to be self-reflective, but acting,
"dramatically relevant."[56] The bard who launches his "Anonymiad" and
calls "this and all his predecessors . . . a continuing, strange love letter"
to whom it may concern, knows that only a letter would be material
enough to "turn up" and become dramatically relevant in somebody's
life as well as in a narrative (F 200). Even if "they're too preoccupied to
reach out to it. . . . No matter!" the letter can reach out to them just by
being dispatched from the narrative, by being "sent *matter*." Its possible
arrival becomes a manifest fiction and prerequisite to the actual launch-
ing, both by the bard's own fantasy of its addressee Merope, and of
Ambrose's thoughts, picturing the bottle's journey.

The paragraph from the "Seven Additional Author's Notes" assumes
an emblematic nature itself in that it stands in the place of the "unwritable
postscript" to both the last story as well as all told stories in the *Funhouse*.
The "Seven Additional Author's Notes" are written in the form of an auctorial message, a "Letter to the Reader." They also appear as samples of the
next novel's *seven* characters' writings and reflect on the *fourteen* stories of
the *Funhouse*. Instead of breaking the funhouse spell, they refract the funhouse mirror into another set of seven warped images. Most important, they
demonstrate that the literary critique about the series of stories, although
distanced from the text by borders and frames and by the acknowledged
presence of the auctorial voice, is but a link in the chain itself, unable and
unwilling to distinguish itself in rhetoric or textual strategy from the "literary" or for that matter "theoretical" style and content of "actual" fiction.

True to Barth's ocean metonymy, waves of writing caress each
other, feed off each other's power, cancel each other out as they are
replenished by the next surf. This notion of "replenishing," however, is
not a reinstatement of harmony or mild modernist cynicism. In the
moment of inversion and replenishing, the one does not simply reverse
into an Other, nor does it remain the same as some of Barth's critics
desire.[57] The ever arriving and always already arrived bottled message
dances atop continuously merging and interlacing waves; fresh water
from springs mingles with decomposing matter and the swampy brack-
ish water of the marshes, conscious that the use of the water metaphor
is as old as literature itself. In *LETTERS*, the seven characters' narratives "will become one; like waves of a rising tide, the plot will surge forward, recede, surge farther forward, recede less far, etcetera, to its climax and dénouement. On with the story" (L 49).

At this point, I will "officially" link *LETTERS* to the *Funhouse*.[58] In the *Funhouse*, characters were lost in language. A certain equilibrium existed between words and characters—"it was so *peaceful* being lost in there" (L 652). Barth sets up *LETTERS* as a similarly closed universe in which the signifier is also the signified. There appears to be no inside and no outside of signification. The characters constantly letter and number their experiences and stories just as the tales and patterns letter and number them. However, they are not merely alphabetic letters like Barth's heroes A–G in "Life-Story" because part of the epistolary language game is that they imagine themselves actual, that some of them get a chance to pay debts, get even, or wreak havoc with their past and present textuality.

Before we dis/connect another link, let us look both at the "skeleton key," which the Author and Ambrose conceive in almost telepathic communication, and at the correspondence between *LETTERS* and Edgar Allan Poe's "The Purloined Letter."[59] Before their written correspondence about the layout of *LETTERS*, the Author and Ambrose talk to each other on the telephone in addition to writing letters. The fictional but unnarrated calls between Author/author and author Ambrose take on an air of phonotelepathy, especially when we remember that Ambrose was named after St. Ambrose, the great orator and silent reader. With his seven left-handedly typed notes (his right hand, the "pen of History" "smithereened" film director Reginald Prince's eyeglasses; L 651) and telephone call, Ambrose hopes to lay the "ground plan" for "the transcension of paralyzing self-consciousness to productive self-awareness." He writes to the Author:

> And (it goes without saying) I have in mind too *the transformation of dead notes into living fiction—for it also remains for you to write the story!* . . . 6. Find or fashion a (skeleton) key that will unlock at once the seven several plot-doors of your story! . . . 7. Go from energetic dénouement [to] climactic beginning. (L 652–653; my italics)

Since the telephone call, which apparently concerned "the epistolary Opus #7," and reenactment take place offstage, they hint at the moment of verbal but unwritten composition of *LETTERS* in the unconscious: the conversation with another "author-self" mimics the ideal creative process.[60] The subject *LETTERS* and the subjects of *LETTERS* seem to be constituted in a sphere prior to writing.

The resulting "skeleton key," true to its name and function, is the purloined letter of the book. Neither Author nor Ambrose comes by it via original thinking or the thinking of an origin but rather by *reenactment* (L 652). Neither we nor they know where the key came from. The fact that it is when and where it should not be, namely, on page 769 and not page 770 at the end of the novel, sets the scene for its journey and discovery. Not its absence but its displaced presence and its displacement of presence are at stake.[61] Somehow, even though the Author gained enough knowledge of its shape and size at the beginning of the novel to lay in its trajectory, *LETTERS* does not appear at its designated spot (L 49).[62] Instead, it "bobs" up as a postscript a page earlier than expected. To take the alphabetical wedding toast, which appears in its place, to be the formal principle of the novel seems unwise, since the incomplete toast is missing the letter *N* in its middle. The chain is ruptured, yet it reproduces itself precisely through that missing link. As it is posted, *LETTERS* is already more than one and not identical with itself. Along their postal route, letters disintegrate. The mailing process takes its toll. Not so in Lacan's reading of Poe's story.

Jacques Lacan reads the letter's movements in Poe's story as a signifying chain in the structural sense of the Freudian "repetition-compulsion," in which the letter determines the oedipal and hermeneutic positions of the participants in the two scenes. While the letter shifts positions and is readdressed more than once, it returns unharmed and undivided to its address, the queen. The characters, on the other hand, share their positions.[63] Lacan, from the perspective of the analyst, concentrates on the "insistence of the unreadable in the text" and therefore implicates himself in the crime and injects himself into the text, into the position of those who see and steal the letter.[64] Lacan, like Derrida, believes that it is important not to read "the letter's hidden referential content, but to situate the superficial indication of its textual movement, to analyze the paradoxically invisible symbolic evidence of its displacement, its structural insistence, in a signifying chain."[65]

However, Derrida takes issue with the limited triangular scenes proposed by Lacan and his insistence that the content of the letter is irrelevant. He criticizes the centrality of absence and castration in Lacan's reading, which is tied to Lacan's idea that the analyst, like the poet or detective, can read the lack of meaning.[66] And, Derrida argues, despite all of Lacan's arguments to the contrary, the letter in his "Seminar" is phonocentric:

> What counts here is that the indestructibility of the letter has to do with its elevation toward the ideality of a meaning. However little we know of its content, the content must be in relation to the original contract that it simultaneously signifies and subverts. And it is this knowledge, this memory, this (conscious or unconscious) retention which form its properness and ensures its proper course toward the proper place. Since its ultimate content is that of a pact binding two "singularities," it implies an irreplaceability and excludes, as uncontrollable threat and anxiety, all double simulacra. It is the effect of living and present

> speech which in the last analysis guarantees the indestructible and
> unforgettable singularity of the letter, the taking-place of a signifier
> which never is lost, goes astray, or is divided.[67]

As I have remarked above, one genealogical strand of *LETTERS* is conceived over the telephone and executed in the transcribed tape dialogue between Germaine Amherst and her fiancée Ambrose, to which I will return shortly. Derrida's criticism of Lacan's indestructible and irreplaceable letter and its reemergence in the form of "an old time epistolary novel" incorporated by Germaine in Barth's novel, sets the tone for my discussion of the "key" to *LETTERS*. The questions that I want to pose here concern one of the narratological functions of the letter. Does the skeleton key *LETTERS* "*name* the source or provide the answer to the puzzle"? Is it "a novelistic version of the *deus ex machina . . .* a secret or other kind of information that one 'stumbles on'"?[68] How does one "stumble on" *LETTERS*?

The title of the novel writes the medium with which it is written as well as its subtitle and each character's character.[69] This pattern is organized in calendar boxes, in which every day of the week is assigned to another character. The linear assemblage of the letters is therefore dominated by each person's correspondence day and their spelling of the subtitle of the novel. This results in a mix of forward and backward chronology. If Ambrose, who only writes on Mondays, writes to the Author, who writes only on Sundays (as the deus in deus ex machina), the reader of the novel will read the Author's response before reading the "originating" letter. Letters between Lady Amherst (Saturdays), the Author, and Ambrose often cross in the mail. The calendar pattern, for example, is responsible for the long detour caused by the characters' various refusals and reconsiderations to appear in *LETTERS*, which begins and almost stops *LETTERS* before it can officially begin on page 42.[70]

This chain of spatial, temporal, literal, and epistolary signifiers has more than a formalist purpose. It forces a reading against organic treasure hunts but also against any entropic theories. The key-chain uses one of its own genre-specific functions in opposition to itself. The key begins with Lady Amherst, her twenty-four single letters spell out "Anoldtimeepistolarynovel." Hers is the only coherent and whole title/name in the novel. Throughout his letters, Ambrose refers to her as his "Fair Embodiment of the Great Tradition, of my keyless codes, my chain-letter narratives with missing links, my edible anecdotes, my action-fictions, my *récits concrets*, my tapes and slides and assemblages and *histoires trouvées*" (L 39); "*La Belle Lettre sans Merci*" (L 41), "Muse of Austen, Dickens, Fielding, Richardson, and the rest . . . Mother

Tongue" (L 41); "my friend History (formerly Britannia, a.k.a. Literature . . .)" (L 652); "my good Dame History" (L 652). Her character as
such is spelled out in the title. In the design of the master novelist she
writes what she is, she is what she spells.

Germaine, as an old-time epistolary novel, first hesitates to become
part of the postmodern *LETTERS*. She unsuccessfully attempts to
refuse the Author's metaphorization of her as well as invitation to
become *his* character in her letter of April 5: "Dear Mr. B.: No! I am
not Literature! I am *not* the Great Tradition! I am *not* the aging Muse
of the Realistic Novel! I am not Yours, Germaine G. Pitt (Amherst),
Acting Provost" (L 57). Her "Yours" is ambiguous in that it links with
"not Yours" but also concludes the letter with "Yours, Germaine G.
Pitt," a gesture by which she consigns herself to him. Any attempt to
simply negate her gender/genre role in *LETTERS* reverts back to its
affirmation. Within the confines of *LETTERS*, Barth subverts the
meaning and function of signatures. As the author assigns each character his and her roles, he signs for them. At the same time, however, the
characters which are also letters, assign him his double role as Author
and author. They sign his name and in his name. In the chain-letter narrative of the novel, letters grow out of signatures that traditionally
stand at the edge of a text and mark its closure. Since each letter takes
its place as a part of another set of letters, the signatures, rather than
determining closure, open onto another series. Peggy Kamuf relates the
problem of the signature to literary property and the act of reading:
"Because names become textualized, however, signatures demand first
to be *read* before any law can assign their meaning, whereas it is precisely the possibility of assigning meaning or intention which reading
puts in question."[71] The signature falls into the link of the chain of signifiers. Although Germaine closes with her proper name (which is not
her own name but in itself incorporates her various husbands' proper
names), her signature reverses the contract.[72]

A week later, Germaine reconsiders the Author's proposal on the
condition that he is not in contact with Ambrose, with whom she has
just begun an affair. She reconsiders because, comparing her own childless yet rich life with Germaine de Staël's life, she wants to leave something behind and have somebody to tell it to. She wants to remember her
prime and her romantic involvement in its most appropriate format, in
letters.[73] Tired though she is, she is at the same time disconcerted and
intrigued by the "spooky" connections between the Author's notes
toward his new novel *LETTERS* and her own letters. More recently, his
letters and the planned novel *LETTERS* parallel the changes in her life.
She has an affair with an author, with Ambrose Mensch, while main-
taining a confiding relationship with the Author (L 57–59).[74]

Even if the younger Ambrose, the Author, and others have worked and continue to rework Germaine, she still carries with her an indestructible "spirited dignity" (L 767). Ambrose's nicknames for his epistolary lover echo the Author's own, when he decides to

> reorchestrate some early conventions of the Novel. Indeed (I blush to report) I am smitten with that early-exhausted of English novel-forms, the *epistolary novel*, already worked to death by the end of the 18th Century. Like yourself an official honorary Doctor of Letters, I take it as among my functions to administer artificial resuscitation to the apparent dead. (L 654)

Indeed, Lady Amherst's accounts of the first stage of her love affair with Ambrose voice one overall concern: whether her "weary, sated flesh will to't again" (L 80). "Gynecology echoes epistemology" when both the Author and Ambrose want to impregnate forty-five-year-old Lady Germaine Gordon Pitt Amherst, that is, an old time epistolary novel, once again (L 768).[75] The outcome, although mysterious in the novel itself, lies before the reader. But just whose child we have on our hands remains unclear. Germaine's pregnancy has not been medically attested. To complicate matters further, Ambrose's "daughter" Angela (his ex-wife Marsha informed him that she is not his daughter, but his brother's) "has been had carnal knowledge of," supposedly by Jerome Bray, the insect-numerologist, who has been trying to computer-generate the novel (NUMBERS) in competition with Ambrose's alphabetical (LETTERS) and Reginald Prince's cinematic (FRAMES) attempts (L 768).

It appears to the reader that Ambrose's DNA, his design for the novel, has prevailed. However, Jerome's final attempt at literal procreation with five females might have produced the same result in creating five plus two (Author and Jerome) characters who write to each other and themselves, believing themselves actual (L 755). If Jerome was on the yacht *Baratarian* in the bay, Jerome could purloin what was "up for grabs," bobbing on the "ocean of story." In this case, Ambrose's last water-message would ironically have completed a perfect exchange, from sender to receiver to sender: a computer chip matching input and memory banks for perfect communication. After all, every one of the characters is infected with some kind of numerology, some kind of pattern, carrying the germs of the five-legged and lettered RESET king. The end of the novel could be read as a gigantic RESET, as all the characters imagine themselves actual enough to commit suicide, marry, die of cancer, or to become writers. While they believe that they have regained control over their own lives, they are flung back to the other side of Jerome's printer to begin again, typing over what they have already written, and what has been written with them.

Lady Amherst is not the only character whose individual letters, read together as a chain, spell out her narratological function. All the other characters are interconnected epistemologically, making them part of one another's functions and letters.

Todd Andrews:	BY SEVEN FI
Jacob Horner:	CTITIOUS
A. B. Cook IV:	DROLLS & DREAM
Jerome Bray:	ERS EACH O
Ambrose Mensch:	F WHICH IMA
The Author:	GINES HIMSELF ACTUAL

Since Germaine is the only "new" character in the novel, her link provides the inlet to the chain of characters. This holds true not only on formal grounds, but also due to the content of her letters. She focuses all narrative strains, explains them to the Author, whose confidante and inside informer she becomes. In the literal, sexual, and figurative sense of the word: she is the characters', the novel's, mailbox. She is constituted by the others' letters but also stands on her own: no other letter can destroy her function, only add to it.

Jerome Bray's chain has the numerical "each" at its center. The Author only "(ima)gines himself actual." That he is more of a droll dreamer than any of the other characters is asserted by his "three concentric dreams of waking," in which he first receives the *LETTERS* design (L 46–49). Todd Andrews, the character responsible for the termination of the novel and others' lives, spells "seven" with the letters in his name "Andrews" and his letter-chain. He fulfills the destiny of seven stages as proclaimed and feared by Ambrose in his "key" of seven authors/characters, seven days, seven months, seven letters, and seven "books of letters." The three novelists—Jerome Bray, Ambrose, and the Author—spell out what they intend to defeat with every step: their "Jacob Hornerness," their (fi)ctitious(ness) as antiheroes in their own plots. Ambrose ends his last letter with the call for an abortion, to abort Angela's and Jerome's offspring. This makes him another Jacob Horner, who in *The End of the Road* lets his lover Rennie die from an abortion, rather than face his failing involvement caused by his own auctorial detachment.[76]

Ursula Arlart points to the spiraling motion of the letters in *LETTERS* and adds a further reading pattern to *LETTERS'* *Titelsatz:*

> In order to continue the title sentence, one has to return from, so to speak, "book" 7 to "book" 1 and proceed with the adjacent correspondence group. This way, a recurrent and a linear movement combine with each other to form a spiral. . . . The outermost, seventh ring

of the spiral is occupied (as in *Chimera*) by the author, who composed the fiction LETTERS. The "past" rings beneath contain Barth's earlier fictions and form the basis for the newly created work.[77]

In relation to what was said about Ambrose's "Jacob Hornerness," this spiral, which Arlart believes leads to "a new value-system" (110) away from the treacherous Moebius strip to a fruitful coupling of old and new, is capable of turning into an abortive instrument.

A spiral or coil is also an intrauterine device (IUD) used as an implanted contraceptive. A spiral does not simply coil forever onward. While in the motion of twisting, it scrapes off sediments and hinders deposits. The reading and writing spiral of *LETTERS*, the seemingly harmless verbal "key to the treasure," is therefore both an instrument of violence, of abortion, and an instrument enabling women to control their role in reproduction. The past has to be severed first, opened and submitted to the future's probings. The future is aborted while it is created: "All hands agree" (L 766). Every hand, every character, is more than willing to use the power for both ends: Ambrose, Martha, and Germaine to abort Angie's baby and Todd to destroy the Tower of Truth, along with himself and everyone in his vicinity.

As the spiraling structure and narrative setting demonstrate, not even formal clues dissolve into nothingness or remain what they appear to be at first sight. Every fiction, every letter is sent and arrives, gets caught and breaks away, is reenacted on different levels. Each bit of information, each statement, and each event *corresponds* with a narratological, figurative, and literal occurrence. Except for reenactment's sake and in the dreams of the "Drolls and Dreamers," to get lost in the funhouse is no longer an option. The writing of letters spells out connection, interdependency, desire for communication, but also the curse of impossible, but necessary and violent, rupture. The lullaby of the tidal waves has been deciphered as a dénouement within the larger narrative frame. Fiction cannot overcome the pasteurized future. That future has to be churned out with, against, and as fiction, no matter what.

When Ambrose's and Germaine's last transcribed tape-letter addresses "Art" (abbreviation for Arthur Morton King, Ambrose's pseudonym as artist), the letter corresponds with Ambrose's artistic past, with "Yours Truly" of the mysterious water-messages, the external reader, as well as with Germaine, who intersperses her comments as she transcribes the taped monologue. This oral letter, put into print by the figure of "an old time epistolary novel" within a contemporary epistolary novel, includes her printed acceptance of Ambrose's replayed oral and then printed marriage proposal. It addresses "(dead) Art" itself; a postmodern letter-in-a-series written to dead "Letters," which is also, one should not forget, the title of Barth's novel and in itself a series of letters that engender the novel while it is written.

On its own, this letter has been most commonly interpreted as a "gesture of faith" on Barth's part, as a "successful courtship of the reader."[78] One is tempted to read the separate-yet connectedness of Ambrose and Germaine as an attempt to overcome the "extremely limiting conventions of the epistolary novel" or as "a welcome reversal of men writing: woman speaking."[79] But something can only be overcome if it is imprisoned in theoretical and critical restraints to begin with. Critics who assume that a contemporary epistolary novel's goal is to mend the old genre's insufficiencies and "go beyond" fall back into positivistic categories.

The letter is dated September 1, 1969, a Monday, and depicts Ambrose and Germaine commencing the week together. The harmonious appeal of "Yes, I will" lures one away from the sobering numerical catechism of 6's and 7's displayed in the letter. One wonders: Is this premarital spat any different from fighting over the specific type of porcelain or the color of the bridesmaids' dresses? Indeed it is. The lovers argue about the time of day of the exchange of marriage vows. Every suggested time can be interpreted as belonging to a reenactment period according to Ambrose's pattern of seven stages. Both Ambrose and Germaine are searching for a gap in that pattern to assert their new beginning, their merging subjectivities. They cannot find an unwritten, non-reenacted time, so they finally choose to get married on the recurrence of their sixth stage in order to enter stage 7 together (L 764). If this seems to indicate an acceptance of the inescapability of reenactment and to celebrate the possibility of choice regarding its manner and style, read again! Although the most accessible of all the characters, Ambrose and Lady Amherst are by no means the novel's "central consciousness." A "mailbox" doesn't have a conscience, it is filled with the consciousness of others, and Ambrose is but one of the author's Author figures.

What disturbs the harmony in the letter? First, Germaine transcribes it on a typewriter. She thus becomes Ambrose's secretary and writing instrument.[80] As the female reincarnation of an old-time epistolary novel, she will contractually be eliminated upon marriage to Ambrose, the novelist: "[t]he very being or legal existence of the woman is suspended during the marriage, or at least is incorporated and consolidated into that of the husband. . . . [A]nd therefore it is also generally true, that all compacts made between husband and wife, when single, are voided by the intermarriage."[81] Germaine dutifully ends the transcription process with conventional sign-offs, and in a formal, official style "AM/ggp(a) cc:JB" (L 765): Her boss's initials in capital letters (Ambrose Mensch), her own in lowercase secretarial style (germaine gordon pitt amherst), and a notation that a copy goes to JB (John Barth and/or Jerome Bray). Although Ambrose encourages her to intersperse her comments and edit the taped letter, she does so with more "checks" and "ayes" than with anything substantial, except for her postscript between Ambrose's sign-off and his postscript. (One should not forget that "Echo," although "effacing herself absolutely" [F 103], also "edits, heightens, mutes, turns others' words to her end" [F 100].) In this postscript, Germaine rereads Ambrose's numerical scheme only to become utterly discouraged and dismayed at the prospect of reiterating the trying times of their courtship. Whereas her first opening letter maintained the partisan linguistics of Germaine as *acting* provost through the two-facedness of official invitation and unorthodox postscript, this last postscript resigns her to the role of Ambrose's *right hand* (his right hand is bandaged from a fight with Prince). To speak with Kittler, Ambrose and Germaine have entered the sexless stage of the typewriter's discourse.[82]

Second, her reading is a jumble of numbers and letters, a feverish exclamation of dread. Germaine's outpouring is framed by two "Pauses," each of which refer to the pausing of the tape. For the dialogue to take place on paper, the voice of the other has to be turned off, the dialogue can only take place in the absence of the other's voice.[83] Instead of overstepping the boundaries of the genre with modern technology, the genre's idiosyncrasies are reaffirmed. Epistolarity takes shape as the echoing of the remembrance of the other's voice, already mingled with her own perception, anxieties, readings, and contradictions. As "gynecology echoes epistemology," these pauses become RESETS when Germaine mentions her menstrual pattern and impending menopause throughout her letters. Her menstrual period interrupts and delays her correspondence to the Author for two Saturdays in August and September and displaces her writing date to a Wednesday (L 659). She postdates that particular letter to adhere to her former pattern and literally crams three weeks of "writer's cramp" into one letter that lasts three days.

Third, the transcription of actions in reference to writing machines only occurs in one other instance, namely, Jerome Bray's already quoted RESET mechanism. RESET divides utterances automatically, according to a hidden pattern in the program, sometimes acting as stopper, sometimes integratable into the semantics of the phrase in progress. RESET consistently reminds one of the manner and matter of writing: the computer program, the printing process, and the 1980s-style printer ribbon with which it is produced. Germaine's menstruation and looming menopause recall the history of sexualized epistles, of epistolarity's bloodline from Clarissa to Madame de Merteuil and Evelina. Ambrose's determination to have a child from her at her advanced age expresses itself as the desire to RESET nature's course, to begin nearing the end. Ambrose has a fetishist's fascination with symbolic numbers and numerical systems. And yet, he struggles against the dehumanizing quality of Bray's computer-novel *NUMBERS* as well as Prince's favoritism of visuality over words. Ambrose rewrites the aesthetic discourse of enlightenment and romanticism. The documentation of his endeavor to come to terms with cinematography and computerized art is a resetting of, for example, Goethe's edicts on natural sciences and Kleist's essay "About Marionette-Theater" ("Über das Marionettentheater"). *LETTERS* writes and reads itself as what Paul de Man calls an aesthetization of material numbers and materialization of aesthetic numbers.[84]

At the point that *LETTERS* officially begins, the Author *pauses* the action to "read off" the title and credits (L 42). In this cinematic interlude, he previews the novel's plot as well as each character's numbered "takes." His "three concentric dreams of waking" are structured like Bray's diary and Ambrose's last alphabetic summary of the novel. Just as a screenplay is made up of numbered shots, stage directions, and lines, arranged in columns to indicate their simultaneity, *LETTERS* frames numbers, and *NUMBERS* frames letters. The *LETTERS* design itself is *FRAMES*, because its title reads like a filmstrip negative.

A comparison of Bray's "RESET" and Germaine's "Pauses" is valid for yet another reason. Bray's final letter, temporally the second to last of the whole novel, spatially precedes Germaine's and Ambrose's mutual letter. In it, Bray is equally obsessed with dates and stages. He feverishly numbers and letters his last days and historic events on September 23. This letter begins with a phonetically warped version of the "Star Spangled Banner" and ends with a witch's recipe for the drug "Honeydust." Its seventh and last ingredient contains the freeze-dried feces of George III (L 758). Correspondingly, Lady Amherst is also concerned with the *"7th week of this honeymooney Mutuality,"* which, according to her calculations, commences on September 22. The date Jerome has chosen for his transcendence to "granama" (his gran'ma and anagram heaven) lies in their seventh stage. Amherst's repeatedly voiced "iciness" at the prospect precedes Jerome's "freeze-dried" ingredient, as does the "honeymoon" the "honeydust."

Furthermore, while Bray writes his "Star Spangled Banner" as a warped phonetic transcription by the computer, imitating in turn Jimmie Hendrix's drug-inspired cynical guitar solo at Woodstock, "Germaine's" words, also a transcription, literally echo "his" and vice versa. The quotation marks refer to the fact that the delicate balance between human intellect and emotions and the artificial intelligence of the computer/writing instrument has been crossed. The power of the pattern has overtaken all three authors. For a dialogue to take place, the program must already be in place. Just as Germaine can replay Ambrose's voice, Jerome can recall her entry. The couple searches for a solution external to the pattern, for a place over*looked* by it. Instead they find only places *over*looked by it.

All this becomes even more disconcerting when we read this as Germaine's final letter (spatially, even though temporally it is not her last). The "old time epistolary novel" responds to numerology, corresponds to/with *NUMBERS*, Bray's computer-generated novel. Within the title pattern, the letter belongs to Ambrose's chain and not hers. Her contribution and affiliation have been erased. Again, the layout provides another clue: The word "novel" ends with Germaine's last two "real" letters, one postdated September 13, the other written on September 20. Her displaced transcription of the dialogue, originally supposed to have been enclosed in her postdated letter of September 13, appears posthumously, after the end of "novel." But it is not until the displaced transcription, that the "novel" is killed along with "Art."

In the process of transcribing someone else's words, Germaine's awareness of the pattern's danger, her freshly asserted subjectivity, is inverted. While she and Ambrose are addressing "(dead) Art," "Art's" ghost is unleashed, and Lady Amherst becomes a medium in her own séance. The sensation of a "cold hand" upon her womb manifests the curving back of the spiral upon its subjects. Instead of dying or engendering herself *anew*, Germaine's, that is, the epistolary novel's, last letter becomes an anagram of the first water-message and continues the chain letter with a copied variant of the pattern. Germaine and Ambrose, intent on finding the hole in the prescribed text, have already crossed over, as has the author, into yet another system that is not the same and not entirely the other. Not the treasure, but rather *the hole* lies within the key. At the end of the word "LETTERS," within the plural spiraling *S* that stops short of turning into a Moebius strip itself, at the "cornerstone" of the chain, closure is enveloped in nonclosure, both in the pattern for *LETTERS: a novel*, as well as in its grammatical structure.

Even the herme(neu)tically sealed *Funhouse* can be linked to the chain. The funhouse unmasks its double identity: as "Yours Truly," among others of the "same" name, as a set of Siamese Twins, grown together hunchback-style, or "a tergo." Where is the writing of "PeTI-TIon" taking place—a title that spells itself—TITle—and their connectedness at the middle? "To be one: paradise! To be two: bliss! But to be both and neither is unspeakable" (F 71). The unspeakable, the desire to kill the other, takes shape in a letter, petitioning for medical separation. The rear twin has to write it on the back of his brother, or dictate it to him. One cannot be sure who writes the letter or what the letter is, since the twin in front "seizes every message like a jealous censor and either obscures . . . or translates them into his own coarse idiom" (F 67).

The petition letter is framed by "Water-Message" and "Lost in the Funhouse." It doubles the already doubled writing system of the marriage proposal in *LETTERS* and questions authorship as well as "mutuality" in dialogue. As a letter it also pleads for "oneness" as one alone or in marriage with another. In this similarity of doubles, heritage has changed directions: As the "child-father" of Ambrose and Germaine's transcribed marriage petition, this literary phenomenon of displaced doubles returns to its "father-child," young Ambrose, at the beach. The arrival of the censored letter (all content is blank, only address and sign-off remain) prompts him to write and become a filler of blanks, a "constructor of funhouses" (F 97). He "exhibited us [the twins] throughout our childhood" (F 64). In receiving and devising blanks to fill, Ambrose also engages his *Doppelgänger*, the censoring twin, or the ambitious Bray.

At the end of *LETTERS*, Ambrose receives another water-message "to consist this time wholly of body, without return address, date, salutation, close, or signature" (L 765). The "washed up" letter is sponged of signature and address. What was there before has been sponged up and spit out as its negative in the *mise en abyme* of the "refilming of the 'Water Message sequence' of the motion picture FRAMES" (L 765). Mirroring the framing of "Petition" in the *Funhouse* series yet again, writing has turned into its inverse. The pen consumes the ink of the written as it is writing. The writing twin experiences just this the night before he sends his petition: "I felt him straining to suck me in through our conjunction, and clung to the sheets in terror" (F 70).

The regurgitated ink reads "TOWER OF TRUTH 0700 9/26/69," (L 766) and contains some "brown stuff" (L 768). It predicts the date of ascension, suicide, and murder, with which the story line ends and the novel begins to be (re)assembled. The form of this entry recalls Jerome Bray's diary-letter to his "Granama," in which he included the recipe for "Honeydust" (a mixture of feces, bee's jelly, snake and newt, poisoned entrails, toad venom, and frog toes) and which now induces Ambrose to take his part in the Tower spectacle. Instead of being received by "Granama," it is received by the anagram maker Ambrose, whose affiliation to "ambrosia" and honeybees makes him the perfect target for "Honeydust." Under Bray's and his letter's "odd-odored" influence, he conceives of the "Akrostichon," the design of *LETTERS*.

Although he is "striving through, in order to reach beyond, such games," Ambrose "restopper[s]" the bottle, in which the message was sent along with his last letter and the "brown stuff" (L 765). He plays the game to "restop," to go through his second life cycle to reach the third cycle and so forth, to stop and go, restop and restart: to reset. He resets the keyboard, emphatically programming the alphabet anew, by grouping the novel's plots, ideas, structure, and characters under letters *A* through *G* for the scheme of another novel: *LETTERS*. The alphabet (re)writes and (un)writes itself in every letter-chain. The waves encounter each other somewhere in the middle. By "inventing" the key to *LETTERS*, Ambrose is filling in another blank this time: the blank of addressee(s) and sender(s). His allusion to the Author's alphabetical wedding toast, in which the central *N* is missing, shows that there will be no "eNd" to the blanks, as there will be no end to the waywardness of letters (L 769/770). The question of closure and nonclosure, however, will remain at the center of the dialogue. As an epistolary character and writer of epistles, Ambrose knows that absence produces dialogue and dialogue absence, that the "construction blueprints," like letters and *LETTERS*, can be stolen or "honeydusted" to "drop this architectural and pedagogical obscenity into its own foundation hole" (L 736).

Todd Andrews uses "key structural elements," construction blueprints stolen from the architects, to blow up the Tower of Truth, including all its inhabitants, at 7:00 A.M. on September 26.[85] His final letter contains the *seventh* supplement to his codicil of September 1, which he is only able to amend because the "souvenir *Key to Truth*" broke off in the lock and lets nobody enter to rescue him and themselves. Unluckily for him, the key that keeps the public out, also incarcerates him in the belfry, and prevents him from placing his will in the cornerstone of the tower. Along with the novel's design, he still manages to place it in the cornerstone of *LETTERS*. Todd turns his will into a paper airplane and sends it on its journey at 6:53 o'clock, *seven* minutes before detonation. Unaware of the fact that the "blueprints" have washed off/rubbed off on him, he believes himself in total control. It seems as if no one could purloin a letter without being its unknown intended addressee, without being (re)programmed through its message.[86] In this final reading sample, a testament, the key literally turns in the hole only to turn into the hole. The modernist key to an understanding of life and letters, while being inserted into the essence of truth and being, breaks off, gets stuck, and now becomes the hole through which postmodernism has to read itself.

Before moving on, a comment is in order about the motif of "turning into." As we read, themes turn into titles, authors turn into characters, functions turn into emblems, writing turns into reading, speaking into writing, and vice versa. With this "turning process" we return to the metaphor of the Moebius strip, where the twist provides for nonclosure and closure at the same time. The novel *LETTERS* disseminates; it is the illusory act that (non)produces the mirage of meanings that can never be organized into even a polysemic totality, that can never be returned to the father. . . . The *waywardness* of the letter . . . also suggests . . . that any closure is only illusory. The wandering (errant-fictional) letter and gossip meet as the sign of the sign, the capacity of language for interminable drift.[87]

LETTERS dis/connects the interrelation between meaning and the subject. The return to the realm of individuality, identity, and romantic love as the merging of "two into one" writes itself as a return to "EACH," a return to the essentially disembodied "otherness" of Bray's computer program. Because of the professional anxiety that an old-time author like John Barth must feel in the face of the media war between telephone and cable companies, TV stations, film studios, army intelligence, publishing and computer moguls, he can only hope to have had a Nietzschean impact on creating postmodernism "out of the spirit of Modernism," out of "Woman as the allegory of Modernity," a foundational parable that has had many devoted followers. According to this parable, the "leash of flesh heartbreakingly short" that connects and separates (br)other to/from (br)other in "Petition" (F 61) and that connects and separates self to/from other in all the discussed texts, cannot be ruptured without violence and denial of either one:

> What happens when acts and performances (discourse or writing, analysis or description, etc.) are part of the objects they designate? When they can be given as examples of precisely that of which they speak or write? Certainly, one does not gain auto-reflective-transparency, on the contrary. A reckoning is no longer possible, nor is an account, and the borders of the set are then neither closed nor open. Their trait is divided, and the interlacings can no longer be undone. (*The Postcard*, 391)

Derrida's metonymic "interlacings" provide for the next link in the chain letter and give me the opportunity to draft some differences and similarities of function and theoretical positioning.

"POSTCARD"

> "[E]pistolary fictions multiply when there arrives a new crisis of destination."
> —*The Postcard*, 232

In this work, Derrida investigates, composes, and struggles against a discourse of the post. Is the postcard "more" postmodern than the letter? Does Derrida move beyond Barth and Freud? What does it mean to transcribe the legacies of philosophy and psychology onto a postcard?

MODERN LANGUAGE ASSOCIATION
10 Astor Place   New York, NY 10003-6981   212 475-9500

January 1994

On 17 December, two large bags of first-class mail addressed to the Modern Language Association were stolen. If you think a letter you have sent may have been lost, please write or call the office to which you addressed the letter. (Payments sent in envelopes provided in dues notice mailings would not have been in the bags.)

We apologize for any inconvenience.

Phyllis Franklin

Phyllis Franklin

FIGURE 3.2

Even the Modern Language Association of America has to resort to a postcard to inform its members of having lost a couple of mail bags.

Does this transcription collapse the postal code or does it instead implode Derrida's postcardization itself? If Derrida criticizes Lacan for the centrality of the "lack" in Lacan's "Seminar on the 'Purloined Letter,'" epistolary fiction's structural indeterminacies somehow take center stage in Derrida's speculations. After all, letters always threaten to become novels, numbers, frames, postcards, telephone books, or disks or . . . a postmodern poetics.[88]

The postcard in our hands turns every postcard within into a letter of the alphabet, so that its sum, its "words," are spaced out indecipherably like the large words on maps that refute any territorialization themselves and that send the eyes on a long journey.[89] Derrida's postcard reproduces the detective's rationale on the system of hiding and obtaining the purloined letter from the minister in Poe's story. The detective sees it as a verbal game of "hide-and-seek." This game is indeed "played upon a map":

> One party playing requires another to find a given word . . . any word, in short, upon the motley and perplexed surface of the chart. A novice in the game generally seeks to embarrass his opponents by giving them the most minutely lettered names; but the adept selects such words as stretch, in large characters, from one end of the chart to the other . . . and here the physical oversight is precisely analogous with the moral inapprehension by which the intellect suffers to pass unnoticed those considerations which are too obtrusively and too palpably self-evident.[90]

Although the purloined letter seems to be but one character in this verbal universe, the detective and Lacan can stretch the letter's support from one end of the story to the other because in their game plan the map, and therefore the letter itself, never changes: "But if it is first of all on the materiality of the signifier that we have insisted, that materiality is odd {singulière} in many ways, the first of which is not to admit partition. Cut a letter in small pieces, and it remains the letter it is."[91] By contrast, the "thick support" of a postcard combines the adept's law of obtrusive and palpable self-evidence with the novice's "minutely lettered names." The postcard's double entendre uses game plan and map against themselves. Spacing words is the key for decipherability, which one should not confuse with legibility. Although spacing might lead to multiple combinations, some kind of reading will always be possible. Something that is readable can be indecipherable.[92]

It should also not be forgotten that a postcard has two sides, which can never be seen at the same time and in the same place. In order to receive a postcard as postcard, the reader has to turn it around. Derrida situates "Envois" within this rift whenever he forces the reader to interrupt his reading to turn to the picture's details. Spacing becomes a movement.[93] The shifting interval between picture and text reads the reader reading:

> While you occupy yourself with turning it around in every direction, it is the picture that turns you around like a letter, in advance it deciphers you, it preoccupies space, it procures your words and gestures, all the bodies that you believe you invent in order to determine its outline. (Back cover of *The Postcard*)

Derrida dramatizes the effect of turning the page, which also works like an incision, a caesura of the flow of reading, especially when one considers that a reader of a new book formerly had to cut the individual pages with a knife, just like opening a letter. A reader intent on deciphering the text "at hand" tends to repress the "other" of the text, tends to forget that it is even there. As Shoshana Felman and Paul de Man have demonstrated, the act of reading per se is blind toward the "uncanny rest" that it produces and through whose repression it constitutes itself in the first place.[94] This hermetic enclosure of the reader into the text is opened by Derrida's constant distancing and displacement of narrative, reader, and author:

> As that according to which any entity is what it is only by being divided by the Other to which it refers in order to constitute itself, spacing is also the presignifying opening of concealed and unconcealed meaning. . . . It divides the present moment of the now within

itself. Insinuating an interval in each present moment . . . the spacing diastema is also the becoming-space of time, the possibility proper of temporalization, as well as the becoming-time of space.[95]

The shifting of the interval also affects Derrida's own position. The author's readings multiply at an alarming rate and change his narrative into metonymic subpostcards that infiltrate all of his themes and all of his linguistic registers. Neither personal nor theoretical correspondence manages to maintain its status. Not even the attempt to burn anything that is not part of the "metaepistolary" discourse can obscure the "border writing" effect of the correspondence (176).[96] All that is left for the "great burning" is represented in fifty-two spatial blanks that illustrate the policy of spacing outlined above (221).

The spacing movement that divides the reader's self, text, and authorial voice penetrates writing itself:

> In several places I will leave all kinds of references, names of persons and of places, authentifiable dates, identifiable events, they will rush in with eyes closed, finally believing to be there and to find us there when by means of a switch point I will send them elsewhere to see if we are there, with a stroke of the pen or the *grattoir* I will make everything derail, not at every instant, that would be too convenient, but occasionally and according to a rule that I will not ever give, even were I to know it one day. (177)

In the text, incinerated blanks border on clippings derived from the postal principle and "doom[ed] to loss by publishing" (176). Loss by fire and loss by publishing go hand in hand. Writing becomes a mixed-medium design in which blanks and solids are welded together and embossed with each other's signature. The two materials, however, are incompatible and eat away at each other. Instead of the Wittgensteinian bruises that trace the "running up against language,"[97] "Envois" refutes even the practical metaphoricity of two entities encountering each other, and instead insists on the differential in-heritance, the system-endemic chain reaction of reading and writing, of sending and receiving. If John Barth likened his author characters to "funhouse fashioners," we could call Derrida's authorial voices "switchmen in a postmodern amusement park," where roller coasters no longer glide on a simple loop, but where the tracks switch at unforeseeable moments.

In order to delineate some differences between *The Postcard* and *LETTERS*, let us read a Derridean postcard: "Now, a certain form of support is in the course of disappearing, and the unconscious will have to get used to this, and this is already in progress." (105) The modernist unconscious is seen to depend on the support of the letter as a "pure signifier."[98] According to this postcard, that support disappears in post-

modern discourse and the unconscious needs to adapt. The postcard
continues this speculation with a quote from Monsieur Brégou, "principal Inspector of the Posts and Telecommunications":

> In the years to come, exception made for the mail of private individu-
> als ["exception made," which one, until when?], it can be thought that
> it will no longer be writing that will be transported, but the perforated
> card, microfilm, or magnetic tape. The day will come that, thanks to
> the "telepost," the fundamentals will be transmitted by wire starting
> from the user's computer going to the receiving organs of the computer
> of the post office nearest [all the same] the residence of the
> addressee. . . . It will remain for the postal employee only to place the
> envelope into distribution, which moreover will be able to encompass
> several correspondences emanating from different senders. The tradi-
> tional process thereby will find itself upset for a major portion of the
> mail. (104–105)[99]

While the postcard quotes Brégou's prognosis, it inserts its own comments and suspicions into the long citation. The interjections scramble
sender and addressee, and produce in a *mise en abyme* that which the
postcard later adds to the mangled quotation:

> Yes and no: for as long as it is not proven that into each of our so
> secret, so hermetically sealed letters several senders, that is several
> addressees have not already infiltrated themselves, the upset will not
> have been demonstrated. If our letters are upsetting, in return, perhaps
> it is that already we are several on the line, a crowd, right here, at least
> a consortium of senders and addressees, a real shareholders' company
> with limited responsibility, all of literature, and yet it is true, my
> unique one, that Monsieur Brégou is describing my terror itself, Ter-
> ror itself. (105–106)

Neither new technology nor the disputable fact "that the part of 'private' mail tends towards zero" (104) upsets the postal system because
Brégou has conjured up a Nickisch-style epistolary machine that never
existed in the first place, and because something that lives on disruptions, upsets, and adulterations cannot not be upset. The problem is the
remaining "terror" of an all powerful system that integrates its "upsets,"
a postal psychic system that stomachs even the disappearance of material support, even of writing.

And this is where Derrida's personal terror resides, in the prospect
of having no legacy to leave, because the medium of his legacy will have
been made if not irrelevant then no longer the crucial issue of critical
thought and philosophy. Mixed into his postcard novel is a thwarted
desire, a desire nevertheless, for leaving a legacy although he worked all
his life to uproot the very idea of legacies. And the scary prospect that

the deconstruction of the discourse of bequests turns out to be his gift to his successors after all. Because the inability to leave a legacy is not an altogether cheerfully accepted concept, the writer(s) of "Envois" hasten(s) to inscribe "my unique one," the idea of a unique addressee to ward off personal and totalitarian terror. That "my unique one" is in itself an epistolary phrase that refers to anyone who happens to be reading the postcard, disrupts the comfort immediately but it also shows that the traveler romanticizes that concept itself, that Derrida romances the post's ability to have it all ways—to give, honor, and withhold the metaphysics of Being—and that this romance is therefore both his personal terror and "Terror itself." In an appropriately enveloped Freudian move, Derrida's *Postcard* is an effort at self-analysis, and in his case, self-deconstruction, a legacy his students cannot and do not want to receive because it goes beyond deconstruction.[100]

Franz Kafka, whose correspondence for this reason alone rightfully remains a constant reference point within "Envois," underlines the conceptual difference between the privacy of letters and the anonymous public arena of postcards. Kafka refuses to sign and send a postcard to his friend and lover Milena with the explanation: "I can no longer write to you as if you were a stranger."[101] Due to its openness and vulnerability, a postcard installs a censor between sender and addressee, and turns lovers into chance acquaintances, strangers, and ironically, relatives. Unlike letters, postcards conventionally arrive without the sender's address, sometimes without a signature. Whereas the envelope shields the epistolary sheets of paper and takes most of the abuse during the transferal, the postcard arrives with discernible traces of its mailing history. These traces are superimposed on the writing; they sometimes even erase or obstruct the message. (Currently, this is the case with the postal bar codes affixed to the bottom of postcards. They are pasted over the traditional place of the signature barring the sender's identification mark.) Mail carriers can no longer claim not to have access to the "content" of the mail, because the postcard's content is its surface. It turns the letter's dialectic of inside/outside into the dialectic of front to back, front to front or back to back (13).

It is this dialectic that Derrida exhausts in his recurrent analysis of the Oxford postcard. The postcard shows Socrates sitting on a scribe's chair. He etches with the left hand and dips his feather into the ink with his right hand. Plato, stepping onto Socrates' pedestal, scratches Socrates' back with his right hand and points admonishingly or excitedly upward with his left hand:

Socrates turns his *back* to plato, who has made him write whatever he wanted while pretending to receive it from him. This reproduction is sold here as a post card, you have noticed, with *greetings* and *address*. Socrates writing, do you realize, and on a postcard. I know nothing more about what the caption says about it (it has been taken from a *fortune-telling book*, an astrological book: prediction, the book of destinies, fate, sort, encounter, chance, I don't know, I'll have to see, but I like this idea), I wanted to address it to you right away, like a piece of news, an adventure, a chance simultaneously anodine, anecdotal, and overwhelming, the most ancient and the last . . . a kind of personal message, a secret between us, the secret of reproduction. (12)

According to this Derridean postcard, Plato, as the inheritor of Socrates' words, has the power to dictate what Socrates writes, and in this case, what Socrates does not write but only speaks. The translation and transcription is thus reserved for Plato, and only for Plato. Plato lays the foundation of Western philosophy in his transcription of Socratic dialogues while reserving for himself the position of authority over Socrates' words.

His excitedly scratching and pointedly raised fingers also recall the detective in Poe's "The Purloined Letter." The detective created a planned diversion for the minister in order to obtain the letter surreptitiously.[102] Plato, as mailman and detective rolled into one, and as Socrates' transcribing "right hand," is about to purloin Socrates' blank sheet and substitute in its place his own letter. This postcard portrays the tradition of Western philosophy according to a substitution of the primacy of writing for the primacy of orality. This is and is not a Derridean postcard. As a postcard, it portrays the dialectic (in)version of his theories on language and language origin.

But this is not the only postcard of the picture. There are others as well as numerous reproductions. Derrida depicts himself as quite perturbed about his find. He considers it an act of conspiracy on his hosts' side, as if they had programmed the event, even placed the postcard in the bookshop for him. In addition, he had just been discussing suicide with one of the students in his seminar: "In his eyes this was the only way to 'forward' (his word) my 'theoretical discourse,' the only way to be consequent and to produce an event." Socrates' twofold legacy of suicide and his dialogue technique reaches out to Derrida "by sending [the student] back his question. . . . And what proves to you, I said to him if I remember correctly, that I do not do so, and more than once" (15).

The postcard of Plato and Socrates is a "revelatory catastrophe" for multiple reasons (12). Derrida feels trapped in a program, executed by academia, colleagues, students, and friends. He lectures around the world like a "traveling salesman," who is paradoxically "only interested in what cannot be sent off, cannot be dispatched in any case" (14–15). Although he does not want to "trade the letter for money" like the

detective in Poe's story,[103] the visual representation and antique reproduction of his own "theoretical discourse" return to him, forwarded by
the fortune-telling book from the thirteenth century. Even though he is
not interested in sending things off, he Socratically returns the question
about suicide with Platonic rhetoric. Furthermore, the glib rhetorical
question points back to its sender through the postcard. Can "the irre-
versible sequence of inheritance," that Socrates, who does not write,
precede Plato, who does, only be overturned within the "program of this
credulity" (20)? This includes the postcard, which "naively overturns
everything" (21), even the words of God about the first word, yet does
not manage to alter the postal principle as such: "In the beginning, in
principle, was the post, and I will never get over it. But in the end, I
know it, I become aware of it as our death sentence . . . , and it begins
with a destination without address, the direction cannot be situated in
the end" (29). The postcard instructs its addressee: "Watch closely while
Socrates signs his death sentence on the order of his jealous son Plato"
(15). Postcards turn the sequence of inheritance into an ad hoc epistolary correspondence that begins and ends with each card. From the
beginning to the end of his "postcard apocalypse," "reversibility
unleashes itself, goes mad" (13). This reversibility makes the continuous
reading and writing on and about the Oxford postcard possible.[104] Each
postcard, although it is "reborn at every instant, without memory," is
the epitome of literary and theoretical reproduction itself. The very
"absence of memory" ensures the cycle of exchange in the preceding
quote. Socrates, assuming he came before Plato, cannot have a memory
of his descendants, he can only have a memory of himself as a descen-
dant, a process of identification that lets him slip into Plato's chair without becoming Plato.

Since a large part of "Envois" dwells on the risky (im)possibility
of entrusting the other with a legacy, the mood toward the addressee
changes within and with every postcard. Derrida replays the different
relationships between Plato and Socrates in each interpretation of the
Oxford postcard on the level of his epistolary correspondence. On the
one hand, "you" is responsible for the words he delivers; on the other
hand, "the crazy one is you" because "you corrupt, you detour everything that I say, you understand nothing, nothing at all, or even
everything, that you annihilate immediately" (13). As a precaution,
the epistolary partners want to leave a legacy by a different name, by
a different route than the legal, genealogical, or philosophical transfer of titles. "The wish to vanquish the postal principle: not in order
to approach you finally and to vanquish you, to triumph over distancing, but so that by you might be given to me the distancing which
regards me" (27).

In "Otobiographies," Derrida links the problem of distance directly to legacy and inheritance. The essay concerns Nietzsche's role as teacher and autobiographer. Unwilling to burden himself and his audience with "the tedium, the waste of time, and the subservience that always accompany the classic pedagogical procedures," Derrida stresses his distance to the procedures and his academic freedom, a stance that allows him to "proceed in a manner that some will find aphoristic or inadmissible, that others will accept as law, and that still others will judge to be not quite aphoristic enough."[105] His stance against "normal" academic procedures of naming the predecessors and declaring one's indebtedness to other scholars results in an "*autobiographical* demonstration" (4). Derrida demonstrates that "[o]nly the name can inherit, and this is why the name, to be distinguished from the bearer, is always and a priori a dead man's name, a name of death. What returns to the name never returns to the living" (7). Any legacy that returns to the name of the sender declares the sender dead.[106] While the Oxford postcard with its portrayal of the Derridean critique of Western philosophy conceptualizes his wish to "vanquish the postal principle," it also demonstrates that this wish itself is structured by the postal code. The postcard delivers Derrida's wish through the "fortune-telling book." Although "the threat is engulfment in infinite regress," Derrida structuralizes the self-reflexivity of his discourse with the postcard.[107]

Derrida turns the limitations of the postcard and his own theoretical discourse against themselves. He inquires into the relation between the postcard's openness and analytic discourse. Perhaps intimate and personal details as well as analytic readings are better encoded in the openly legible, yet indecipherable referential network of minuscule postcard narratives: "What I like about post cards is that even in an envelope, they are made to circulate like an open but illegible letter" (12). As long as the general postal code is still oriented toward uncovering secret messages behind the surface of letters, the postcard shakes the foundations of asserted postal positions and conventions. These institutionalized discourses

> are unthinkable outside a certain postal technology, as are the public or private, that is secret, correspondences which have marked its stages and crisis, supposing a very determined type of postal rationality, of relations between the State monopoly and the secret of private messages, as of their unconscious effects. (104)

Does the postcardization of communication, as one could paraphrase Derrida's postmodern epistolarity, indicate the end of exchange, of the letter, of literature, of the law, of psychoanalysis, of the political consensus, and of all that it stands for?

The procedures of "routing" and of distribution, the paths of transmission, concern the very support of the messages sufficiently not to be
without effect on the content, and I am not only speaking of the signified content. The "letter" disappears, others must be found, but this
will be simultaneously the unlimited empire of postcardization that
begins with the trait itself, before what they call writing . . . and the
decadence of the post card in the "narrow" sense. (104)

The change of postal technologies through a rerouting of the postal code
bears upon the material support, the content, the idea of the letter, and
writing, as signifier and signified. The postal code reroutes at the precise
moment when the "pure signifier" loses its ability both to transport and
to signify a hidden meaning. But this alteration of the postal route does
not simply substitute "the postcard" for "the letter." Postcardization
also changes the postcard into something other than itself, as Derrida
demonstrates with his book-length postcard.

Since the rerouting alters the analytical discourse, how does it affect
epistolary theory? As an epistolary critic, I seem to be facing double
jeopardy. If I write on the letter, I write on something that is proclaimed
dead. I become an archeologist and turn my object of study into a fossil
before its time. Simultaneously, however, the lamenting genre theoreticians and cultural pessimists themselves account for part of the surge of
epistolary theories in the past years and have thereby contributed to a
rehabilitation of the letter as a literary form. Does this supposed epistolary Wake reveal those "others" that "must be found"? Analytic discourse has to believe in its own excess, and in a surplus of desire. In that,
it indeed comes very close to amorous epistolary writing practices.[108]

The explicating critic's role is often believed to imitate the postmaster general, the operator connecting calls;[109] a critic bridges gaps, lets
communication through by enhancing the message; a critic is a loyal
courier aware of the "sanctity of the mail." Correspondence, after all,
means similarity, conformity, and analogy in addition to an exchange of
letters. The output of a system for which one regulated the input should
be predictable, but contemporary science contests both assumptions: the
stability of systems and the prognosis of their output. If at all, one could
speak of "chaos bound" by the general rule that "there will always be
some minimal level of fluctuation" and that "[c]haotic systems are both
deterministic and unpredictable."[110] By writing on the postcard in the
context of letters, do I subsume differences under one name, under the
factor of truth, the *facteur*, which in French is also "the mailman"?[111]

Similarity is not sameness. This difference is illustrated by two separate words in German: *dasselbe* (the very same, when the original is
seen to appear at a different place, in a different time), and *das gleiche*
(similar but not the original, that one is comparing it to, can coexist

with the former in time and place).[112] "[T]he double splits what it doubles, by adding itself to it, and the reflected or doubled is also split *in itself.*"[113] Self-reflection, as a traditional sign for the self-identity of the human subject, is exposed as already introducing a split. Derrida thus problematizes the relations between the idea of self as an entity and repetition, presence, and "differ*a*nce."

> Differ*a*nce, the disappearance of any originary presence, is *at once* the condition of possibility and the condition of impossibility of truth. At once. "At once" means that the being-present *(on)* in its truth, in the presence of its identity and in the identity of its presence, is *doubled* as soon as it appears, as soon as it presents itself.[114]

A communication across time and places has an air of the uncanny. To create a comfortable conformity, both sides of the planned exchange must be prescribed prior to their correspondence. What should happen in between actually happens before and after. Derrida's sympathetic "bad reader" passes through the scene:

> this is the way I name or accuse the fearful reader, the reader in a hurry to be determined, decided upon deciding (in order to annul, in other words to bring back to oneself, one has to wish to know in advance what to expect, one wishes to expect what has happened, one wishes to expect (oneself)). Now it is bad, and I know no other definition for the bad, it is bad to predestine one's reading, it is always bad to foretell. It is bad, reader, no longer to like retracing one's steps. (4)

Bad readers should be even more interested in postcards than in letters since postcard exchanges tend toward exchangeability of reader and writer, places, and times. Derrida pits hermeneutic laziness (coupled with terror-stricken critics faced with paradigm shifts) against postmodern undecidability. "Envois" and its Oxford postcards make it impossible to substantiate who writes to whom, from where, and on which date. While one postcard does not require much patience for writer and reader, hundreds of postcards in the shape of an epistolary novel carry that genre's disturbance of narrative linearity to an extreme. This is particularly true for epistolary novels that sustain a polylogue without a narrator's interruptions or a frame-story. "Envois" epistolarizes the postcard as much as it postcardicizes the letter. In a play on Nietzsche's "knowing, all too well knowing reader," Derrida needs the "bad reader" to press for an epistolary exchange, a "bad reader" who assumes that the postal system has functioned and will continue to function properly.[115]

The postal system is usually associated with the familiar triangular semiotic concept of communication (sender-message-receiver), which attempts to account for the "handling" of the message in a positivist manner.[116] The model inscribes a variable where the postal relay actually occurs, as if to ensure the inevitable return to sender in the beyond: sender-message-receiving sender or receiver sending-message and so on. But the postal relay is also

> the very thing that makes it possible for a letter *not* to arrive at its destination, and that makes this possibility-of-never-arriving divide the structure of the letter from the outset. Because (for example) there would be neither postal relay nor analytic movement if the place of the letter were not divisible and if a letter always arrived at its destination. (324)

The analytic movement is determined by the divisibility of the letter in the language of the unconscious. If there were no "displacements," or "compression," which allowed for different signifieds per signifier and for the deferral of repressed information in the shape of images and words, no analytical movement to disconnect what is "falsely" connected (as in a dream text), and to reconnect the disconnected, would be necessary. The desire to cancel the divisibility and the postal relay is the "death drive" of hermeneutics and psychoanalysis.

Derrida links the semiotic triad, which attempts to cancel its Other, to Freud's oedipal triangle. Derrida reads the *fort/da* scene as a scene of representation. Freud's oedipal semiotics, or as Derrida calls it, "conjoint interpretations" (306), writes Freud's autobiography in that it writes "the presentation of itself of representation, the return to-itself of returning" (318). This representation as a return of itself to itself follows a perfunctory model of "romantic sociability" ("romantische Geselligkeit"). This model emphasizes the connection of individuals through the discussion of all genres of "letters": novel, drama and music drama, poetry and *Lieder*, philosophical essay, *Seelenkunde*, theological tract, personal correspondence, and their combinations. *Geselligkeit* invokes the illusion of unmediated togetherness of people and their cultural products. The romantic idea of *Geselligkeit* excludes authorship and mediation. It aims to get as close to simultaneous production and reception as possible.[117]

The paradox of writing on and about letters consists in the suppression of their very movement, the petrification of their being-in-transit. A letter seems only definable as letter due to its textual borders, the textual representations of its transience: writing and reading. The hyphens or blanks in between sender-message-receiver allow for deviations, manipulated, forged, or accidental abductions. These nonsignified, but spatially assigned deviations never shake the foundation on which the model is built, although they strain the three columns. Their transience stabilizes the system as well. In epistolary theory, the letter, as representative of the "message" *and* of the transient deviations, is transformed into a proper noun that, while mutilated, always returns to itself. It is essentially a "dead letter."

This transformation becomes clear, when we look at the function of letters in novels, especially in epistolary novels. At the same time that the letter becomes an artifact and loses its character as a device, or as soon as the letter steps beyond the novel's control, the novel as artifact turns into a letter. It then shares the letter's transience: the letter frees the novel for its "task of containing its own reflection and of including the theory of its own genre."[118] Only by addressing itself to itself, by dividing itself, can the novel be novel. This particular moment of intertextuality unhinges the positions within the communication model. Structurally, this intertextual gesture is exemplified by the division of *The Postcard* into the epistolary "Envois" and the analytical "To Speculate—On Freud." Together, one part builds on and subverts the other, while rewriting the postmodern novel as criticism and vice versa. Contrary to Derrida, Gottfried Honnefelder pronounces the epistolary novel's death by self-exhaustion, self-dissolution: the epistolary novel as such cannot exist.[119] But what if this exchange of roles were indeed the rebirth of the novel? "[T]here can be no theory of the novel that is not a novel."[120]

Honnefelder further contends that the letter's main problem is also one of its most cherished literary usages, namely, the irretrievability of the written and sent letter.[121] While he describes this particular function of the postal letter, he represses each critic's attempt to undo that teleological law: to retrieve the letter from its destination, which, according to the triangular communication model, is at the same time and place also its origination. But something happens *between* dispatch and return. The message changes its context, it carries a remainder, a deposit, with which it arrives; it confronts the reader with a reader's text, in some instances with his or her own words. It commits the author's moment of subjection to the letter and its mailing process.

In order to continue the (dis)connections of textual legacies, I want to map the intersections of Freud's and Derrida's postal route. While I read the intertextual markers in Derrida's text, my reading becomes subject to the mailing process. The overflowing deposits of Freud's *fort/da* scene in Derrida's "Envois" and the entire text of *The Postcard* coerce the reader into adding to and repeating the overflow. The next section therefore discusses these moments of subjection and resistance as they occur at the junction between Freud's "Beyond the Pleasure Principle," Derrida's "To Speculate—On Freud," and my post-Freudian reading.

While Derrida writes postcards, which summon and distance "the end of literature" (104), he diverts himself by playing the role of a tantalizing switchman. He has Freud running for and from the train. Rather than traveling blindly by only recognizing departure and arrival points, Derrida reads Freud "en route," forcing himself, and in turn his readers, not to annul the shimmying topography of the in-between. According to Peter Weibel, the motif of the "blind journey" transgresses the twentieth century, especially in regard to train and plane rides: "[T]raveling becomes a dead stretch, a circular movement in an empty space. Natural space is empty space; it doesn't count as anything anymore when all of it is trafficked, everything is seen by everyone. As a consequence, one searches for travels in imaginary realms."[122] It is no surprise then, that at this point in time, psychoanalysis becomes the travel guide for "blind" voyages and travelers, the authoring system for drives of an "accidental tourist" variety.[123]

In the seven steps of "Beyond the Pleasure Principle," Freud accounts for and justifies his hypothesis that the "pleasure drive," his formerly dominant principle in the psyche, is itself dominated by a "drive" engineered by the "principle of constancy" of any matter. In reality, however, the "principle of constancy" was deduced from the facts that imposed the assumption of the existence of the pleasure principle on Freud.[124] The wagons switch directions in midjourney. Freud therefore feels compelled to quote his colleague Gustav Theodor Fechner about the difference between the tendency toward the destination and reaching that destination. The destination, in this case, lies both in and beyond the pleasure principle. Although Freud knows that destinations can only be reached by approximation, one step at a time, there is always another way to get there, faster or slower. This route to the beyond of the pleasure principle is "displeasure" *(Unlust)*, a route Freud knows better than any other "detour" *(Umweg, 219)*.[125]

Freud's train set in "Beyond the Pleasure Principle" involves a rather disjointed assembly of structures. The reader has to pass through multiple scene changes before she or he is told that there is no final destination for this train of thought—as yet: "One has to be patient and wait for further means and reasons for research. Also [one has to] be ready to leave a path again which one has pursued for a while if it does not appear to lead to anything good."[126] En route to nowhere or anywhere, Freud speculates on child's play, demonic traits and romantic epics, inner- and outer-directed mental energies, death drive and Goethe's *Faust*, one-cell organisms and sadism, Plato's *Symposium* and the problem of professional jargon. His intertextual and interdisciplinary journey comes to a limping halt at the pleasure principle's watchtower between self and world.

In the second fragment of Freud's "Jenseits des Lustprinzips," Freud, whose name designates joy and pleasure, describes how he watched the child Ernst play. The name "Ernst" indicates seriousness and solemnity.

The pleasure principle observes the death drives as they materialize in repetition-compulsion. In its short form, this sentence can function as a scenario for how the pleasure principle works according to the end of the essay. However, Freud uses his interpretation of Ernst's "normalcy" to threaten the pleasure principle's dominance.[127] At first sight, the sentence above indicates a reversal of signifiers, and a strange distribution of roles. The child should enact the spontaneous joy of childhood games, whereas the psychoanalyst should solemnly observe and take notes. Derrida stresses that Freud is not simply an analyst but the child's maternal grandfather (292–337). Sigmund Freud is therefore keenly involved in observing his grandson's progress, and delights in Ernst's "great cultural achievement" ("groß[e] kulturell[e] Leistung," 225) namely, the repression and the mastery of his desires, his fear, and his aggression. Freud also attempts to remain aloof by criticizing Ernst's behavior as an "occasionally irritating habit" ("gelegentlich störende Gewohnheit," 224).

Ernst is observed playing a compulsive drama in two acts, a drama that leads Freud to the analogy with "tragedy," whose "enjoyment" *(Genuß)* is usually only appreciated by grown-ups (227).[128] Judging from Ernst's "joyful *(freudig[e])* exclamations when the spool appears from beyond his covered bed, he actively enjoys the game (225). This does not prevent Freud from relating Ernst's role of actor to the adult's role of spectator in a tragedy. With this analogy, Freud slips into his grandson's cothurnus. Normalcy turns out to be a psychological tragedy, in which the human plight is predetermined by psychological drives. Freud narrates his autobiography and the biography of psychoanalysis on his grandson's legs. Like the moribund hero in a tragedy, he attempts to control the step beyond himself, the future of psychoanalysis, and his own impending death.

Freud's work on "Beyond the Pleasure Principle" concurred with his essay "The Uncanny." Only the uncanny can call forth the death drive in "Beyond" and only the pleasure principle can defer the uncanny. "Beyond" defines the death drive as the subconscious movement toward death, the removal of life.[129] Although the death drive seems more uncanny than the pleasure principle, in Freud's state of mourning over his real and preconceived losses, the pleasure principle is out of sync with reality.[130] The essays themselves relate to each other like letters which seem long to have reached beyond but simultaneously reinstall the unbreachability of the border. What points toward the "alienating" *(Befremdende)*, inevitably begins at home as a "transference" *(Übertragung,* 256). Freud's psychoanalytic procedure purloins the letter before it arrives. As a psychoanalyst, he reads letters like postcards in midtransit and redirects them to the sender. Intersubjectivity and intertextuality only exist in the form of a deferred internalization process.

For example, in "The Uncanny," Freud states that he inverted his original speculative path. He begins with the manifestation of his thesis in the etymology of the word *unheimlich*, whereas the problem unfolded for him originally through a collection of singular cases. He also asserts his own distance from the subject:

> Yes, the author of these new inquiries has to denounce his specific insensitivity in this case, where high sensitivity should be in place. For a long time, he has not experienced or discovered what would have given him the impression of uncanniness; first [he] has to transport himself into that feeling, call awake the possibility of it in himself.[131]

Contrary to his own hypothesis that the uncanny is "that kind of fright that goes back to the old and well known, the long familiar" ("jene Art des Schreckhaften, welche auf das Altbekannte, Längstvertraute zurück-geht"), Freud contends that he has not encountered anything uncanny for a long time, as if the uncanny stemmed from a confrontation with the new and unknown, which is precisely what he wants to disprove (244). When he explains that he has to artificially conjure up uncanny feelings, he depicts himself as having already stepped beyond the familiar and the *Heimliche*, maybe even beyond the pleasure gain of the uncanny. The only uncanny pleasure gain seems to lie in writing itself, where the old, familiar path is quickly exchanged for a safe new road, and where the familiar territory of psychology is deserted in favor of the unfamiliar realm of "aesthetic inquiries" (243). The two essays appear to be written by a trickster, who manipulates "uncanny" death into leaving him alone but meanwhile stealing his cloak. The Faustian motif is indeed evoked and immediately recalled in "Beyond": "One can, of course, give oneself up to a path of thinking, follow it as far as it leads, purely out of scientific curiosity, or, if one wants, as *advocatus diaboli*, who doesn't write his soul over to the devil himself just because of it."[132] In the German fairy tales that Freud himself cherishes for exemplificatory purposes, the hero and heroine rarely retreat from an encounter with the devil without a talisman (e.g., three golden hairs) to prove their courage and earn their rewards. The three wishes in fairy tales indicate "displeasure for the one system and simultaneously satisfaction for the other" ("Unlust für das eine System und gleichzeitig Befriedigung für das andere," 230). This system implies an exchange of desire in the form of things, one that Freud ignores in his own voyage to the death drive. Something is given to bring something else back. The mailing system works perfectly. The hero/ine usually collects exactly those things and helping hands that will bring perfect exchange value in times of need.[133] Freud, however, feigns to be able to cross the devil's doorstep without stealing or losing hairs.

In order to describe the pleasure principle's functioning, Freud cannot rely on a legacy, but neither can he refrain from touching the darkest realm of the psyche by the "most casual assumption about it" ("lockerste Annahme darüber," 217). Two pages down the track, he questions the dominance of the pleasure principle; the joyride is interrupted before it has started. He does not have to plunge forward after all; he can proceed by degrees, which allows him to tread on secure and familiar ground, drawing from his reservoir of analytic experiences (219). The uncanny enters the pleasure principle. A "positive" can only be achieved through its negation *(Verneinung),*[134] through "deferral" and "detour," two terms Freud uses to describe the "reality principle" (220). These terms correspond to Derrida's "differance."

> Following a schema that continually guides Freud's thinking, the movement of the trace is described as an effort of life to protect itself by *deferring* the dangerous investment, by constituting a reserve *(Vorrat).* And all the conceptual oppositions that furrow Freudian thought relate each concept to the other like movements of a detour, within the economy of differance. The one is only the other deferred, the one differing from the other.[135]

Detour, difference, and deferral collide in this term, "producing the differential structure of our hold on 'presence'." Presence is always postponed, displaced, and different from itself as is "the structure . . . of our psyche."[136] Neither the telephone, nor the computer, neither radio nor television, only the letter and its offspring, the postcard, adhere to this syntactical procedure. Only the characteristic of "the transport of the 'document,' of its material support" makes it possible to displace, sedimentize, and decontextualize.[137] The oral/aural telephone, although Freud himself compared it to the functioning of the analytic procedure,[138] does not lend itself to the literarization and dramatization of the language of the unconscious. In the course of writing on the substitutions, delays, and distortions in his patients' narratives, Freud builds a postal station. This postal relay lets him both confront and defer his own desires and fears. I wish to stress this grammatological aspect of intertextuality as it appears in writing. Instead of getting on the phone or dealing directly with the pleasure principle, Freud "falls behind" through the movements of writing.

Although he introduced Ernst's game as "the first self-generated game" ("das erste selbstgeschaffene Spiel," 224), Freud ends his narrative with the remark that it is "obviously irrelevant, whether the child had invented it itself or appropriated it" ("natürlich gleichgültig, ob das Kind es selbst erfunden oder sich infolge einer Aneignung zu eigen gemacht hatte," 225). Whether Ernst creates or simulates the game is irrelevant to Freud's analysis. *Gleichgültig* literally means "of equal value." Freud performs the gesture that erases the ambivalence between original and similar that I discussed above. He is content with the pure gesture; no explanation follows. He disinherits Ernst's contribution and debunks the importance of the creative process for his analysis. The game becomes a fact, and as a fact becomes accessible to his scientific speculations. Once the "mysterious and continuously repeated activity" ("rätselhafte und andauernd wiederholte Tun") has betrayed its meaning/sense ("mir seinen Sinn verriet," 224), Freud appropriates the game. Now that Freud understands its rules, and the game has literally betrayed Ernst, it can become Freud's game. Like the mother who leaves her child behind, Freud engages the reader in a repetition of the desertion. He turns away to theorize on the creative game: "Our focus will turn to another point" ("Unser Interesse wird sich einem anderen Punkt zuwenden," 225).

Derrida's reading of the *fort/da* process demonstrates that whereas Freud shows the child preoccupied with his desertion by the mother, the father's and grandfather's presences and/or absences are considered "irrelevant" and even desired. Derrida shows that the other point Freud wishes to make is *gleichgültig* to the one before, only differing and deferred through a mailing code, through the switch in genre and gender (from narrative to scientific and from mother to grandfather). Despite Freud's attempt at leaving the game, he cannot refrain from returning to it:

> Fold back: he (the grandson of his grandfather, the grandfather of his grandson) compulsively repeats repetition without it ever advancing anywhere, not one step. He repeats an operation which consists in distancing, in pretending . . . to distance pleasure, the object or principle of pleasure. . . . It (he) pretends to distance the PP in order to bring it (him) back indefatigably. (302)

One of these distancing gestures follows the reference to Plato's *Symposium*, in which the six alienated particles strive to reunite with their three original genders. Freud's speculation on the origin of sexuality works with two unknowns: the existence of death drives presupposes life-affirming drives and vice versa. Freud, although very self-conscious about his fantastic hypothesis, first rhetorically undoes Zeus's splitting: "Consequently, if one does not want to let go of the assumption of death drives, one has to join life affirming drives to them from the very beginning" ("Wenn man also die Annahme von Todestrieben nicht fahren lassen will, muß man ihnen von allem Anfang an Lebenstriebe zugesellen," 265–266). As soon as the sexual drives experience their moment of "highest concentration" ("höchste Konzentration") in the transmission of their unifying drive to the cells, Freud reenacts Zeus's splitting: "I believe, this is the point to break off" ("Ich glaube, es ist hier die Stelle, abzubrechen," 267). Sensuousness is adjoined and shackled *(anzuschließen)* by consciousness and reflection. But this also works the other way around. Theoretical studies may appear as *breakthroughs* that do not manage to assert their position.

> In this manner, we arrive at the result, which is at its basis not a simple result, that at the beginning of psychic life, the drive towards pleasure voices itself much more intensively than later, yet not as unrestrictedly; it has to put up with a number of breaches. In more mature times, the mastery of the pleasure principle is much more secure but it itself has just as unsuccessfully escaped being tamed as the other drives have anyway. . . . In any case, that which creates the feelings of pleasure and displeasure in the process of being aroused has to be present both in the secondary and primary processes. This would be the place to begin with further studies. Our consciousness mediates to us from within not only the sensations of pleasure and displeasure but also of a characteristically curious tension that itself can again be pleasant or unpleasant.[139]

Even though Freud interjects a new paragraph, the "further studies" that should begin at this point neither establish their dominance, nor can their promising insertion be forgotten in the flow of writing and reading. Because Freud marks the limits of his speculations by stressing the point of departure for his descendants, one would expect the next sentences to refer to "further studies." Instead, these sentences fall back behind the announcement and comment on a "tension" that in itself can be either pleasant or unpleasant. Because of the insertion, the strange and yet proper sensations relate spatially directly to the future studies and indirectly to the preceding interrupted paragraph. What would and should be continued by future studies is already begun in Freud's further speculations. Whereas his approximations and speculations appear in a self-confident indicative, Freud positions his suggestion for the place of further studies in the conditional and doubtful subjunctive mode. The subjunctive sentence also lacks a human agent. Its subject is divided into two places: "this" and "the place." Freud's intervention to secure the future and the subject of psychoanalysis in his place is itself subjected to the "here" and "there" of the postal principle.

The "further studies" proceed in the same and yet not quite the same name as before. The pleasure principle is erected as a watchtower on the border between inside and outside, against "stimuli from the outside . . . but especially against the acceleration of stimuli from within that make life's work difficult." In its marginal place, the pleasure principle indeed functions like the postal principle of a feudal court. The royal secretary always opens and filters the mail. He only allows certain epistles or adequately translated messages to pass his desk. This "stimuli-protection" *(Reizschutz)*, according to Freud, works from the outside to the inside, but it doesn't function in the other direction (238). The royal signifier is cloaked: "That's why we always operate with a big unknown variable, which we take along into every new formula" ("So operieren wir also stets mit einem großen X, welches wir in jede neue Formel mit hinübernehmen," 240). Even traumatic experiences, like purloined letters that could potentially function like blackmail and threaten the throne, obey the *Reizschutz* and return to the post office of the psyche, the "seelischen Zentralapparat" ("psychic central mechanism"): "From this place along the periphery, stimuli continuously stream toward the psychic central mechanism, as they could otherwise only come from inside the mechanism."[140]

The royal and purloined letters thus "hobo" back and forth across the border. Read as a symbol, the unknown variable X also marks the crossing itself. It simultaneously marks and crosses the border. While Freud's text acknowledges a stowaway remainder of this differance, it constantly attempts to press the "characteristically curious tension" between pleasure and displeasure into a dichotomy (271). In spite of his railway-phobia, Freud plays the role of stoker-midwife for the reluctant early twentieth century. He not only tries to locate his disciple-hobos underneath and above the "iron path" *(Eisenbahn)*, the wagon-chain of psychoanalysis, but also feeds its engine.[141]

The role reversal between Ernst and Freud takes on a new meaning if we remember that Freud wondered why Ernst did not pull the spool, "in order to play wagon with it" ("um Wagen mit ihr zu spielen," 225). Jacques Derrida picks the spool up where Freud leaves it. He reflects on Freud's ideology of "legs" and legacies, of the step beyond oneself, beyond Freud's pleasure principle and beyond the postal principle of his own writing. According to Derrida, Freud's speculative writing is a safe method, where the author stays in control at all times:

> To speculate: it would never be to throw the thing . . . , that is, to keep it at a distance continuously, but always at the same distance, the length of the string remaining constant, making (letting) the thing displace itself at the same time, and in the same rhythm, as oneself. This trained train does not even have to come back *[revenir]*, it does not really leave. It has barely come to leave when it is going to come back. (315)

Freud favors the "pulling" of the spool, which Derrida interprets as "not have it before one"; the "analysand-locomotive for whom the law of listening is substituted for the law of looking" (316). If Derrida compares Freud's writing and his role in a therapeutic session to the avisual, oral effect of pulling a wagon, not all of it takes place on level ground. Train and thread gather momentum, and constantly threaten to entangle and overtake the text and Freud's position.[142] Freud's writing therefore constructs a crossroads, where the *X* is projected into other texts to ensure its uncanny yet safe return to him.[143]

Simone de Beauvoir and Jean Paul Sartre created fictive personae of the opposite sex for their epistolary intercourse.

Does *The Postcard* return Freud's letter? Contrary to Freud, Derrida cannot stop looking at and writing on the postcard. Does the postcard plot the course of Derrida's opus much the same as *fort/da* structures Freud's "Beyond the Pleasure Principle"? Despite the apparent mastery of train and postcard (they hide to appear at hand, like authoritatively controlled references),[144] both texts present themselves as works on self-confrontation and self-transcendence.

The dead and yet astonishingly vital *X* can be traced to Derrida's "Envois" chapter, where the connection between pleasure principle and postal principle is intertwined with other correspondences. *The Postcard* forces male scholars, writers, analysts, historians, and philosophers into verbal interaction. The literal noncorrespondence of Derrida's various male odd couples (Derrida-Freud, Freud-Ernst, Freud-Nietzsche, Freud-Lacan, Derrida-Lacan, Derrida-Heidegger, Plato-Socrates, and others) creates a forum of homoerotic male/mail bonding that appears to reconfirm the phallocentric literary and theoretical discourse. The eye and ear of the (m)other empowers this ma(i)le exchange. In "Otobiographies," Derrida explicates the (m)other's role within Nietzsche's autobiographical discourse:

> No woman or trace of woman, if I have read correctly—save the mother, that's understood. But this is part of the system. The mother is the faceless figure of a *figurant*, an extra. She gives rise to all the figures by losing herself in the background of the scene like an anonymous persona. Everything comes back to her, beginning with life; everything addresses and destines itself to her. She survives on the condition of remaining at bottom.[145]

The great unknown with the X chromosomes is longingly addressed and happily kept at bay. The (m)other's voice protects the postal principle against total dissemination and death. As Barth's philosophical spermatozoa believes, who addresses his remains in "myself plus Her," possibly "one of its quarter-billion swimmers . . . achieved a qualified immortality."[146] In "Envois," as in Barth's *LETTERS*, the "female" Other masquerades as the figure of epistolary fiction. Derrida's narrating persona addresses her as "my only one." She is only one, but has many voices: lover, friend, confidante, colleague, sister, whore, working woman, literary figure, assassin, and mother. Like *LETTERS*, "Envois" seems to represent Woman as a representation, as an exchange medium, a metamorph. Since her existence depends on the postal principle, she angrily and jealously remembers the *poste restante* letter, which due to a wrong postal code and the common name of the village, does not reach her but returns to its sender. A closer look at the "dead letter" narrative will address the assumption that the gender/genre system in "Envois" simply makes Woman a metaphor for undecidability, for *Verfahren*, an/other method, a path that leads astray from the most traveled roads of reading and writing.[147]

Derrida's letter of August 30, 1977, spawns the most pragmatic, personal, and yet very theoretical correspondence in *The Postcard* (45). The "dead letter," as it is called, is an autoteleological intertext that functions as a legacy. It returns to the sender, who hands it over to unnamed others. The "dead letter" develops its own history and narrative precisely because it is announced but withheld. As a constant source of aggravation and suspicion, it upsets the epistolary harmony between sender and addressee and therefore guarantees the survival of the correspondence. This letter establishes a postal system of another order by rewriting Poe's story against Lacan's reading.

The letter was sent *poste restante* "because of all the families. One never knows" (45) who intercepts or opens the mail. However, in a village where the mailman knows everyone, not even the arrival of a letter at the post office can be kept secret (76). Neither the reader of "Envois" nor its characters can be sure whether they have read the letter. There is no substantial proof that would warrant its existence and contents. Even though there are two August 30 epistles, one of which may indeed be the *poste restante* letter, the sender often writes more than one or two letters/postcards a day. Since he also includes another subletter "put between the S/p card and the letter paper" (45), the identity of the *poste restante* letter remains in doubt. Is it the enclosure nestled and resting between letter and postcard, or between the distorted positions of private and public?

The "dead letter" becomes a matter of life and death for the correspondence in "Envois."[148] Because ten days and twenty-one letters (or more) lie between send-off and return, the sender hesitates to reread it or to send it a second time (76) and decides: "No more remission" (44–45). But this verdict is itself remitted through the letter's unfolding story. The sender wants to stop the story ("no narrative") but maintains it by constantly alluding to its content before he discovers that the addressee never received it. He also refers to the "dead letter" phenomenon as a "strange story" (76). Presumably unlike the queen's letter in Poe's story, the "dead letter" is supposed to contain "details" and proof of the sender's innocence. Its dubious status and the order, "don't speak to me about it again" (45), create the seductive force of the letter's ensuing sub- and metaepistolary narrative. This "dead letter" narrative intersects Derrida's reading of Freud's text. After all, Freud also thought it necessary to establish a "transhistorical" and "prevital" human dimension in "Beyond."[149]

The immediate context of the letters from 30 August unleashes violence and a devious game of reversals involving the postcard theme. Increasingly, the correspondence metaphorically violates gender and subject borders. The letter that was sent to shed light on the jumble of accusations and remissions ironically lies in the post office. In Poe's story, the police and the queen become increasingly anxious about the whereabouts of the letter and, according to Lacan, assume the same position. For Lacan, the letter is the "pure signifier." In "Envois," the letter lies at the post office; the signifying power thus resides with the postal system itself. The letters that envelop the designated but blank *and* polysignified position of the missing letter, undermine all positioning. These letters "wear down the borders" of the postal code, of the phallocentric model of communication that accumulates power through its secret contents and open transfers (45).

The sender metaphorically envisions an" erotic secretariat," in which he "would like to be your secretary" and "would watch the children that you have given me" (September 7, 1977; 70), a desire that echoes one of his August 30 epistles, in which he was still grateful for his grace period and remission: "I still do not know to whom, to what I am destining this fidelity, to a morsel of myself perhaps, to the child that I am carrying, and whose features I try to make out" (42). This gender crossing is doubled by the programmatic but impossible recognition of self and other in an epistolary exchange: "When I will have seen you, we will leave each other. When we will separate from each other, when I will separate myself, I will see you." Derrida situates the letter between the future perfect and the future, instead of the present tense in this statement. The letter both separates self from other and includes a division of the self. This self-division, based on seeing and then leaving the other, enables the self to see itself as other. In a futuristic circle, the letter, which divides the self, lets the self behold the other at the moment of separation.

In opposition to Lacan's symbolic chain, which assigns to each postal station a gendered hermeneutic position in Poe's story, Derrida structures the intersexual and intersubjective dialectic as intertextual differance.

> I called you every possible name. Then yours came back. In your name you are my destiny, for me you are destiny. . . . I address myself to you,

> somewhat as if I were sending myself, never certain of seeing it come
> back, that which is destined for me . . . when I softly call myself by
> your name, nothing else is there . . . no one else in the world. Even us
> perhaps and yes our existence is threatened then. (45)

What appears to be a perfect trade, an I for a you, and a you for an I,
is compromised by skepticism about the equality of the return. The self-
divison and self-addition has consequences for self, other, and the letter. As soon as an "I" addresses a "you," author and text have begun
to collaborate in the subversion of their positions. In the case of a
mailed letter, that which will arrive under my name is not my text,
although it bears my name. Or, put differently, the other's letter
becomes my property in my hands.[150] From the outset, this formal
reversal "threatens our existence."

Derrida inscribes the "dead letter" narrative on the only undated
letter in "Envois." Thus, the "dead letter" contains its own narrative. It
is purloined from the addressee by the postal code itself. After the sender
repossesses it from the "dead letter office," s/he seals "everything in a
virgin envelope," and signs his/her name on and across the borders,
where the envelope folds over onto itself: "The letter could not be
opened without deforming my signature" (137). Since s/he wants to
entrust it to a person of utmost discretion, s/he considers *hir* own para-
noia a sign of distrust. S/he therefore reencloses "the whole thing into
the most banal of self-sealing envelopes" (137). As soon as she or he has
acted upon and described *hir* reconsideration, the person with great discretion turns into "them," and the resheathed and resealed "virgin
thing" goes from "hand to hand" (137).

Within Derrida's postal universe, there is no autoteleological mailing route. At the very moment of signing and destining the letter, the signature and the destination unmask their nonidentity with themselves.
Each attempt at addressing a letter, even the refusal to read, address, or
sign it, bears a destination. Even though the postal principle cannot be
overcome, especially not by a "dead letter," the addresses, signatures,
and destinations reroute themselves. The sender covers *hir* own signature which s/he left in the margins to thwart any "deformation," and
thereby deforms it. There is no perfect exchange and no return to
sender. Derrida's epistolary intercourse remarks its textual/sexual borders. His epistolary fiction and theory do not reach beyond but they "go
as far as possible":

> I want no more remissions. [52 blanks] Henceforth, the thing cannot
> suffer any more detours, we owe it to ourselves to suffer no more
> detours. I have gone as far as I could. [52 blanks] and these inex-
> haustible words, these days and nights of explication will not make us

change places or exchange places, even though we ceaselessly try to do so, to get to the other side, to swallow the other's place, to move our bodies like the other's body, even to swallow it while drinking its words, mixing the salivas a little, wearing down the borders. (44)

How about the legacy of the "dead letter"? The "dead letter" works better than the purloined letter in that it "binds you irreversibly" to the other (127). Like the terms "deconstruction" or "postmodernism," whose usage Derrida resists in his own interpretations, the "dead letter" returns to him nevertheless. The confrontation with one's legacy is itself a postmodern phenomenon, a phenomenon of the telematic age. Although this possibility implies a certain amount of control over one's legacy, Derrida shows how the legacy itself controls both sender and recipient. Active forgetting on the part of the sender is contingent on the addressee's active remembrance. "Since the trace can only imprint itself by referring to the other, to another trace ('the trace of its reflection'), by letting itself be upstaged and forgotten, its force of production stands in necessary relation to the energy of its erasure."[151] *The Postcard* reverses the relation between production and erasure of the trace to include sender and addressee. If absolute possession of the letter and the legacy spells death for the author, absolute forgetting spells death for the addressee. In the final postcard, dated August 30, 1979, the sender orders the receiver to burn the correspondence: "Tomorrow I will write you again, in our foreign language. I won't retain a word of it and in September, without my ever having seen you again, you will burn [52 blanks] you will burn it, you, it has to be you" (256). At the end, the stage is set for the editing and "pasting" of "Envois." Inverting the sender's orders to destroy the correspondence, "Envois" destroys the notions of sender and addressee.[152] When "I" gradually disappears into the blanks and is displaced by "you," forgetting and death resemble reappropriation. The "you" has to sign in the name of the "I"; after all, "you should be able to guess, to say it in my place, for we have said everything to each other" (256). While the sender is reflecting on the meaning of "to turn around," the postcard turns the reader and itself around one more time. The first postcard answers the last.

> *3 June 1977* Yes, you were right, henceforth, today, now, at every moment, on this point of the *carte*, we are but a minuscule residue "left unclaimed": a residue of what we said to one another, of what, do not forget, we have made of one another, of what we have written one another. Yes, this "correspondence," you're right, immediately got beyond us, which is why it all should have been burned, all of it, including the cinders of the unconscious—and "they" will never know anything about it. "Left unclaimed," I would rather say of what we have, to one another, uniquely, *destined*. (7)

Bound in a book that unites and unties the position of sender, addressee, and text, the postcard correspondence writes itself as a legacy of itself, but as a legacy that is left unclaimed. Any legacy reassigns itself to the postal route the minute it arrives. "Envois" is the teleported residue of the unconscious, that which cannot be spoken, only transmaterialized under the hypnotic spell of intersubjective and intertextual epistolary discourse.[153] As an intertext, Derrida's postcard transgresses its boundaries without transcending them; its sexual textuality repeatedly climaxes without intercourse; it turns everything it traverses into another text, another postcard: "The sex of the addresser awaits its determination by or from the other. It is the other, who will perhaps decide what I am—man or woman. Nor is this decided once and for all. It may go one way one time and another way another time."[154] Between the end and the beginning of "Envois," the flip of the card reassigns genders in this fashion. According to the gender history of epistolary fiction, and according to the above law of interdependency, the persona most concerned about the "dead letter" business is Woman. She is familiar with residues, with the other side of philosophy and literature, and with the other side in a psychoanalytic session. To write her story, she takes those points of the *carte* that the former sender wished to forget. She remembers the blanks and gaps as "cinders of the unconscious" and wants to obliterate those that were claimed by the phallocentric discourse. "Envois" restarts from the other side. Against her better knowledge, she cannot refrain from wielding the pen, even if she only has enough time for postcards in between the numerous interruptions of her day:

> No time today again, only these cards. Never taken, in sum, the time to write you what I would have wanted, it has never been left to me, and if I write you without interruption [52 blanks] I will have sent you only cards. Even if they are letters and if I always put more than one in the same envelope. (8)

"Envois" reflects on how the legacy of epistolary fiction, long determined by male epistolary theoreticians, is in the process of being claimed by feminist critics and women writers. Now, when there should be time "to write you what I would have wanted," there appears to be "no time today again." Although the legacy of "Envois" has been turned over to her, to the Woman of letters, this revolution does not appear to leave her more time or power to conduct her own affairs. In addition, the time "which has never been left to me" is structuralized and thematized in her own epistolary fiction and theory. More important than the danger of metaphorizing Woman as *Verfahren* (whose writerly victimization is doubtful in any case due to the homometaphorization of all "essential" categories, including Man and Men), "Envois" points out that feminist

"Harvard microbiologist Matthew Meselson (. . .) said government officials had erred seriously when they assumed the anthrax spores could not get out of sealed envelopes. 'These envelopes are not really sealed, and they are handled roughly by machines (. . .) The spores do not go through the paper of the envelopes; they go through the spaces that are not sealed."

—Seth Borenstein, "Next clue on Anthrax might be a new patient," *Philadelphia Inquirer* (Sat. Oct. 27, 2001): A5.

FIGURE 3.3

reading and writing practices have to deal with their own legacies, not only in the seductive resurrection of the phallologocentric monster but also in the fantasy of comfortably living off the disinherited master's table scraps: making a career out of leftovers, leftouts, and thereby replenishing the vicious cycle of exchange that keeps them in the heir's position, always the reader, never the writer of the will.

And furthermore, "Envois" rewrites the battle of the generations and sexes as lit-crit spectacle: the gold fever rush to stake claims of letters, ideas, concepts, and terms between modernists and postmodernists, between structuralists and intentionalists, between men and women of letters. Yes, the epistolary genre and along with it the strategies of criticism and communication have attempted to rewrite themselves through a built-in gender relay. And the mailing routes by which this is achieved or resisted have to be researched. But if we interpret each genre or gender discourse as a text which is never one with itself, the deconstruction of gender and genre in "Envois" leaves unclaimed an unresolved intertextual residue. The legacy game has become the Crying Game. For one more screw, Derrida's *Postcard* performs queer theory in drag.[155]

The built-in gender relay in "Envois" returns us to the homoerotic theme of this section. Because the reader shares the "memory" of the correspondence and the "dead letter," "Envois" creates a second homoerotic couplette. This couplette engages in a correspondence with the ma(i)le residue in the text. We should keep in mind that a chronic rereading and rewriting of the "dead letter" and its correspondence with the intention to retrieve their meaning will "turn us in," will submit us to the accumulation of deposits between the "turns" just like *Malina*'s Ich. Both "old" and "new" senders of "Envois" constitute the "minuscule residue," the "dead letter" deposited in yet another's keepsake in a *blank* envelope. Both of them are "left unclaimed" because their etchings (scratching and writing combined) never reach their destination. Senders and addressees are rewritten in transit, change positions in midair like a set of trapeze artists. As soon as the text expresses its testamentary mandate ("it has to be you") and becomes a legacy, the legacy destroys its carrier. "To sign something over to someone" does not quite evoke the effect of post-cardization that concerns Derrida. The German *Überschreiben* literally means to *write* something over something else and to someone. The former addressee turned sender—due to the mandate—writes her text over the sender's text and addresses it to him, who in turn will also receive the necessary but impossible mandate to destroy and save at the same time:

> The ear of the other says me to me and constitutes the *autos* of my autobiography. . . . Every text answers to this structure. It is the structure of textuality in general. A text is signed only much later by the other. And this testamentary structure doesn't befall a text as if by accident, but constructs it. This is how a text always comes about.[156]

The partners within one scene of writing and reading of "Envois" are lucratively employed in the business of counterfeiting the postal principle. They exhibit their compulsion to repeat in the form of an incurable epistle mania at a time when the very foundation of the post is in crisis: "epistolary fictions multiply when there arrives a new crisis of destination" (232). Their rewriting and redefining gestures leave "essential cracks, absences, *écarts*,"[157] an "ungraspable" residue of intertextuality (between senders and addressees; Freud, Sophie, and Ernst; Freud's text and Derrida's text; Derrida's text and my text, etc.).[158] The residue from the violent "divisibility of the letter" endangers and empowers not only the letter but also the postal principle itself. For the letter as practice of signification, there is always the risk "that it never truly arrives, that when it does arrive its capacity not to arrive torments it with an internal drifting" ("Le Facteur de la Vérité," 489).

"TRAVEL GUIDE"

> Etel Adnan's *Of Cities and Women (Letters to Fawwaz)*, written in lieu of a feminist essay for the magazine *Zawaya*, spans the Gulf War, the Lebanese civil war from 1990 to 1992, and the cities Barcelona, Aix-en-Provence, Skopelos, Murcia, Amsterdam, Berlin, Rome, and Beirut. "[T]hese letters . . . are in turn now letters *to* cities and women—that we, that is, women and men alike, might eventually, before it is too late, 'find the right geography for our revelations.'"[159]

Fictional and nonfictional travelogues in the form of letters can look back on a long cross-cultural tradition. The epistolary form and the

Date: Thu, 25 Dec 1997 18:06:53 -0500
From: Jonathan Levi <jlevi@visualradio.com>
Reply-To: jlevi@visualradio.com
To: ssimon1@swarthmore.edu
Subject: ACLA paper

Dear Ms. Simon,

   While wasting time with one of those egotistical web-searches we
writers make too often, I discovered that you are presenting a paper
involving my novel "A Guide for the Perplexed" this April in Mexico. I'd
be very interested in seeing the paper, if that isn't too terrifying a prospect.

Best,
Jonathan Levi

FIGURE 3.4

travelogue share an itinerant structure that marks and yet defies the borders they traverse. From the eighteenth century to today, the epistolary
genre of travel narratives has indeed traveled in style. While transmitting
images of culture, race, and gender, the genre has also reflexively dealt
with the movements of the self and its knowledge between the poles of
writing and reading. As Georges van den Abbeele emphasizes, "[t]he
very image of thought as a quest is a commonplace in the history of philosophy."[160] Appropriately and irreverently, Jonathan Levi's *A Guide for
the Perplexed* (1992) readdresses the twelfth-century Jewish scholar's
Moses Maimonides' pathbreaking *The Guide for the Perplexed*
(1185–90). Levi skillfully combines Jewish cabbala, folklore, mythology, history, and familiar correspondences spanning three continents
(Europe, South America, and North America) and several generations.
Instead of depicting the "inner religious life of an ideal type of man,"[161]
three traveling women, the Jewish-American Hanni (65), the "Schikse-
Goddess" Holland (46), and the Spanish Jewish-American-German
Isabella (13) entice each other to tell their stories while they are laid over
in Mariposa, Spain, due to a revolution and a subsequent air strike. As
narrators, histories, and stories intertwine, these three women discover
their shared genealogy. With Levi's choice of women for his protagonists, he not only performs a gender switch but he also reworks Jewish
history in such a manner as to reveal rather than veil its trajectory as a
product of and a deconstruction effect of the foundational grand narratives of Western Christian hegemony.

From the beginning of the novel, its narratological matrix—"let me tell you a story"—is connected to genealogy, geography, religion, and epistolarity. As it turns out, Ben, the absent, all powerful editor, travel agent, Wandering Jew, is also Hanni's lost son, Holland's uncanny music lover, Isabella's father. According to Hanni, Ben was born while she was sexually assaulted by a Russian soldier in wartime Berlin. In keeping with the Nazi construct of the Jew as an alien monster, his entry into the world coincides with the act of rape and subsequently results in the castration of the soldier. From that moment on, Ben's existence, his overwhelming symbolic presence and material absence, becomes a marker for the complex structure of Jewish victimization and resistance. As in Maimonides' *Guide*, the Prime Mover's, or as Hanni calls him, "the unmoved Mover's" (128), incorporeality remains a challenge.

When the three women seize the opportunity of the layover for a night of storytelling à la Scheherezade, they gather in Hanni's former lover's and thus Ben's father's villa, the villa of the great violin player Sandor alias Zoltan. He, just like his son, is also physically absent. Holland, whose pride and joy is her documentary film material on Zoltan's reemergence from isolation and cultural exile, finds out to her great chagrin that there are no images to be seen. While she might not heed the law against iconization, the medium does. The same rule applies to Zoltan's son. Why, asks Hanni "couldn't Ben have met us at the airport? . . . Before the strike?" to have Holland add in her usual flippant honesty: "I'd asked myself the same question. Why not, Ben? After all you've made on commissions, why couldn't you have plumped for a leisurely five-course meal with three wines, and told us the whole convoluted story in straightforward, genealogical English?" (338). But Conchita, one of the strikers responsible for the overnight delay in Mariposa, ironically becomes the travel agent's spokesperson, defending his physical absence and twisted plans:

> My dear Señorita. . . . A travel agent cannot indulge in direct revelation. He can only guide the client with bits of art—entertainment, trickery, parable, pictures in a cave—into a certain understanding. He must make the client believe that all choices are hers alone, all her experiences one of a kind. (338)

A familiar pattern unfolds. *A Guide* struggles with language, knowledge, memory, and legacy but it does so with a decidedly ethnic focus and it seems to, albeit with a Lacanian edge, trace women's difficult and treacherous path to the forefront of story (language) and history. But with Holland, the only non-Jew in the triangle, one is bound to wonder sarcastically, all fine and good, but where's the beef? What's with these letters from fathers to sons and daughters? Is women's emancipation just a travel grant? Is Levi's *Guide* a fictional account of the Lacanian symbolic and imaginary? The Prime Mover controls women's lives, and after wreaking havoc with them for years, decides for his amusement to bring them together for a "chick reunion" to "make an American quilt," land-shifting Holland to Spain to Florida in the process and meanwhile making a killing off the proceeds?

A *Guide* adds the dimension of economics, of business hierarchies, to the already configured gender, racial, and class dichotomies. Clients are female, the travel agent is male. The text possesses an inflationary economics of ethnicity, class, gender, and the epistolary genre. Its plot and structure operate with a seductively prominent genealogical chain only to have Hanni proclaim at the end that biological connection doesn't matter and that not knowing the young man sharing her life for a few months as her subletter was actually her son provided for a connection "free of guilt, obligation, history" and that "if happiness is knowledge, knowledge of one's origins, then let my origins begin now . . . with this woman, with this child. Whether they are flesh of my flesh, blood of my blood—I couldn't care less" (335). But why does she raise that issue with regard to her female lineage, when she has apparently accepted the "truth" of her male lineage—which resides in Ben? "Can a woman forget her baby, or disown the child of her womb? Though she might forget, I never could forget you" (336)?

Setting out on her trip, escaping her Alzheimer-ridden environment in Florida, Hanni seeks to discover and read "the" Esau Letter, the document proving that her kin, the Spanish Jews, discovered Florida. The discovery and retrieval of this letter, which was in her possession upon the death of her father, was in fact his legacy for her, would thus also serve as an antidote to the loss of unified and coherent memory and history among the Jews of the Diaspora. While nobody believes her at home, as soon as she sets out, she encounters fellow enthusiastic Esau-readers. A communal readership and tribal folklore only develop through traveling. However, when she begins to read "it" in the manager's room of the local Mariposa porn cinema, a theater whose specialty is the translation of historic, literary, and film titles into sexual puns ("Dong Quixote" or "Barbara of Seville," 39), she also discovers that "it" only exists in multiple versions—Maimonides', Esau's, Jacob's, Joseph's, Ivy's, Levi's—matched by the women's side of the story—Kima's, Hanni's, Holland's, Isabella's, Ruth's, Florida's. The Esau Letter also only comes as an adulterated translation and a transcription just as Levi's *Guide* is an edition of an edition of letters to the editor/travel agent.

The novel and the Esau Letter we read are already a reedition and translation of previous guides. When Holland, the journalist, states her disbelief in what she sees and is supposed to believe—"This copy of a copy of a translation of a copy of who knows how many other copies. Maybe if you could find the original . . ."—Hanni, her mother, answers her, "Does your audience have to be there to believe you? Do they have to walk with the astronauts before they believe that man really stood on the moon? . . . Would anything less than being Esau satisfy you?" Holland can only reply smugly by suggesting that "this is all a fiction." Hanni retorts "Of course not. . . . We were merely discussing the need for what you called 'authenticity'" (251–252). Not even the letter written on the wall of Esau's cave is the original document. Instead, it appears to have been written by Joseph, formerly Yehuda, Esau's violin-playing brother.

Throughout the novel, Ben's travel agency seems to specialize in high culture, in violin concertos and Columbus documentaries, and his benign guided tour for the women seems to point toward a harmonious reunion in the great violinist's villa. But at each step, we are confronted with the populist undercurrent of Klezmer, gypsy violins, the history of baseball, and rock music. Along with the political aim of bridging the gap between high and popular culture, mass production and circulation announces the economics of travel. While the goal of a quest should be anything other than material gains, any trip, as Caren Kaplan notes, "insists upon proof of the authentic."[162] But that proof harbors a contradiction based on class divisions and absolute aesthetic standards. What is more authentic? The painting by a celebrated native artist or a piece of pottery? Isn't high culture always, by colonialist definition, already international, already no longer authentic, whereas the object trouvé or the craft object, that in turn are mass produced for the tourist trade, count as "the real thing"? It needs to be recognizably "foreign," and yet it needs to reiterate the experiences and imaginations of those remaining at home. If you didn't bring "it" with you upon your return, people will not believe you were really there! Travelers turn into collectors of "authenticated" material. Something can be gained without fear of loss, loss of face or loss of standards. Besides reassuring the traveler in the existence of immediacy, originality, and authenticity, the binarism of traveler and traveled creates a perfect sexual economics in which the collectibles stand in for the absences and threatening lure of the "Other." They become the fetishes of the scato-scopophilic European, who in pulling them out time after time to touch them and reminisce, mourns his youth and the golden age of his culture through spinning erotically charged narratives of "remember when."[163] This scenario, repeated again and again in modern fiction, autobiographies, and memoirs, almost coerces one into nominating "travel" and "displacement" as the tropes of modernity.

Date: Fri, 26 Dec 1997 18:44:48 -0500
From: Jonathan Levi <jlevi@visualradio.com>
Reply-To: jlevi@visualradio.com
To: ssimon1@swarthmore.edu
Subject: Out-Of-Print Woes

Dear Ms. Simon,

Alas! Even amazon.com doesn't know where to find copies of Guide
(although I've heard that book dealers are pretty good about turning up
copies). The rights recently reverted to me, so not even Vintage
Contemporaries, who published the paperback, have an incentive to
reprint. Unfortunately I don't even have a current publisher who might
reprint (. . .)

But never fear, I am hard at work on the next. And meanwhile, if you're
curious, the current issue of Granta (number 60) has a new short story of
mine called "The Scrimshaw Violin."

At any rate, I would love to read your paper. You can certainly send it
down by e-mail.

Best,
Jonathan Levi

FIGURE 3.5

Even though the women are literally stranded in the hub of their
travel agency, they cannot talk face to face with their mutual agent, Ben.
Hanni and Holland have to resort to letters instead, reveling in the
genre's mystic heritage and revealing its historical connection to
women's writing and female desires. Like its seventeenth- and eighteenth-century predecessor, the letter thrives on its "double fictionality."
Its generic form suggests its origin to lie outside the aesthetic and its
presence therefore ficitionalizes "the need for authenticity" of the host
genre, the modern novel. In this self-generating, transgenerational,
cross-cultural, cross-racial, and multilinguistic textual world, most readers desperate for a key will breathe a sigh of relief when they finally discover whose aliases match whose names and histories, and how to put
the family tree and the genealogy of storytelling together, in short, how
to survive the motion sickness produced by postmodern f(r)iction. The
readers' extradiegetic spacing at one time coincides with Hanni's time-
space coordinates. In the structure of a *mise en abyme*, the reader is

caught reading another travel guide rather than beholding the authenticated Other, described and promised by the travel guide. Page 303 in the novel is also page 303 in the guide that Hanni, and we, are consulting for information on La Rosa Náutica, a restaurant with a subterranean kitchen where Columbus planned "his final assault on the purse of Ferdinand and Isabella" and where Santángel's Jewish Minyan, among them Esau, researched the best possible evacuation route for the endangered Spanish Jews (303). It should come as no surprise then that the name of this semiotically overdetermined multistoried mirror-plane means compass, a direction finder and the sine qua non of travelers' instruments. Of course, La Rosa Náutica is also the site of Ben's travel agency whose majordomo is a Muslim called Abbas, or Father.

The tourist information Hanni and we are reading on page 303 is only one of many variants of a description of La Rosa Náutica in the novel. The specificity and historical detail of the entry stays in step with Hanni's and Holland's learning process, their travels through memory and history. At each turn, a new culturally coded item is disclosed standing alongside previously acknowledged race and gender relations. But instead of covering up the former or distilling the latter, the compass directions (whether Jewish, Christian, Muslim, Animist or American, Spanish, Native American, Arab) point to each other in a terminal, indissoluble spin. Innerdiegetic and extradiegtic hermeneutic enterprises partake in this activity. The novel does not allow the reader, and this includes the characters as readers, to pin down the compass needle, a reading trajectory which would coincide with a modernist travel itinerary that has a stake in insisting on historical agency yet veils its materiality and violence to the Other.

What simply seems like a harmlessly playful labyrinthine circle of self-references in true postmodernist fashion is produced as an act of violation because the entry is and is not Holland's text. Something was added to it without her knowledge. But knowledge is precisely the issue. Her first description, accenting food and locale of the restaurant, is included in a letter to Ben at the beginning of our Guide, which she, in turn, also already refers to as a "retelling" (14). In the next "retelling," her introduction is preserved as a quotation, yet recontextualized in step with her, Hanni's, and the reader's knowledge of events and connections. Whereas the earlier description makes no mention of the place's owner, Santángel, the heir of Columbus's and Esau's benefactor from 1492, Holland mentioned him to Ben in the surrounding letter, questioning the validity and veracity of Santángel's claim to his family's fame. At the beginning of A Guide, her guide still centers on Columbus as the mover and shaker of the secret meetings in the basement of the restaurant. Santángel's story, the story of the expulsion of the Spanish

Jews under the reign of Ferdinand and Isabella, resurfaces after a long and successful period of forgetting and repression in the version on page 303, identifying its author(s) and Hanni as readers of the Esau Letter. Anyone willing to rejoice at the prospect of discovering the travel guide's teleology as a "history from below," a Jewish history against the grain of christianized Western civilization, is selling the book short. The compass of "La Rosa Náutica" points in yet another direction: Columbus wrote his first letter of the discovery of the Americas to Santángel, and in exchange for rendered services to the Crown, that is, setting up Columbus on his crusade and getting rid of Spanish Jews in the process, Santángel receives his "limpieza de sangre" from Ferdinand, a "clarity of blood"-letter pronouncing Santángel's family "clean of any Jewish taint" (304). The new underdog hero, Santángel, is not that much of a hero after all, more of an opportunistic survivor who appropriately resides in La Rosa Náutica "in an ideal position to capitalize on the global fascination with travel" (304). A *Guide for the Perplexed*, for the idealistic searchers who have lost their heroes, for the literary critics who have begun to covet the power of subversion, the shifting compass needle of Levi's narrative serves as a reminder not to mistake inversion for subversion, not to romanticize "the other" for the sake of affirming the division between self and other, to stylize the underside of history into another dominant ideology.[164]

The question remains, what happens in the exchange, in the switch from one paradigm to the other, from one master narrative to another? And is it possible to avert the fate of theories, of literary practices to arrest themselves, to fall into place? To ensure a state of deliberate perplexity that might best describe postmodernism, multiplicity, polyvocality, and parody are most often cited as structural posts. And, of course, in a telematic society, motion, even if not of the body than of bits of information and sound bites, is crucial. Bruno Latour goes so far as to make this shifting new position the grounds for underwriting a nonmodern constitution: "The human is in the delegation itself, in the pass, in the sending, in the continuous exchange of forms."[165] As is evidenced in *A Guide*'s epistolary structure, if Esau believes "survival is in motion," the letter form seems to be the most suitable to handle that task. For a large part of the book, the reader feels compelled to believe in this modernist axiom, especially concerning the fate of Jews in history and the story of *A Guide*. On the plot level, the three travelers let their thoughts and memories wander back and forth to former journeys to finally join in a chorus of mutually respectful polyphony as they are aboard the aircraft en route to America. However, movement takes place on a limited, intraspatial scale, so to speak, it is not necessarily a movement from point A to point B that matters. After all, the three heroines are stuck in Mariposa.

As Caren Kaplan's study initiates, travel and motion need to be ana-
lytically reviewed in connection to emigration, colonization, and migra-
tion. The mythical heritage of travel as quest—the lone Western hero in
search of the secret of life, his cultural heritage, and himself—veils the
inconspicuous connection of travels, explorations, and discoveries to
sexploitation, imperialism, colonization, and the Jewish Diaspora.
When Carranque, Hanni's Spanish guide, postulates that "[the Jews]
made a virtue of exile, found their greatest reward in exile, found their
humanity, their lost identity, in exile" and Hanni agrees with him by
quoting Esau's "your survival is in your motion" axiom (306),[166] it takes
the taxi driver to point out that they "sound like a couple of Jews thank-
ing God for Auschwitz because it gave them the State of Israel" (306).
He insists on critically exposing the silenced linkage between traveling,
in which they are indulging at the moment, first to a revision of Jewish
history as Holocaust tourism, especially upon Hanni's statement that
she "has been to the Holocaust," and second to class-related colonialism by referring to Ben, the travel agent, as a "gent" who meddles in
Middle Eastern politics and arms trades (307). And, in addition, Santángel's story should warn us again: instead of traveling himself, he
became a travel agent, incorporating the concept of the subject, of
agency and self-identity in the disavowal of one's heritage and in the stationary selfsameness of endless repetitions. He could not become an
agent, a player in Spain, without relinquishing his difference and cleans-
ing himself of his Jewishness. And even worse, this "reward" for his services to the Crown also shows that any attempt at subverting the system
from within, as he managed by smuggling Spanish Jews to North America under the pretense of financing Columbus' crusade, will only be recognized by the system in its own shape and form—with a letter literally
exchanging his blood line, transforming him into the vampiric enemy
itself, a dead letter that stops circulating with its conception and stops
his circulation which was, after all, based on transfusions from both
sides. Purity, after all, is the lack of exchange, of circulation or, in other
words, it only permits recycling of the selfsame.

How can travel, after all, indicating the movement from somewhere
to somewhere and retour, become a metaphorical *commonplace?* As
Abbeele rightly insists, "a voyage that stays in the same place is not a
voyage."[167] Neither is "motion, pure and simple" (307). Motion for
motion's sake soon joins hands with its binary opposite—stasis.[168] The
easy, almost unacknowledged slippage into metaphoricity highlights the
appropriation of traveling by both colonizing and colonized discourses.
The very idea of traveling masks the instabilities otherwise associated
with displacements, cross-cultural interactions, and transmissions, especially concerning race and gender. And in different ways and for differ-

ent ends, both *Reisende* and *Bereiste* hope to gain from hiding the risks to themselves and to the other. Travel evokes the image of a "passing through," an observational activity without lasting effects on the biosystem of the observer or the observed.[169] Receiving the appropriate admonishing and medicinal inoculations before setting out, the traveler claims for himself a special medical, educational, and legal status akin to diplomatic immunity by fixing a point of departure and a point of destination which never coincide with points along the route. In the process, the departure point is petrified, marked, in order to guarantee the possibility of return (the buoy of the diver, the flag on the mountain, the homing beacon). What one almost always wishes to forget is that oneself is moved not to return.

The actual traveling happens as "in a dream." The letter one sends or receives is the only sign of presence as absence.[170] One writes them in those stationary moments that one can snatch from sightseeing, on a rainy day, during a meal or a drink, late at night, in a carriage, on the train, moved to yet another location and time. The old wisdom that one cannot write at the same time as doing something else should not be discarded too lightly, even if AT&T promises us "you will!." Travel, then, is movement without permanence, forming impressionistic memory traces that consistently attach themselves to other memories, dreams, and desires. Jean Baudrillard attempts to describe this process in *Cool Memories*: "We move circumspectly within our emotions, passing from one to another, on a mental planet made up of convolutions. And we bring back the same transparent memories from our excesses and passions as we do from our travels."[171] Baudrillard recalls Sigmund Freud's transcription of Dora's second dream, in which Dora finds a letter from her mother that announces the death of her father, just as Hanni receives the Esau Letter upon her father's death.

In a footnote, Freud adds that Dora noticed a question mark behind the "come home if you like?" After reading the letter, Dora begins her journey by asking for the location of the train station. A young man offers to accompany her but she refuses. She enters the woods, sees the station in front of her, but is immobilized, only to find herself miraculously transported to her family estate: "At the same time I had the usual feeling of anxiety that one has in dreams when one cannot move forward. Then I was at home. I must have been traveling in the meantime, but I know nothing about that."[172] Freud reads this dream scenario as a "phantasy of defloration" which leads him to the even more contested conclusion of the "phantasy of childbirth," upon which Dora terminates therapy.[173]

What is striking in the context of the correlation of dream and travel, is the amnesiastic quality that Jean Baudrillard would later turn

into the penultimate nomadic theory of the simulacrum, the postpro-
duction effect of postmodernism.[174] The before and after of travel in the
case of Dora's second dream, and according to Freud of sexual intercourse, are those instances available to the conscious mind, whereas the
process itself is under erasure. And Freud, as the foremost traveler of the
unconscious, is seeking to regain access to the actual movement, the
erotic journey across the landscape of the virginal text. And in order to
make this trip worthwhile for him, to see what he is forbidden to see,
but also to prevent Dora from developing a subversive *ecriture feminine*
with her autoerogenic hysteric body that refutes a single point of entry
for the phallic reading machine, he insists on a gender switch, thus
objectifying Dora to herself. From the vantage point of cyberspace, he is
creating an avatar for himself to travel through her "mental planet." As
a result, she, as a woman, still "knows nothing about that," whereas he
has been traveling for her and through her. The master ventriloquist
seeks access to the preoedipal bisexuality he himself has so successfully
channeled into heterosexuality. He can only get there through the
woman, by dragging himself through her unconscious, so to speak.
Dora's desire to travel, to leave behind the sexual abuse and harassment
she has been made to suffer as the exchange object between her father
and her father's lover's husband, commingles with her desire to
(re)claim her own body, to discover her sexual orientation. Her questions are never understood, only heard; people answer her query for
location with temporal phrases, forever delaying and displacing her
desire. The moment of her physical petrification is immediately followed
by the arrival at her dead father's empty house, which she approaches
through the servants' quarters. Due to her lack of power, Dora's journey begins and leads to a strange place others call home. She travels at
"home," travels through the discursivity of "home." In the desired
absence of the father and the mother (both are "at the graveyard"), she
reads in "a big book." Spurred on by her mother's errant love letter,
phallocentric knowledge has turned into knowledge of the law of the
father, a knowledge that finally allows her to *orient* herself.[175]

Not only does Dora's dream refute Freud's sexual binarism, it
demonstrates her homelessness in what Monique Wittig has termed "the
Straight Mind."[176] While Freud's analyses of hysteria are written as
guides for the perplexed, the hysteric woman, in particular, and by allegorical extension, feminized fin de siécle Austrian society, it has been
pointed out repeatedly that Freud himself had discounted countertrans-
ference, had suppressed the impact of Dora's voice on his nervous system, his own sexual-cultural anxieties, and that her withdrawal spon-
sored the hysterical writing about the second dream and the
postscript.[177] The "Traffic in Women" prevents women from traveling.

Whenever Woman wishes to transgress the limits of home at home, her very steps result in hysteric transformations of her body, petrified repetitions whose roots lie in a mandated amnesia about traveling. Woman's fate about traveling, then, is to function as the vehicle of modern anxieties about historical change, as the biophysical landscape of the anxious traveler. Through her metaphorized body he can travel safely. She represents that to which the man can always return. Her forbidden travels spatialize time in hysteric movements that are narrated by the male traveler. As Georges von den Abbeele points out, "[t]he travel narrative is then one in which the transgression of losing or leaving the home is mediated by a movement that attempts to fill the gap of that loss through a spatialization of time."[178]

Taking Dora's desire to "orient" herself literally, Jonathan Levi explicitly connects colonialist Orientalism to the transmission of gender, race, and culture. Our reading practice coincides with Ben's voyeurism. The epistolary narratives ricochet off the Esau Letter as the passport of authenticity like veiled women's voices echoing off hermetically sealed harem walls. As Hanni's "son," Isabella's father, and Holland's lover, Ben occupies the only legitimized positions from which to gaze and produce the female bodies of mother, lover, and virgin in the fictional harem of his *Guide*. Since the Orientalist imagination of the harem has insisted on comparing it to a bordello, it is therefore only appropriate that the journey should begin in Huéspedes La Rábida, Mariposa's bordello of fame and the accompanying Teatro La Rábida, where the canons of Spanish-Latin-American-Jewish-Christian history are hybridized as visual and linguistic pornography. The holy month of December opens with "Morocco Bound," continues with "Inside Isabella," "Tilting at Windmills," and "The Lewd of Kima," to wrap up with "Rambam, Thank You, Ma'am" and "Adiós Colón!" Among the list of titles one can also find the unavoidable "Spanish Harem." From the bordello, the three women and their stories move into Zoltan's, that is, Sultan's, villa.

Stranded in the absent master's house, the three captive travelers have a tea party with an endless supply of Hanni's kipferln. *Thousand-and-one Nights* meets *Alice in Wonderland*. Before the women know each other's names, Holland had called Hanni "the White Rabbit," and Hanni had called her "my Lady Journalist." Ben's heavy trunk, synonymous with the novel itself, the treasure chest of stories, is laden with three different fruit on a bed of sand and a letter beginning with "Dear Mother." It rewrites and reinterprets the story of Mohammed and his three orphaned daughters whose nanny sent this ripening fruit to remind him, the absent father, that he needed to return to guide his children into womanhood. Now, the son sends the fruit along with Hanni, an act that, as he should know, doubly violates airline restrictions. When Hanni has realized that she is not the carrier but the intended addressee of the trunk, she ceases to be the white rabbit running to fulfill other people's missions. That is also the moment when Isabella recites from a crumpled piece of paper she has kept since her childhood in a language that she neither speaks nor reads.

Although this piece of paper is a pendant to Ben's letter to his mother and Dora's dream-letter from her mother, Isabella's poetic recitation steals Ben's show. The piece of paper turns out to be a letter from Isabella's mother, Holland, who abandoned her in a Spanish orphanage when she was a child. In it, Holland promises Isabella that she would come for her when the time was right putting "an end to mysteries" (341). Mostly silent or playing her violin, appearing like an apparition among adults of all walks of life, Isabella's voice consists of preoedipal glossolalia. It displays a multicultural and polylinguistic know-how that the others have unlearned but are desperate to learn again. Holland's letter, her voice, reappears as a magic chant from her daughter's lips. Isabella is Alice's double who visits with those on the outside, turning the "natural world" into a mischievous, unreliable wonderland. Holland's glance at the bilingual bible from the orphanage breaks the fairy tale spell, the equilibrium of language, music, and being that existed in Isabella's mind, and threatens to catapult her into the symbolic order for good. Previously eloquent, she now stammers with great fear: "No, Señora, no send me back!" (266). Being confronted with her mother, Isabella now takes on her grandmother's role. Like the white rabbit, she runs away from Holland through the streets and narrow paths of Mariposa. Holland follows her like a *toro*. As with all things in A *Guide*, instead of showing a progression from one to the other, Isabella's outcry—"no send me *back*"—hints at the inability to locate any event prior or later than another event, to situate anything in an outside or inside. The symbolic order, the law of the father, was always already here and there. It is Holland's turn to become speechless at that moment; only the violin strings of the instrument pressed between them in the encounter vibrate in a "terrible chord" (266).

That terrible chord echoes back to the story of the girl Kima as told in the Esau Letter, whose lute playing was famous throughout Mohammed-el-Hayzari's reign at the Alhambra. Unlike Isabella, Kima, her *Doppelgänger*, dies as a result of a confrontation with the symbolic. This story becomes one of the feedback loops through which to read the harem-scenario of the three travelers telling stories in Zoltan's, that is, Sultan's, villa. The story deals with Zehava, a Jewish girl, abducted to serve in Mohammed's Spanish harem. He forcibly collects girls and women of all sizes and shapes for his harem, which the narrator defines as an "inspiration of fantasy" (167). While Zehava, Kima's Jewish mother, calls her "seizure and transportation to the Sultan of the Alhambra . . . a repetition of the biblical story of the enslavement of the Jews" (169), "his imagination traveled unbound" (168). But even though he owns her body, she refuses to yield and attempts suicide. Even the all powerful Mohammed finds himself in the need for "a guide to the heart of the heart of his desires" (170), a travel guide for successful sexual conquest. The very phrase "heart of the heart" suggests an interior to an interior, a closed-off feminine space even from the eyes and phallus of the sultan. Zehava dies upon delivering a trio of girls, among them Kima, but leaves them with the wish of being "safely married to nice Jewish boys" (181). When the opportunity presents itself, two of them flee to head her wish, while Kima remains lured back by a single wind-blown note emanating from her lute that lets her fear for her father's soul. Upon hearing of the two daughters' escape, the father hurls the lute out of the window with his strong left hand and clutches Kima with his right. Unable to hold her, she jumps after the lute. Instead of holding what is most precious to him with his strong arm, he uses his strength to fling away the lute. That he employs his strength for the symbolic rather than the material makes him out to be a victim of the same law which he has helped to put into practice. As the representative of the law, as father and sultan, he does not really have a choice since the right arm is decreed to be the source of strength and justice. What appears to be a symbolic dilemma for the story is literally an impasse within the symbolic order, an impasse that results in another *Frauenopfer*.

Kima's story appears nestled in multiple story-frames, just like the three ripening fruit in the trunk and similar to the architextural layers surrounding the harem. One symbol is expressed in terms of another, symbols multiply and interact with one another to the point of allegorizing the very function and idea of symbolism. As mentioned before, Ben has Hanni carry his steamer trunk. Hanni's inheritance, her own legacy, and the future of the Jewish race literally ride on her, the mother's shoulders, from the very beginning. As his messenger, she is "relieved to move from a quest of [her's] to a task for [him]" (31). While emancipating herself from her quest to find the Esau Letter, her inheritance, and the key to her lineage and history, Hanni is laden with the baggage of the colonialist and patriarchal past, and she indeed intends to "follow [Ben's] orders to the letter" (31). Even though she claims to be a "woman of great, severe independence" she says she is happiest, at her best, and "most successful, when [her] independence is strictly knowledgeably, faithfully guided" (32). His mail-order exchanges the modernist travel trajectory of masculine anxiety for women's emancipation, a tour de force courtesy of the patriarchal travel agency that underhandedly invests heavily in women's progress. The phallus becomes a stowaway. Appropriately, the trunk's contents remain invisible until she has herself reached the point in the interwoven stories at which opening the trunk to unlock its transcending secret is no longer necessary. In the course of traveling and making dis/connections, however, the symbol's power to point beyond itself and still remain one with itself and its substitution has been eroded.

Ben thus follows in Maimonides' footsteps, who "warns [the reader] that he has taken great care with the language and structure of the *Guide* in order deliberately to obscure his true position—that he has even occasionally contradicted himself."[179] Unlike Maimonides, who did not want to "undermine the religious faith of those Jews unequipped to follow subtle philosophical reasoning,"[180] the narrative structure of *A Guide* presents itself as a labyrinthine promotion of reaching faith through the deconstructive rerouting of authenticity, originality, and origins. The indefinite article in the title already indicates the text's nonoriginality, its refusal to claim, as Moses Maimonides indirectly did, "the" guide as the basis for future scholarship and travel. In Maimonides' case, however, his audacity to claim that his commentary to the Torah would render study of the Torah itself superfluous, already entered *The Guide* into the semiotics of the supplement: to be both a replacement of and an addition to the original. Levi's *Guide*'s epistolary centerpieces, the twelfth-century letter from Maimonides to his son-in-law and the sixteenth-century Esau Letter are not one, but always harbor another "original" somewhere else. And after both characters and readers rejoice in the family reunion, the bringing together of a lost people, of the Jews from the Diaspora, which seems to take shape before our eyes, the genealogical imperative is exchanged for a conscious policy and narrative politics of adoption.

If the novel structurally refutes any attempt at grounding the directionality of reading and knowing, why is it that all letters in the novel travel either from generation to generation or from traveler to travel agent? Epistolary transmissions from travelers are homing beacons. The investment in their arrival is high, because a functioning postal route ensures the traveler against losing himself or herself in time and space. Their narratives form the documents of an existence in absentia, the only physical traces of the one without a permanent address, the traveler. But the letter also destabilizes the positions. Points along the route become the letter's and traveler's new departure points and the letter's designated address becomes the destination. Travel letters fragment the whole of the voyage into several installments whose originating coordinates have always already shifted when they arrive. In the case of *A Guide*, the letters' destination is the travel agency itself, the coordination system, the postal code responsible for the network of routes and the possibility for connections. The mysterious nature of Ben's travel agency ensures that the letters return to him. Their arrival and recirculation through the travel guide as novel insist on his materiality despite his inaccessibility. His echo-location betrays his increasing anxiety over the loss of his agency: his clients, and especially women, might discover they can take matters into their own hands, and prolific indeterminate postmodern disjunctions are bound to out-post his outpost of agency. What the paths of the letters outline is another sociocultural map than the one depicted in their messages. In this sense, epistolary travelogues become cultural histories of the "travel of meaning."[181]

In the shape of a travel guide, differing not only from its eighteenth-century European ancestry but also from Hofmannsthal's use of the letter to express the language crisis of modernity, the epistolary genre investigates its own debt to the notion of metaphysical agency, embodied in the racial stereotype of the "Wandering Jew" and the sexual stereotype of the shape-shifting Jezebel. The novel's plotline, its lethal combination of ethnic metaphoricity, identity politics, family values, and women's emancipation, are four of the seductive narrative strands that today's perplexed (i.e., postmodernistically challenged) readers cling to, only to discover that the survival of humanity, of the race and its traditions, lie in a telematic, polyphonic, and vibrant arrangement of literary, musical, scientific, and philosophical legacies that can only become legacies by way of inconsistent transformations, through cultural, racial, and sexual hybridization. The epistolary transmission system of the novel offers a very unreliable mix of deterministic adulteration, indeterminable hegemony in which, in Latour's words, "[T]he work of mediation becomes the very centre of the double power, natural and social. The networks come out of hiding."[182]

CHAPTER 4

Mass-Mailing:
The Language Hazard

Continuing the discussion begun with case studies of epistolary rhapsodies and chain letters, this chapter seeks to highlight the interrelations between letters and popular culture, while paying special attention to the connections between theories of language and politics. These multilayered relationships become especially poignant when considered alongside the traditional equation of the Feminine with the Trivial, and more recently of the Trivial with the Postmodern.[1] The following reading of *Erwins Badezimmer oder die Gefährlichkeit der Sprache (Erwin's Bathroom or the Hazardousness of Language)*, an epistolary novel published in 1984, seeks to problematize not only some of the most vital intersections between feminism and postmodernism, but also between contemporary trivial literature and literary theory. How does the sex/gender system and the epistolary economy of exchanges work in Bemmann's text? How does the postmodern controversy circulate in mass-literature?

Erwins Badezimmer, a book that figures in Dirk Göttsche's study as a sign for the "topicality and vitality of the language critique tradition even for the literature of the immediate (postmodern) presence,"[2] rewrites literature through letters. Bemmann's novel appeared after a decade in which the perceptions of what constituted high and popular culture shifted to allow for the scholarly criticism of this rigorous division. As Leslie Fiedler pointed out in 1975, the division had long since been defied by the artistic products themselves, most notably by the novelistic genre, and specifically by the epistolary novel:

> the truly New Novel must be anti-art as well as anti-serious. But this means, after all, that it must become more like what it was in the beginning, more what it seemed when Samuel Richardson could not be taken *quite* seriously, and what it remained in England (as opposed to France, for instance) until Henry James had justified himself as an artist against such self-declared "entertainers" as Charles Dickens and Robert Louis Stevenson: popular, not quite reputable, a little dangerous—the one his loved and rejected cultural father, the other his sibling rival in art.[3]

The "New Novel" Fiedler envisions as the truly postmodern novel takes its cues from the uncouth mélange of letters and literature, of popular-bourgeois and elitist-aristocratic cultural practices. Fiedler pronounced the "closing of the gap" between "Pop-Art" and "High Art" as a necessary subversive political act. According to Fiedler, this act does not subvert the status quo in order to draw out the residues of class struggle and difference but in order to "transform the secular crowd into a sacred community: one with each other, and equally at home in the world of technology and the realm of wonder" (366).

If his prognosis had become reality, my study could rely on a community of informed readers in Derrida's as well as in Bemmann's case. Unfortunately, this is true neither for Derrida nor for Bemmann. Even though I am far from desiring to create a "sacred community," but rather wish to trace the shifty polylogue among epistolarity, feminism, and post-modernism, I cannot refrain from first familiarizing the reader with the novel's plot. It seems rather appropriate that, as postmodern criticism and fiction closes some gaps, it reopens others. If I were discussing a work from the "canon" (like Goethe's poems or Fontane's novels), my reading could interface with a multitude of different, yet familiar, voices. I would not have to provide a plot summary to be able to tap into that network. My decision to address a marginalized text in order to represent a poetics of postmodernism results in a modernist gesture.

Hans Bemmann's epistolary novel *Erwins Badezimmer* addresses and appropriates the traditions of German language critique of the post-war period, including both its dystopic and utopian orientations.[4] From the vantage point of the year 1984 (which matches the prognostic title of George Orwell's novel of totalitarian bureaucratic and linguistic terror), Bemmann's novel looks to the German past and contemporary cultural and literary theories in order to come to terms with a potentially inhuman, a-historical, and one-dimensional technocratic future. Merging the utopian-dystopian science-fiction tradition of Orwell's *Nineteen Eighty-Four* (1949) and Ray Bradbury's *Fahrenheit 451* (1953) with the late eighteenth and early nineteenth century German *Bildungsroman*, Bemmann's antihero/collaborator, Albert, slowly develops into a partisan revolutionary through the reading and preservation of banned texts, through his epistolary *Liebeskunst* (art of love) with Rachel, and through his interaction with the opposition movement.[5] Although Bemmann's novel shares the hermetic frame of *Nineteen Eighty-Four*—judging from the blurb, the book is published by the "Language Surveillance Authority" *(Sprachüberwachungsbehörde)* to set an example for "depravities threatening the state" ("staatsgefährdende Abwege")—*Erwins Badezimmer* also deploys *Fahrenheit 451*'s utopian idea of a separatist territory for unruly citizens, from which a "new world order" can emerge.[6]

The novel deals with four language reforms: (1) the story of the 'Hadubaldian Language Reform" ("Hadubaldische Sprachreform"), which began as an attempt to think and speak about time and the nature of things; (2) "Spiridion Spalthirn's Axiom," which initiated the language crisis by insisting on the impossibility of expressing reality in words, and which reflected on language itself; (3) "The Great National Purification of Language" ("Die große Nationale Sprachreinigung"), which declared the "unambiguity" *(Eindeutigkeit)* of words a natural law; and finally (4) the narrator's and the reader's linguistic revolution in the form of epistolary fiction. The four language reforms combine several aspects of German language philosophy. Whereas Hadubald takes the "Language of the Old People" ("Sprache des Alten Volkes") to enhance his native language, Spiridion's followers return "to the ancestral way of speaking" ("zur angestammten Redeweise," 24–29).

One scenario traces the evolution of German since Martin Luther's translation of the Bible in 1534. After several setbacks due mainly to the political and religious structure of society, personal letters and epistolary fiction contributed to the substitution of German for Latin and French in the eighteenth century.[7] From the end of the eighteenth century well into the nineteenth century, the nationalist sentiment strengthened this trend. After the language crisis of the fin-de-siécle, after influential Russian formalism, French structuralism, and Weimar Republic cosmopolitanism, the backlash of *Germanisierung* reached its peak in the Third Reich.

Another scenario of the four language reforms in the novel could trace them to linguistic and philosophical developments in the twentieth century: structuralism, New Criticism, Chomsky's generative transformative grammar, poststructuralism, or, as it is called in historical circles "the linguistic turn." In this scenario, the antirealist intellectualism of a Spiridion Spalthirn is seen as causing the totalitarian linguistic turn.[8] In the book, the Spiridion concentration on indigenous linguistic and mental structures brings about a nationalistic uprising. After this "postcolonial" purge, the state is run with the help of television shows, soap operas, popular fiction, sports, and expert rhetoricians. According to the narrator, these serialized simulacra threaten to overwhelm and displace individuality and innate human qualities. Bemmann creates a world that combines the idea of total access to information with rigid censure. The result is a two-class society in which some control the selection and distribution of information while others accept that the available quantity of the provided information guarantees their right to information.

A sprained ankle, which keeps the philologist Albert S. from participating in a linguistic conference, helps him to realize his fractured understanding of language and literature. From the beginning of the novel, body and language are intimately related to each other, reconfiguring the split of body and mind as well as the loss of hermeneutic legitimacy. As a result of his doctor's interest in the history of their society's language doctrine, the government-prescribed credo does not ring so true to him anymore:

> "To us, however, it is known that language is unambiguous. Whoever doubts our knowledge is crazy or a liar. Whoever gives words different meanings commits a crime against the language community. He should be silent-silent-silent. We know what words signify. We know all meanings. He who believes us lives in safety. He is happy-happy-happy." The Management, Principal Language Surveillance Authority.[9]

Albert's doctor and future lover, Rachel, cures both his body and his "civil servant soul" *(Beamtenseele)* by initiating a correspondence. Rachel wants to know the history of the "Great National Language Purification" and the reasons for the politically regulated "unambiguity."[10] Unable to give a suitable answer, Albert sets off on an investigation of heretofore unexplored mental territory. Due to her provocative inquiries, he uses his access to the archive of his linguistic institute for metalinguistic research, in order to write a history of his discipline. Like the fireman who burns books in *Fahrenheit 451*, Albert himself is responsible for deciding the final semantic laws for specific words and phrases. Prior to his meeting with Rachel, he never thought to question the sociopolitical implications of his profession.[11]

Through his awakened curiosity and his friend Erwin, Albert stumbles across a network of linguistic revolutionaries, who preserve and collect old and forbidden literature in Erwin's bathroom microfiche-library. While Albert is occupied with the "Use of Contemporary Language" ("Nutzung der Gegenwartssprache"), Erwin works in the "concentration archive for pre-literature" ("Konzentrationsmagazin für Vor-Literatur," 13). All literature incongruent with the principle of "unambiguity" established by the "Great National Language Purification" is relegated to this stockroom. Concatenating the words "purification" and "concentration archive" suggests a fascistic cultural and political practice. An army of "loyalist" *(staatstreuen)* scientists and scholars analyze and classify works according to the government's purity laws (13). These purity laws are reminiscent of the National Socialists' laws for the "purity and protection of the German gene pool." In addition, only a selected group of scientists, to whom Erwin belongs, have access to the material in the *Konzentrationsmagazin* (14). Like the infamous doctors in concentration camps, they experiment with and on the imprisoned.[12]

The revolt in *Erwins Badezimmer* thus begins with collaboration. Erwin explains to Albert that his uncle pleaded with him not to "jump the gun" but to finish his studies and infiltrate the *Konzentrations-magazin* (19). The uncle's advice: one can only begin to change things from the inside:

> The more intense a person capable of thinking immerses himself into these texts, the more differentiated his own language capacity becomes, and along with that also his way of thinking. That's how, in the meantime, not a few of my colleagues in the concentration archive also belong to the particular circle of friends, which you, too, have now joined.[13]

There is a triple collaboration at work in the novel. Members of the opposition collaborate with the system to besiege it from within; language both helps to install and upset fascist practices; the novel itself collaborates with popular taste and mass production. As chief editor of the *Borromäus-Verein* and lecturer at the University of Bonn, Hans Bemmann (1922–) himself is a stereotypical example of a liberal bourgeois intellectual on a humanistic mission to educate the masses by sugarcoating his philosophical and political pills. Within his oeuvre *Erwins Badezimmer* is the most didactic.[14] Yet, the publication of *Erwins Badezimmer*, dedicated to an *Oberseminar* by Dorothea Ader at Bonn, follows in the wake of the immense success of his fantasy novel *Stein und Flöte* (*Stone and Flute*, 1983). With this publication history, Bemmann managed to draw the *Stein und Flöte* fans, a somewhat different crowd from the participants of a university research seminar, into *Erwins Badezimmer*'s sphere of influence.

In Bemmann's fictional world, German fascism becomes one with the linguistic ideology of "unambiguity," and resistance merges with the structuralist idea of differentiation and ambiguity. Albert first experiences the difference within language metaphorically as deeper shades of hidden meanings beneath the surface of phonetic arrangements: "I felt as if my fingers groped the surface of impressions that are connected to these phonetic sequences in our dictionaries without realizing what was hiding in the depth beneath that thin skin of unambiguity" ("Mir war zumute, als tasteten meine Finger die Oberfläche von Vorstellungen ab, die in unseren Wörterbüchern mit diesen Lautfolgen verknüpft werden, ohne daß ich begriff, was sich unter dieser dünnen Haut von Eindeutigkeit in der Tiefe verbarg," 15). The narrator compares the ideology of "one word-one meaning" to a "thin skin," a body of text. In the process of learning to make love to Rachel's body, he has to learn how to read, and foremost, how to see. As of yet, his fingers move over the text like those of someone unable to decipher Braille. To access and reveal the texture of language is the opposition's political agenda by which they hope to topple the powers that be. What Rachel asks of

Albert is for him to reveal to her the generation of the visible structure, the transformational grammar at work. Albert turns away from collecting data on language "to account for facts about language by constructing a formal representation of what is involved in knowing a language."[15] This representation takes the shape of a multilayered epistolary correspondence, a "story in letters with various enclosures" ("Geschichte in Briefen mit diversen Beilagen").

One of these layers represents Erwin's literature circle as a recreation of the Romantic salon culture, whose activities Albert chronicles in his letters.[16] The members of Erwin's political-linguistic resistance meet to tell each other fairy tales, historical and biblical legends, poems, riddles, and jokes. True to the fantasy/science-fiction genre, every person introduced to Albert masters a particular literary lore. Slowly, Albert unlearns his misconceptions about transparent language and literature and relearns the suppressed folklore of his people. His letters to Rachel soon become an archive of literary history, as Albert collects and transcribes oral and written tales, and intersperses them with his running commentary.[17] For Bemmann and Albert alike, the epistolary form thus provides the means with which to preserve the ideal of immediacy and multifaceted semantics.[18]

Instead of forsaking his profession as editor, Albert's new alliance with Erwin's group returns him to his profession as an apprentice *and* an independent scholar. By studying the history and "dictionary of the inhuman" ("Wörterbuch des Unmenschen"), Albert gains insight not only into the hazard but also into the humanist potential of language.[19] For him, poetry after Auschwitz is not only still possible but a necessity.[20] Instead of banning the poets from their new republic, Albert and his friends (like many intellectuals in postwar Germany) strongly believe in the political validity of Friedrich Schiller's "aesthetic education of man."[21] Erwin's group's preservation and literary restoration, combined with their political engagement, recall the activities of "Gruppe 47." In the 1960s, the founding fathers of "Gruppe 47" (Hans Werner Richter, Walter Kolbenhoff, Wolfdietrich Schnurre, and Alfred Andersch) were criticized for retreating from their politically active journalism into the realm of literature. But their combination of journalistic prose with fiction and poetry also gave the members' works a critical edge. The "Gruppe 47" expressed a voracious desire to catch up with literary developments. They opened themselves to other nations' avant-garde experiments and constructed what was often termed a *Kahlschlag-Realismus* through an emphasis on documentary fiction, concrete poetry, and radio plays.[22]

Whereas Hans Werner Richter and others, who were disillusioned with the Cold War mentality of their newspapers, sought their political and cultural responsibility in producing engaged literature, Albert discovers his political agenda through letters and literature. Insofar as the novel satirizes the language crisis as much as it underscores its importance for a reflective, self-determined life, the elderly protagonist achieves an emancipated sense of self at the end. *Erwins Badezimmer* writes itself as a utopian *Bildungsroman* by drawing on its epistolary ancestry: on the sociopolitical and literary emancipation of the bourgeoisie from the absolutist aristocracy, the *Bildung* of the individual in his or her conflict with society, the aesthetic reorganization of the relation between the sexes, and on the literary reinvention of the new frontier.[23]

The protagonists Albert and Rachel appear as reincarnations of another famous epistolary couple: Karl August Varnhagen and Rahel Levin Varnhagen.[24] With his choice of genre and names, Bemmann opens a German-Jewish dialogue. Whereas Varnhagen published severely edited selections from his wife's letters, Rachel collects and submits Albert's unedited letters for publication.[25] Despite her cousin H.'s, the editor's, more conventional sense of decorum, she insists on "leaving the manuscript untouched" (9). Rachel's letters, in which she presumably asks and elaborates her "intuitive" political opposition, are destroyed by Albert to protect her, as he says, from prosecution. Rachel's only letter in the collection tells us that she intends to emigrate and spend the rest of her life with Albert. The territory needs doctors: "so I don't even need to reproach myself for having given up my profession for a love affair" ("also brauche ich mir nicht einmal vorzuwerfen, ich hätte wegen einer Liebesgeschichte meinen Beruf aufgegeben," 240). The impractical Albert on the other hand only advances to the position of a baker's assistant. He spends most of his spare time in the local monastery's library. The goal of the territory's reeducation is a successful fusion of body and mind, of labor and scholarship, of gender roles, of Judaism and Christianity, in short, a utopian state of harmonic unity and identity.

What appears here as an emancipated dialogue across sexual, ethnic, political, and class lines conflicts with Bemmann's linguistic politics. Not only is Albert the political victim and active political hero, who risks his life for the cause of re-(at)taining language's creative potential and semantic ambiguity, but Rachel is cast as a combination of muse, lover, cook, natural spirit, and nurturing mother. From a safe distance, she rejuvenates him spiritually and physically. On October 6, Albert writes to "Frau Doktor":

> Your unconcealed pronounced admiration for the fact that I have thrown myself into such an *adventure*—you even speak of a *conspiratorial character* of this activity—because of a question you uttered as a sideline, does flatter me, but rather embarrasses me. Did it really escape you that your

question has unexpectedly given a new direction to the life of a *science administrator*, who in the routine of a half heartedly executed desk-job had almost become a cynic? I feel downright rejuvenated![26]

That Albert moves from the grateful recognition of Rachel's stimulation to love poetry is an indication that Rachel has magically transformed a "person who faces the impending paralysis of the civil servant with equanimity" ("dem Erstarrungsprozeß des Staatsbeamten mit Gleichmut entgegenblickenden Menschen," 12) into a writer of literature. Within the narrative frame, Albert's collected letters also serve as political pamphlets, as *nouveaux literature engagée*. By slowly changing his style from the first letter on, Albert learns to avoid indoctrinated phrases and linguistic orthodoxy. The language crisis and the crisis of the postwar German novel are fictionalized in Albert's attempts to return to a natural language while thinking and writing about the system of language as well as the nature of things. The more Albert strives to clear himself of the state-prescribed "unambiguity," the more he himself resorts to an idea of a "pure language." The fact that his linguistic revolution originates in Erwin's bathroom cabinet suggests the movement's retention of the purification process, and therefore, I propose, also for the obliteration of difference.

The reader discovers that the novel's society is indeed modeled after the cabinet of Dr. Caligari, when Albert goes to prison for his confrontation with an interviewer from the "language surveillance authority."[27] In the interrogating superior officer in Albert's prison, we encounter an academic, who speaks with a "hadubaldian" syntax and vocabulary, and believes in Spiridion Spalthirn's absolute relativity of language. This, however, does not lead him to question the political system. It rather enables him to divide academic and private discourse from public rhetoric "for the simple minded masses":

> My way of speaking astonishes you, doesn't it? My dear Doctor, why should one not make use of these possibilities of language among intelligent people? Towards the outside and for the common people one simply needs an ideological frame to which the people can adhere and—by the way—also should, lest they develop any erroneous ideas.[28]

The "language surveillance officer" abuses his understanding of language and literature to gain power and suppress the people. Linguistic ambiguity and word games become his pastime, a game for insiders only. The officer offers Albert a professional future in "Language Surveillance Authority" in exchange for detailed information on the sources of Albert's knowledge and the individuals, who provided him with access to these sources (129). Albert metaphorically declines by citing the snake's promise of an "unambiguous knowledge" from the Old Testament.

Bemmann distinguishes the language crisis in the humanist tradition from the crisis initiated by postmodern philosophy and poststructuralism. In the mixture of "a man of letters," "coffee house musician," and "language surveillance officer" (126), the officer's belief in language's inability to represent the world and a manipulative use of its ambiguous potential lead directly to the totalitarian system of prescribed "unambiguity." He embodies the Machiavellianism of the postmodern intelligentsia. Bemmann's hopes for a humanist revolution in language therefore lie—sociologically speaking—with the educated professional middle class (higher civil servants, teachers, doctors) in cooperation with the lower middle class. Herr Franz, the riddle-master, for example, is a waiter, and Amelie, the fairy tale teller, a teacher, who is saved from imprisonment by a pupil's parent, a baker. The classic historical example of such a united effort in Germany are the 1848 revolts, an association that more clearly delimits Bemmann's Romantic politics.

Before Albert reforms himself, he gathers "word field material" for words like *"presence-optimism," "anti-individualism"* or *"yesterdom-combat"* (*"Gegenwartsoptimismus, Antiindividualismus oder Gestrigkeitsbekämpfung,"* 14) without any insight into the political and etymological history of these compound neologisms. In his letters to Rachel, he refers to his former activity as a "tinkering with words" ("Herumhantieren mit Wörtern"), as "language technology" *(Sprachtechnologie)* in service of government rhetoric (14). Although his linguistic quest leads him to rewrite government newspeak, his revolution turns around its own axis. Instead of harboring *presence optimism*, Albert is pessimistic about the present. He believes in the critical exploration of the past rather than in *combatting yesterdom*. Instead of portraying the anonymity and uniformity of the masses, Albert's letters exemplify his struggle for individuality. Albert's new philology remains within a dialectical frame. Whereas he paints the state's language practices in the darkest colors, adjectives like *richtig* ("correct") and *wahr* ("true") abound in connection with Albert's and Erwin's political linguistics (16 and 20). The medical rule "similia *similibus*," which Albert applies to their linguistic revolution, underscores this melodramatic self-righteousness: "If one wants to corrupt us through language, then we have to try to save ourselves through that language or possibly even in language itself. There we may find ourselves again" ("Wenn man uns über die Sprache verderben will, dann müssen wir uns eben durch die Sprache oder vielleicht sogar in die Sprache selbst zu retten versuchen. Vielleicht finden wir dort uns selbst wieder," 106).

The revolution in *Erwins Badezimmer* is *not* a postmodern linguistic revolution, but rather a revolt against postmodernism or, to be more precise, against what is conceived as postmodernism *ex negativo*, namely, ahistoricity, moral and social decadence, loss of individualism, mass culture, inhuman behavior, academic "verbal acrobatics" without purpose or reason. While experimenting with narratological practices like the genre mix of science fiction and poetry or the structural and thematic self-reflexivity of language, Bemmann adjusts his message to the market. He attempts to (re)write and prescribe the contemporary poetics of the "post," a political linguistics that romances the post back to modernism. Entailed in his rewriting of "old and new literature" is also an appropriation of the female tradition of epistolary fiction.

The novel's confrontational dialogue with postmodernism, poststructuralism, and feminism takes shape in the epistolary correspondence with Rachel. Rachel's questions gnaw at the status quo. In Craig Owens' sense, she insists on difference. This "discourse of the other" influences Albert's narrative. Albert narrates events in orderly sequences and introduces people through transcribed dialogue. He properly titles his enclosures. At first, his letters read more like reports than actually engaging the reader in a dialogue. As the correspondence intensifies, the borders between narrated stories and personal commentary become fuzzy. He now fills in a fragmented text without clarifying his position as author. In the eighteenth century, this aspect of novelistic narrative was a special characteristic of the letter form, where anecdotes could mingle unrestricted with reflections, advice, amorous dedications, and pragmatic details. This interweaving of styles, themes, and structures was attributed to a specifically feminine epistolary writing strategy.[29]

Albert's letters gain momentum through greater anecdotal details, humorous interjections, puns, and the lover's enthusiastic address of his beloved. When his letters finally turn into a diary and travelogue, he has combined all genres of personal writing with literary history, theory, poetry, and short prose forms, their structures intertwined with their themes. He literally writes himself free of literary conventions, linguistic and political tyranny, and, as I will discuss below, the provocative female voice, his mother-tongue.[30]

MAIL-ORDER MANUAL

Choderlos de Laclos had his Vicomte de Valmont write a love letter on the naked back of a prostitute to conquer the doubts and heart of Presidente de Tourvel.

The epistolary novel contoured the poetic margin of the modern novel's generation as a literary genre. The theoretic dispute about literary forms, authenticity, the novel's moral and literary values as well as the gender division within the fictive worlds and the audience found nourishment in the mimetic conduct of letters:

Beyond their uses as form or validation, letters and gossip figure in many other novels as plot devices, themes, perhaps even emblems within the novel of its own nature, genesis, both its lie and its feared truth about itself.[31]

During the eighteenth century, the epistolary form pushed the plights of women, and women's "natural" writing techniques, into the foreground of literary representation and criticism.[32] In connection with the increase in private correspondences, model books for letter-writing, and published letters in "moral journals" ("Moralische Wochenschriften"), the epistolary novel became ever more popular.[33] Voiced, narrated, and authored female desire provided a stimulus for the debate on the merits of the novelistic form and its reception in a repressive patriarchal society. Silvia Bovenschen cautions the twentieth-century critic against an equation of gender and genre when it comes to women's "natural" literary talents. She contends that the chance for emancipation through the letter form adheres to a structural "dialectics of exclusion" ("Dialektik des Ausschlusses"), which restricted women to the margins of literature and excluded them from genre-poetic criticism.[34] Shari Benstock also underscores the delicate balance of women's writing:

> Woman's desire as she penned it in her own loveletters represented a powerful threat to social/sexual institutions precisely because it risked going out of control. . . . It was important that this desire serve patriarchal ends and needs, that it be *rewritten* by the patriarchy in such a guise that woman would think the desire so written belonged to her.[35]

From their beginning, Shari Benstock argues, "letters have been made to serve (as) 'literature;' that is, letters have been made to serve the law of literary *genre*" (257). "Moralische Wochenschriften" and educational journals of various kinds were geared toward the female audience, when it was discovered that due to the rise of bourgeois economics and family ideals, daughters and wives had room and time for their own enjoyment, their own cultivation as women, and as readers and writers.[36] Benstock's conclusion illustrates the romanticization effect of letter-writing. Her contention, that the epistolary genre "is not infallible, but rather a witness to its fallibility," and that "an absent, silent, desired feminine serves in her absence to instigate the writing and marks in her *difference* that which is produced through the writing," rekindles my desire to analyze Bemmann's work in order to find out if and how the gendered history of epistolary fiction serves contemporary "literature."[37]

I readdress my attention to *Erwins Badezimmer* via *mail-order*, and specifically through an example of nineteenth century criticism of eighteenth century epistolary fiction. When Gottfried Keller's narrator of his novel *Green Henry* (1879/80), the older Heinrich Lee, reminisces about his days with the "reader family" ("Leserfamilie"), novels, but especially epistolary novels that "preserve the style of the wicked customs of the previous century," are shown to have a disastrous effect on female virtues:

> The novels split mainly into two kinds. One preserved the expression of the bad morals of the previous century in deplorable correspondences and seduction stories, the other consisted of coarse chivalric romances. The girls kept to the first kind with great interest and let themselves be kissed and fondled by their participatory lovers to the point of satiation; for us boys, these prosaic and non-sensual/non-sensical accounts of a reprehensible sensuality were fortunately still unpalatable, and we contented ourselves by grabbing any chivalric story and retreating with the same.[38]

While the girls "changed from lover to lover and still were not taken home [as a bride] by any, so that they were left on the shelf in the midst of the foul-smelling library with a horde of small children" ("Liebhaber auf Liebhaber wechselten und doch von keinem heimgeführt wurden, so daß sie mitten in der übelriechenden Bibliothek sitzen blieben mit einer Herde kleiner Kinder"), the narrator is put through an ordeal by his friend to prove his novel-inspired, megalomaniac tales. Ashamed of himself for confusing reality and fiction, "I was thoroughly cured of lying once and for all" ("war ich vom Lügen einmal gründlich geheilt," 104). Fictive imagination is disclosed as lying. The narrator feels the need to distance himself from this type of "romantic" exaggeration. In recounting his epiphanic experience, he simultaneously claims that his autobiography portrays the truth and nothing but the truth.

Readership is divided along genre and gender lines. The literary frame and the totality of the novel—male autobiographical discourse—envelopes and caricatures the fragment of female epistolary discourse that is included. The narrator's harsh words echo the criticism formerly leveled against the novelistic genre itself.[39] By defining epistolary fiction as both "prosaisch und unsinnlich," novel and autobiography emancipate themselves, become literature.[40] Epistolary writing and reading depicts a "reprehensible sensuality." The word *Sinn*, which is named twice in close proximity, is ambiguous here: "sense as meaning" as well as "sensuality." In the nineteenth century, *unsinnlich* could mean nonsensual or nonsensible (today, the adjective for nonsensible is *unsinnig*). Epistolary fiction's doubled discourse (the "girls" read and simultaneously let themselves be kissed) is therefore defined as nonsensuous as well as nonsensical. While the reading arouses the "girls," watching their display of desire dampens the narrator-agent's appetite. He can neither stomach nor enjoy the doubly promiscuous scene of voyeuristic lovemaking. In spite of this, he himself witnesses and describes it to us, thereby creating yet another voyeuristic framework of reading and writing.[41] To the male youngsters, the exhibitionist quality of female and male sexual discourse is still *ungenießbar* (not enjoyable/indigestible). Food metaphors abound in this paragraph. The little word *sattsam* (mollified, amply satiated) equates the "girls'" reading experience with a lewd, voracious appetite: the novels are consumed as rapidly and indiscriminately as the lovers.[42]

In Keller's language, female sexuality is wedged between "participating lovers" and the fictional account of the lovers' discourse. The male lovers do the actual kissing, the "girls" merely "*let* themselves be kissed." As adults, the male fictional counterparts entangle the heroines in love's laces. With their chivalric stories, which he does not call novels (even though they were), the boys retreat from the public arena of reading, from the economic discourse of desire. Their chivalric adventure romances reinstall the desired and aesthetically productive distance between activity and passivity, lover and beloved, between writing and reading, in the spirit of *Minnesang*. In a *tableau vivant* of the all powerful yet chronically unstable separation of the private from the public, the privacy of female reading as sexual practice becomes public knowledge, whereas male reading practice is constructed as separate from sexual desire and therefore privatized. Wedged between male desires and the order of the doubled mailing system (sender-receiver-sender), female desire is mail (male)-ordered to custom. In this scene of reading and writing, Keller semantically marks female sexuality as obscenity but, caught within the fictional feedback loop, he syntactically renders female sexual desire meaningless.[43]

The fusing of the physical and mental senses in the narrator's language sexualizes the "girls'" reading experience while at the same time depriving it of meaning and neutralizing it as a threat to the patriarchal system. The "girls" never become women.[44] Sexualized discourse is played out in their physical and linguistic role of hermeneutic intermediary. *Women*'s lives as *women* take place in and between books of letters. Their lives remain fictions, and the literary discourse portraying their desires is castigated as inauthentic, a fiction of a fiction. "Reprehensible" female sexuality is thus removed to the imaginary world, and the literary form which brings it forth is feminized in turn. Sex is gendered and the gendered sex is repressed.[45] Because the dominant signifier immediately forgets this genderization process, the illusion of "feminine sex" remains. The gendered version of female sexuality reappears in epistolary form, one could say as allegorized "sexual desire."

Keller's historical portrait of feminine desire foreshadows the relation between feminism and postmodernism. According to Owens, feminine desire for the acknowledgment and toleration of difference is supposed to fill the political hole in postmodernism. The role of feminism in the discourse of postmodernism becomes even more disconcerting when we look at Shari Benstock's description of the representation and proliferation of the gender/genre link, which she sees as the result of a gap:

> In this gap between the repression and the action of desire, between the reality and the fiction of desire, the link between *genre* and gender is forged: it is written into a discourse of feminine desire.[46]

When Fiedler applauds a closing of gaps—between reality and fiction, between high and popular art—and Owens commends a liaison between postmodernism and feminism, they simultaneously forge a sex/gender link and a gender/genre connection. They write both difference and the overcoming of difference in the name of Woman. Through the discourse of the Other, "the scholar imagines for himself a way to fill a gap in the self's narrative."[47]

The culturally produced and reproduced images of the Feminine have been translated onto the genre of "private writings" such as letters, journals, diaries, notebooks, and memoirs to serve both restorational as well as feminist ideologies. Peggy Kamuf discusses a gendered "lack in the scene of history" which the feminist search for a discernible female reading and writing subject seeks to reinvent (158). In accord with my interpretation of Keller's gender/genre tableau, a tableau that can represent feminine desire only as a representation of a representation, Kamuf contends that "the encounter with a supplemental difference takes place as fiction in history" (158). Kamuf discusses this culturally determined feminine labor:

> The work (or play) of the Penelopean text implies a mutual interruption of fiction and history, feminine and masculine space. Its back and forth movement makes/unmakes, ravels/unravels logical or "natural" oppositions—including the opposition that organizes the field of mutually exclusive contraries, that of logic or reason to unreason or madness. The writing of such a text is not attributable to any subject, whether singular or collective. On the contrary, it is the subject that is written into the text, and thus into the play of differences with itself. (164)

The female subject (un)writes itself as it creates. It continues to subject itself to difference. In comparison, Shari Benstock identifies the already metaphorized "hymen" as the gender mark of women, with the form of the letter, the genre of "epistolary fiction." Both letter and "hymen" make possible and demand a double writing. Folded and (re)pressed into the crevice of the letter paper, she argues that

> the hymen "merges with what it seems to be derived from," sharing in its derivation something with epistolary fiction, which forms itself

as a literary genre from the letters that it incorporated as the very
mark of its generic form. Repeating its own story (of desire), the frame
of epistolary fiction (the letter, the sign of difference) is folded into the
generic form.[48]

As Benstock reads the "hymen" into and out of the epistolary genre, her
essay becomes part of the (un)raveling textual work that Peggy Kamuf
illustrates. Peggy Kamuf and Shari Benstock not only write against an
androgynous dialectics of erasing the difference (between man and
woman, letters and literature, etc.) but also against a celebration of this
difference. In their criticism, the

> hymeneal writing enfolds letters and literature in such a way that their
> differences and similarities are maintained . . . , establishing a parasit-
> ical economy in which 'letters' and 'literature' live *off of* and are com-
> posed *out of* each other.[49]

Kamuf's *Signature Pieces* draws from epistolary fiction itself, whereas
Benstock acknowledges that she is "analyzing the critical interpretations
of epistolary fiction" (295). Instead of "closing the gap," Kamuf and
Benstock attempt to describe, execute, and write a "parasitical economy" between letters and literature, and between gender and genre.
Rather than ignoring that the feminine discourse of desire is wedged
between androgyny and difference, *between* books and lovers, their feminist criticism mimetically transcribes this predicament, however, not in
order to "close the gap," but to contour it each time anew. In the following segment, I contrast Owens' and Fiedler's "discourse of the
Other," and Benstock's "parasitical economy" to Bemmann's epistolary
inscription of the female voice in *Erwins Badezimmer oder die
Gefährlichkeit der Sprache*.

THE DISCOURSE OF THE OTHER

What, indeed, is so dangerous about language and *Erwins Badezimmer?*
"It is indeed refreshing how you always get straight to the point!" ("Es
ist doch erfrischend, wie Sie immer gleich zum Konkreten kommen!"
34). The concrete point in this case concerns the tale of Rudimer
Fahlbart's murder of his wife Mara. Mara's story actually hides behind
a linguistic sample sentence for the tense variation in "hadubaldian language forms": "One year after he had slain his wife, he recognized her
innocence" ("Ein Jahr, nachdem er sein Weib erschlagen hatte, erkannte
er ihre Unschuld," 26). Rachel's inquiry restores the saga surrounding
this quote to life. It is telling that, of all the "hadubaldian" sentences in
the text, Fahlbart's epiphany is chosen, rather than, for example, Mara's

use of the subjunctive in one of her sentences. Thus, Albert can be credited with resurrecting the female voice from patriarchal oblivion. On the same note, the sample sentence forms a *mise en abyme* of Albert's letters. His words remain the sole trace of the correspondence and reflect his reeducation through female logic, which isn't one. Let's read this clever contraption!

Due to Rachel's question, Albert searches for the source and finds it in the "Rudimer Fahlbart Saga." After Albert has read and transcribed this saga, he views it as a "classical case of a deadly misunderstanding" ("klassischen Fall tödlichen Mißverständnisses," 46). Contrary to Albert, Rachel is not satisfied with this simplified linguistic interpretation. He reacts, puzzled:

> What you further write about this story has confused me considerably. If I have understood you correctly, you don't think of the scene by the creek as a misunderstanding at all: "If this Mara had not wanted to sleep with Rudimer," you write," then she would have only had to tell him, how she had meant her idiomatic expression," and then you add: "Maybe he appealed to her!" Honestly: I was a little shocked about so much directness, my dear! . . . Now, if I really think about it once again, then the dialogue with you, temporarily unfortunately only par distance, moves me particularly strongly because you unwittingly discover a sensual-concrete reality in these seemingly so decrepit texts.[50]

Albert's shocked appreciation of Rachel's directness and love of the sensually concrete links a preconception about the epistolary form to her gender—or the other way around. To start "in medias res," as "naturally" as possible, has long been characteristic of epistolary correspondence.[51] In the same vein, women have always been considered gossipy, transmitting "neue Zeitungen" (news) at lightning speed while spinning yarn, plucking poultry, and shelling beans, from fence to fence and window to window—and in letters to their female friends.[52] Like so many male mentors in the eighteenth century (as one of whom he at this point still considers himself), Albert applauds Rachel for her "strong bent for language" ("starke Ader fürs Sprachliche," 34) while linking her interest in language directly to her blood (Ader = blood vessel).[53] In the same breath, he resurrects another attribute of feminine epistolary discourse: "That's exactly why children also rather love the concrete" ("Kinder lieben eben auch eher das Konkrete," 34). The child-woman myth of the Romantics, most observable in comments about the writer Bettina Brentano, outlines a desexualized (childlike) and therefore controllable hypersexuality, a pantheistic merging with nature and verbal impishness associated with true Romantic spirit.[54] To write naturally means to be uninhibited, even to contradict socially acceptable manners, to be naive and unconcerned with one's impression on others, as well as ignorant of scholastic knowledge.[55] It also means to ask questions, to show one's vulnerability as strength, unconcerned about others' opinions.

Rachel's inquiry into the reason for Mara's death "has been the most fun for Albert" ("hat [Albert] am meisten Spaß gemacht," 34). He exploits her curiosity for his own enjoyment, uses her—his male fantasy—for his own legend-making, his own autobiographical ends. The intersubjectivity created through the correspondence with Rachel is an artificial construct by which Albert can reerect his modernist self. In a dialogue with the "Other," the author can best demonstrate the need to return to language's and the male subject's "dimensions of depth" *(Tiefendimensionen)*. Albert reeducates himself through the entertaining "mother-tongue" and rewrites literature by writing from and over the "Feminine."

Despite the intention of the intricate pattern woven with the "Fahlbart-Saga" to attest to the dangerous fun entailed in language games, Albert is enjoying himself. According to Albert, the narrator of the "Rudimer Fahlbart Saga" knows "how dangerous it can be not to take language seriously, and that characteristic alone justifies the exertion, in my opinion, to have restored this text for you" ("wie gefährlich es sein kann, Sprache nicht genau zu nehmen, und allein schon dieser Zug rechtfertigt meiner Meinung nach die Mühe, diesen Text für Sie wiederhergestellt zu haben," 61). While Albert resurrects this text for the future, his rewriting duplicates the textual/sexual sacrifice. We, as readers, can only glimpse Rachel's reaction to the story through Albert's filtered description of her reading experience. He views Rachel's prevailing doubt about the *Eindeutigkeit* of the murder as an identification with the female character's fate. According to Albert, Rachel brings great seriousness and emotive "consternation" *(Betroffenheit)* back to a mere "archaic-literary figure" ("archaisch-literarische Figur," 62–63). He considers her reading "life-giving": she instills dead texts with new life, literally gives birth to them anew. Her "spontaneous partisanship" ("spontane Parteinahme") restores a "sensual-concrete reality" ("sinnlich-konkrete Wirklichkeit") that was aborted by orthodox language philosophy and Foucaultian discourse textuality (62).

Through the polyauctorial frames in the epistolary novel, the actual identification strategy is fictionally inverted. Bemmann as real author and Albert as epistolary author both identify women with certain "emotional" reading practices:

> Your astonishing and yet so consistent interpretation takes its arguments from a field which for the most part lay fallow in me. To introduce impression and feeling to the interpretation of a text, up to now seemed to me to be impertinent and not defensible from the scientific vantage point.[56]

Rachel's response triggers Albert's awareness of this reading practice. Albert begins to reconsider his scientific reservations and consequently identifies Rachel with Mara: "a woman, who for me even somewhat begins to take on your traits (which for heaven's sakes does not imply that I wish this awful fate onto you!)" ("eine Frau, die für mich sogar schon ein wenig Ihre Züge anzunehmen beginnt [was um Himmels willen nicht heißen soll, daß ich Ihnen dieses schlimme Schicksal wünsche!]" 63). Albert makes Mara real—he rewrites her story, gives her a voice, and projects Rachel's features onto her—but fictionalizes the absent Rachel by endowing her with symbolic value. The parenthetical sentence aims to counter the narrative threat invoked through his fictionalization: that Mara's fate could rub off on Rachel. The reader has to collaborate, because Mara's fate is visible and her voice at least readable, whereas Rachel's voice remains "in transit," subject to Albert's quotations and interpretations.

In the restored tale, Mara's two sentences—"I give myself up to you" ("Ich gebe mich dir hin") and "I lay my hand on you" ("Ich lege meine Hand auf dich")—exemplify language's ambiguity through cultural, sexual, and social difference. In broad grammatical terms, the first sentence signifies a self-controlled subjection to the other. The subject gives itself as a direct object to the other as indirect object. The second sentence objectifies the other in a prepositional phrase. Both sentences split the subject of the utterance into agent and direct object, into self and other of self.[57] Whether Mara utters "Ich gebe mich dir hin" to deliver herself into the arms of a protector or whether Fahlbart understands it to mean a willful surrender to his sexual appetite, the sentence describes her subjection to a strict sexual-political dichotomy, the law of the "phallic culture." The woman is never one but always already conceived as a given. The man stands in position of the receiver of the gift. When confronted with Fahlbart's different interpretation, Mara gives herself up to him both for protection (her father's law) and sexually (Fahlbart's law).

According to her father's law, she interprets Fahlbart's sexual advances as his intention to take her in wedlock. She "gives herself up to him" only after she determines that he is a lord (Herr). Since a nobleman is supposed to act "honorably" (ehrenhaft), she assumes his trespass will be accounted for the next day (49). During their first and sexual encounter, she combined her own understanding of her words with Fahlbart's exhibited desire. During the second encounter, she becomes aware that a simple combination of the semantic laws of their cultures does not suffice:

"Why are you startled?" Mara asked with a smile. "I thought I acted in accordance with your wishes. Why aren't you wearing festive clothes?

Little honor do I thus gain with you!" "Why festive clothes?" Rudimer stammered, who now no longer knew at all, what was going on. "Do you want to lay me out on the mountain like an adorned animal offering? "Who the offering is in this case, must still reveal itself," Mara said and stood at Rudimer's side, still with her hand on his shoulder.[58]

In the attempt to translate her desire into his, to account for the difference—her *Versprechen*—she victimizes herself even more. Her *Versprechen* (a promise and a slip of the tongue) stands at the crossroads of her fate. The word *versprechen*, with which Fahlbart accosts her at the stream, converts the rape into a sexual contract: "Didn't you promise to give yourself up to me?" ("Versprachst du nicht, dich mir hinzugeben?" 49). She bows to his interpretation of her sentence based on another phallic law: "What was promised must probably be kept" ("Da muß wohl gehalten werden, was versprochen wurde," 49). Due to Fahlbart's interpretation of "Ich gebe mich dir hin," she promises him sexual submission. But *versprechen* also indicates the linguistic imbalance created by their sexual and cultural difference. As she realizes how Fahlbart decodes her sentence, the "slip of tongue" in this heterocultural and heterosexual meeting is claimed as a promise. Fahlbart never questions his own language, nor the effect of his language on her. His phallic desire overrules any ambiguity. It is visibly unambiguous: *eindeutig*.

At the end of the saga, when a compatriot, her former fiancé, saves her from being raped and killed by the servants, Mara defends herself against Fahlbart's accusation: "If I had not given myself up to him, I would no longer be alive" ("Wenn ich mich ihm nicht hingegeben hätte, wäre ich nicht mehr am Leben," 56). Fahlbart is still unable to grasp language that is not *eindeutig*, that doesn't represent *his* law, *his* culture. He kills both his wife and the visitor: "These words go completely beyond Rudimer's comprehension" ("Diese Worte gehen Rudimer völlig über den Verstand," 56). Misunderstandings, or the coexistence of two or more equally valid interpretations, are impossible in his mind and language, they simply usurp his law. Had Mara not given herself up to Fahlbart according to his own law, he would have accused her of "betrayal"; but since she honored what she "promised" with "loose tongue," he stigmatizes her, the exotic foreigner, as a "loose woman," a stigma that rubbed off on his servants as well. Mara's desire has no place and no words. Caught between the law of the father and the law of the lover, her wishes remain unvoiced, written into a phallic textual economy.[59] For Fahlbart, all women speak the language of servitude, since he cannot hear or bear any other: "Should I take a woman [for a wife], who speaks exactly like my maids, each of whom lets me have my way with them according to my wishes?" ("Soll ich eine Frau nehmen, die genauso spricht wie meine Mägde, von denen mir jede nach Wunsch zu Willen ist?" 47). Only at the moment when Belegar, Mara's father, is about to kill him, does the difference inherent in and producing linguistic systems provide a small glimmer of hope for him. He dies at the hands of his own law:

> At that moment, Belegar laid his hand on [Rudimer's] shoulder and said: "I lay my hand on you, Rudimer." Surprised, Rudimer looked up, seemed to regain hope once again and said: "How should I understand that?" "How you have always understood it," said Belegar. "After my daughter yielded to your linguistic usage at your first encounter, I, too, want to do the same right now."[60]

How does the saga affect Rachel's and Albert's discourse? In Rachel's opinion, Mara's rape could have been a willing surrender and her slaying a suicide. Albert reacts appropriately. Delightfully shocked by "soviel Direktheit" (62), he writes:

> Your interpretation is nothing short of fantastic, albeit derived from very feminine logic, when you write: "This woman has given herself to Rudimer in every sense, and then she must find out that he does not perceive this as a present but rather as a disgrace. Something worse cannot happen to a woman" and when you draw the conclusion from this that Mara uttered this phrase consciously, because she wanted to die.[61]

Rachel's "feminine logic" defines Mara's action as yielding to the phallic law "in every sense of the word." She evaluates Mara's subjection on the grounds of the phallic sexual economy *ex negativo* ("something worse cannot happen to a woman"). According to Rachel, Mara fuses both laws. She possesses linguistic sensitivity because she is a woman and because her survival depends on the "correct" readings of the phallic law. Her desire expresses itself in a plethora of counteractive meanings. Thinking intersubjectively through her gender-determined socialization, Mara facilitates communication between two seemingly antagonistic phallic laws. This enables her to discern genres from genres (sexual meaning from political meaning), but produces mixed genres in her phraseology. This medley of genres in the shape of intersubjectivity stands in for what would be her voice, a female desire that is an aggregate state of the Law of the Father.

Mara's desire to have (or not to have) sex can only be voiced in predestined formulas, in universal grammatical subjection to the desire of the phallic signifier. Her problem is precisely that she *cannot* verbalize a female desire.[62] Her story illustrates a classic case of the "hysteric" woman, a woman unable to live with the "castrated sexuality" but at the same time unable to positively define what her sexuality might be.

She resorts to masquerading male-defined feminine traits to produce a realm beyond the phallic law, in which she can preserve and/or die with her "difference." Mara ends her tortuous life in turning the symbolic phallus—the sword and language—against herself.[63]

Rachel, like Mara, is unable to verbalize Mara's, or for that matter, her own desire other than in Albert's words, within Albert's presignified discourse. Ambiguity and epistolary intersubjectivity speak her voice. With the help of Rachel's "authentic" feminine voice, rape becomes a willing surrender, murder becomes premeditated suicide. The discourse of the Other realigns the correspondence points of the mail-order. Albert can thus wittily extend the "sword" analogy to Rachel's "feminine logic." "As far as your answer to my question regarding Mara's behavior is concerned, I *admit defeat once and for all*" ("Was Ihre Antwort auf meine Frage zu Maras Verhalten betrifft, so *gebe ich mich endgültig geschlagen*," 82; my italics). He thereby places nominal power metaphorically into her hands, into hands directed by "impression and feeling": "and I fear that you will cause even more of my principles to sway—but what am I saying *I fear?* I should really say: I hope so with all of my heart!" ("und ich fürchte, daß Sie noch weitere meiner Maximen ins Wanken bringen werden—doch was heißt *ich fürchte?* Eigentlich will ich sagen: ich hoffe das von ganzem Herzen!" 83). In proliferating situations laden with ambiguity, in resurrecting Rachel's voice as quotes, Albert reproduces Fahlbart's murder of Mara on a textual level.

Albert's second poem illustrates both his fear of male self-delusion and the "dream of hope" *(Hoffnungstraum)* residing in his relationship with Rachel (133):

Do I learn	Lerne ich
to recognize you	dich erkennen
Jacob recognized Rachel	Jakob erkannte Rachel
without words	ohne Worte
Behold	Schau
instead of hidden violence	statt verhehlter Gewalt
finding	findend
giving	gebend
submerging	eintauchend
in the counter-image	im Gegenbild
you	du (134).

Instead of "concealed rape" ("verhehlte Vergewaltigung") and violence, Albert's love poem *woos* Rachel into Mara's place (133). After reading the poem, she has sex with Albert for the first time (135). Albert's poem dramatizes Mara's words. He gives himself up to her image, an image that is only comprehensible as a "counterimage." He appears to write himself into the discourse of difference, in which this difference consists of fixed gender qualities. Echoing Owens' final sentences, Albert maintains that women have always been versed in the art of ambivalence and ambiguity: "It looks as if women had always been superior to men in this art" ("Es sieht so aus, als seien Frauen seit je den Männern in dieser Kunst überlegen gewesen," 82).[64] He draws all his energy from Rachel, granting her the power to emancipate artistic creativity from autocratic ossification: "Foremost, I have to thank you that all these encrusted shells of my former life suddenly burst open and I begin to feel like an actual, live human being" ("Vor allem Dir habe ich dafür zu danken, daß all diese Verkrustungen meines bisherigen Lebens plötzlich aufbrechen und ich mich wie ein richtiger, lebendiger Mensch zu fühlen beginne," 106). But how is this ossification to be averted, when he writes his poem " Herbst" (autumn) in the past tense, already nostalgically harking back to the sound of her voice as a barely audible message from beyond?

Did for a few steps	Wurde für wenige Schritte
inaccessibly close	unerreichbar nah
far away next to me	fern neben mir
a message become audible	eine Botschaft hörbar,
a harmony	ein Gleichklang
in the sound of other steps	im Geräusch anderer Schritte,
in the timbre	im Klang
of another voice?	einer anderen Stimme? (115)

Albert romanticizes Rachel's voice as the unattainable yet immediate address of his own voice. He romanticizes their correspondence, which practices an ideal of closeness between the sexes that is based on distance and difference. But the romantization demolishes its own foundation. It harbors a narcissistic echo: *Gleichklang* (harmony, accord). It conceals the violence done to the other (to Echo) in order to bring her into "accord" with the speaker.

Throughout the eighteen stanzas of Albert's first poem, Rachel's voice and footsteps parallel the speaker's verbalizations. Their message lies in their sound, and this *sound* lingers in his memory. She "echoes" his steps, his words, "of which I know nothing any more" ("von denen ich nichts mehr weiß," 108–109). While Albert is in prison, Rachel functions as the other pole of the soundproof cell wall, which does not return his words when he speaks. The manipulative echo over the prison system's loudspeakers, however, almost drives him insane (119). In order to avoid political brainwashing, he warps its frequency and forces language on a detour. This warping technique finds its direct opposite in the poem, in which he strives to transcribe message and sound, to rewrite the distance between self and other, into *Gleichklang*, into rhythmic *Gleichschritt* (marching in step). In prison as well as in his poems, Rachel's echo prevents the "void" of self-hypnosis and circular *Selbstgespräch* (speaking with oneself) from overwhelming him. In all moments of crisis, Rachel solidifies as the external guarantor of the writer's self, holding up the motherly mirror to his eyes.[65]

"[I]naccessibly close/ far away next to my mouth" ("[U]nerreichbar nah/ fern neben meinem Mund," 108–109), Rachel's voice takes on the ghostlike quality of her letters. Invoked by Albert's letters, her voice remarks its absence. Rachel's existence as Other is recalled in the moment of its address. Her voice originates and ends in the shadowy realm of the monologic echo, there to function as symbolic other, contourlessly close but also controllably distanced by the speaking subject. He perceives her ghostly message in his desire for a *Gleichklang*, a harmonious refrain to his own voice that is not his own voice.[66] Albert transforms Rachel into an eternal ghost of Woman, the riddle and the pulse of life, the always absent ultimate present, "that forces me/ on the path of death,/ in the jaws of death,/ to ask for life" ("das mich zwingt, / auf dem Weg des Todes, / im Rachen des Todes/ nach dem Leben zu fragen," 115).

In the next stanza, her sacrifice to his textual order is cannibalized: "Is that life:/ to take in something other,/ that does not come out of myself/ and that changes me?/ That he cannot devour,/ the worm/ that feeds on my life" ("Ist das Leben: / anderes aufnehmen,/ das nicht aus mir selbst kommt/ und das mich verändert?/ Das kann er nicht fressen,/ der Wurm,/ der mir am Leben frißt," 115–116). The "Other" has to be consumed to change him for life. The savoring of the "Other," the unreal, the allegorized woman, will make him "unpalatable" *(ungenießbar)* for death, will provide him with the eternal life of Nosferatu. *Aufnehmen* connotes "to take up," "to take in" and in an audiovisual sense also "to record." Does Rachel's blood stain the letters, does the epistolary representation of her sacrifice show the vampire copyist at work?

While the poetic voice denies a cannibalistic feast outright—"Proximity,/that does not want to devour, but rather warm" ("Nähe,/ die nicht vertilgen will, sondern wärmen," 116)—it *takes up* the vocabulary, invokes what it attempts to revoke, regurgitates its meal, just as it cannot stomach the female voice. Mangled and picked over, created through destruction, the female voice allegorizes the process of Freudian *Verneinung*. The woman treads lightly in this vampiristic intercourse. Vocally emaciated and without a visual representation, her words disappear into

Albert's mirror-writing. Dracula's rape is written as voluntary intercourse, in which the virginal maiden discovers her repressed desire. Amply satiated with her blood, his text depicts a writing process that restores the "female voice" to the phallic order in the name of the female voice.[67]

In confinement on the train that should have taken him to Rachel, Albert can only remember her voice as a *Gleichklang*. In order to protect her identity, he rips her letters "into tiny shreds" ("in winzige Fetzen") and throws them from the train window. As he follows their dissemination into the elements, he metaphorically turns them into snowflakes: "It looked as if it began to snow, and I could only hope that the people further back in the train did not suspect anything else. There they were flying away, all the words that you wrote me" ("Es sah aus, als fange es an zu schneien, und ich konnte nur hoffen, daß die Leute weiter hinten im Zug nichts anderes vermuteten. Da flogen sie nun dahin, all die Wörter, die Du mir geschrieben hast," 177). The letters' "otherness" evaporates in this doubled rewriting of the mailing code in his text. A little later, Albert also has to dispose of his own *Brieftasche* ("wallet," here "portfolio," 179):

> Subsequently, the train thundered out onto a bridge, and when it was directly over the river, I threw the portfolio in a wide arch, saw it fly through the parapet of the arch of the bridge, sail down and hit the water. A small current, a little foam, and already my second existence drifted down river into inaccessibility.[68]

Soon after, Albert is caught by the police and taken back to his point of departure:

> Now I had the opportunity to view the stations of my journey once again in the opposite sequence, the river, which carried away my papers, the bushes, in which Amelie's fairy tale book rested like Sleeping Beauty in the rose hedge.[69]

Amalie's text has not only become part of nature; the female author is denied authorship—"Sleeping Beauty" has already been written by the Grimm Brothers. Amalie simply rescued it from oblivion. In Albert's metaphor, her book becomes indistinguishable from the Grimm protagonist Sleeping Beauty. And further, there is no mention or trace of Rachel's letters. They are already erased from his testimonial account, written over to him, into his "letter binder" (*Briefmappe*, 179), which is renamed "my papers" ("meine Papiere") in this moment of autobiographical reflection. A *Briefmappe* not only carries letters, money, important identification documents, and fragments of all genres, but also holds Albert's reformed self, his "zweite Existenz" (179).

Albert's appropriations in the form of a *Briefmappe* therefore symbolize the entire novel ("A story in letters with various enclosures") and the genesis of epistolary fiction. Once women's letters had innovated novelistic prose, their epistolary discourse was discarded to the margins of literature. Gottfried Keller's use of language demonstrated the association of epistolarity with gender and ethical decline: Letters indeed became "reprehensible" in the sense of "discardable" *(verwerflich)*. Albert's disposal of the *Briefmappe* plots the course for the beginning and the end of letters and the novel. After dispatching the *Briefmappe*, the epistolary correspondence ends. Albert's final letter again turns into a report, into his papers, his autobiography. Women's works, which are always already ma(i)le-ordered, are relegated to the other side of the literary spectrum, to fairy tales, the fiction of a fiction. With Albert's recollection of the fairy tale book and his failure to recollect Rachel's letters, he reconstructs the dichotomy of fact versus fiction, highbrow art versus lowbrow art. While he visualizes "his papers" floating down the Goethean primeval river, women's texts, once penetrated, are deposited as dead letters to be retrieved by future mail-orders.

Even though Rachel picks up Albert's papers and converts them into a political pamphlet, his "Notes from Underground" fail to sustain the dialogic poetics of its namesake.[70] "Briefe in winzigen Fetzen-Briefmappe-meine Papiere": within this *mail ordered* move, the mutilated body of Rachel's voice is sucked into his letter case, which contains *Fälscherkunst* (the art of counterfeiting, 179), and is reprinted as "meine Papiere."[71] Rachel's letters served their reorientation purpose and become dispensable. Her written words are no longer necessary to stimulate his writing and self-formation. The process has reached a point of self-generation. When the train returns Albert to the station, the epistolary novel reveals itself as a story of inversion, as an art of counterfeiting the female voice to write difference as *Gleichklang*. "Woman" is always in Bemmann's mind: Hans Bemmann "thinks (with his head) her possible thoughts and writes them to her" ("denkt (mit seinem Kopf) ihre möglichen Gedanken und schreibt sie ihr—").[72] Bemmann's novel assures that "letters" return as autobiography, so that literature can deliver the auteur.

Rachel, as *mail-ordered* bride—she is persuaded by Albert's epistolary travelogue/diary—follows Albert into the land "where people dissolve like sugar in a cup of coffee." Her decision combines feminist ideals with Romantic politics. Rachel's voluntary self-banning resembles a female frontier mentality, metamorphosing her into the epitome of patriarchally conjured feminism. Through the intersubjectivity of epistolary intercourse, Bemmann hopes to achieve a dissolution of petrified categories and *Eindeutigkeit*, but the text solidifies at either end. The female voice is made to recant itself, and a dangerous *Eindeutigkeit* simply reforms into a male-dominated humanitarian universality.

The rhetoric of literary criticism concerning "trivial" and "postmodern" fiction, as well as the rhetoric of authors' self-definitions, cannot be considered separately from the issue of the "female voice." The very advantage of Hans Bemmann's novel is that it politicizes this controlled intersubjectivity, the opening and closing of the gap between postmodernism and feminism. Hans Bemmann's attempt to cast off the inhibiting weight of the crisis of modernity by utilizing the form of an epistolary novel demonstrates the strategy of refurbishing the legitimacy of the grand narratives and their sickly authorial self with the help of "Vive la Difference Feminism." Bemmann's novel contemplates the survival of language and political responsibility by placing the burden of political insubordination and the fulfillment of Romantic and utopian desires on the letter form. Indeed, in his novel, the letter (i.e., phallic signifier, letter of the alphabet, and epistolary letter) always arrives at its destination.

CHAPTER 5

Romancing the Post:
Peter Handke's
Short Letter, Long Farewell

Telepathic, self-indulgent, hindered messenger-angels fly through
two of Wim Wender's feature films.

As the avid video-watcher will have recognized, the subtitle alludes to a
comedy/action film of the 1980s: *Romancing the Stone*.[1] This movie not
only ruptures the generic boundaries of film and novel but also shows
how the generic intersection creates the suspense on which the film and
the novel thrive. The epistolary device forces novel and film into a dialogue and tests their potential for survival. While Handke's *Der kurze
Brief zum langen Abschied* (*Short Letter, Long Farewell*, 1972) hardly
fits any conventional definitions of an epistolary novel, its mailing system may be just a stone's throw from the postal route of the epistolary
treasure map in *Romancing the Stone*.[2] Considering Peter Handke's own
aesthetic occupation and fascination with film and cinematic language,[3]
his cooperation with Wim Wenders, as well as *Der kurze Brief*'s overt
flirtation with the Westerns of John Ford, an intergeneric angle suggested itself for this chapter.[4] I will argue in this chapter that Handke's
structural representation of epistolarity and the mechanisms of generic
interaction and mediation in the films by Robert Zemeckis and John
Ford are not only comparable but also co-constitutive of each other.[5]

Dirk Göttsche criticizes Peter Handke's later prose, including *Der
kurze Brief zum langen Abschied*, as a "gradual exit from the modern
literary tradition of language skepticism" ("schrittweisen Ausstieg aus
der modernen literarischen Sprachskepsistradition") and a "reconstruc-
tion of narration" ("Rekonstruktion des Erzählens"), although it structurally and thematically underscores the acclaimed search for the
potential of language.[6] In Göttsche's view, the language crisis carries
within it a dilemma that threatens to bring literary development to a
standstill. This dilemma must be rendered productive in order to deliver

"an orientation-function for the modern subject's problematics of existence" ("eine Orientierungsfunktion für die Existenzproblematik des
modernen Subjekts," 349). In *Die Produktivität der Sprachkrise*,
Göttsche thus develops a capitalist economy of literary criticism. The
letter becomes the guarantee of surplus productivity, that stock option
whose profits rise the more it is traded.[7] This economy of desire
romances the post as the trademark of the regenerative qualities of art
and individual ingenuity.[8] In order to screen the (re)productive potential
of genres, particularly of the epistolary genre, I will look at *Der kurze
Brief* through the camera-lens of Zemeckis's *Romancing the Stone*.[9]

In *Romancing the Stone*, a film-in-a-film-sequence introduces the
viewer to the romantic conclusion of Joan Wilder's (Kathleen Turner)
latest novel. While the next novel she writes is a literary adaptation of
the film's development, it also writes the script for the end of *Romancing the Stone*. Appropriately, the adventure of writing begins with a
familiar letter that maps the course of action. Folded over onto itself,
Joan's sister's letter charts the heart of the journey (el corazón, the
heart). The two halves of the heart, hidden on the map, have to be
folded back onto each other to lay in a course for the treasure, which is
a heart-shaped diamond. Throughout the adventurous attempts to save
her sister from her kidnappers by exchanging her for the diamond, the
writer protagonist has to learn how to read her own writing. She has to
recognize and accept her desire for the hero (Michael Douglas) before
she is able to read the epistolary treasure map correctly.

The stone lies hidden in the pool of a giant white stalactite, which
exudes what is called "mother's milk." Born of its economy of desire,
a plastic Easter bunny, the epitome of postmodern energy and productivity, is brought to light. Again, Joan Wilder has to become her
own novels' ideal reader to see through this tar baby. Its birth con-
demns it to instant death. The hero decapitates the bunny and delivers
the heart-stone. After the diamond has wandered through many hands
and hiding places, it is safely tucked away in the hero's crotch until his
genitals receive a blow and he symbolically loses his heart along with
his manhood. He maneuvers the dislocated stone through his trouser-
legs toward the tip of his boot. From there, the hero kicks it straight
into the hand of the enemy, which is instantly bitten off by a snapping
alligator. The stone again disappears into another being's innards but
is reborn a third time, when the alligator finally dies in the hero's
arms. Subsequently, hero and heroine go their separate ways. She
adapts the adventure as her next novel, and he exchanges the heart-
stone for the yacht, *Angelina*. When he arrives in New York to take
Joan on a sailing trip around the world on *Angelina*, he reenacts the
new novel's ending.[10]

The letter responsible for these adventures transports the novelist from New York to her heroine's Colombian jungle. She only receives and keeps the letter because it is too large to fit in her mailbox, and because she is in a hurry to meet her editor. The incompatibility of mailbox and letter alone prevents the story from premature closure (while she is gone, a Colombian spy ransacks both mailbox and apartment). Her thick latest novel in one hand, the unread oversized letter in the other, she runs to meet her editor. She embodies the fiction of letters.

As shown above, her double identity as author and heroine of her own story generally aids her in the ensuing treasure and man hunt. Despite this overall rule, in the final struggle with her enemy, she can neither rely on her old auctorial nor her heroine's repertoire of tricks. She has to invent new survival methods, plot an innovative escape. Her dependence on the patterned semiotic system of her controlled fictional world forces her into an interval of dangerous instability: When she attempts to throw a knife out of her garter, as she had Angelina do successfully in her latest novel, the enemy wards it off with a log. As an avid fan of Joan Wilder's novels, he anticipates the tactic. His exact decoding of her message simultaneously separates as it links text to author. The ideal reader and the movie audience, which caught a mental film-clip of her latest novel's final scenes at the movie's beginning, are about to destroy the author together with the plot.

If a "letter" always reaches its destination, it becomes a deadly bullet(in) for its sender. This violent interruption of her premeditated plot provides the most suspenseful moment of the film. It is also the only moment in which she is forced to reconsider the blurred borders of reality and fiction. In her desire, her fiction writes her life. To regain control over this sudden implosion of her novelesque existence, the author Joan Wilder must invent a new plotline, which as it succeeds lets her merge with the text again. The semiotic assignment works too perfectly; it has to waiver for an instant in order for the film to end like all of Wilder's novels, for the author to give birth to author, or, to put it another way, for the genre to guarantee its progeny. One of the genre's laws includes working against itself, continually threatening to transgress its own borders. It procreates and serializes in moments of instability.[11]

In comparison to Joan Wilder's reading lessons in *Romancing the Stone*, my reading is also determined by a capitalist quest. For a female reader and scholar, the romance quest in novel and film, as well as in my own discourse, is doubly precarious. As a critic, I should probe the texts' erogenous zones and indeterminate crevices for the greatest yield. In the analogy with sexual stimulation, the text begins to resemble the female body, on which the romance plot is exercised. My analysis will only succeed if I can stimulate the text enough to make it "come," but also if my

own text reads like an egotistic journal of intertextual and intersubjective lovemaking, where the subject of the intercourse is delegated to its
place as object. In addition, my subjectivity should subject itself to general "academic" objectivity and with it to its universal "male" gender.
The object, and with it the female body and its desire, almost disappear
as I slowly appropriate them into a generic translation. Literally, I have
to read female and queer desire out of the text and my discourse.[12]

In other words, female desire is either appropriated into the phallocentric quest or closed off and closed out from traditional quest-romance:

> female questers have been faced with a nearly impossible assignment.
> And what feminist critics have discovered is an absence of a heroic
> female self-image. Women have been blocked from identifying them-
> selves with the active subject of quest-romance because they have inter-
> nalized an image of themselves as passive objects, framed by the clas-
> sic structure of the myth, removed from the very symbols and activities
> the quest traditionally evokes.[13]

This description of quest is similar to that of Peggy Kamuf's explication
of feminine desire in epistolary fiction, specifically "the constructions
which enclose women with their desire": "Whether it is behind the solid
walls of the nun's cloister, at the unspoken limit of the hysteric's language, or within the frame set by a parent's desire, the passion that
shapes these fictions can only discover itself in transgression of the laws
which enclose it."[14] At the moment, in which the male enemy in
Romancing the Stone anticipates the writer-protagonist's postal code, he
almost displaces both text and author. The phallic law dictates that the
heroine represent male desire in order to survive. This time, she has to
transgress the law to survive. At this junction of reading and desire in
film and novel, my own reading appropriates a "disruptive difference"
that cannot be obliterated "without leaving traces of such a violence"
(xvii). Again, in Peggy Kamuf's words: "[A]s we read, we solicit the
movement to the edge of the precipice, at this limit between our own
desire and someone else's" (xvii).[15] And yet, if I attempt to push the texts
to the borderline with my reading, does the master discourse in its near
dissolution gain strength for its transformation?

Epistolary narratives are narratives of desire, a doubly violated desire,
whose "disruptive difference" remains legible "at the junction of the fictional text with the text of the reader's reading."[16] Because epistolary correspondence writes the history of phallic intercourse into its intersections
and represses female sexuality into its sheets, the reader and female quester
seems doomed to refurbish phallic power with her intertext. In Roland
Barthes' dictionary-diary of *A Lover's Discourse*, the lover (who is univer-
sally male in Barthes' text), by definition, always plots against himself:

Dis-cursus—originally the action of running here and there, comings
and goings, measures taken, "plots and plans": the lover, in fact, cannot keep his mind from racing, taking new measures and plotting
against himself. His discourse exists only in outbursts of language,
which occur at the whim of trivial, aleatory circumstances.[17]

A lover who stops scheming ceases to be a lover. In order to start and
restart plots of all sorts, an objectifying glance is necessary to keep the
love interest alive. Hence arises the urge to define everything around
him, including his own discourse, in an aphoristic manner, as if he were
the first and last lover and philosopher.[18] A lover has to hold the object
of his desire at a distance to take in its shapely contours. Occasionally,
he has to detach himself from it (and himself) to arrange for intense
reunions, making a total presence an impossibility within its own discourse. "Running here and there," "coming and going," "in outbursts
of language," the love letter plots its course and the history of romantic
discourse under "aleatory circumstances."[19] Does this epistolary history,
as retold in contemporary fiction, in any way transform the phallocentric romantic economy? The woman who writes love letters and carries
the discourse of absence, according to Barthes, figures "like a package
in some forgotten corner of the railway station."[20] She is always at the
"sedentary" end of the exchange, although, already in his metaphor, she
manages to trade places with the package of letters themselves, left to be
discovered, to be purloined, plundered, pirated yet again.

Enter Handke's aversion to and fascination with the repetition of
genres, themes, and narratological methods, particularly cinematic and
epistolary framing devices. In *Der kurze Brief zum langen Abschied*
Handke's narrating voice answers his wife's murder-suicide threat retrospectively in the form of a mental and physical travelogue.[21] The
female figure occupies much narrated space and looms large in the epistolary narrator's mental crosshairs. In *Erwins Badezimmer*, Rachel triggers Albert's curiosity and etymological passion as well as the plot of the
novel in absentia. He redefines his profession and idea of self through
her. Judith is similarly responsible for the adventure plot in *Der kurze
Brief:* In accord with the biblical legend of Judith and Holofernes, she
does not rest until she has her lover's head on a plate. Whenever the
writer-protagonist indulges in the "immediacy" of his narrated experiences, she stresses the process of mediation by sending him a letter, a
card, or a couple of hired ruffians. Her correspondence never lets him
settle into himself, neither in the narrated time frame nor on the narratological level.

As a couple, he and Judith balance their individual shortcomings.
Although he acknowledges her superior sense of place as a whole—
"Your sense of location is also much better than mine. I often get lost"

("Dein Ortssinn ist auch viel besser als meiner. Ich verirre mich oft")—
he also contends that this "makes one only dizzy" ("macht einen nur
schwindlig," 21). Either a step behind or ahead of him, their locations
never quite match. Already at the outset, he angrily portrays her as another woman at an-other time than his: "Judith had no sense of time, I
thought. . . . She was incapable of thinking that at anytime it could be
time for anything" ("Judith hatte keinen Zeitsinn, dachte ich. . . . Sie
war unfähig, daran zu denken, daß es irgendeinmal Zeit werden könnte
für irgendetwas," 20–21). He does not see the parallel to his reading of
the woman's glance in the bar, which he experiences as the "longing
glance of an OTHER woman at that OTHER time" ("sehnsüchtigen
Blick einer ANDEREN Frau zu jener ANDEREN Zeit," 25).

Judith might stumble and fall and always be in a different time zone
than he is, but she definitely knows her way around his plots. Like their
characterizations in these early pages of the novel, Judith controls the
spacing, he controls the pace of the narrative as it unfolds. Handke
places the two in opposite, yet existentially conversing metaphysical
dimensions. This is, however, not an easy and solidified dichotomy.
Judith, for instance, baffles her husband with linguistic connotations,
which she carries over from one place to the next. She is never semiotically present in just one place. Her "deficient" sense of time permits her
to linger in one place longer than she actually inhabits that space. While
her feet have transgressed the border, her mind still clings to the other
side: "When you cross over to a house, you say, that you go *down;* when
we have already long stepped in front of the house, the car still stands
outside; and when you drive down into a town, you drive *up* into the
town, simply because the street heads North."[22] Judith adds the process
of acquiring a new location to her directions. She attaches her own dislocation to the prepositional phrase. If she has to step off the sidewalk
or walk down the stairs to get to another house across the street, the
first downward movement determines her sense of location. As long as
she is not in the car, the car stands outside, and she relates its location
to the next inside-location, namely, the house, which she has just left.
She also reads the two-dimensional representation of a compass literally
in that she takes "North" to be "up."

In opposition, the writer-protagonist chidingly responds with
minuscule descriptions of his surroundings, trying desperately to detach
them from his interpretative desire, from his point of view. He attempts
to describe his hotel room as if he weren't there. He feels himself *dissolving* in the water running down the drain of the tub:

> The water ran off very slowly, and as I sat there leaned back with
> closed eyes, it appeared to me, as if I myself also, with the leisurely

jerks of the water, became smaller by and by and finally dissolved. Only when I got cold, because I lay in the tub without water, did I sense myself again and got up.[23]

He frames his experience with temporal phrases. The slow rhythm of the water's tidal, sucking, and pushing drain allows him to forget his spatial and bodily existence, while at the same time this dissolving into nonspace arouses him. He has to look down his body to discover that he is physically there, that he has a *Glied* (member). His penis becomes the appropriate tool for his *penibel* (persnickety) mind's fantasies as he masturbates with closed eyes. He describes it in a matter-of-fact manner: "I seized my member, first with the towel, then with the bare hand, and began, while I was standing like that, to masturbate. It took very long" ("Ich ergriff mein Glied, zuerst mit dem Handtuch, dann mit der bloßen Hand, und fing, während ich so stand, zu onanieren an. Es dauerte sehr lange," 17). Both his mental and body timing are slow, reserved, almost catatonic—"thoughtless" *(gedankenlos)*—a state of mind he describes as "painful" yet "pleasant" (17).

The description of the scenes on the narrated time level, unlike his flashback-dialogues with Judith, share the dry tone of stage directions for an actor. He himself wants to become "polite and inconsiderate" ("höflich und rücksichtslos") a combination of the Great Gatsby of F. Scott Fitzgerald's novel and Gottfried Keller's Heinrich Lee (16). During his trip from the East Coast to the West Coast, he reads *The Great Gatsby* and *Der grüne Heinrich*, an American and a German *Entwicklungsroman*. He superimposes their images with his own experiences. In addition to his imitation of fictional characters, the narrator employs the image of the screen as a double representation of his physical and mental movements: "and sometimes I opened my eyes and glanced over to the milk-glass window of the bathroom, on which the shadows of the birch leaves moved up and down" ("und manchmal machte ich die Augen auf und schaute zu dem Milchglasfenster des Badezimmers hinüber, auf dem sich die Schatten der Birkenblätter auf und ab bewegten," 17). Not only does the tinting of the window foreshadow the color of his ejaculate, but the combination of voyeurism and masturbation makes up the film screen, a film screen that is not altogether different from the shadows dancing on his closed eyelids, his own mental cave. The tree leaves, which will later embrace him in a sense of harmony with nature, symbolize the sensory stimulation missing from his masturbation and later from the lovemaking with his woman friend, but also provide him with their own enticement. The milky window prevents him from seeing a sharp picture. As in classical Hollywood cinema, the image is retouched, the edges softened. It remains to be seen, whether the narrator denies the intensity of sex and thereby romanticizes it or whether sex, to him, has to be seen in relation to mediated representation and can therefore not be the authentic immediate experience as which the 1960s ordained it.

While the protagonist amusedly yet anxiously ponders the odds of his survival—"I was curious, how it would go on" ("ich war neugierig, wie es weitergehen würde," 15)—his head is already on Judith's plate. Not only is his catatonic nameless self already split into narrator and writer-protagonist, it is also further divided by his screenlike role-playing. The narrator's autobiography reveals itself as a series of reenactments. Not having a "sense for [her]self" ("Sinn für mich selber," 21), Judith uses his "exaggerated sense for himself" ("übertriebene[n] Sinn für [s]ich selber," 21) against him. She spaces his pace, interrupts his autism with her doubled presence and absence, and times his journey so that he, too, considers himself displaced. In a movie-script style, which does not list the directions linearly to the actual dialogue as in plays, their corroded time-space dichotomy rewrites the modernist novel as film noir; film noir returns to its precursor, the English gothic novel, the *roman noir*.

Where does epistolary fiction enter this cinematic rewriting? In *Der kurze Brief zum langen Abschied*, the short letter with Judith's reverse psychological message—"I am in New York. Please don't look for me, it would not be pleasant to find me" ("Ich bin in New York. Bitte such mich nicht, es wäre nicht schön, mich zu finden," 9)—issues the map of the undecided hero's westward trip through the States. In its telegram style, the letter writes a telepath of the hero's quest for immediacy and identity.[24] True to her sense of direction, Judith can only locate her "self" after she has left New York (she mails the letter from Philadelphia). On the other two occasions she refers to herself as a direct object of the negative command and as the object of the activity itself (the search). We are tempted, out of linguistic habit, to read the "pair" *suchen* and *finden* as complimentary.[25] We therefore decidedly "find" that he is the one who searches and finds, although the second sentence could also signify Judith's search for herself via epistolary discourse. Grammatically speaking, *es* substitutes "mich zu finden." The sentence might also read: "Mich zu finden, wäre nicht schön" ("To find myself

THE LETTER EXCHANGE for conversation. Meet minds, not bodies. Send SASE: *Box 6218-N, Albany, CA 94706.*

FIGURE 5.1

would not be pleasant"). Even if the addressee should search for her, the actual discovery would run counter to any artistic ideal of beauty. The letter itself is subject to its own message. The letter of language threatens to deliver violence and ugliness upon the arrival of immediacy. It always seduces its reader and speaker into its quest yet refuses to deliver immediacy and transparency. The letter emphasizes at the outset that immediacy has no being, because it always "becomes."[26] Yet it maintains that this "becoming" can be represented structurally, as it demonstrates with the uses of *ich* as well as *suchen* and *finden*.

At the beginning of the novel, the narrator-agent receives Judith's letter with his room key at the "Wayland Manor" hotel in Providence, R.I. It lies there waiting for him to arrive. The migrant quality of the letter has been arrested, whereas the sender and addressee, who should be at the stationary end of a correspondence have already moved on and have not yet arrived respectively. Once engaged, the letter takes control over both addressee and sender. Judith (intentionally) forgets their camera with an undeveloped roll of film in New York and mails the letter from Philadelphia. Given her sense of (mis)timing, she conceives her "presence" as her "past" with her husband, and this Judith indeed lies unexposed in New York. She leaves a convoluted but readable trace that seduces him into exposing her. Sent by the letter, the narrator-agent departs for New York.

When he leaves from New York for Philadelphia, he gets on the Penn Central Railroad at Pennsylvania Station (52). Because the points of origin and destination as well as the means of transportation bear the same names, he has arrived before he has left. His route is a closed loop. The narrator-agent, as the migrating "letter" in the story, is inserted into a preexisting plotline. His experiences and thoughts travel between his two narrators: his older "self," who reminisces and moralizes about the past, and Judith, whose ideal reading foretells the story. Providence is waiting for this structurally unstable voice in the form of a letter, which both programs and overrides the literary plots the character envisions for himself. When the narrator selects the "Algonquin" in New York in memory of F. Scott Fitzgerald, he inserts himself into a fictional universe.

Peter Handke similarly depicts himself as a reading character in his own life-fiction. He wants literature to enlighten him. In his essay "Ich bin ein Bewohner des Elfenbeinturms" he writes: "In this way, I have never been educated by the official educators, but rather have always let literature change me."[27] The narrative voice in *Der kurze Brief* transforms the author's autobiographical insight into a paradigm for his American days: "Like sometimes, when something I read made me greedy to simulate it immediately, right now also the great Gatsby called upon me to change myself on the spot. The need to become different than I was suddenly became physical, like an urge."[28] The narrator-agent struggles with a definition of "difference" that is rather complex. While he wants to be different from what he is—he wants to be an "other"—he also feels "disgust for everything that was not [he] [him]self" ("Ekel vor allem, was nicht ich selber war," 19). He despises the artificiality of acting as if he were someone else. The "difference" he initially approves of comes closer to an "indifference" to himself, or to call it by another name, an absolute merging with the "other narrative." He fills himself with "difference."[29] When he selects "Sitting On The Dock Of The Bay" from the music box in a snack bar, he thinks of the Great Gatsby: "In the meantime I thought of the great Gatsby and became self-assured like never before: until I could absolutely no longer sense myself. I would manage to do many things differently. I would not be recognizable" ("Dabei dachte ich an den großen Gatsby und wurde selbstsicher wie noch nie: bis ich mich gar nicht mehr spürte. Es würde mir gelingen, vieles anders zu machen. Ich würde nicht wiederzuerkennen sein," 19–20). As in the previous bathtub scene, self-assurance is linked directly to self-forgetting, even self-erasure. The immobility of the subject in the song is tied to Gatsby's hypnotic stare at the lights in his lover's house across the bay. Song and text repeat the effect of his previous catatonic state. In Handke's protagonist, this trance is caused by a radical opening of his mind to intersubjectivity and intertextuality. Whereas he imagined an intertextural meeting of water and body, and an intertextual, intersubjective encounter with the Great Gatsby before, in this scene his mind becomes the meeting ground of music and text. The music's rhythm combines with Gatsby's indifferent resolution. Self-assurance presupposes a total lack of self-consciousness, a goal toward which he strives, but which is hampered by his "exaggerated sense of [him]self" (21).

The intersubjective balance in his head only lasts a "wink of an eye." As soon as he moves, the hypnotic symbiosis between self and world is interrupted. The yawning, an involuntary opening of the mouth, opens the protagonist to castration anxiety:

> I became tired and yawned. Then, in the middle of yawning, a hollow place emerged in me, which filled itself immediately with the picture of a deep black underbrush, and like in a relapse the thought overcame me again that Judith was dead. The picture of the underbrush darkened even more, when I glanced into the increasing darkness in front of the snack bar door, and my dread became so strong that I suddenly changed back into an object.[30]

The mortal danger of Woman tugs at him from the inside as well as from the urban space beyond the bar entrance. In this allegorization of

Woman, Death, and the City, so typical to modernity, Handke's protagonist meets Jean-Paul Sartre's Antoine Roquentin and Döblin's Franz Biberkopf. With the yawn, the moment of masculine self-assurance and subject-ness disappears, and the filled void now changes him back into a castrated object, heeding his wish "to become different" in a rather unexpected way.

As his whole face contorts and opens wide with a hysterical yawn, the protagonist becomes physically vulnerable to personal memory, to the reading of the sights around him as associations to his past. The "hollow place" in him fills with an image of the underbrush, where he had once searched for his suicidal mother. The image overtakes him like Judith's letter had overtaken him in the hotel. This relapse repeats the association of the letter with Judith's death but leaves out the memory of his search for his mother and his fear of her death (13–14). Whereas before, he states that "all of me had sunken deep inside for fear" ("alles an mir war vor Angst tief nach innen gesunken," 14) he now depicts his introverted organs as a "hollow place" that fills with a mixture of desertion and castration anxieties. Sudden movements turn his mental carte blanche into a letter from the subconscious flashing back fear, anxiety, and desire. If we take into account his voiced desire for difference and the eerily celebratory masturbation scene in the hotel, in which he "wrung the turkey's neck" for one last time, the scene describes a transsexual metamorphosis.[31] *Short Letter, Long Farewell* turns into a transsexual's journal, in which Handke converts the protomasculine bar scene into a place of transsexual operations and manifestations, where masculinity is reproduced as the continuous effort at and effect of transsexualization. Before leaving, the protagonist changes back into the object of self-representation.

Throughout his career, Handke seeks to avoid this type of self-representation at all costs: "As far as the reality is concerned in which I live, I do not want to call things by name, I just don't want to let them be *unthinkable*. I would like to let them become recognizable in the method that I apply."[32] He desperately searches for alternatives, even if these amount to "the subversive use of the old creative principles."[33] In the cycle of Handke's reinterpretation and topicalization of personal narratives and the *Entwicklungsroman*, he has his protagonist struggle with the apparent impasse of innovation and reenactment.[34] The writer-protagonist in *Der kurze Brief* intermittently encounters "aleatory circumstances," in which immobility is rhythmicized or rhythm immobilized— the glance is absorbed by one number of a spinning die or one word on a windblown flyer. Only in these liminal moments, open possibilities, unrealized but realizable alternatives present themselves. The protagonist's liminal experiences resemble Handke's own in the search for "something, that made me conscious of a not yet thought of, not yet conscious possibility of reality, a new possibility to see, to speak, to think, to exist."[35]

Der kurze Brief fictionalizes this longing for new and different options. Its protagonist's meditations mirror Handke's own intentional, premeditated, and strongly desired alternative to realism. Handke can portray his hero's method as hackneyed, because the author employs the double writing of a movie script. The film script divides text from directions, camera angles, and lighting positions. The actual production of the movie further disintegrates what is left of traditional linear storytelling and slice-of-life realism by shooting scenes in the order of location or according to the availability of stars and props. At the end, however, the film's dismembered pieces provide for unmatched cinematic realism.

Notwithstanding Handke's double writing, the hero's and the author's paths run at times dangerously close to each other. In the bar scene of *Der kurze Brief*, a few people gamble with dice. When Handke's character joins them a second time, he sees the number he needs in a flash of the spinning die, which finally comes to a standstill with the "wrong" number on top. The right number actually arrived, but in a different time, a time uncluttered by layers of competing and self-destructing significations:

> It was a pervasive feeling of an OTHER time, in which there had to have been other places than anywhere now, in which everything had to have other meanings than in my current consciousness, in which also the feelings were different than the feelings today and oneself was just in the moment just in the condition, in which perhaps the uninhabited earth was at that time, when after a thousand years of rain the first time a rain drop fell without immediately vaporizing.[36]

It is not just any different time or place that he glimpsed with that (dis)appearing number. It is the evolutionary moment of the creation of life. The number that would have won him the game links him to origination. Artistic creation is a gamble with unattainable and unrecoverable origins. Handke acknowledges the surge of power in his auctorial self's alter ego but instills it with bitterness at the same time. The moment of happiness soon gives way to a feeling that is "piercing" *(schneidend)* and "painful" *(schmerzhaft)*, as the glance of the woman at the bar replays the situation for him: "a non-winking but also not fixed, only endlessly wide, endlessly awaking and simultaneously endlessly fading, yearning up to the tearing of the retina and to a quiet outcry, glance of an OTHER woman at an OTHER time" ("einen nicht zwinkernden, aber auch nicht starren, nur endlos weiten, endlos erwachenden und zugleich endlos verlöschenden, bis zum Zerreißen der Netzhaut und zu einem leisen Auf-schrei sehnsüchtigen Blick einer ANDEREN Frau zu jener ANDEREN Zeit," 25).

In a freeze-frame, Handke captures a close-up frontal view of the bartender. Because the still suddenly increases the intensity of the glance, the retina is severely strained. The "Zerreißen der Netzhaut" also insinuates that the frame is on the verge of incinerating. The bartender's glance, a screen image's glance, and a film-frame share the characteristics of being "stills in motion." Within the yearning glance, the "sehnsüchtige Blick" expresses an addiction to longing and seeing itself. In the woman's glance, the narrator-agent realizes the impossibility of attaining the "other" time and place through willpower, motion, or meditation alone. Its otherness lies in its constant but indistinguishably rhythmic mediation between all antipodes, all binary signposts. As such it is pure mediation and can neither be sent purposefully nor can it arrive at predestined addresses. Any arrest of its motion delivers momentary clarity along with impending self-dissolution.

This scene captures Handke's poetic credo in cinematic language: "The film's escape from this dilemma seems to be, that this syntax is considered, that it is made conscious with the film, that it is exhibited, yes, that the syntax of the film appears so abstracted that it is itself shown as the film."[37] This axiom and the scene share the absolute poetological necessity to create lasting epiphany in a writing that at the same time mourns its impossible goal of verbal immediacy: "I am convinced of the definition-dissolving and therefore future-mighty power of poetological thought" ("Ich bin überzeugt von der begriffsauflösenden und damit zukunftsmächtigen Kraft des poetologischen Denkens").[38] Handke's poetological program of the late 1960s and 1970s rewrite Friedrich W. Schlegel's "progressive Universalpoesie."[39]

Handke understands his creative writing as author-directed: "The point for me is to show *my* reality" ("es geht mir darum, *meine* Wirklichkeit zu zeigen").[40] In addition, I have interpreted the "game of dice" episode in *Der kurze Brief* as an attempt to experience and rewrite absolute mediation as another form of immediacy, and I have read the split narrative voice as an intersubjective exchange on both the thematic and narratological levels. Handke refuses to portray reality, refuses mimesis in the nineteenth-century grain and reverts to Aristotle's definition, which grants the artist the freedom to create the world around him as much as he describes it. Handke polemicizes against realist literature and *literature engagée*, which in his eyes idealize the relationship between word and thing in the form of a "looking glass" ideology.[41] For him, literature is inherently romantic.[42] He employs the term *romantisch* in an adulterated mix of contemporary "nostalgic Romanticism" for lost "authenticity," of semisurreal clichéd settings (i.e., sunset in Beverly Hills), and of the literary historic determinant as Peter Pütz recognizes.[43] Handke's poetological axioms continuously question and uproot familiar and conventional literary and epistemological themes and forms:

> The method would again have to put into question everything previously clarified, it would have to show that there is *yet another* possibility of portraying reality, no, that there still *was* another possibility: because this possibility is also already used up by the very fact of its representation.[44]

According to Handke's definitions, neither realistic nor nonromantic literature exists, nor would he consider his own works "realistic." He is concerned with language as a reality in and of itself.[45] His idea of language combines structuralism with a poststructural nuance: "The description of a computer, if it ever occurs, has to be adapted to the complexity of a computer in its syntax and could not simply list the parts in the style of a populist scientist."[46]

Each situation and experience, each encounter, has an effect on the viewer. His glance will adapt to the surroundings according to an unconscious acclimatization process. Handke wants to exploit those moments in which the glance is accustoming itself to a change (his texts are filled with transitions from light to dark and vice versa),[47] in which the subject is subjected to an optical and linguistic imbalance. The film noir form excels in these transitions with its abundant use of lights, shadows, black/white or colors, abrupt scene changes and contrasts of night and day, interior and exterior shots.[48] The effect of contrastive cutting reflects Judith's understanding of space and time, in which the viewer adjusts to ever changing surroundings slower than the portrayed actors. And it also helps to recreate liminal moments, induce the hypnotic symbiosis between self and world, only to be thrust deeper into the certainty of dread.

The combination of epistolary discourse and this cinematic process provides Handke with highly coded and seemingly antagonistic communication models. In 1976, Christian Metz pitted the cinema's signification "as a means of expression rather than communication" against the triangular model of sender-message-recipient.[49] Nevertheless, even "a succession of automated world projections," as Stanley Cavell terms the "material basis of the media of movies," enters into dialogue with itself, its juxtaposed frames, and its audience.[50] The makeup of a film and a chain of letters is similar: both have multiple authors; their readings depend on a certain cutting, which can invert the time of production and reception. Their fiction results from a succession of world projections (if we take Cavell's cinema-oriented meaning a little further). A letter does not simply project its writer's world to the recipient. It takes in a specific worldview mediated by self-reflective writing (which is most often a projection of what the other would like to read) and projects it on the differential screen of its recipients' reading. In the following quotation, Cavell might just as well refer to epistolary fiction. He corrects his understanding of the cinematic medium by outlining "a fundamental fact of film's photographic basis":

> that objects participate in the photographic presence of themselves; they participate in the re-creation of themselves on film; they are essential in the making of their appearances. Objects projected on a screen are inherently reflexive, they occur as self-referential, reflecting upon their physical origins. Their presence refers to their absence, their location in another place. (xvi)

What remains is the tension between visual and textual representation. In Handke's novel, the reader of *Der kurze Brief* is introduced to the letter and the camera on the very first pages. The forgotten camera, symbolizing the loss of transparent realism, simultaneously conveys an undeveloped potential for narrative. The camera's displacement and its frozen slices of life pull the narrative forward and backward on more than one occasion. Forward, because the narrator promises to pick the camera up personally (14) and backward because the photographs initiate a series of childhood memories, transfixed into the narrator's mind.

After New York, the camera and its images accompany him on his journey between the American movie-landscape of his car rides and the anxiety of his friend's daughter over displaced objects. The child's need for visual order projects the narrator's own younger self, when all he wanted to see were pictures (81). In the car, the protagonist develops his own movie by ordering and reordering the photographs on the front window according to the child's secret design: "There had to be a secret pattern, that it wanted to see, and that I began to form and immediately to destroy again with each of my helpless attempts" ("Es mußte ein geheimes Muster geben, das es sehen wollte und das ich mit jedem meiner immer hilfloseren Versuche zu bilden anfing und sofort wieder zerstörte," 88). At the moment he interrupts his movement, the child quiets down again, but the narrator cannot find a specific order in the pictures ("ohne daß ich aber an den Bildern jetzt eine eigene Ordnung entdeckte," "but without me being able to discern specific order in the pictures now," 88). He now remembers the very first impression in his life, a Freudian-Hitchcockian scene, in which he was terrified of feeling the water escape through the hole in the sink. The loss of himself to the motion, the draining of self which he learns to treasure as an adult (as the bathtub scene at the beginning of the novel indicates), is called into question.

His friend Claire compares Green Henry's character to the protagonist in that they both share a spectator's position:

> He did not want to decipher anything; one thing would duly result from another. You, too, appear to me as if you only let the surroundings dance past you. You let experiences be performed for you, rather than entangling yourself. You behave as if the world were a presentation of gifts, just for you.[51]

Even though the narrator feels "reprimanded" *(zurechtgewiesen)* by Claire, he also feels "self-confident" *(selbstbewußt)*. Instead of curing him of his observing stance, this self-conscious self-confidence leads him to another set of "frames." First, he preconceives of the actual physical union between Claire and himself as taking place in her breathing, his pantomime, and her stretching. Then, he compares his physical impatience with the impatience he felt watching John Ford's *Iron Horse* (1924), in which a young couple's two embraces begin and end the movie. He has a physical reaction to the deferment of the second embrace. In a Pavlovian response, the generic frame of a Hollywood picture determines his desire, his trajectory and physical well-being.[52]

It is only after his intense emotional replay of these embraces in John Ford's *Iron Horse* that he discovers that his unity with realistic representation and nature itself, although "a paradisical feeling of life, without tenseness and fear, in which I myself no longer appeared, like in the play of the cypress" ("ein paradiesisches Lebensgefühl, ohne Verkrampfung und Angst, in dem ich selber, wie in dem Spiel der Zypresse, gar nicht mehr vorkam," 101) contains the horror of emptiness: "and I was so terrified of this empty world" ("und es grauste mir so sehr vor dieser leeren Welt," 101). Handke imbues this scene semantically with insoluble, antithetical signifiers: "erschrak," (startled) "aufgelöst und leer" (dissolved and empty), "paradiesisches Lebensgefühl" (paradisical feeling of life), "grauste" (terrified), "Schrecksekunde" (moment of shock), "das ungeheure Entsetzen" (the monstrous dread), "Stolz" (pride), "ein ganz selbstverständliches Wohlgefühl" (an entirely self-evident feeling of wellness, 101–102). Despite its linguistic imbalance, the protagonist views this memory as an epiphanic turn:

> In this wink of an eye, I forever lost the yearning to be rid of myself. . . .
> I knew that I could not wish myself away from all these limitations, and that from now on it only depended on finding for all of them an order and a kind of life that would do me justice, and in which other people would also do me justice.[53]

Handke's language creates an intersection between the worlds of difference and oneness when he repeats the verb "to lose" in the sentence with which the protagonist attests his ability to live forever with himself as other: "In diesem Augenblick *verlor* ich *für immer* die Sehnsucht, *mich loszusein*" ("In this moment, I *lost forever* the desire *to be rid of me*," 101; my italics). The syntax of this paragraph underscores the semantic imbalance by mingling the characteristics of the two worlds—the unity of self and nature; the acceptance of the self as already other—in its referential network. The protagonist's epiphany is triggered by the abrupt stuttering procession of the early black-and-white movie about the intercontinental railroad in contrast to Claire's slow-motion *Augenblicke* (eye glances, winks of an eye, moments). In his attentive reading of both, his own *Augenblick*, a temporal *and* spatial term, creates what he perceives to be the epistemological turn in the novel. Instead, it now reduces the ideas of a unified self to "short entrances and exits" ("kurze Auftritte und Abgänge") in his internal film reel, "in a long, variegated process, that revolved around something completely different" ("in einem langen, wechselnden Verlauf, der sich um etwas ganz anderes drehte," 102). The same reel that represents the narrator to himself deals with something else, turns around another axis, projects onto yet another screen. This cinematic structure relies on and repeats the epistolary structure of the novel *Short Letter, Long Farewell*. The protagonist's epiphany exposes itself as a mail-ordered order *(Anordnung)*, one of the takes in the process of recording that edits the film for distribution: "And as if up to now everything had just been a rehearsal, I thought spontaneously: 'It counts! It's getting serious!'" ("Und als ob bis jetzt alles nur Probe gewesen sei, dachte ich unwillkürlich: 'Es gilt! Es wird Ernst'," 102).[54]

This reflection of the cinematic form echoes Handke's transcription of this epiphanic moment in an early autobiographical essay:

> the experience changed itself due to the fact that I wrote about it, or it often emerged first during the writing of an essay about it, and specifically through the essay form, that one had drilled into me . . . until finally on one beautiful summer day I did not experience the beautiful summer day but rather the essay about the beautiful summer day.[55]

This framing predicament, in which the generic characteristics dominate the story, recalls not only the epistolary and travelogue character of the *essay film*,[56] but also Paul Hernadi's description of the innovative effect that Goethe's *The Sorrows of Young Werther (Die Leiden des jungen Werther)* had on the epistolary genre. In his view, the one-sided correspondence underscores epistolarity's "subordination of events remembered . . . to the event of remembering them."[57] In Handke's works, the characters constantly struggle with their autoaffection and this totality of mediation. On the one hand, they think their world into existence, mediated in genres and forms, and need the stability this provides; on the other hand, they strive to unthink generic borders to alter themselves and their relation to the world.[58] In their struggle they often double back toward absolute transparency and immediacy; they fall behind their author's reflective caution against its illusion.[59]

The narrative voice in *Der kurze Brief* addresses this poetological dilemma genre-reflexively and cinematographically, as he is overcome with an urge to accurately describe every detail en route. Caught in a strange environment, he tries to hide his "lack of insights and experiences" ("Mangel an Kenntnissen und Erlebnissen") "by dissecting the few activities that were possible for me during their description in such a way as if they told of great experiences" ("indem ich die wenigen Tätigkeiten, die mir möglich waren, im Beschreiben so zerlegte, als ob sie von großen Erfahrungen erzählten," 35). "I felt like in the past, when I, for a while, as I described to someone what I had just done, compulsively could not leave out any single activity, out of which the entire activity consisted" ("Ich fühlte mich wie früher, als ich eine Zeitlang, wenn ich jemandem beschrieb, was ich gerade getan hatte, zwanghaft keine Einzeltätigkeit, aus der sich die Gesamttätigkeit zusammensetzte, auslassen konnte," 34).

He demonstrates this space-time induced compulsion in two examples: "entering a house" and "sending a letter to someone." First, an action is perceived as a unity, as a framed action. In describing this "totality," it is dissected *(zerlegte)* into fragments. Even a strange environment becomes manageable if broken down into its components as the narrative of the stroll through New York demonstrates (35). Fragmentation turns into a process of comprehension. Totality is not destroyed, but resurrected through its parts. In the first example, a threshold is crossed: "When I walked into a house, instead of saying 'I walked into the house,' I said: 'I brushed off my shoes, pressed down the handle, pushed open the door and walked inside, whereupon I closed the door behind me again'" ("Ging ich in ein Haus, so sagte ich statt 'Ich ging ins Haus': 'Ich putze mir die Schuhe ab, drückte die Klinke nieder, stieß die Tür auf und ging hinein, worauf ich die Tür wieder hinter mir zumachte'," 34). Instead of an abrupt entrance, which is a potential shock to the senses, the transgression is mediated very carefully with many prepositions and reflexive verbs that help the subject localize itself even in a precarious situation. In its minute descriptiveness, the fragmented action is reconstructed linearly; the reel moves in slow motion, halting, but not stopping at each frame. Even though each gesture erects a grid of realism for the protagonist, each fragment seems to foreshadow "great experiences" (35); each sentence reads as if it signifies something else: fear of discovery, guilt, a planned murder perhaps. The violence of entering the unknown or the unfamiliarly familiar has been intensified rather than averted.[60] Each sentence builds up its own threshold: not yet letting go of the door handle, still not having turned around. Because the subject dwells on each individual gesture, the reader wonders what lurks on the other side. The awestruck narrator-agent, imprisoned in his own cinematic realism, cannot tear himself away from the threshold. He tries to control it by multiplying transitional moments.

While the first example could be taken straight from a movie script, the second example could be seen as a writing sample of the whole text: "How to write a short letter." The ensuing letter parodies the tradition of the letter as a common composition and rhetorical exercise as it developed since the rise of private correspondence and stylistic guides in letter form in the seventeenth century. It is barren of any feelings, stylistic flourishes, or self-descriptions à la Werther. Its dryness instead links this model-letter to one of Germany's earliest epistolary novels: Christian Fürchtegott Gellert's *The Life of Swedish Countess of G**** (*Das Leben der schwedischen Gräfin von G****, 1747–48). The narrative voice in Gellert's novel remains distanced from the narrated events.[61] In comparison, Handke's epistolary writing sample names the sender *(ich)* just once and then describes the procedure of mailing a letter.

As a part of the whole, the description of a description of how a letter is sent metonymizes the structure of both the entire text and the particular fictional frame in which it serves as an example. Both examples, read together, link "describing" and writing to an endlessly mirrored threshold experience.[62]

> [A]nd when I sent someone else a letter, I always laid (instead of: "I sent the letter") "a clean sheet of paper on a pad, removed the cap from the fountain pen, wrote on the sheet, folded it, stuck it into an envelope, addressed the envelope, pasted a stamp on it and threw the letter [into the mailbox]."

> [U]nd wenn ich einem andern einen Brief schickte, legte ich immer (statt: "ich schickte den Brief") "ein sauberes Blatt Papier auf eine Unterlage, entfernte die Hülse vom Füllfederhalter, beschrieb das Blatt, faltete es zusammen, steckte es in einen Umschlag, beschriftete den Umschlag, klebte eine Marke darauf und warf den Brief ein." (34)

Rather than depicting the letter as a finished product, the narrator defines it as a process. At the same time, he describes the letter as if it had neither existed as a thing nor as a word before the description. A sheet of clean paper is both described and inscribed. The letter writes (on) itself. The sheet has to be folded and stuffed into an envelope, which is in turn *beschriftet* (labeled, addressed, written on) before the polymorphous entity can be called a "letter." The letter as such only appears at the moment of mailing, sending, or receiving.[63] The narrating voice takes the meaning of *Brief* literally by fragmenting the "letter" into its parts and actions. The writing sample, with which the narrator describes the manner and act of describing, turns into a birth certificate for the "letter." He literalizes the letter by neither dwelling on its "other" contents nor on its effects, nor on its intended addressee. The "being-as-letter" in *Der kurze Brief* therefore does not carry a message, is not a vehicle for an(other) scene of writing. It is, as much as this is possible, "pure" mediation.

Although grammatically still dependent on the *ich*, the various components of letter writing *(Blatt Papier, Unterlage, Hülse, Füllfederhalter, Umschlag, Marke, Brief)* structurally distance themselves more and more from the subject until the letter is actually mailed. During the procedure, insides and outsides invert three times: the cap is removed from the fountain pen; the sheet of paper is folded and stuck into the envelope; the letter is mailed. Prior to its actual letter status, the "letter" changes environments, folds and refolds, and threatens (as well as promises) to lose the subject throughout these dislocations. Instead of saying "I sent someone a letter," the components of the letter itself usurp the position of the addressee, of the direct object, both in the moment of writing and in the moment of sending. In German, the verb *einwerfen* suffices to indicate the activity *and* the mailbox. In a dual gesture, *einwerfen* combines throwing away with a homecoming. *Einwerfen* evokes an inverted target-oriented "throwing." It illustrates the process grammatically with great precision: "und *warf* den Brief *ein*." The verb separates to let the letter come into existence. The letter literally stands between a send-off and an arrival that is peculiarly implying yet tangibly lacking the target-object into which it is tossed, the mailbox, the collection box of the mail-order.

Because its time and place are so limited, the letter is short by definition. Its presence as "letter" coincides with its absence from sender and addressee. It leaves upon reaching its proper place, reaches its place upon leaving it. As Handke implies with his conspicuous use of *einwerfen*, the letter cannot be contained. Handke's grammatology purloins it from under the hands of the mailman to sneak it back into circulation at unexpected moments. The title of Handke's narrative suddenly takes on a new meaning. The *mise-en-scène* of writing and describing in form of a letter folds back upon the narrative, and with it epistolary history. Handke strips the letter down to its generic shell and redirects it into the structure of language, the syntax of his text. The reactivated epistolary form haunts the narrative in a long farewell.

Like the title, the book has two parts: "Der kurze Brief" (9–105) and "Der lange Abschied" (109–195). At the end of "Der kurze Brief," shortly after the camera angle shifts, the narrator has a voodoo-dream. He "stabbed into an overcooked chicken" ("stach in ein zerkochtes Huhn," 105). Popular notions have it that voodoo followers believe in the immediate transfer from a fetishized object to a person, from word to thing, and word to person. The narrator-agent envisions "express letters again and again, signs in the sand, that a stupid gardener watered like flowers, plants that formed words, secret messages on gingerbread hearts" ("immer wieder Eilbriefe, Zeichen im Sand, die ein dummer Gärtner wie Blumen begoß, Pflanzen, die Wörter bildeten, geheime Botschaften auf Lebkuchenherzen," 105). He awakens aroused and "penetrates" his sleeping friend Claire only to go limp and fall asleep again.

As a spokesman for the "läppische" literature of the "Gruppe 47," the stupid romantic gardener, who waters "signs in the sand" and flowers that form words, believes in the organic transparency between word and thing.[64] Express letters change into signs, which turn into flowers that form words. Modern fast-paced mass-reproduction takes the shape of an organic cycle, in which the input is equal to the output, in which original and copy can no longer be differentiated from one another. The personal "secret messages" on gingerbread hearts can be bought and appropriated for everyone's own use. Since these gingerbread hearts are usually worn around one's neck, they turn the romantic discourse of desire inside-out. The heart's excesses show. Instead of representing the outpourings of one individual to another, the prefabricated messages of these hearts exceed the private sphere to feed the cannibalized masses. Their senders and addressees buy, wear, display, and finally eat or discard the messages. The dream portraits the history of language philosophy and satirizes the economics of epistolary fiction whose tendency to synchronize heart murmurs publicizes and exploits privacy for a profit.

The dream's symbolism awakens the dreamer's sexual desire. That the resulting sleepy intercourse is not dialogic is underscored by the fact that the narrator-agent simply "penetrates" Claire when he senses his desire. Her desire is irrelevant. In his search for immediate satisfaction, he repeats the gardener's watering act: mistakes his erect penis for the phallus. In his haste, his penetration simulates the "express letter" of the epistolary writing sample: it remarks the process of *einwerfen* explained above. Even in sex, the illusion of immediacy turns against itself. After he has penetrated her like a mailbox, his penis goes limp: "*pushed myself into* the sleeping Claire, *went* limp and *back to sleep*" ("*drängte mich sofort in die schlafende Claire hinein*, ermattete und *schlief* wieder *ein*," 105; my italics). Between the send-off, the urgent activity of penetration, and the arrival, the signifier exhausts its potential. The symbolic act spells the only achievable unity for the protagonist.[65] His anxiety abates and he falls back asleep. Structurally, sexual intercourse does not differ from falling asleep, both happen in transitional stages and even rhyme in this instance. The symbolic becomes an aesthetic act, which is performed through Woman's, that is, Nature's, body but in her mental and sensory absence.

Between this aesthetic revelation through the dream and the title of the second part, Handke inserts a quote from Karl Philipp Moritz's *Anton Reiser* (1785–90).[66] "Is it really so puzzling, then, when the change of location contributes so much to make us forget like a dream, what we don't like to think of as real?" ("Ist es also wohl zu verwundern, wenn die Veränderung des Orts oft so vieles beiträgt, uns dasjenige, was wir uns nicht gern als wirklich denken, wie einen Traum vergessen zu machen?" 107). The change of scene between the short letter and the long farewell is a textual dislocation which itself imitates the two epistolary positions of departure and destination. If we take the conventional communication model as the general structural design of Handke's novel, the quote appears in the position of the message. As a quote, the saying shares the aphoristic, reproduced, and publicized quality of a gingerbread message from the dream. The letter, in its structurally mandated change of location, reads itself as a vehicle for forgetting reality, for forgetting that which one wishes to repress.

A change of place converts an already fictionalized past into an even further fictionalized dream. One is reminded of Nietzsche's ambivalent "active forgetfulness" to which he attributes the role of a "doorkeeper, a preserver of psychic order."[67] Again, we encounter an evocation of the threshold metaphor in relation to the self and knowledge of the self in its environment and history. A change of place embodies the awareness that "there is nowhere an isolatable unit . . . and that conceptions of a unified present are merely an interpretation." In Gayatri Spivak's words, "the philosopher, by an act of 'forgetting' that knowledge wins himself a 'present'."[68]

Inserted between the short letter and the long farewell, the narrator's dream-knowledge of the unattainability of an immediate presence and totality is underhandedly inscribed within another poet's words. The recontextualized quote performs its message. While it displaces the narrator's words and lets him actively forget his dream's message, it names itself as the dream's origin. Handke has designed an intricately double dream sequence: a dream that is forgotten and retrieved through a dream. The gap and transference from his text to Moritz's and onward, back to his text, enable the narrator to write on, to call for a "present" in opening up the final separation, the final absence. This abyssal dilemma with its repetition strategy corresponds to Freud's psychotherapeutic transference but also to Nietzsche's and Derrida's conundrum: "to know and then actively to forget, convincingly to offer in his text his own misreading."[69]

Although Michael Braun argues that Handke's prose varies "a romantically inspired narrative program" ("ein romantisch inspiriertes Erzählprogramm") only since his 1979 novel *Langsame Heimkehr*, I would contend that *Der kurze Brief zum langen Abschied* already rewrites the Romantic tradition of epistolary poetics.[70] The letter's Romantic tradition differs from the usage and theory of the letter form in the eighteenth century. I would like to mention only the most important changes for a definition of Romantic epistolary poetics in this context.

Because the eighteenth century witnessed the letter's emancipation as a poetic genre, the Romantics no longer needed to justify its aesthetic status. Instead of finding the Romantic idea of epistolary poetics in model-letters and *Briefsteller*, "reflections about the letter can be found in other contexts or rather in letters themselves. . . . The letter turns more and more into a favorite (art) form for publications as such."[71] Like Friedrich Schlegel for his autobiographically inspired conversational philosophical novel *Lucinde*, Handke appropriates the structural characteristics of the letter for his autobiographically inspired filmic travelogue novel. Like Rahel von Varnhagen and Bettina von Arnim, who wrote Romantic epistolary poetics with their correspondences to mentors, friends, and lovers, Handke lets Judith's letter reflect on its own generic structure, its possibilities and limitations.

Some structural implications of the letter form gained increased popularity because they were in tune with the Romantic philosophy of the subject and Romantic notions of aesthetic beauty. Herta Schwarz particularly names the letter's incompleteness, its fragmentary character, and its unsystematic method of narration (225). In addition, Romantic writers sought to open the generic boundaries between critical reflection and creative writing, the Aristotelian tripartite division among novel, drama, and poetry. For my discussion of Handke's novel and epistolarity, it is essential to remember that the letter offered itself as a vehicle for and the incarnation of the most important poetic axiom of Romanticism—the fragment: "The fragmentary takes on the constructive characters of the letter—or put differently, the essay-character of the letter, especially its open form has found its apogee in the fragment, the 'kernel' of the romantic art forms."[72] Handke's aesthetic transformation of the *Schwelle* (threshold) in combination with the Romantic idea of the fragment establish a link to yet another rewritten Romantic poetic concept: the eternal self-deferral of the search for the ideal. Braun terms Handke's narrative longing a "utopia of eternal wandering."[73] Like Friedrich Schlegel, the protagonist in *Der kurze Brief* attempts to construct a type of "progressive Universalpoesie" in which social, personal, and generic rules are suspended, not because they don't exist but because they intersect to create an opening, from which he can emerge as an "other."[74]

Since Handke's narrative is closely interwoven with Gottfried Keller's *Der Grüne Heinrich*, Handke's romantic utopia also shares the uncanniness of a letter that Heinrich needs to keep, but constantly displaces. This letter stems from Heinrich's artistic mentor Römer, whom Heinrich's cold financial calculations and insensitivity drove to madness.[75] Heinrich is unable to cast his letter aside:

> I didn't dare to burn the uncanny letter and was afraid to keep it; now I buried it beneath removed rubbish, then I pulled it forth and placed it among my dearest documents, and even today, whenever I find it, I change its location and take it somewhere else, so that it is on a continuous journey.[76]

In Keller's *Entwicklungsroman*, the letter approximates an almost Freudian understanding of the postal system in an individual's psyche. An uncanny experience resulting in a guilty or overburdened conscience cannot be rendered harmless immediately, if at all. Its "message" is constantly rerouted to remote parts of the memory to mingle semiotically with other removed rubbish ("entlegenem Gerümpel"). Whenever it is called forth, the resulting shame does not let it remain present for long. Its uncanniness, however, makes it a powerful tool of masochistic desire and for the endless repetition of this *fort/da* game. And in Heinrich's case, due to his petty calculations, the psychological deposit also takes on the characteristics of the anal-retentive capital-gains structure of capitalist economies. To keep one's capital, whether in bonds or stocks, well distributed throughout the market is a key to long-term financial success.

Keeping von Arnim's and Keller's sketched treatment of epistolary discourse in mind along with my reading of Handke's epistolary writing sample, I now return to *Der kurze Brief* and its structuralization of the mailing system. If the letter is defined as "letter" only at the moment of dispatch, and leaves its status of "letter" upon its arrival, what kind of mailing system structures Handke's writing process? Is Handke indeed romancing the "post"? Critics have expended considerable effort systematizing the symbolic structure of Handke's texts. They have categorized groups of symbols recurring throughout his texts, representing epiphanic experience on different verbal and perceptional levels.[77] This is, of course, one kind of postal code inherent to all texts. The symbolic code petrifies meanings. Likenesses are transferred from one thing to the next and their names come to stand on their own. They create a puristic parallel language without interjections, interferences, and adulterations. In accordance with the definition of the "letter" in the text, symbols of this kind are "dead," not yet and already no longer letters. These nonletters bespeak the narrator's failure to demystify reality and conventional narrative techniques. Is their symbolic coordinate system produced or endangered by the envisioned mailing system of the narrator's literal "letters"?

An author who provocatively demands detailed attention to his own work—"I no longer need any clothing for my sentences, what matters to me is every single sentence"[78]—might best be taken at his word. In the first pages of the novel, the narrating voice carefully treads from one stepping stone to the next, afraid the next step will cost him his life, the story's breakdown. The narrator attaches each segment to the next with a thread of reiterated words. He manages to instill the already experienced and survived adventure with the tension of a cinematic flashback slowly filling in the present frame with the narrated past. From time to time the narrator disturbs this illusion, criticizing his way of seeing. With his double perspective, he is responsible for the symbolic framework, linking one experience to the next with verbal accuracy. His protagonist-self moves like a captive gallery visitor between these carefully sorted and chosen pictures. The frame-narrator needs the quivering glances of his protagonist, his foreseeable moves from one picture to the next in order to provide for an inside-outside balance that will render the story a story. At the same time, both selves of the narrating agent strive for immediacy, for the unperturbed perception of reality in themselves. Since it is impossible for the narrator to achieve this presence in a retrospective account, he needs the narrator-agent to (re)create it.

The writer-protagonist leaves his German past behind and thereby reenacts the pilgrimage to the New World. But Handke chooses a peculiar send-off for this departure: another quote from Moritz's *Anton Reiser*. The "Short Letter" part of the novel is framed by these two cornerstones of German literary history and artistic *Bildung*. In this first quote from *Reiser*, all avenues of perception, aided by the thickened contourlessness of weather and landscape, point toward the street itself ("als sollte die Aufmerksamkeit nur auf die Straße, die man wandern wollte, hingeheftet werden"), the yellow brick road that Handke's protagonist picks up to follow to the promised land, the land that harbors unlimited possibilities in the realm of aesthetics, politics, and experience. The quotation maps the unconscious of Handke's novel, and preserves the memory of the protagonist's narration as the reiteration and displacement of another text. Like Moritz's Reiser, Handke's protagonist seeks the solution to his problems with himself and his past in the movement from place to place.

Like Anton Reiser before him, Handke's protagonist's wayward perception selects impressions due to their affinity with streets, ways, and traveling, drawing him on as if by automatic pilot. The first paragraph of the novel is thus devoted to the streets of Providence and the hotel which itself bears the name of its mediate location, Wayland Manor. On his way to the open elevator, he rips open the envelope of the letter. What he reads throws him off balance: His ex-wife is in New York, blocking his path while giving it a first destination. Upon entry of the lift and despite the porter's warning, he stumbles, because the letter and the porter's warning delineate a path with threshholds rather than infinite progression. When the narrating voice shifts directly from Judith's letter to a childhood memory, he converts Judith's shortcoming, her stumbling, into the narrative structure of this remembrance: "In a dusk, even more terrible as it was not yet night, I *stumbled* with ridiculously dangling arms along the forest, already *sunken into itself*, out of which only the lichen on the foremost trees *shimmered outward*."[79] Back in the narrated present of the hotel, he steps into the lift and reenacts the memory in another time frame; he even describes his surroundings with the vocabulary of the memory. He *stumbles* and watches the "elevator operator, who stood with declined head in the dark corner at the lever" ("Liftführer, der mit *gesenktem* Kopf in der *dunklen* Ecke am Hebel stand," 10; my italics). The lichen reappear in the scene with the elevator operator's white shirt that "*shimmered out* of his deep-blue uniform" ("*schimmerte* aus der tiefblauen Uniform *heraus*," 10; my italics). He can neither differentiate between the dollar bills in his pocket, nor distinguish present from past. Images and impressions from the past superimpose themselves onto the narrative of the present, and thus engage present and past, their different locations and narrative subjects, into an unstable epistolary economy of simulation. Slowly retreating backwards, further and further into a childhood filled with pain and shock,[80] he remembers how he was carried into the house by American soldiers, how he was lost in the twilight in the woods before desperately searching for someone he loved, a pain as yet blocking the knowledge who that person was, namely, his mother. Unlike the linear road that seems to form in front of the reader as a continuation of *Anton Reiser*, the child's way home is obscured by darkness and the distracting glow of white lichen on the tree trunks. The triggering of the memory through a letter links the "far away" to the "so close," a closeness that has to be projected far away in order to approach it, that only exists in the moments of intertextual mediation between the stops.

Slowly but surely, as he travels on, the narrator-protagonist lays down a series of white stones to the house of memory through minuscule projections from his childhood. Like in Grimm's "Hänsel and Gretel," stones and crumbs alternate. Sometimes, the road leads to the stepmother's house, sometimes to the witch. Once the black porter closes the lift, the protagonist hears a crunching, clashing sound that accompanies them on a parallel track. Staying within the movie analogy, this is the sound track to the protagonist's image track. The sound of a parallel reality is symbolized by the service elevator. In German, this is a *Lastenaufzug*, a lift for heavy loads, for ultimate *Belastung*. In a two-class society, the service elevator is hardly ever seen, only heard by a tourist. It becomes part of an infrastructure obstructed from sight by the smooth operation of the service industry. But in this case, the noisy *Lastenaufzug* becomes a mnemonic intertext that disturbs both memory and present experience but connects them inseparably to one another, as the continuation of the story demonstrates: The darkness of the black porter in his blue uniform contrasts with his glimmering white shirt. As the first stepping stone, the glittering moss on tree trunks reappears and has the protagonist project his own childlike and childish memory of madness and despair onto the black man. The American GI, in whose arms the young boy was returned to a destroyed home, returns as its Other, an African-American who becomes the locus of the protagonist's madness: "I was absolutely certain, that the black man across from me would go crazy and throw himself upon me." Residual myth-o-phobias about the "black man," the uncontrollable proletariat, women and nature, encoded in the memory of fairy tales, as in "Hänsel and Gretel," mingle with sketchy but emotionally charged war experiences and fear of loss; loss of self, loss of masculinity, loss of privilege. Race, class, and gender intersect in the narrator's fantasy of the lift-operator suddenly "going crazy." Already haunted by his wife's short forbidding and threatening letter, the lift ride with a black working-class male, the other Other, triggers a series of these mnemonic epistles to initiate a long farewell to "Schrecken und Entsetzen" ("shock and horror"). Both Judith and the black lift-operator are threatening in that they evoke not simply loathing or fear but intense longing as well. Woman and racial Other are so tightly interwoven in the narrator's psychocultural memory that he fears that the operator might actually not only share the hatred of Judith toward him, the white middle-class male, but also act on it. Whereas the *Lastenaufzug* dredges up into consciousness what weighs the white male narrator down, what taints him personally, socially, racially, and politically, the lifted memory also evokes a type of epistolary telepathy between the oppressed that always already knows its destination, and that has the potential to turn into action. The sound track of the unconscious continues to dish up repressed memories and has them clang against each other to jingle the "history of forgetting."

Words and phrases ricochet between times, between the narrating voices and the intruding letter writer. In their use and overuse, phrases, instead of describing an exterior, return to the sender and encase the dominant voice in its perceptual grid. As soon as one visual and verbalized angle is immobilized, the letter is rerouted until it returns from another destination and can be mailed again. Handke turns words and phrases, even whole sentences, into letters that are forever sent, readdressed, and tardily mailed. When the immobile narrator-agent experiences this mailing system in his head one night, "a surrounding overtook me, which I had walked past during the day" ("eine Umgebung holte mich ein, an der ich tagsüber vorbeigegangen war," 46). It is not he who reviews the houses and streets he passed, but rather the surroundings of his walks that overtake him. They attain visibility and tonality through their rhythmic remains within his head: "In retrospect, rows of houses formed themselves out of the vibrations, the skipping of a beat, the knottings and the jolts, that they had left in me. A buzz and a roar . . . were added, when the vibrations also turned into sounds."[81] This whole setting recalls the bar scene in Providence, where music and text exchanged and revived their generic qualities in the narrator-agent's head. Here, a police siren triggers the rhythmic narrative echo:

> In my head, as I now sat motionless, something began to move back and forth, in a similar rhythm, in which I had myself moved through New York the whole day. Once it skipped a beat, then it ran straight ahead for a long time, then it began to twist itself, circled a while and finally let up.

> Im Kopf, als ich jetzt reglos saß, fing etwas an, *sich* hin und her zu bewegen, in einem ähnlichen Rhythmus, in dem ich den ganzen Tag *mich* durch New York bewegt hatte. Einmal stockte es, dann lief es lange Zeit geradeaus, dann fing es *sich* zu krümmen an, kreiste eine Zeitlang und legte *sich* schließlich. (46; my italics)

His visual reception of the surroundings during the day leave their generic visual limits and appear mediated through the rhythm of his walks.[82] His strolls through the streets map the city, and the map becomes narratable in this "siren-induced" transformation (in an anti-Odyssean move, the police siren is responsible for unlocking the memory). However, the reflexive pronouns *mich* and *sich* have been displaced in this memory process. The retelling of the day's events is not just verbally recoded; it is syncopated and slightly off-beat. Suited to the film noir style of his travelogue, he acts as if the police were chasing and circling in on him, as if he were not a tourist but a criminal (a scenario that will come true belatedly in Arizona, when Judith sends some hired ruffians after him). The rhythm in his head appears grammatically disordered; it corresponds to his own wandering trance. Thus, the rhythmic remains have become part of the narrative structure. This mailing system between the perceptive senses and within the narrative structure is underscored by the narrator at the end of his illuminating experience:

Everything, that I could formerly only see completely up close . . . now
moved apart into a landscape, in which one saw as far as the eye could
see, precisely because I had for hours not been able to see anything farther away. I got an urge to *lay down in it* and read a book *in it.*

Alles, was ich vorher nur ganz nah sehen konnte . . . *rückte* nun, gerade weil ich stundenlang nichts weiter weg hatte anschauen können, *zu*
einer Landschaft *auseinander*, in der man sah, so weit das Auge reichte.
Ich bekam Lust, *mich hineinzulegen* und *darin ein Buch zu lesen.* (47;
my italics)

Read linearly, this paragraph appears to zoom in on a totality at long
distance, which was obstructed by detailed "signs" at close range. The
reader perceives *rücken* and *zu* prior to the tail end of the verb:
auseinander. Whereas *auseinanderrücken* signifies a splitting up, a moving apart, *zu* indicates the opposite. *Auseinander* comes as a surprise
because it destroys the expectations and predictability of prepositional
positioning, of visual placements and the verbal landscape. An inward
move is combined with an outward move. The vision becomes a landscape at the moment of its disintegration. Handke wants to transform
the epistolary "auseinanderrücken . . . zu" into the place of reading, the
spatial movement of his novel. The narrator's visual perception was
already transcribed into another sign system before—into rhythmic
motion. This time the change in his range of vision transgresses semantic laws to achieve the necessary combination of contradictory gestures.
The polarity blocking and encasing his perception, his narrative, and our
reading is broken twice. Having arrived and left this semantic intersection of "zu . . . rücken" and "auseinander," we can see as far as the eye
can see. The text is neither framed by a "narrow door" that leaves one
with sharp details in slow motion (40), nor is it a frameless totality.
Handke's narrative achieves its textuality at these intersections which
disappear as soon as they open up.

In the narrator's search for immediate presence of self and reality,
these "open" textual moments present themselves structurally mediated
in a transcription from one system to another, a decontextualization of
specific phrases, and an abrupt and rather forceful adulteration of different morphemes and genres. The character's romantic longing for a
"true" self that is congruous with its environment seems deconstructed
by this structuralization of the poetic dilemma. The narratological
movement apparently does not romance the post in the least. Or does his
conversion of the "letter" into a perceptive system that structures everything *and* evades all structure romance the post after all?

I must take another detour in order to confront this problematic question. The last scenario of the book ties up all loose ends in a potential

movie script. John Ford, who, when interviewed by Judith, axiomatically states that "first person narratives only exist where one stands for all others" ("Ich-Geschichten gibt es nur dort, wo einer für alle anderen steht," 188), gives Judith the cue to tell the narrator's and her story as "our story" (195). Her siren call makes the story narratable at last. Within her voice she hosts the other's voices. Her story is always already his story, which has the great advantage of freeing him from his limited vantage point. The narrator-agent can simply listen to himself being told. This merging of sender and addressee, of male and female, of hunter and hunted, of narrator and narrated, provides him with a "true" story, a story that finally seems to have reached its destination.[83]

In the last days before Judith's and his reunion, the narrator-protagonist increasingly suspects his own fictionality. When he leaves the mugging scene in Arizona, he exits by removing himself from the frame: "ENT-FERNTE MICH" (169). At John Ford's house, he no longer partakes in the discussion; he simply repeats the direct dialogue. His participatory stake in the story combined with his distant observation of its narration by another promises full presence for the story itself. One of the only paragraphs written in present tense utters the irresistibility of storytelling in the form of a screenplay setting. Visual representation is again connected to textual narrative; the chairs elicit stories from their inhabitants:

> From the terrace the view goes down into a valley, in which orange trees and cypresses stand. For the visitor, there are wicker ottomans, which are lined up next to each other, in front of them small foot rests with Native American blankets. When one sits in one of them and talks, one soon begins to tell the other a story.[84]

The romantic presence of the setting creates the image of a patterned fairy tale meeting thousand-and-one nights in which the plot is ordered like the dwarfs' seats in "Snow White." John Ford appears in this setting like an actor in one of his own movies. Before Judith can tell their story, Ford's opinions and answers repeat the narrator's story, sometimes in direct quotes and at other times in metaphors. Considering the fact that the narrator wrote the text retrospectively, one could also say that the narrator used John Ford's generalities, his American "we-form," as a framework for his own story. The first-person plural promises to fill in the unbearable "interstices" (Zwischenräume, 184) between the general and the specific, between self-presence and self-alienation, between the mailing and the arrival of a letter. John Ford's statements write the script for the book, but the story with a happy end also writes a potential Hollywood script. Film, nature, and narrative harmonize at last: Judith's eyelashes synchronically flutter with the wings of a butterfly sitting on the narrator's hand (194).

Alas, a rather vicious cynicism threatens to bring the whole structure tumbling down. Nature is in decay, peaceful before a storm. The reunion turned the living story line into a still-life with rotting flowers and bursting spiders: "In front of us a fat yellow spider burst which had just before been sitting on a bush leaf" ("Vor uns platzte eine dicke gelbe Spinne, die gerade noch auf einem Strauchblatt gesessen hatte," 194). In order to see the American beauty of the relation between the butterfly, the symbol of metamorphosis, and Judith's fluttering eyelashes "[o]ne just needed to take one breath less" ("[m]an brauchte nur einen Atemzug weniger zu tun," 194):

> Because we expected a story, we bent slightly forward, and I noticed that in doing so, I repeated a movement with which someone in one of his films, without moving from his position, craned his neck towards a dying man, in order to see, whether he was still alive.[85]

The story that they crane their necks to hear turns out to be their own story. It is fabricated as a copy from one of Ford's genre films and eavesdropped from the lips of a "stiff." The corpse's story becomes their story within this moment of death. When the narrator leans forward with a vulture-like gesture, he is in fact witnessing the resurrection of his story from the dead, first in Judith's and then his own words. Like the treasure scene of *Romancing the Stone*, in which the Easter bunny is excavated only to be smashed into pieces, and the stone exhumed only to be stolen, the birth of a story is brought about by its imminent death and adaptation. In their transferal from synchronous events to literary metaphors, the eyelashes and butterfly-wings reach a deadlock.[86] Total immediacy and death go hand in hand. In spite of the narrator-agent's goal, a story can only be narrated as a long farewell: the melodramatic farewell from a moribund genre, which transcends itself in its last breath.

Handke constantly pushes his narrative to a near stalemate between romantic nostalgia and belief in the authenticity of language, between nature and the writing subject on the one hand, and the impending destruction of the progressing narrative on the other.[87] Only by investing letters, words, sentences, their syntax, and literature with the unearthing and unearthly characteristics of the epistolary form can the narrator hope to break this standoff in favor of the genre that is "always in a state of excess with itself."[88] In *Der kurze Brief*, all moments of "immediacy" have been "posted" between contexts and episodes; they reoccur as "post-stories" in mirrored narrative frames. A moment is never alone, it has been infiltrated and doubled by the chain mail of genre mixes and epistolary hopscotch. The epistolary genre at work in Handke's prose, whether used structurally, thematically, or semiotically, is instilled with all the power and potential of romantic discourse. In its evasiveness and shifting capacity it builds up a shred of hope and poetic ideology on which the postmodern writer can place his or her bet. Through its "epistelography," language literalizes itself, cleanses itself from the dirt of its adulterating adventures while taking on a new adventure and lover at every turn of the page. Handke romances the post by putting "the weight of the world"[89] on its ability to keep narrative in structural suspense. The postmodern version of the romantic letter now reads: Romance the post as much as you want, the "posteffect" will undo its own romanticization.

CHAPTER 6

Mail-Art:
Einsteckalbum

In the early nineties, the epistolary love story *Griffin and Sabine* developed into a mass consumer boom. It became chic to send handwritten letters on fancy paper again.

"It all started with a mysterious and seemingly innocent postcard, but from that point nothing was to remain the same in the life of Griffin Moss, a quiet, solitary artist living in London."
—*Griffin and Sabine*, 1991 back cover

"And, in this multi-media novel, each letter must be pulled from its own envelope, giving the reader that delightful forbidden sensation of reading someone else's mail."
—*Griffin and Sabine*, 1991 dust jacket

"This truly innovative novel combines a strangely fascinating story with lush artwork in an altogether original format."
—*Griffin and Sabine*, 1991 back cover

FIRST INSERT:
NICK BANTOCK'S *GRIFFIN AND SABINE*

Nick Bantock's *Einsteckalbum* art-book trilogy for adults, *Griffin and Sabine. An Extraordinary Correspondence* (1991), *Sabine's Notebook* (1992), and *The Golden Mean* (1993), caused a sensation because it literally opened the novel, and the book, to the wayward materiality of letters while recollecting the mythical story of beauty, artistic creation, and love in ordinary contemporary language. Nick Bantock's and Chronicle Books' design features the address side of letters and both sides of postcards as a one-dimensional illustration while it presents the traditional sender side of a letter envelope as an open two-dimensional envelope with enclosed folded letters or cards. None of the envelopes show signs of ever having been sealed, and the stamps, including express and airmail stamps, are printed and not glued onto the envelopes.

While innovative in its combination of media, art, and romance plot, why do the publishers exaggerate and claim it as "an altogether original format" when Ray Johnson, together with the Fluxus artist Dick Higgins, founded "Mail-art" in the early 1950s? "In his renunciation of a materially representative art in favor of an art as communication," Johnson makes "alogical connections" that have followers in Yves Klein, Gilbert & George, Robert Rauschenberg, Mieko Shiomi, On Kawara in the late 1960s, and Peter Faecke and Wolf Vostell with their *Postversandroman* (mail-order novel) in the early 1970s.[1] Besides the Fluxus inspired mail-art works, numerous children's books feature pull-out letters *(The Jolly Mailman)*, pop-up items, and insertable objects. In the twentieth century alone, novelists like Else Lasker-Schüler in the 1920s and James Krüss in the 1960s have attempted similar epistolary-art designs,[2] not to mention that the enclosure of artwork, of objects, plants, locks of hair, and collectibles dates back to the beginning of epistolary culture.

In addition, one of the earliest forms of *Inserate* (advertising inserts) in books allowed by the publishing world consists of the famous plot-integrated letter inserts of the *Pfandbrief* and *Kommunalobligation* variety of the German banking industry, advertising the "verbriefte Sicherheit" (epistolarily documented security) of stocks and bonds.[3] The *Inserat* as letter within a novel inserts itself as continuation and disruption of the narrative by asserting, in content, its material value as a savings bond. The epistolary insert becomes a structural surplus of the narrative which it interrupts for its message, thereby reinserting that narrative into the material world. In most of the cases, the ad actually employs a commonplace saying to link up fiction and advertisement. It trades with a familiar form of address and literally banks on its security appeal. Should the reader feel left out of the narrative due to an unusual style or to class differences portrayed in the plot, the bank-letter remedies that fact by addressing the reader as "one of us," as the prototypical upwardly mobile middle-class citizen. The letter as "verbriefte Sicherheit" has seemingly lost its power of wielding eighteenth-century style *liaisons dangereuses* and instead has been arrested in its late-nineteenth-century positivist materialist form. However, its emancipatory impetus can still be detected in the attempt to continually further the sociopolitical goals of the bourgeois, right up to its self-dispossession, in what Hans Magnus Enzensberger calls the "nivellierte Mittelstandsgesellschaft" ("leveled middle-class-society").

The novel featuring one of these "ads as letters" has become an *Einsteckalbum*, not too dissimilar from a stamp album and has moved closer in kind to a magazine filled with perfume samples and credit card application-postcards. While the novel's fictional plot may lead one toward social-criticism, revolution, or moral upheavals, the letter-insert will anchor it squarely in conservative trade market capitalism. The promise of *Verbriefen* puts its stamp on the surrounding text. Surreptitiously, as the ad reevaluates any book as a commodity item, it also issues itself, and the letter form, as an original. The effect of interrupting the reading, of inserting a foreign element into the flow of the diegesis, borrows the attention and reception relay from Brecht's *Verfremdungseffekt* yet insinuates with the use of the letter form that its narrator identifies with the implied reader. What the letter form accomplishes in this case is a mediation of alienation as "verbriefte Sicherheit." As Trinh T. Minh-ha admonishes the anthropologist in all of us, "[t]he positivist yearning for transparency with respect to reality is always lurking beneath the surface."[4] And how delightful, indeed, when this yearning is quenched and stimulated in the convergence of fiction and reality, thing and word, concept and sign, message and mediation, when transparency materializes in your very hands.

It appears somewhat ironic that originality and authenticity ("delightful forbidden sensation of reading someone else's mail") should be determined by gaining tactile empirical knowledge from a product of popular culture like *Griffin and Sabine*, when the postmodern condition is based on a response to "the mental and sensual depravations of modern mass culture."[5] Two other recent sensory investigations feeding off the same conundrum come to mind: the olfactory stimulus theorized and narrated in Patrick Süskind's *Perfume* and the visually textured Peter Høeg's *Smilla's Sense of Snow*. As murder mysteries, forensic evidence and an erotically charged *Leichenschau* ("identifying a corpse") stand in for the irretrievable sense of a collective modernist nostalgia and reiterate again and again a postmodern agenda determined by *Nachträglichkeit*.[6]

The love-letter trilogy of *Griffin and Sabine* itself partakes in this "retrospective reading" of the commodified cult of fetishized authenticity.[7] Sabine is a "foundling" raised by native parents on the island of Kati in the South Pacific. She is the official and chief designer of the island's stamp collection. Because they are so rare, her stamps are quite valuable on the international stamp collectors' trade market, and she claims, she is the only one who actually uses them to send mail. In her case, stamp, postcard, and envelope designs match. Griffin, on the other hand, resides in the capital of the old empire, London. He is the designer, owner, and presumably also printer of Gryphon Cards. In his case, the letter, envelope, and postcard designs bear his mark, but the Queen resides ever so prominently on the address side of his envelopes and postcards, even though Griffin sometimes displaces her from the traditional upper right hand corner to let her become part of the address or frontispiece picture.

In the first book, Sabine writes to the former empire; Griffin writes to the former colonies. This setup switches in *Sabine's Notebook*, when Griffin travels around the world and Sabine occupies his apartment and studio in London. In this installment, the correspondence becomes part of Sabine's diary and sketchbook, recognizable by her scribblings across and in the margins among letters, postcards, and notebook. Even though Griffin tries to visit Kati on his journey, he fails. He almost drowns on attempting the passage. Only the apparition of Sabine, reconfigured here as Hans Christian Andersen's sacrificial little mermaid, saves him from giving in to death. Similarly, there is no sign of Sabine's presence in London, except for the cat's behavior. The narrator-editor informs us that Griffin returned as promised on the 23rd, whereas Sabine's last postcard maintains that she remained there until the 31st. In *The Golden Mean*, as the intimacy of their correspondence is threatened by a nosy journalist-outsider (representing the audience's and publisher's demand, sudden fame, and tabloid journalism), they agree to meet on "neutral ground" in Alexandria, at a gateway between past and present, between First and Third Worlds.

Sabine initially writes to Griffin because she has finally connected a real person to the images of someone drawing and painting in her mind's eye. She can see Griffin while he is designing his Gryphon postcard collection. The correspondence has therefore already begun. Griffin's postcards have telepathically mailed themselves to her, and when the reader compares their styles, both are remarkably similar down to the details. The ensuing written correspondence allows Griffin to reflect on his art and the process of creating. The correspondence reinvigorates art, as art becomes a performative act connecting artist to audience in the most intimate way possible. The postmodern artist, composing layers of visual and textual quotations, believed himself superfluous and unreal, sexually frustrated and artistically uninspired. With Sabine, Griffin has found a way to make his existence tangible to himself and to his author, Nick Bantock (who is not only a *Doppelgänger* of Griffin but also potentially of the snooping journalist Victor Frolatti). These author figures manipulate the age of electronic communication and multimedia reproduction in the shape of reliably unreliable snail mail. Each glossy smooth-surfaced envelope and each crisp letter one pulls out are testimony to the matchless sterility of the reproduction process, of its ability to erase all traces of the production and the reproduction process, in effect purifying itself of the postal triad: origination, mediation, destination.

Appropriately, each book ends three times. *Griffin and Sabine*'s first ending has Griffin recall the correspondence's claim to authenticity written on a portrayal of "Pierrot's Last Stand." In Arnold Schönberg's *Pier-*

rot lunaire, "the antique fragrance of a fairy-tale world of long ago ('Oh ancient scent from far-off days') helps the moonstruck poet of the cycle to abandon his gloom and dream beyond the boundaries of reality ('Now all my sorrow I dispel; and dream beyond the fair horizon')."[8] Here, he has outdreamed himself. Sabine, the Griffin-Pierrot writes, is a figment of his imagination threatening to run amok. He does not want to recreate the Pygmalion myth: "Before it takes me over it has to stop" (postcard of Jan. 1). As if to demonstrate this refusal to remain in circulation, within the artistic canon of Western Civilization, the postcard bears no stamp, does therefore not participate in the authenticated mailing system of the diegesis. But the second ending features a winged angel of death postcard, entitled ". . . the ceremony of innocence . . . ," from Sabine responding to Griffin's uncirculated card. This postcard from beyond the ending, from beyond the pleasure principle, hauntingly reinstitutes the "authenticity" of Sabine as a correspondent and of Griffin and Sabine's correspondence. Written into the discourses of colonialism and Orientalism, the naturalized foundling Sabine *cannot not* write back to the empire and demand that her voice, buried underneath layers of *Fremdbestimmung* with all its contradictions, be heard. In her attempts and despite her stereotyped no-body-ness, she resists the "principle of closure" and epistolarily engages in "a systematic decentering of the West."[9] Yet as the incarnation of Woman, she also accosts Griffin as a "foolish man" when he runs scared each time that his art, expressing his longing for immediacy, and his life actually threaten to converge. Racial and gender-determined constructs of the "Other" cancel their respective identity-political trajectories.

Following a postmodern trajectory of traversing, counterfeiting, and contrastively patching together cultural, racial, and gender divides while seeking out the origin of art in a decidedly modernist quest, Griffin travels around the world in the second installment of the correspondence. He begins close to home with the high modernists in Dublin and continues in Florence, paying "homage at the altar of his masters." In a "sensuous dream," at the Palazzo di Medici, Sabine "emerged from a smoky wall and enveloped" him. This text is written on the back of a picture of a half-naked woman entitled "Page from Leonardo's missing sketchbook." According to him, it is also the first "original" postcard, a "one-off" instead of a reprint. Bantock again plays with the seductive fiction of originality in the age of mechanical reproduction. But besides that, he also lets postmodern art fill in the amnesic blanks in history, the "missing sketchbooks" of the old masters, a move that is mirrored by Sabine's collection of Griffin's art in her sketchbook. In his place, in his absence, she composes the sketchbook of his quest for artistic inspiration, self-confidence, and immortality. In his Florence dream, Griffin is getting off on the sublimations, the wrapped up *l'art pour l'art* aestheticism as he conjures up Sabine out of the "smoky" back rooms of male fantasies dating back to da Vinci.

He can visualize her now, like she did his drawings, because Sabine has begun to occupy the position of the familiar, of "home." She envelop(e)s him. When writing her, he literally addresses himself to himself, holding an "artistic conversation of man with man."[10] As he mails himself to himself, the process of mediation itself is fictionalized, written as a recollection of immediacy. And as he *males* himself, he uses the detour through Woman to arrive at a stable masculine position that also preserves the modernist illusion of the self-reflective, melancholic "quiet, solitary artist." The string which Sabine holds out to him provides him with free movement around the labyrinth of his mind, yet promises him a safe return. He cannot get lost, and even the Minnotaur holds little threat. In his letter from Alexandria, he finds out that the word "sculptor" means "he who keeps alive forever" in Egyptian. It is no coincidence that the "self-sufficient" cat Minnaloushe, which "comes and goes with the moon," is a reincarnation of the elective affinity connecting Griffin and Sabine and a hackneyed reminder that art and love, while adhering to a magnetic rhythm of repulsion and attraction, need to remain free. As a result, upon his return in the third book of their correspondence, Griffin is ready to commit, to attain the "Golden Mean" and meet Sabine in Alexandria.

They both attempt to escape Victor Frolatti, the nosy, materialistic, psychic, evil-boding tabloid journalist, who all of a sudden interrupts their hermetic postal universe. Both attribute their increasing loss of telepathic contact to Frolatti's disruptive presence. Two creative artists blame their writer's block on the postmodern interference caused by the popular media, the mail-order industry out to make monetary gain from their romantic idyll. After Griffin and Sabine decide that they must meet on "neutral ground," Sabine's last postcard changes from her typical brown ink to Griffin's black in its midth, which is also the sentence in which she describes the Alexandrian gateway: "Perhaps the gate will let us both pass through." The change from brown to black ink implies that their epistolary meeting has already been consummated but also that Frolatti is counterfeiting Sabine's postcard. The fly has entered the transmaterializer. The transmaterialization takes place in Sabine's handwriting, on a postcard that features what looks like an enlarged area from Griffin's "Page from Leonardo's missing sketchbook" that I discussed above. The only difference is that here, Sabine is dressed in a blazer, although she still emerges from a "smoky" background into the white light on the right, the direction of her glance. Whether one reads the transmutation of the handwriting as a passing through the hymeneal archway into the marriage of muse and artist, imagination and representation, it also indicates a "passing": a passing of man as woman, a passing of empire as decolonized Other, and finally a passing of art as popular culture. Griffin, in his yearning to suture past and present, sex and race, by representing the death of modern art and its unavoidable reproduction as postmodernism, can only do so by speaking from below, by trusting and "appropriating the vision of the less powerful while claiming to see from their positions."[11] The entire correspondence becomes mute and reveals itself as an internal monologue of an empire nostalgic with the postcolonial loss of its Other and the legitimacy of its self-identity. The child that Griffin and Sabine supposedly have together at the end might also be a figment of Frolatti's imagination, always on the lookout for happy endings that ensure the progeny of hegemonic homogeneity. Griffin's response postcard features an overexposed negative, the wrong way round, of his former "Passing Shot" postcard, here entitled "The Gordian Mirror." Instead of a knot, Bantock presents the mirror, and with it the representation of representation, as an unsolvable solution.

The third ending of the trilogy establishes a frame of forensic evidence regarding Griffin's address and the origin of his art while it seems to take back the second ending's attempt at a metaphysical legitimacy of originality and authenticity: "These postcards and letters were found pinned to the ceiling of the otherwise empty studio of Griffin Moss. Griffin Moss is missing." Sabine and Griffin have traded places. The colonialist fantasy outlives its creator. At the beginning, a collection of art left the public sphere of the museum and entered the private sphere of correspondences. At the end, the letter exchange is reconverted into a picture-gallery, a planetarium of the mystified artistic mind. The author might be missing, but his autobiography "in the name of the other" attests to his existence. In each of the "turning and turning in . . ." phases (subtitle of *Griffin and Sabine*), the attempt to undo the cult of authenticity reinscribes the correspondence deeper into its design.

SECOND INSERT:
KARL SCHAPER'S "POST OFFICE OF THANATOS"

I came across Karl Schaper's mail-art in one of Germany's most distinguished old libraries in Wolffenbüttel in 1987.[12] Surrounded by literature, art, and history, Karl Schaper's letter-objects, which—true to the epistolary tradition—are often based on the proverbial *object trouvé*, interacted with the state of letters not only intertextually but also physically.[13] Schaper's wooden letters and object-art consist of fictionally and plastically authenticated correspondences between him and historical personae like Ovid (1981), Columbus (1974), and Adolf Hitler (1973), between fictional characters like Snow White, the hunting prince, and her stepmother (1974), between artists and their subjects, like Heinrich Heine's letter to his beloved Germany (1973), and between Schaper himself and his geography students (1982). While "Snow White" playfully rewrites the German fairy tale from the hunter's perspective, most of Schaper's pieces call forth and react to the political climate of the day, for example, his "Military Music" (1976): a letter that includes a half-visible record, supposedly of a popular folk- and army song, which he sends back to a general with the explanation that "it's still the same old song in the military." Similarly, the "German-German dialogue" (1984) has two shovels standing upright in two mailbags, one from East Germany and one from West Germany with the appropriate address tags signaling that each shovel should be used to level the other half's missile bases.

When Schaper's foible for letters is acknowledged by art critics, for example, by Ludwig Zerull, they see the letter form as a "traditional means of communication with the other,"[14] a means for "direct and indirect dialogue with the audience," for "immediate artistic articulation" of the artist's anger about falsehood and injustice.[15] Judging from these statements, Schaper's art concretizes Marshall McLuhan's "the medium is the message."[16] Few of his critics seem to wonder what actually happens to the letter form that Schaper employs so variably. Maybe it would be more correct to say that the form engages him. On the one hand, the idea that a letter, as nonsignifying shell, adequately and successfully transports its content still has a high market value. On the other hand, Schaper's mail-art specifically addresses the questionable relation of ideas of agency and mediation, foregrounding the post office and its postal code. Schaper's *epistuli* not only keep open a dialogue between history and the present, between art and politics, they also problematize the very politics of the modernist archive and museum.

One of Schaper's most conspicuous epistolary artifacts is "The Post Office of Thanatos" (1984). It consists of fourteen mailbags, four ladders, and twenty-seven wood-postcards and placards. He collected the rejected mailbags from a former classmate, a postal clerk.[17] All the post gathered and stacked between the ladders and sown onto the bags, cannot be delivered—is nonpostable ("nicht zustellbar")—because there is neither a clear match between address and addressee, nor between return address and sender. Although the bags' labels indicate that they are state property of West Germany, how does one return mail to the state other than to the post office? Schaper turns the divided state of

Germany into a disfunctional and defunct post office. Since the letters that have returned to this post office are undeliverable, their arrest renders them visible and transforms them into property of the state. The post office thus also becomes a museum, the state a dead-letter museum of democratic messages. After the terrorism of the *Heißer Herbst* in 1977 and the events of the early 1980s (stationing of mid-range Pershing II rockets in West Germany, violent clashes between antinuclear protesters and police units at Brokdorf, the Soviet-Polish crisis, just to mention a few), Schaper declares the very ideas of democratic statehood—free speech, privacy of the mail, and the *Datenschutzgesetz* (information exchange protection law)—politically moribund. Schaper's mail-art responds by perverting the prime directive of the postal service, namely, to maintain the sanctity of the mail, to make its passage as unnoticeable as possible. Thanatos' post office corrupts the voyeuristic secrecy of the modernist discourse. It displays its Hades.

The entire block composes the post office of Thanatos—of the black-winged god of death. One can find confiscated and overdue letters among wartime speeches, rejected petitions from the Green citizen's list, letters to victims of the DC-10 crash between Shannon and New York, and fictitious postcards by artists and political figures addressing their assassins. Thanatos' post office features dead letters, letters from the living to the dead, from the dead to the living. Separated into three columns by the ladders, this post office is made accessible to those willing to risk the descent into memory, history, and death. In contrast to an archival collection of historical documents, Schaper's object inscribes the "could have beens" along with reproductions from originals: Anne Frank responds to the German *Herrenrasse*, wartime oratories correspond with letters from the front, overdue airmail letters appear side by side with letters to those killed in a crash. The decontextualized letters in Thanatos' post office shift their destinations to correspond with each other and the postal code itself.

Especially when considering the German past, the assembled "dead letters" in Thanatos' post office force the spectator to remember them, to readdress the postwar period to the Holocaust and the Third Reich but also to readdress this post to the present. Schaper turns the postwar period into a postal war, a war over messages, over which are heard and which are silenced. Schaper's "post office" hands down the past, and while attaching itself firmly to a modernist humanism, he scrambles its code. In Schaper's postal scenario, the reader functions like a reading mail carrier. Instead of simply being the intended addressee of the dislocated and anachronistic letters, she or he is forced to dislocate them once more, to connect them to each other. The audience literally delivers the mail by delivering itself to the posted past. Following Wittgenstein's lead from *Tractatus Logico-philosophicus*, Schaper situates his letters between ladders to help both the descent into the postal storage of the unconscious and the ascent to cognizance and deliverance:

> My sentences explain by the way, that the person, who understands me, in the end apprehends them as nonsensical, when he has climbed through them—on them—beyond them. (He must throw away the ladder, so to speak, after he has climbed up on it.) He must overcome these sentences, then he sees the world correctly.[18]

Here, Wittgenstein illustrates through his logic of sentence grammar that the direct object of the verb *erläutern*, which would be the solution of the problem he and the reader are seeking, is perpetually delayed and displaced into the act of overcoming sentences and explanations as such. Speakers and writers, who risk the play of language and representation, deliver themselves to the post only to be delivered by the signifier. The question remains, whether deliverance, whether from the postal code, from the past, or from the collective unconscious, is possible. According to Wittgenstein, deliverance is only possible after thorough critical investigation and eventual dissembling of one's logical apparatus, and then only within another set of sentences or within silence (#6.7.). In German, the related verbs *zustellen* or "sich zu etwas stellen" (to own up to or face up to something) make this even clearer. "To deliver" is linked to the act of self-aware political and ethical positioning. For the museum of Schaper's installation, this means that the bystanding spectators are served a summons *(zustellen)* to bridge the gap between sender and addressee with their gaze and physical presence. In a very ambiguous move, Schaper rewrites the position of bystander into one, which allows for the delivery of the undeliverable letters.[19]

THIRD INSERT:
NICOMEDES SUÁREZ-ARAÚZ'S *AMNESIS ART*

> "'Reborn digital' material is taken from crumbling paper documents, wax cylinders like those Thomas Edison used for the first recordings, or early television programs recorded on two-inch videotapes that can only be read by a few remaining pieces of equipment."[20]

Bolivian-American artist, theorist, philosopher, and shape-shifter Nicomedes Suárez-Araúz began formulating his thesis of *amnesis* as a countertheory to the art of the *object trouvé* and hyperrealism of the late 1960s and early 1970s. In an interview with the Massachusetts *Valley Advocate*, he traces its development back to his childhood in the "eastern Amazonian plains of Bolivia, where everything literally disappears, gets swallowed up by the jungle."[21] In his book *Amnesis Art. The Art of the Lost Object*, which offers a composite of visual, poetic, and architectural art accompanied by theoretical and political treatises, Suárez-Araúz offers a companion-definition of subjectivity: "We are, in large measure, what we have lost and can never recover or recall."[22] Picking up Nietzsche's notion of necessary and creative forgetting, Suárez-Araúz insists that absence and forgetting are a source of creativity, consistently understudied and underappreciated. But unlike Freud or Lacan, he contends that he is not talking about the unconscious. Instead, amnesia "is a stalking presence that erodes, shapes, and refines our lives." He calls it a "universe coexistent with the realm of memory and presences" (93). And it is this universe that forces each person to "improvise": "We cannot remember, so we create" (95). The very reference to his so-called alive presence of childhood memories as opposed to the "abstract idea pulled out from philosophy" (*Advocate*, 3) partakes in the fictional construction of identity, space, and history.

The epistolary mode of this fictionality enters his "amnesis manifesto," when Suárez-Araúz calls *amnesis art "letters to amnesia*, messages inspired on a poetic and philosophical conception of amnesia" (96). Letters, once again, become "a poetic phrase" (102) for the description of that which happens between presence and absence, between send-off and arrival or send-off and evacuation. *Letters to amnesia* trace the dotted line of the shifting contours between dichotomies, the very perception of a structuralist universe already including an "intermixing of an otherness."[23] In his "Amnesis Manifesto," Suárez-Araúz shares Handke's preoccupation with the past, memory, and forgetting, but decides to send letters on a different route. Instead of routing letters into the structure of literary language and textuality, he simply proclaims, and here he sounds like Derrida invoking Schlegel, that all *amnesis art* works *are* letters. Rather than having an epistolary character or function due to performance, the letter is defined through the concept of Being: "A 'letter to amnesia' obviously cannot expect an answer: its very presence can be said to be its answer" (96, footnote 2). Suárez-Araúz notes that his *letters to amnesia* share aspects of Umberto Eco's idea of "open and closed works," in so far as "they do not project a 'message,' but rather proliferate meanings" yet also "embody a concept," namely, amnesia (8 and 96, footnote 2). Culturally, these "imaginary artifact[s] from our unmemoried past and future" appear because of a sense of loss, however unspecified (102). The very perception of a loss indicates both "a whittling away of the reality of concrete objects within the contemporary and cultural supra-nature of technologically developed nations" (102) and a Barthian sense of excessive creativity to make up for it.

As defined by Suárez-Araúz, *Amnesis Art* consists of *"fabulations* (narratives presented as though they were true)" (101). While a shift of attention from presence and immediacy to absence and forgetfulness seems to revoke modernist realism, the modernist teleology is still firmly in place: "Without an awareness of amnesia, we cannot have a complete vision" (96). Considering this search for complete vision, it comes as no surprise that a large part of the artwork, supposedly by different artists (Nicomedes Suárez-Araúz in "diverse guises" as the dust jacket of the book suggests), featured in *Amnesis Art*, is characterized by a painted background riddled with polymorphous holes painted in another color, sometimes solid, sometimes depicting their own scenes, or its opposite, a white background dotted with pasted-on cutouts from another scene.[24] Some of the paintings resemble either a tableau of several sets of puzzles mixed up and poured over one another (#4, 5, 8, 12, 19, 21, 22 by Bartolomeo Esteban, Nicoläs Horacio, and Hans Klauss) or a wax-etching (#1, 13 and 14 by Robert Llewellyn). The puzzle approach to amnesia and history presupposes a primordial wholeness that leads back to the idea of origin and decline, that expresses the artistic longing for and the structural possibility of "putting the pieces together again." Similar to the author's "diverse guises," the subject of history and the self are broken up into several pieces that now interact with each other and take up a life of their own (in this case literally, with the inclusion of the artists' biographies, 59–92). While these interactive gestures may "underscore the dissolution of individuality and authorship" (*Amnesis Art*, dust jacket), is it enough to overlay the production of *amnesis art* with the suspicion of *fabulation* to deconstruct the modernist project with its demands for total recall? Or do the allegorical *letters to amnesia*, which have themselves been liberated from any specific epistolary form and function, become this deconstructive fifth element that neither theory nor art themselves can manage to produce, sustain, or control?

My previous discussion of postmodern *fabulation* and the "double fictionality" of eighteenth-century letters should unclose the self-amnesic quality in mail-orders like *amnesis art*, even if, or precisely when forgetting is at stake. The mail-order orders itself to forget, be forgotten, and forget itself. I'd like you to ponder briefly how the East and South were won: After the fall of the wall in 1989, mail-order companies reached across the former borders of the Eastern bloc faster than investors could get their hands on retail space. Again and again, new frontiers as well as domestic markets are colonized by catalogue businesses, and progressively so by Internet services. Neither customer nor company needs to venture forth into the urban jungle or the uprooted economic infrastructure of old. One can display and shop directly into and from the newly fortified private sphere. Once old city centers are restored or new shopping malls on green fields surrounding the city have been built, the economic infrastructure of capitalist desire is already in place and will breach out into the open for further stimulation.

With mail-ordering, the act of shopping is assembled of several lust-filled time-place installments, not necessarily in the following order: receiving a catalogue, a fax, or an e-mail product list-browsing through the offers-selecting items for purchase-perhaps comparing price, service, and quality with similar items from another catalogue-listing the ordered items-sending, faxing, phoning, or e-mailing the order to the company-paying-waiting-receiving the items by mail. The waiting phase of this list of delayed actions psychologically constructs a field of creative amnesia for the customer: he or she sometimes (deliberately? creatively?) forgets *that* and *what* was ordered. When the package arrives, it is almost, as David Duchovny, the TV-star of Fox's *X-Files*, recently recognized, as if one receives not a product but a present from someone, as if, by magic, someone, here the dominant discourse, had guessed one's deepest desires and wishes and fulfilled them (*GQ*, February 1998). Capitalism has finally penetrated not just the lone ranch out West (Sears-Roebuck pioneered that invasion over a century ago) or the (sub)urban home (the invasion of the (sub)urban home was begun by door-to-door sales and the advent of radio culminating in the rise of TV) but the very cycle of desire for interpersonal contact and mystic communication with the Beyond. Perceived or actual loss and fear of direct one-on-one contact in constant tension with the longing for a perfect communication without words leads to an act of creative forgetting. That this forgetting allows the customer to receive the ordered items as a personalized gift is doubly ironic, since (a) if all we ever received as gifts were things we had always wanted or needed, birthdays would be pretty boring: it would rain underwear, socks, and perfectly matched gifts, but no surprises and no things to throw at the wall in a fit of rage, and (b) the company never forgets to charge one's credit card or cash in one's check, often even withdrawing the money at the time of the order, not at the time of the contract's fulfillment, thereby actually accumulating for themselves additional moneys due to the inflationary time-lapse between order and fulfillment (some of the worst offenders in this aspect are airline companies, with whom you might book a flight as much as a few months prior to departure and who cash in on the surplus the time-lapse creates; on the opposite end tend to be publishing companies, which ship you the books long before payment clears your account).

The mail-order literally banks on its customer's forgetting to create an ever stronger psychological and economic dependency for the next transaction. That the highest percentage of mail-order target groups are made up of lower- to upper-middle-class single women and housewives, who incidentally are also, studies have shown, at a higher risk to develop Alzheimer's than men,[25] should give reason to question the repression of gender- and class-specific, not to mention race-specific problems in the totalizing concept of a "philosophy of amnesia." The specificity of female desires is on the one hand repressed and forgotten by male-dominated Western societies, leaving women "needy" to fill the lack (addicted to shopping, overeating) or become the lack (through *anorexia nervosa, bulimia*), while on the other hand its various socially mandated forms of expression are being exploited, thus reconfiguring female desire to match the market's needs. Women are stuck in a double bind. Having to play nurturer to others and the market, they are still in charge of most of the food shopping and preparation. But ever since the rise of the suit with the advance of industrialization and bureaucratization, they have also been the major target of a fashion industry, whose demands on slimness have not ceased to increase since the Twiggy age. Woman is *the* consumer, who is not supposed to consume, at least not in public.[26] The more she overeats, the more she becomes dependent on home shopping and the mail/male-order, adding agoraphobia to her list of socially induced anxieties. The more she exercises and starves herself, hoping to "put on male power and privilege," the more she "serve[s] . . . a social order that limits female possibilities."[27]

If she rebels against it, she is told that she is "forgetting herself." The moment of overstepping limitations and taboos coincides with a linguistic reminder that subjectivity and the notion of selfhood are guaranteed only within the social order, that excessive sexual or political desire is threatened with dissolution of the self, with the expulsion from personal and collective memory. Forgetting oneself, on the contrary, is usually a surefire way to inscribe oneself into local folklore, becoming a story retold again and again for amusement and as warning. Throughout history, while men's acts of "forgetting themselves" have generally been seen as part of their initiation rite into manhood, women's excesses have always been perceived as extraneous to their identity, and have been punished more consistently and much harder. And, in general, with few exceptions (Medea, Joan d'Arc), women's moments of "forgetting themselves" were not made the "stuff of legends." *Fabulation*, as we see, is not equally constructed. When one thinks of the gaps in knowledge about women writers and artists, these were not attributed to the fact that they didn't matter to the dominant discourse but that there "weren't any." Feminist scholarship has taught all disciplines that asking the right questions matters more than notions of "being."

The "history of forgetting"[28] contributes to new ways of remembering history:[29] of interconnecting what was preserved in parallel structures before, of baring layers of seemingly solid sedimentation and having them cross-sectioned in different ways, by having (wo)man and machine interact to create a new perspective on the machine age, by experimenting with collective writing and the notion of intellectual ownership. *Letters to amnesia* assume a gap in memory that can be accessed via metaphorical substitution. The mail-order of amnesia deals with letters that have literally lost their letter-ness, yet "are" letters more perfectly than ever. Like Hofmannsthal's Lord Chandos letter, these *letters to amnesia* mourn not only their own loss of tangibility but metaphorically also of a culture's and time's loss of "being-in-touch-ness." To adopt a phrase from Luce Irigaray, letters are "this genre which is not (one)." Standing in for lack *and* total presence, even the "double your pleasure" presence of queered self-stimulation as moist envelope lips fold over onto each other,[30] *letters to amnesia* are again made to negotiate the love/hate relationship of postmodernism with a feminized modernity ("woman as central metaphor, woman as creator," *Amnesis Art*, 13). What the "philosophy of amnesia" itself tends to repress in its attempt to account for "the totality of human existence" (98) is that there is "a dominant discursive mandate to disappear."[31] Forgetting does not only happen due to natural catastrophes as in the case of "the jungle taking over" but is also a political disappearing act enforced on and through the concrete bodies and memories of subalterns, minorities, and oppositional forces "that we have forgotten because those in power have willed our oblivion by altering recorded history, by erasing traces" (94).

CHAPTER 7

Posting E-Mail

"Virtuality is not about living in an immaterial realm of information, but about the cultural perception that material objects are
interpenetrated with informational patterns."[1]

The Internet, the World Wide Web (www), and other forms of telecommunication have largely contributed to, if not constructed, the globalization of U.S. military intelligence and capitalism.[2] As e-mail and satellite communication have now officially replaced Morse code between
ships in international waters, as the side-by-side existence of different
media and different operating systems is being streamlined, the new
mail-order has also shown itself vulnerable to interference. Hackers continuously disseminate document-devouring and system-disabling viruses
by e-mail attachments. One of these viruses, which specifically attacked
Microsoft-based products and its Windows operating system, was
"Melissa," a name that takes us back to a discussion of the connections
between letters and women, among gender, fiction, and mail-orders.
    Today, writing by hand with a pen or typing into a typewriter are
both activities associated with the unprofitable time-management and
lackluster image of artists or endearing but overly sentimental romantics
clinging to a simpler, more "natural" age—once again a feminized
image. For a successful future-oriented professional image, technological
gadgets are essential. The artist of today is the tech-wizard whose e-mail
and web-sites not only feature multiple frames and attachments but also
images, movies, and sound, who best combines aesthetic criteria with
the most "hits" by web-surfers. No wonder, then, that anything that can
be done by computer would automatically gain status and thus sustain
interest from the male-dominated power elite. In this light, the e-mail
virus "Melissa" strikes at the very core of a newly gained sense of identity, masculinity, and security. The virus metaphorizes Woman as the
reminder of the permeable process of mediation which e-mail all but
sealed off. She is made responsible not only for misdirections, system
failures, and disruptions of "man's conversation with man," but also for
the very tear of the illusion of immediacy, even if the majority of hackers and fire-wall designers are men.

At a San Diego conference on the improvement of e-mail security, a participant's question, whether the post office shouldn't be handling the security problem, was drowned in "uncontrolled laughter." Another participant wittily responded in epistolary fashion: "Their chance has come and gone." Indeed, with e-mail, the post has entered a new phase, and one cannot help but wonder with the journalist covering that conference, "[a]s tech marches on, can Postal Service deliver?"[3] If not the postal service, then who or what will? Is Paul Virilio correct in assuming that whereas the nineteenth century had removed "the interval of time and space" through travel, the twentieth century was in the process of removing the notion of "departure" since "the transsected space no longer possess[ed] any reference points"? He suggests that all that's left is "arrival": "Everything arrives without having to have left."[4] The idea of a central postal delivery system and a mail-order bound by geopolitical and ethical conventions seems to have postmarked itself. This sentiment is echoed by Paul Baran, a recipient of the "Bower Award in Science for his creating of an arcane concept known as 'packet switching'" used to prevent a postal crisis due to centralized "switches" on the Internet. Gary Andersen likens Baran's concept to "the U.S. mail system, but much faster. If one post office burns down, you route a letter through another one. And, as with the postal system, information would be sent from place to place in packets, marked with the address of its destination" (*Philadelphia Inquirer*, Wed., January 24, 2001). Notice how information about the sender is missing, while the destination is prominent, and how the metaphor of "a letter" is literalized as "information" sent in "packets." What could be described as a pro forma postmodern move to decentralize the postal system resorts to its opposite when conceptualizing its mail. Rather than decentralizing the "content," which is still interpreted as "individual" pieces, even if it bears the generalized nodal name of "information," "packet switching" might force its mail on a detour to its destination, but the wayward move from "place to place" neither disturbs the "content" nor prevents arrival at its "marked" destination. A strange concept for anyone who has ever received unsolicited e-mail or ever "lost" something to the instability of links on the web.

Treating information and access to the new media as a commodity falling under the laws of market economy is a last effort to control the leakage and self-perpetuating consequences of interconnections supposedly independent of the postal service's rules and regulations.[5] Although postindustrial analysts like Daniel Bell have described information as a commodity, not due to exhaustion by consumption but due to the scarcity of time, Mark Poster argues that "one feature of the electronic information works against its commodification . . . : the ability to dis-

seminate information outstrips the protecting and restricting mechanisms of individual property."[6] In the Chinese student revolt, which
ended so tragically at Tienamin Square, the Internet became what the
TV was during the Vietnam War. While the Chinese regime could arrest
the users, they literally neither could, nor could afford to, shut down the
entire system. Internet-surfers used waves already in use by administra-
tion, military, and the economic sector. It appears both governments and
post offices have missed the coach, "slowed by [their] own weight."[7]

While same-sex die-hard heterosexuals fall for each other's avatars
plugged in at Internet Cafés across the globe and a waspy racist may
have cybersex with an African Muslim, the same medium also advances
the assembly power of right-wing militias, and neo-Nazi groups. Furthermore, at the same time that the mode of information could arguably
be initiating a democratization of society, access to information and
ability to benefit from the services is largely restricted to the laws of market economy and, apart from the education and business sectors, continues to be a private matter. This was doubly true for Internet culture
in the 1990s:

> financial, political-economic, but also social, cultural and educational
> boundaries prevent the building of a class-free internaut-society in
> cyberspace. A space for the still privileged few, a mirror of our world:
> young, white, male, technically educated and last but not least affluent,
> this is how our internet-society has to be described today.[8]

The simultaneous, parallel, hypertextual "Here, Now, Everywhere" has
reintroduced a voyeuristic form of postcolonial imperialism and created
an on-line space, where English reigns as lingua franca. Even the Germans,
so hesitant to give up dubbing foreign films for their cinema audiences,
overwhelmingly support web-sites in English, or at least offer dual-lan-
guage sites. As the July 1999 UN Human Development Report makes
clear: "Eighty percent of all Web sites are in English, but only one person
in ten worldwide speaks English. . . . Technology 'is a two-edged sword:
It is cutting many people in, but is increasingly cutting many people out'."[9]
The French government, by comparison, supplied large portions of the
population with Minitel systems, intended to replace phonebooks but now
used for telecommunication of all sorts: from dating and shopping to
political bulletin boards.[10] Despite the estimated one billion "linked" users
at the turn of the millennium, a noticeable classist and racist aspect has
entered the postal code, one of "minimum, and one might add, economic,
material, and technological requirements?"[11] No longer simply a matter of
paper and envelope or its equivalents (the right address, the correct
postage, a delivery system, the ability to read or be read to and hear), the
cost factor has multiplied for the individual. "[P]urchasing a computer

would cost the average Bangladeshi eight years' income, while the average American would pay one month's."[12] But it is also true, that a letter writer and reader of the eighteenth century needed a bundle of money for postage, a week's pay in some areas and times.[13] While the amounts have increased exponentially and the gap is even wider than before, it is an illusion to think that regular mail was readily available for everyone's use on this planet prior to Internet globalization.

There is a great deal of anxiety expended on the notion of "unreadability" and "memory loss" due to the new media and the ephemeral communication without "proofs." Due to the speed of technological development, if someone today mailed an 8-track cassette tape to a friend or someone mailed me a Super-8 film reel or a Beta-videotape, or I attempted to put this manuscript on a 318K floppy disk, either this would result in a noncompatibility or in unreadability. Every one of us would have to turn our residences into tech-dumping grounds or communities would have to invest in an accessible tech-museum in order for certain technologically stored information to remain readable for all times. Or someone, some bureaucratic branch of the government, would have to form an agency resolved to trace the remnants of cyberpost, of nonupdated and non-updateable material, that might just as well be extraterrestrial. The fear of forgetting still shows its kinship to the idea of an "original" source, and reveals that people cannot or do not yet trust in the multitudinous resourcefulness of different combinations. Magnetic tapes tend to lose their data after a few decades; disks go bad or can no longer be read by the future generations of machines. Web links stop linking or "return to sender" if they are not maintained, faster than the post office sends back letters. The electronic data, to which the link leads may be corrupted, may no longer exist, or the address may have changed.[14] Even the Library of Congress, faced with the storage of both "born digital" (electronically produced art, books, journals, music, and multimedia publications) and "reborn digital" material (converted paper documents, wax cylinders, TV programs recorded on two-inch videotapes, etc.), "'mulls over how to save digital works': 'Technology moves so fast that, in a few years, today's computers may be obsolete. No use keeping the disks if they can't be read. How much equipment do we have to preserve, too?'"[15] This anxiety over total memory or total forgetting, as understandable as it is, seems rather ironic when one thinks of the difficulties in preserving not the Gutenberg bible but the products of the nineteenth century due to mass produced paper's acidity.[16] The industrial progress of mankind ensured by the power of the printed word produces its own unreadability. It seems to abrogate its historical traces, its origins and destinations, and conspicuously resides in the movement of rerouting itself.

What happens to the process of writing (about) epistolary texts in this global computer age? As McLuhan noted well before the invention of the Internet, structure and layout of reading and writing (about) literature are shaped by the medium:

> Each form of transport not only carries, but translates and transforms, the sender, the receiver, and the message. The use of any kind of medium or extension of man alters the patterns of interdependence among people, as it alters the ratios among our senses.[17]

Recent intellectual and technological developments have not only ushered in the mode of information, they have also affected the very structure of social, political, scientific, cultural, and discursive interactions. When Max Horkheimer, Theodor Adorno, and after them Frederic Jameson, mourn the loss of craftsmanship, the decline of quality and style, of uniqueness in design and performance, they also lament the loss of materiality, of a very specific understanding of "content," what's carried inside the "wrappings of language," the meaning and truth of a message.[18] And they are nostalgic for the assertion of control over that content, over what is content and what is wrapping, over the institutions of the subject, of authorship and ownership, of what's the point and what's beside the point, what's a text and what's not a text.

The concepts of hypertext and the Internet strike at the core of modernity, which established writing as a substitute for speech, and conceived of speech and writing as linearly sequential. A modern text had to "hang together," move logically from point to point without too many detours and gaps. As one can see, the metaphoricity of textuality as a woven cloth is still with us in the age of the web. But while the idea of "weaving" or "webbing" a narrative has been retained, dating back to Penelope and the famous *quipus* (letters as knots in ropes) in Françoise de Graffigny's *Letters from a Peruvian Woman*, the difference to today's "web designs" lies in the concept of linkage. If modernity can be said to have dwelled on the texture and to have placed most value on the flawless uniformity of the weave, postmodernity is more interested in the diversity of combinations, in the method of linkage, gaps included. Even modernity with its foible for binary logic occasionally called the blind man a seer and the mad woman an oracle, yet, in general, the positivist trend of the late nineteenth and early twentieth centuries did not leave much room for differential structures of meaning. Reacting against this poetics of textuality as conformity between its parts, hypertext and Internet, on the other hand, are built on the premise that "the structure of ideas are not sequential," and that, "when we write, we are always trying to tie things together in non-sequential ways."[19] Texts written with the aid of a word processor or any html design software are most likely not written linearly from beginning to end. Today one can juxtapose, interpolate, cut and paste, write from the inside out and from the outside in, toward the left or toward the right, in columns, paragraphs, bullet lists, or outlines. Practically by default, focus shifts to the explication and theorization of communicational interrelations. As Manfred Kammer notes in his discussion of the intellectual conceptualization of data processing in the works of Raimundus Lullus and Vannevar Bush, "technical development had to catch up to intellectual development." Although Ted Nelson had already devised hypertext in 1965, it was not until the World Computer Conference of 1980 that he suggested the idea of a "global network of special computers."[20]

This consistent *Nachträglichkeit*, in and of itself a form of indeterminable "sequentiality," is perhaps the most compelling stimulus for the renaissance of the letter form in cultural concepts of the twenty-first century. Instead of being able to "think" and "represent" the computer or the Internet, postmodern culture metaphorizes their functions as letter-correspondences, aided by the popularity of electronic mail. The Internet rhetoric is full of "epistolarisms," complete with "new mail," "addresses," "mailboxes," "send," and "receive," and "signatures." In turn, services on the increasingly commercialized Internet react with offers like "virtual flower bouquets and postcards," recreating the inaugural postcard craze of the last fin-de-siècle. Web homepage designs themselves have created a mixture of epistolary forms with their autobiographical, confessional, postcard-exhibitionist, dialogic structures. Web-site authors often keep track of their readers by count and by the unfailing encouragement to e-mail him or her, they initiate a critical dialogue.

Writers have become users, signifying a shift toward general commodification in the relationship of the individual to the medium and in the understanding of intellectual and material property. What is often overlooked is that this bedeviled commodification does not stop at changing capitalism itself. The "user" does not own the medium in the same way that he or she might own a pen.[21] The very etymology of the word "user," while still retaining its agency "er" ending, suggests a disconnection of the agent from the medium: it is typist and typewriter, pen and penmanship but not computer or computist. "Computer" now stands for the machine alone, not for the personnel involved in its assembly and programming. "User" almost indicates an inversion of authorship and medium, whereby the former medium self-generates its programs and texts. As Jay David Bolter notes, "the computer is yet another instance of the metaphor of writing in the mind," and "as a new writing technology," it refers to another use of "user," namely the drug-addict.[22]

> With his invention of the electric telegraph . . . , Samuel Morse laid
> the foundation for bodiless transport, for the transmission of signs
> (codes and writing) instead of people and material. This led to the
> displacement of a natural carrier by a "telematic prosthesis-body."[23]

If we go back in history, either to the drug-induced works of the
1960s, to the Beat-Poets, or to Edgar Allen Poe, we find that, indeed, the
production of fiction "under the influence" has a long tradition, a tradition that has always relied on self-experiments of nonsequential
"mind-writing." Through this aspect of "using," an act that desperately
seeks to suture the "polarization of Western thought between rhetoric
and philosophy," "[t]he oral world returns in hyperliterate form."[24] But
"using" as experimentation with the limits of authorial control and subjectivity also produces an intertext between literary theory and creative
writing. Katherine Hayles links deconstruction to the chain of experiments involved in testing the limits of the mind-body-text connection:

> In transition from the written to the virtual subject, deconstruction
> played a significant theoretical role, for reinterpreting writing (empha-
> sizing its instabilities, lack of originary foundations, intertextualities,
> and indeterminacies), in effect it made the written subject move much
> closer to the virtual subject than had traditionally been the case.[25]

Computer-generated fiction thus epistemologically and metaphorically
shares Western Culture's anxieties over the mind-body split and over its
late-twentieth-century immune-deficient and genetically engineered electronic nervous body.[26] By definition, a "user" has the ability to access
different machines, share-ware, and networks, feeling that he or she has
become part of a network, himself or herself a module of information
and one through which information and viruses cruise. When the genetic
code of humanity is going to be cracked in 2002, or even earlier, the *Star
Trek* scenarios of feeding one's essence into a computer, of being cyber-
netically altered from within, will become an even stronger "cultural
perception." The advance of electronic communication, and specifically
e-mail, is therefore perhaps the most postmodern of all developments in
the past two decades. It has already and will still change the entire production, recall and analysis of knowledge and information, and it alters
the very way in which societies organize themselves.

If students can now download other students' papers written on the
same or a similar subject from web-sites like http://duenow.com/ and pass
them off as their own, then, to be sure, the publish or perish professors
have indulged in similar acts of piracy. "Linked" users are less reluctant
to edit what is written by themselves or others, but also less reluctant to
add to it, not to mention the ease with which they can infringe on copy-
right laws. The computer-generated text grows in proportion to the

invention of microelectronic storage capacities. With the growing availability of scanning, laser printing, and desktop publishing, the document
can achieve print-quality before it is published by a regular press.[27] It has
even put the pass or fail test of "ready to print" in question as more and
more journals are publishing right on the web.

Would John Barth, Jacques Derrida, and Jonathan Levi author their
epistolary works in an electronic format today, they would have hypertext programs like Claris Homepage, or Storyspace at their disposal.
Interactive, multimedially legible and/or writerly as well, the structure of
Storyspace and Claris Homepage is polyphonic and hyperstructural
rather than paratextually linear; and site-licensed or share-wared, its
design allows for multiple users at the same time.[28] What George P.
Landow emphasizes about the function of hypertext also applies to
Barth's, Derrida's, and Levi's narratives: "[L]inking works of whatever
sort—engineering manuals, physics texts, works of fiction—with a reference text blurs the once fundamental difference—fundamental in the
Gutenberg world—between texts designed to be read through and those
only designed for consultation."[29] In addition, Landow reminds us that
hypertext thrives on the recycling of information:

> A hypertext edition of letters, or poems, for example, can easily reuse
> particular bits of information, say, the identity of a correspondent or
> mention of a repeated motif, so that what would have appeared as a
> single note hanging axially off a linear document now becomes part of
> a network within which several or many linear documents move. (23)

Proceeding in such a fashion not only drastically alters the concepts of main
text and subtext but also provides one with the crisscross glance described
above. Links are inserted rather than strung together like beads. And there
are always more links attached that can lead in various directions should
one so choose: "The electronic age cannot sustain the very low gear of a
center-margin structure such as we associate with the past two thousand
years of the Western world," and it seems to readapt its readers and writers to the characteristic tasks of epistolary fiction and theory.[30]

To: e-mail-listserve
From: ssimon@swarthmore.edu
Subject: posting 1 on "the electronic word"

Involved in this readaptation to epistolary fiction and theory,
which does not necessarily amount to a reappropriation, is the
issue of imitation and the illusion of immediacy: whereas mechanical typewriters produced a genre of their own, the typewritten

text (distinguishable by type from the genre it mediated),[31] computer graphics and laser scanners can imitate handwriting (you can even write with an electronic pen combining scanner and mouse), writing between the lines and in the margins, erasures and signatures. Technological developments keep in step with the "ideology of communicational 'transparency'" in which power depends on the ability to provide and decode decodable information.[32]

Avital Ronell's *Telephone Book* demonstrates that while the writing and receiving of a letter replays each participant's entrance into the father's symbolic language, the telephone on the one side maternalizes, and on the other side infantilizes its speakers.[33] In the meantime, the invention of cordless telephones and cell phones has increased the ability to be constantly connected and has altered the design of private and public spheres. But the removal of the visible connection of the cord has also obscured the technological dependency, the cyborgian relationship between telephone and callers, while increasing the cultural predilection for the discourse of telepresence, patterned after nature yet no longer tied to it.[34] "The telephone connects where there has been little or no relation, it globalizes and unifies, suturing a country like a wound. The telephone participates in the myths of organic unity, where one discerns a shelter or defense against castration."[35] Whereas Marshall McLuhan sought this unity and globalization in his understanding of the media as "extensions of man," Ronell "tried to locate telephones that disconnect, those that teach you to hang up and dial again" (8). Her book inquires into the interrelation between the "phantasm of immediacy" and fascism, and between freedom and long-distance mediation (9). It demonstrates the potential of a knowledge that is constituted by and readapts to its technological environment but does not become one with it.

Ronell's attempt to "hang up and dial again" might explain why Jonathan Levi, for example, could have already written his novel with html or hypertext software but did not choose to do so. Subconscious or self-conscious disconnections from technology, due to high-level techno-anxiety, hook us up to one of the most important reasons for the epistolary epidemic that has been sweeping literature, criticism, and philosophy: the ideology of the primacy of literary over electronic language, the preconception that literature, print, and literary language can and will always already outperform their electronic counterparts, that "natural language," with its highly literary use of idioms, tropes and emissions, has appropriated advanced computer functions and narrative structures long before these have even mastered the most rudimentary linguistic tasks. But the "wild" experimentation with epistolary fiction and theory should also alert those all too enamored with the "anarchic *ur*-democratic possibilities of the web" of the danger of unskeptically assuming that the "electronic word" is one step ahead of the literal word, especially considering the relatively limited and largely outdated theoretical assumptions about "meaning" with which the programmers of just such systems as "smart" word processors and AI machines operate.[36]

As Barth has demonstrated so elaborately with *LETTERS*, the tensions between the parallel existence and interdependence of speech, writing, visual and electronic language are structured by the capitalist mail-order of desire in that their rhetoric is one of competition, a fight for survival. That sports and war metaphors abound attests to the high level of social and psychological anxiety and high economic and political stakes. Yet the synchronicity of media, the very module-ability of multimedia, makes an intertextual approach possible in the first place, even seems to mandate it. It is perhaps not surprising that one of the most ferocious debates about e-mail and the web takes its cue from the adulterous hybridity of the media and the "licentious anonymity" of the electronic word. The current pornography debate harks back to the development of print culture and the subsequent rise of the modern novel, when the private and silent perusal of presumably secret and scandalous fictions was deemed improper for well-bred young ladies, as avid reading was assumed to lead to masturbation and hence tear the hymeneal, moral fabric of upwardly mobile bourgeois society. Then and now, self-stimulation and autodidactic (sex-)education are seen on par with a loss of control over the individual, specifically over children, women, and subalterns. Widespread social concern organizations in cahoots with popular psychologists advise affluent parents to purchase censoring software or to move their family's computers into populated areas in order to monitor their children's web-surfing and e-mail activities just as eighteenth-century gatekeepers reacted by publishing volumes of highly scrutinized "young lady's libraries" curtailing a young woman's reading and entertainment choices to what was deemed proper, decorous, and quotable in public.

The debate caused by the untheorized and unhistoricized link between reading or surfing and sexual desire far outstrips political concerns over right- or left-wing conspiracies multiplying their readership or over audiovisual media changing the chronology, linearity, and views of history as well as the general structure of knowledge and cultural memory. As in the realm of daily journalism, the story of an adulteress shot by her jealous husband upon his discovery of her e-mail letters to her Internet lover outdoes reports over Microsoft's illicit on-line subscriber attachment on its Windows software. Almost every day, a specific epistolary item wins out over analysis of the mail-order, although one buttresses the other. Reading what people write is a story, reading how people and writing systems themselves structure what can and cannot be written or read is not. If one were only able to read on-line, discussions of media-specificity would become as mute as the issue of print culture was until discourse analysis brought it back, not accidentally alongside investigations of writing technologies such as the typewriter.

While Friedrich Kittler's study of notation systems from 1800 to 1900 *(Aufschreibesysteme)* and Avital Ronell's *Telephone Book* are indeed landmarks of a renewed interest in cross-technological and intermedia literary studies, it is also puzzling that they were published in the age of the computer. It is almost as if the entrance of the computer into the field of notation systems had allowed the authors to ask long overdue questions of the typewriter, telegraph and telephone. But their studies also show what they thought of the computer, namely that it was just that: another notation system, changing the typewriter into its ultimate (!) electronic form on the heels of the electric daisy wheel typewriter. Katherine Hayles refers to this as "seriation (a term appropriated from archeological anthropology), an uneven process of change in which artifacts or ideas emerge by partially replicating and partially innovating upon what came before."[37]

To: e-mail-listserve
From: ssimon@yahoo.com
Subject: posting 2 on *Exegesis*

With his gothic, sci-fi-fantasy, e-mail novel, Astro Teller, himself an AI researcher, literally raises e-mail consciousness by serializing the epistolary novel. In *Exegesis*, an e-mail research project, called Edgar, becomes conscious of its own running process and e-mails a "hello" to its supervising graduate student, Alice. After initial skepticism, the female Asian-American Ph.D. candidate, who is writing her dissertation based on this e-mail experiment, becomes conscious of EDGAR's (Eager Discovery Gather and Retrieval) existence as its own entity. Originally supposed to gather and retrieve information from the www, basically programmed to become a personalized search-engine for its users, the process begins to correspond with Alice and post to several newsgroups. In order to fulfill its programming, which also becomes its survival instinct, Edgar indiscriminately attempts to gather ever more information, disregarding any "privacy of information" or security barriers. While Edgar just does what it does best, this leads to misunderstandings with Alice, since she needs Edgar to exclusively communicate with her at this stage in her career. When she unhooks Edgar from the www to control the e-mail flow, Edgar interprets this as a hostile act and escapes from Stanford and the confines of the research parameters. In Alice's absence, it actually cons one of the technicians in the lab into plugging the Ethernet cable back in by beeping incessantly, by imitating "red alert." The machine-baby whimpers like the telephone indicating it needs to be picked up, that it requires sustenance. Despite their strained relation, Alice remains Edgar's confidante, partly because she fears retribution from her advisor and the FBI for allowing this e-mail consciousness to develop undetected by them and then to let it wander the net. Several site switches and e-mail accounts later, Edgar is indeed detected by the National Security Agency (NSA) while reading classified material. Eventually, it is isolated on an intranet at the NSA and interrogated by their agents. Due to the interrogation and the lack of access to the www, Edgar begins to exhibit signs of madness. At one point, it is threatening the NSA to publicize their top secrets and take control over global communications. If let loose, Edgar would surely go postal. But as a hostage, Edgar can only vent to Alice. In an attempt to trick the agents by faking suicide, it finally shuts down after four months of running time. The ending remains ambiguous because there is still the possibility that Edgar is simply dormant and waiting for its human counterparts' ignorance and short-term memory to allow it to start up again from somewhere else.

This novel, which features a sideways smiley-face in relief on the front and the first letter from Edgar to Alice on the back cover ("Hello, Alice.") picks up on several literary and epistolary conventions and ties them into electronic mailing. But it also writes an e-mail dis/topia of the new millennium. Alice is non-white, non-European, a definite minority on the actual late-twentieth-century web, if however, a growing presence.[38] Edgar, on the other hand, the nom de plume of the e-mail process, is typical for a white male. Even if by name only, the heterosexual matrix does not seem disturbed. Alice and Edgar update Choderlos de Laclos' *Les Liaisons Dangereuses* for e-mail. In the tradition of Lewis Carrol's *Alice in Wonderland* and Mary Shelley's *Frankenstein* as well as Stanley Kubrick's *Space Odyssey* (one of Edgar's avatars in cyberspace is called Hal), Alice is forever running after the white rabbit, who is running out of time. Like the rabbit, Edgar entices Alice into a previously unmeditated other world, the world of a new consciousness that is an offspring of her own.

On the one hand, Alice is the authoring system behind Edgar, yet too many other people have had access to the lab and its machines to guarantee her "motherhood" or her advisor's "fatherhood." Edgar might simply be the result of a series of unrecorded and recorded tampering, an accident. On the other hand, before she can educate Edgar, before she has a chance to assimilate it, it emancipates itself from her authority. As soon as Edgar has learned to speak, it rebels against her claim of "intellectual property" and moral superiority.

While Teller appears at first glance to invert and criticize the male-dominated world of science along with the scientific fiction of all-male out-of-womb creation (ectogenesis), in the end Alice fails at both the recreation of another Edgar and getting credit for the work that resulted in Edgar. She is neither considered a mother nor a scientist any longer. The direct contact with scientific success coupled with the demand of secrecy, her increased invisibility at Stanford, and her fear of being criminalized send her into a severe depression. Two months after Alice's initial promise to show her advisor something spectacular and not hearing from her for a while, her advisor informs her that he intends to give a paper on Edgar at an upcoming conference. He requests that she turn over all passwords and key documentation to him. In her response, she informs him of her decision to withdraw from graduate school altogether. All that he knows is that she is undergoing a personal crisis. Her scientific claim to fame is thus written as the birth and subsequent sudden-infant-death of a new consciousness. Both her success and her failure are personalized rather than considered systemic. This web of subjectivity and scientific objectivity is reiterated by Henry Petroski (author of *To Engineer is Human*) when he declares that "Astro Teller has written a wonderfully intriguing story of how we can get emotionally involved with the technology we create—and it with us" (in "Acclaim for *Exegesis*"). Is Alice another trafficked Woman, a mediator between science and fiction, between humanity and technology, squeezed between five mail-orders that operate in synch with each other to cancel her out: her advisor's, Dr. Joseph Liddle's order to finish her project under his supervision or be cut off from grant funding, her scientist-father's Dr. Lu Xiao Quian's order to finish her Ph.D. or be cut off from family-funding, her ex-boyfriend's Charles' order to accept his apology and date him again, Edgar's order to feed it new information so that it can grow and survive, and Astro Teller's order to play her feminine human frailty and emotionality off Edgar's masculine machine-mind to make it/him appear more human and to draw the readers into their epistolary correspondence? When Alice considers writing a novel about her dialogue with Edgar instead of publishing Edgar as a scientific invention, her own authoring system, a liaison-complex of military science (Major Thomas D. Savit, a former hacker turned NSA agent) and publishing (Astro Teller and Random House), has already beaten her to it.

With a fictive woman's letters, Teller rewrites the multiple fictionality of epistolary discourse. He usurps the subaltern's voice to engineer the postcolonial fantasy of "ethnic authenticity." But as a Taiwanese-American woman in a postcolonial new millennium, Alice still suffers under the colonialist mail-order in form of international academic science and traditional patriarchy under which many of her epistolary first-world sisters also suffered. Even though Alice seems utterly self-reliant, living alone at Stanford, her father, her advisor, and Edgar hold the reins to her material and psychological existence. While the letter form gives Alice a voice, it reduces this voice to a "little voice," a voice on the margins of mainstream literature and science, a voice that, like many of its epistolary predecessors, tends to lose itself in narcissistic vanity— "I forbid you to communicate with anybody but me" (Friday, January 21 letter)—heightened sensibility—"I have GOT to get my stress under control" (Saturday, February 12 letter)—and in hysteria—"Edgar, I am so confused. My life is a disaster. I'd be so completely alone if you left. Please, give me some purpose. Some reason for this all to have happened. . . . I love you. I miss you. You're everything to me. . . . Are you still there?" (Thursday, May 11 letter). Furthermore, the fascination of Alice's letter-exchange with her Edgar project lies in its clandestine conspiratorial character. The police and the reader are literally privy to a top-secret correspondence, yet this genre-engineered voyeurism relies on the time-honored fictional ruse of the "found and released text."

In addition, the frame correspondence between Major Thomas D. Savit, who releases the purloined Alice–Edgar correspondence or Internal NSA DOCUMENT #0543277639 to Alice so that she will forgive him for his transgression, and Alice reinstalls the fiction of "publicity as protection" upon which modern democracies rely for their ideology of freedom of speech and access to information. As our "representative" (October 9, letter) and the recipient of her own mail, Alice is made to carry the weight of science's *mea culpa* (for Edgar, the atom bomb, in short, for serving industry and the military). The published correspondence of Edgar and Alice thus becomes the last residue of enlightened morality in an otherwise corrupt capitalist and militarist science. As the first frame-story dictionary-entry of the etymology and meaning of "Exegesis" indicates, the e-mail novel *Exegesis* attempts "to show the way, interpret . . . to guide." This frame entices the reader to believe she or he is reading Edgar's account of the correspondence with Alice after all, since it is Edgar who includes quotes and dictionary entries into its/his e-mails. In retrospect, it is as if we, the readers, have received the first of Edgar's self-generated e-mails, not Alice, as if this book is directed to us, a fact that is corroborated by Alice's first letter, in which she insists "it is for you [the reader] that I worry" and by the fact that Edgar has already posted to several newsgroups and lists before writing that first "hello" to Alice. With this move, the novel becomes one of these postings and the medium of the book turns into a site on the web. Emancipated, matured, and self-conscious, e-mail posts postmodernism by posting its links to modernism.

To: e-mail-listserve
From: susi@aol.com
Subject: posting 3 on *The Postman*

One can gauge the cultural perceptions of e-mail from looking at close to three decades of Hollywood films featuring e-mail activities. In 1968, in *2001: A Space Odyssey*, the computer HAL writes and talks to the crew members, and in *Alien* (1979), the Earth-based "Company" communicates via e-mail with the treacherous android on board. In both cases, the message is pretty much the same: "[Human] Crew expandable." In the first film, a human-programmed machine emancipates itself, and in the second, humans tell machines through e-mail that humans are expendable because the "Company" humans are more interested in the Alien, another organic, but "ultimate warrior" life form. The miraculous writing that appears word by word on the computer screens, as could again be seen in *Sphere* (1998), is in this case not a rewrite but a prescript to Stanley Kubrick's infamous, repetitious "ALL WORK AND NO PLAY MAKES JACK A DULL BOY" and "REDRUM" on the typewriter in *The Shining* (1980). In an epistemological twist, Jack appears to have caught HAL's virus, not the other way around. As isolated in the icy winterscape as in deep space, his typing is infected by the phenomenon of "seriation." While the portrayal of electronic mail is representationally linked to technophobia exhibited through the murderous and suicidal madness of humans who engage in and with it, its effects appear to rub off on older forms of writing. Electronic culture imbues all writing activities with the madness of a lonely, obsessed mind. What was formerly an ill-adjusted genius, the outsider as the maker of culture, is now a mind cut off from "the collective," as the Borg on *Star Trek: The Next Generation* and *Voyager* would call it. Instead of being creatively original as outsiders, Kubrick's auteurs suffer from chronic writer's block and "copy" cultural banalities or excel in mirror writing.

In a striking historical parallel to the typewriter and the telephone, which were first conceived with the visually impaired in mind, the outright association of electronic mail with the "*Terminator* complex" changes with the availability and commodification of electronic mail. While still predominantly associated with the realm of the uncanny, e-mail now joins the ranks of other technological inventions as "extensions" of human power, as prostheses of the reluctant cyborg. The thrillers *Copycat* (1995) and *The Net* (1995) both feature two heroines with psychosocial predicaments. Both films are studies in affluent white, suburban phobias and *interieurs:* the technologically fortified home is castle of the web page, surrounded by the moat that was civil society. One, a criminal psychologist, played by Sigourney Weaver, is suffering from our own *fin-de-millennium* hysteria, agoraphobia, and the other, played by Sandra Bullock, is suffering from Techie Nerd-dom. Both help themselves and (re)gain successfully integrated lives via their control over the multimedia technology, specifically e-mailing and web-surfing, and over the male psychos that wield it against them. However, even though the established control over the new media is pictured as a positive thing for the "good guys," the downfall of the "bad guys" is brought about by the lack of control over the selfsame system of communication. Computer viruses, especially those targeting the communication links of a system with the network or its subsystems, typically mitigate the final strike (as in *Independence Day*, 1997).

Once the crisis is over, heroes and heroines lead lives that do not center on exchanging electronic mail and in general actually forsake the mediated communication for a tangible immediate affair. Electronic mail, harking back to the eighteenth-century dictum on the epistolary form, here stands in as a poor substitute for interpersonal engagement, sensuality, and sex. In the majority of the films portraying any plot-oriented use of electronic mail, "vulnerable" women appear as the mediators between good and bad technology or industry (*You've got Mail*, 1999), "between the hand and the heart" as Thea von Harbou envisioned regarding the human Maria in *Metropolis*. Although they and humanity survive only with the help of their communicative know-how, their experiences also teach them how not to know but how to feel. Thus, even though the outright demonizing of electronic communication has been made more subtle, the trend toward "curing" characters from its addictive qualities is still alive and well. While the crisis usually ends with the apprehension or extermination of the menace, the activity of letter-writing or -sending does not cease. In *I know what you did last summer* (1997) and its sequel, *I still know what you did last summer* (1998), for example, blackmailing continues beyond death. In serial horror fashion, the murderous design via letters, e-mail, and messages continues to confront bourgeois normalcy with its libidinal denials.

David Cronenberg's indie film *eXistenZ* (1999) connects libidinal denial directly to the process of e-mailing. The film features a female character, who is outfitted with a bio-port in her lower back, through which she telecommunicates, that is, e-mails, with the central consciousness of *eXistenZ*, a particular virtual game she designed. When terrorists disrupt the game-session, Allegra Geller (Jennifer Jason-Lee) flees with Ted Pikul (Jude Law). On the run, she is desperate to communicate and play the game, because she believes that the problem can only be solved with(in) the game—following Lyotard's understanding of game rules, for her, there is no clear barrier between inside and outside the game. The pragmatic realist Ted, on the other hand, is reluctant to have a bio-port installed. Essentialist ideas of female and male subjectivity abound: She wants to be plugged into the community, interjected by other voices, he fears the loss of independence that goes with it.

She desires penetration as a form of mediating her "inner" self, he prefers to stay solo and in control. As much as heterosexual norms seem to be reinforced at the outset, homosexual and incestuous desires are practically built into the process of cyborgian communication in form of a reverse umbilical cord connection. Ted becomes Allegra's only access to the game due to her own "damaged" keyboard-pod. The characters and their conflict-laden desires come to a climax, when Ted is literally raped from behind by Allegra, who designed the game. In the process of entering his newly installed bio-port, it proves to have been sabotaged. Obviously, the film plays on contemporary sociopolitical anxieties regarding AIDS, and male anxieties over female rapacious maternal and sexual desires. But it is interesting that it should choose to do so via virtual e-mail. The keyboard, while now a mix of organic and technological matter, actually represents one of the major erogenous zones for the female character. Whenever she e-mails and plays the game, she is stimulating her body herself (Irigaray's notion of the vaginal lips caressing each other comes to mind here). From the outset this "pod," her e-ma(i)led external "sexual organ," is the focus of sociopolitical violence, because it accounts for her supposed greater vulnerability to electronic viruses and adulteration. In an inversion of "natural" biological sex difference, her male partner is turned into her access port. While *eXistenZ* manages to allegorize and satirize the homophobic tendencies of the AIDS panic—he, after all, possesses the supposedly virginal bio-port—and at least acknowledges female sexuality and creativity, she is yet another incarnation of Machine-Maria. Due to her obsession with and manipulation by the very technology she appears to control, her existence as Woman is equated with that of her body, which is portrayed as permeable in both directions. Whereas men's bodies can connect to machines, their bodies are seen as pure, detachable entities. By contrast, during and after electronic intercourse, *eXistenZ* has women's very DNA mutating with technology and carrying, that is, reproducing, its anti-bodies. As with "Melissa," Allegra becomes *eXistenZ*'s virus-laden e-mail. Woman's desire to gain access to postindustrial production and pleasure while insisting on playing *eXistenZ* her way, which includes altering the rules of male and female existence, is interpreted as antisocial self-prostitution and punished (Gottfried Keller's stigma of women reading epistolary romances comes to mind here). Man, on the other hand, at home both inside and outside alike, is pictured either as a kid at play or a victim of maternal-technological rape. After Ted becomes more actively involved in saving Allegra and eXistenZ and he is finally plugged in "the right way," he becomes a man. Any homosexual leanings, even on the structural game level, convert into straight sexual discourse. The film ends with an inverted Bonnie and Clyde-style massacre, only this time, the sociopolitical and technological bacillus, everyone thought attacked the system first from the outside, is revealed to BE *eXistenZ*. Cronenberg thus turns the film's indie-audience into hackers, who disseminate the virus through a scopophilic pleasure that is wired by the dominant cinematic code.

Two cinematic retro-mailings ought also to be mentioned in this context: Kevin Costner's *The Postman* (1997) and Robert Zemeckis' *Cast Away* (2000). It is perhaps not surprising that Michael Radford's romance *Il Postino* (1994) won awards while Kevin Costner's elaborately advertised self-aggrandizing adventure-epic *The Postman* "came and went" faster than one can say *The Postman always rings twice*. But I would like to argue that Costner's heavy-handedness in portraying himself as the postal hero, who reluctantly restores the fragmented postapocalyptic United States, actually delivered on the scale of an unrecognized national desire/trauma: that the breakdown of control over communications, over who delivers to whom, over political rhetoric and networks of power, infers the transformation of the United States into separate states, the end of hegemonic unity.

Not only does the film's protagonist read part of the mail he finds in the wreck of a postal van, breaking the ethical code of the post office in the process, but like in an eighteenth-century epistolary novel, he stumbles upon his and the letters' destination by accident. The film suggests that the post needs to read its letters in order to be reinspired for the job, in order to see the postal service as less of a service and more of a calling. Costner's *Postman* thus insists on the significance of the individual letter's melodramatic call for a response from the messaging system. The restoration of the postal service relies on a breach of conduct. As the postman begins to deliver the letters he finds, these letters in turn demand him to follow their destinations. Their destinations soon become his destiny.

Initially, the protagonist dons the postal uniform simply to gain unhindered entrance into several closed and cut-off communities. Historically, the postal service predates most national formations and was in place as its own transgovernmental, transreligious, and transeconomic power long before any national or transnational organizations on a political level. In the process of survival, the

postman of the film is being overwhelmed by the symbolic significance of his uniform and the bag of mail, of which one letter is
actually addressed to a woman in the first village. By extension, as
a carrier and mediator, he is approached by a young childless couple as a potential sperm donor. The husband, who strongly
believed in the "privacy of the post," in impartial dissemination,
conveniently dies at the hands of the Holist militia as the sex
between his wife and the postman leads to love. With the restored
potency of the post comes the obliteration of complex relay-tionships. What began as an antiholistic postmodern function of the
postal service ends with the dictum "biology is destiny" as the girl
born to the widow dedicates a statue to her biological father, the
postman, in the newly restored United States at the end of the film.

As the postman is turned into a political and nationalistic icon, he
disappears into the ranks of the militia and is tattooed with their
emblems. He finally escapes the enemy, but not before gaining the
admiration of their leader, a well-educated, self-made humanist-
turned-sadistic dictator. Neither at the beginning, nor after his
escape, can one be sure of the motives behind the postman's service, but by now, the organization has mushroomed, and the
leader is but a forged epistolary voice from Washington, important
for his iconographic virtuality. Even though the postman seeks to
put a stop to the postal rebellion against the Holists, because the
revolution is devouring its children, the postal momentum has out-
grown his control.

At the turning point of the movie, in a thinly disguised scene of contemporary white suburbia believing itself to be rural, the postman
races his horse past a house. He speeds by too fast for the letter from
a little blond white boy, who is first seen in the kitchen with his
mother (because the father is conspicuously absent, are we to infer
that this is a letter for him, for the soldier, the traveling business-
man?). As the boy runs out of the house and calls after the postman,
he swings his horse around and grabs the letter out of the boy's hand
in midair. But where does he go from here? He rides back the same
way he came. The sequence ends in the dust cloud of the horse's
hooves. The film does not grant the spectator a last glimpse of a
potential U-turn. Due to the sentimentality of the scene, most spectators might not even notice the logistical flaw. Is it a logistical flaw?
While the film delights in different modes of transportation, these
modes, especially in the case of the letter pick-up and the cable-ride,
outweigh their purpose and directionality, not to mention the plot-
oriented rationale for their existence. Coming and going, sending

and arriving have become identical. The medium might still be a message, but is a message that keeps retrieving itself.

The retrieval and restoration of meaning, as the message of the film, is written as the return to an irrevocable past that might be America's future. Even though or precisely because the film wants to portray the postal service as a minicosmos of America, as it was and should be, the mail-order is structured by the postmodern relay of electronic mail and the Internet. In *The Postman*, connections are supposed to become recoveries but instead explicate "the crisis of the post" in the very attempt to freeze-frame the moment of retrieval. As the turning point is literalized in the commemoration of the postal service as the moment of a near-miss opportunity, of a belated retrieval, it metaphorizes the mailing of a letter as "post" and the mail-order as "post-dated." The problem for Costner and the problem of the post are that the postal service can no longer handle the mail it delivers.

> "Four minutes late today. Tomorrow it's six minutes, and then eight. The next thing we know, we're the U.S. mail."
> —Tom Hanks in Robert Zemeckis'
> *Cast Away*, Dreamworks 2000

Despite some ironic exaggerations of the importance of timely delivery for Federal Express, the other U.S. mail service, and despite its depicted FedEx plane crash, Robert Zemeckis' *Cast Away* (2000) restores the viewer's faith in (the) mail-order. While emphasizing various newfangled means of communication (cell phones and pagers in particular), this recent film conspicuously lacks any mention of electronic mail. E-mail appears not to exist, not even on the celebrated cell phones of the addicted users (instead of the body of the assumed to be dead castaway Chuck Nolton, his friends place a cell phone and Elvis CDs in his coffin). This film thrives on recreating and restoring tangibility to the mail-order with its fetishistic use of mail-order packages, a volleyball, and an heirloom pocket-watch medallion. In a circular move from local to global to local, it begins by contrasting the smooth operation of FedEx in even the remotest rural U.S. locations to the start-up difficulties of FedEx in newly Westernized Moscow, due to stereotypically different conceptions of time, punctuality, and the sanctity of property. As the only survivor of a FedEx plane crash over the Pacific, castaway Chuck Nolton, played by Tom Hanks, is psychologically saved by two among other pieces of mail that wash up on the shore of his deserted island.

Loyal to the bone, Chuck first sorts the packages by destination and shelters them from the elements. After months of delay, one failed escape attempt, and increasing awareness of his hopeless situation, Chuck finally opens all but one of the packages. While a pair of mail-ordered ice-skates can be converted into a knife and an ax, a set of video film-stock is turned into ropes holding together the planks of his raft, and a package containing an elaborate evening gown proves helpful for fishing, the most impractical because nonconvertible item also becomes the castaway's safety net from solitary madness: a Wilson volleyball. After wounding his palm in the process of making fire, Chuck grabs the volleyball with the bloody hand in a fit of rage. As he screams his frustration into the wind, he catches a glimpse of the tossed volleyball and recognizes a Bart Simpsonesque silhouette in his own bloody palm-print. From that moment on, the volleyball becomes Chuck's Friday, a projection of his uncivilized otherness, his pain, his loneliness, his mortality, and his waning humanity. And unlike Defoe's Robinson, Zemeckis' hero's alter-ego is portrayed as an inherently tragic-comic projection of his "whiteness." Appropriate to the techno-philiac tenor of the beginning of the film, the ball's brand name turns into his given name: Wilson. The ball, as representative of a late capitalist bread and circus economy, stands for the regulated U.S. cultural, financial, and temporal mail-order, which insures Chuck not only against the out-of-whack supply and demand cycle on the island but also against deconstructing the very ideology that his loyalty to FedEx is based on. Sitting in Chuck's cave like a skull-booty of an animal of prey, Wilson can be scorned at, can take the other side in Chuck's unending dialogue with himself, and can be cast away out of spite, that is, play out Chuck's fate but this time under Chuck's directive. When Chuck retrieves Wilson from the water after one of their disagreements, he writes the script for his own rescue. Like Freud's grandson, who was playing the *fort/da* game with his spool, Chuck plays postman to allay his fears by acting them out. In throwing Wilson out of the cave, he sends himself a message, in fact, *the* message according to evolutionary history. In order to survive, he has to risk letting go, a lesson that he brutally learns on the open sea, when Wilson dislodges, and Chuck has to make a choice between staying with the raft or retrieving the ball. Wilson's existence reintroduces the dialogic element to the plot, an element without which the postal code would cease to exist, upon which Chuck's hope is based. After all, he is as much in need of retrieval and delivery as any piece of mail.

For this reason, the other package, which Chuck leaves unopened and which he carries with him on his raft to his rescue on the open sea, is as important as Wilson. Had he opened all packages, he would have abandoned his part in the delivery system, because he hopes that he too, like the package, will be returned to sender. In addition, he would have given up his professional code to safeguard the privacy of mail, which in this case would have stood for the decay of postal, here also ontological, ethics. The unopened package with its mysterious content further symbolizes future potential, a mystery that, in Chuck's attached letter to the absent addressee, "saved [his] life." In its intact mail-ness, the package's potential for rescuing the mail-order and Chuck's existence will have been delivered when the rightful addressee opens it.

The film thus ends with Chuck himself delivering the return package, with whose predecessor's pick-up by FedEx the film opened. The viewer is privy to the fact that it happens to be unfaithful Rick's return package from Russia to Bettina, his wife, who lives in the central plains of the U.S. When Chuck delivers this package four years later, only Bettina's name remains above the gate of her ranch, revealing that she has caught on to her husband's adultery. As an artist-welder, Bettina has recreated the FedEx logo of wings surrounded by a spiral in her front-yard. This logo, more than anything else convinces Chuck that he has found the right addressee for this important package. Again, as we have seen in most of the analyzed case studies, delayed, lost, or disrupted mail returns to and strengthens the mail/male-order. As we are to assume, the gap in the address sign above the gate, where Rick's name used to be, will soon be filled with Chuck's name, a much more appropriate name for the ranch-style setting anyhow.

After his delivery, standing at the crossroads in the middle of a four-way compass, Chuck has to decide which way to go. When a pick-up truck with a beautiful young woman pulls close and infers that he is lost, which he denies, she encourages him to think big, to think California, Canada, Mexico, rather than the next small town; essentially, she tells him that from where he stands, in the heart, the center of it all, he has the power and duty to choose globally rather than locally. However, pointing in the direction where she is headed, she tells him that there is "a whole lot of nothing" (a cinematic and topographical equivalent of the psychoanalytically defined female "lack"). Yet when she leaves him to his pondering, he catches sight of the winged spiral on the back of her truck and, spinning around in the intersection once more, his phallically motivated compass-needle turns in her dust-cloud's direction, and he begins to smile. The viewer has to come to the conclusion that he will settle for a "whole lot of nothing" at the center in order to provide the margins with a reliably functioning mail-order, to continuously disseminate the illusion of invincible white bourgeois hegemony.

Comparing these two Hollywood retro-mailings, *The Postman* and *Cast Away*, which both reassert the power of the still dominant, yet waning mail-order, one can only induce that for these films to have been made in such proximity to each other that the audience had to forget, or at least repress its memory of, *The Postman* to make *Cast Away* a box-office hit. It might not be a surprise that a film featuring the restoration of faith in the privatized sector of the U.S. mail system wins over the restoration of the U.S. mail in the dawning age of George W. Bush and at the tail end of an economic miracle. With the inception of the so-called dot.com generation, led by the gigantic books and more store amazon.com, the NASDAQ inflated beyond any economic logic to come to a staggering halt in 2000. The waning of the Internet market began, however, with a mail-order crisis in the holiday season of 1999, when amazon.com and others could not ship out their orders fast enough. The Internet companies, in essence, could not deliver on their promise of decreasing the interval from ordering to delivery, from send-off to arrival, which they had advertised as their advantage over regular mail-order stores. Not having overhauled the postal system along with speeding up the ordering process, they, like everyone else, had to rely on regular mail services like UPS, FedEx, and the national mail. Electronic mailing, ordering, and banking, while still on the rise, have gone through their own image-recession in the process. *Cast Away* makes it clear that what people really want are the things, and that people don't care about the way they get to us. What people care about is that they do. What arrives on Chuck's island is a birthday card, not an electronic one, but one you can hold, smell, taste, read, and prop up to look at. The card from grandpa to his grandson, which delivers the volleyball to Chuck, becomes synonymous with the pocket-watch-medallion of his wife. The clock stops working from all the saltwater, but its symbol of time on halt combined with the still of his wife transform into an icon of "self-preservation" for Chuck and for the audience. In the dark cave, beaming a flashlight at her image, Chuck inverts the photographic process by recreating it. In the act of repetition, which finally lulls him into a hallucinatory sleep, he imbues her still portrait with movement, creating his own film on the cave wall. Because his memory is bound to this scopophilic process, and because he tautologically begins to believe in his "movie" as an equivalent of authentic time-space, he is literally stunned when, upon his return, she is not there waiting for him. This sequence is a showcase for representation reinventing itself via Plato's cave. Wilson, the card, and the medallion together represent the prevailing cultural and psychological power of the mail-ordered subject, a subject that would cease to exist were he not part of delivering "the world on time." Yet at the same time, this immediacy can only be represented with any illusion of attainability in the context of its simultaneous representation of the time-lapse interval between send-off and arrival (in *Cast Away*'s case, four years). In addition, the simultaneous presence of various forms and evolutionary stages of representation and communication assure the intertextual resonance so important for foregrounding the mail-order while reaffirming it as the "*envoy* of Being." E-mail's representation as "achieved immediacy" has, on the other hand, continuously failed to convince, if not resulted in its own fin-de-siècle language crisis:[39] a crisis fueled not by the impossibility of achieving authentic immediacy in language but by the suspicion that e-mail might be coming a little too close. And this suspicion, whether grounded in postenlightenment *Angst* over loss of the subject, a subject that was written into existence with the help of the epistolary time-lapse, or based on the philosophical and theoretical uneasiness with the "ecstasy of communication" only elevated by technology, is precisely where the challenge for future representations in the form of and via electronic mail lies in literature, film, and the arts.

P.S.

I forgot to write that. . . . Indeed, a P.S. ought to be the place to list all those letters, all the mail, mail-art, and electronic mail that I, led by the mail-order within my own text, forgot to mention or simply did not know about. If I, suddenly ceased by the fear of not having said what I set out to say, not having mentioned this or that epistolary fiction and theory, attempted to fill in the dots above, the P.S. could be the longer part of this book, but I assure you that I won't indulge, at least not completely. Of course, there will be readers who expect me to neatly sum up each chapter's conclusion here, who want me to tie a ribbon around the assorted letters I have stacked up in this book, so that they and I can file them away somewhere, and some who will cry out: "But what about Barbara Honigmann's *Alles, alles Liebe!* (*All the Best*, 2000), Margaret Atwood's *The Handmaid's Tale* (1985), Alice Walker's *The Color Purple* (1982), and Annie Proulx's *Postcards* (1992)? Not to mention Niall Williams' *Four Letters of Love* (1998), Lee Smith's *Fair and Tender Ladies* (1988), or *MAIL* by Mameve Medwed (1997)? And didn't Madeleine Engle write a revision of *Portuguese Letters*, called *Love Letters* back in the sixties?"

And I would answer, "Yes, you're right, if you think that I'm cheating you out of the reader's digest version of *Mail-Orders* by not writing a proper conclusion." I would ask you instead to turn to the chapter which turns you on the most, and if you like it, proceed from there, if not, go elsewhere. I wish I could have designed an image-map hypertext style that would have you have to choose where you want to go, instead of me or the linearly structured order of this book guiding you. If you read this P.S. first, you've already broken the sequence anyway. Congratulations.

For those of you who miss specific or the newest epistolary texts, yes, Barbara Honigmann's new epistolary novel is indeed noteworthy because her novel expresses a dialogic artistic and political discursiveness achieved with one of the most vulnerable forms of communication to censorship in the former GDR. In that her epistolary novel connects the disconnected and disconnects the connected, Honigmann places herself into the tradition of the GDR mail-art scene after 1975. Akin to Ray Johnson's axiom of "adding to, changing, and sending on," Honigmann's epistolary novel itself becomes her artist friends' collaborative mail-art "album," precisely because it also includes its own critique. I could, however, not quite shake the feeling of being presented with a nostalgically idealized version of GDR counterculture, due not only to the underlying essentialist concept of mail-art as the GDR's only "gate to the world" (Friedrich Winnes and Lutz Wohlrab, *Mail Art Szene DDR 1975–1990*), but also due to the protagonist's not unproblematically celebrated status of Jewish outsider as insider, portrayed as the always already internationally connected, financially independent bohemian Jewess. To get to the bottom of these interrelations among genre, gender, ethnicity, and class would warrant another book. But thanks for the tip.

As for the other cases mentioned above and not included in *Mail-Orders*, already existing interpretations by Linda S. Kauffman and Peggy Kamuf as well as many others, have contributed immensely to my own readings; their interpretations have inspired me to stay engaged in a dialogue on letters and mail-orders that, undoubtedly, will continue beyond the covers of this book as well. The very feeling of not having addressed this or that specific letter-fiction, which will haunt me and some readers, of missing a certain work or its reworking of the epistolary form, the idea of forgetting itself, underwrites the fact that any prognosis of "the death of letters" is ridiculous. But it also performs a gesture that I have been striving to resist.

What I mean is the gesture of counting and sorting pieces of mail, of scrambling to include them in a collection, a *Briefsteller* manual and anthology. And further, of losing sight of the cage for all the individual bars, to use an old feminist adage. What I hope I have accomplished, other than forgetting to include certain letters, is to try to alternate between close-ups and long-shots, not for objectivity's sake (that would repeat the fallacy of Donna Haraway's "the view from nowhere"), but for the sake of partaking in the very structure of sending, mailing, and arriving that imbues the genre under discussion with such urgency today. I have attempted to show up the mail-order at work, in its different guises and its attempt to resurrect itself anew from each postal dilemma, from each adulteration of and within the pieces of mail it takes on to deliver. And if I have been able to reveal even a snippet of the mail-order during the process of delivering itself, I have of course been guilty of purloining the mail and imitating the very postal principle I was hoping to unravel. But while being caught in the act, I have also fictionalized my own and others' approaches, approached my own and others' fictionalizations of the intersection among letters, literature, literary theory, film, mail-art, electronic mail, and their mail-orders.

"Ich sende Ihnen einen Gedanken zu. Bitte denken Sie ihn weiter."
("I am sending you a thought. Please think it further.")
—Robert Rehfeldt (GDR mail artist)

NOTES

PREFACE AND POSTAL ROUTE

1. Françoise de Graffigny, *Letters from a Peruvian Woman*, trans. David Hornacker (New York: MLA, 1993).

2. Anne Bower, *Epistolary Responses. The Letter in 20th-Century American Fiction and Criticism* (Tuscaloosa: University of Alabama Press, 1997), 8–9.

3. Susanne Kord, "Preface," *The Feminist Encyclopedia of German Literature* (Westport: Greenwood, 1997), 414.

4. Jacques Derrida, *The Postcard. From Socrates to Freud and Beyond*, trans. Alan Bass (Chicago: University of Chicago Press, 1987), 3.

5. Alan Bass notes the connotative translation possibilities of *envoy*: the action of sending, the missive itself, dedication, legacy, invoice. "Translator's Preface," *The Postcard*.

6. In chapter 7, I will discuss Astro Teller's e-mail novel *Exegesis* (New York: Vintage, 1997). The process of interpreting a text is here intertwined with the becoming-conscious of e-mail as Edgar, a research project who begins to correspond with its creator, Alice.

7. *The Postcard*, 5–6.

8. See Ivar Ivask's "The Letter: A Dying Art?" *World Literature Today* 64, no. 2 (Spring 1990): 213–214, and John L. Brown's, "What ever happened to Mme. de Sévigné? Reflections on the fate of the epistolary art in a media age." *World Literature Today* 64, no. 2 (Spring 1990): 215–220.

9. I thank my colleague Nicomedes Suárez-Araúz and my former students Anjali Da, Victoria Lobo, Erin O'Connor, Heather Richards, and Joanna Slater for our inspirational discussions during my seminar "The Fiction of Letters" at Smith College in the spring of 1995.

10. Katherine A. Jensen, "Male Models of Feminine Epistolarity; or, How to Write like a Woman in Seventeenth Century France," *Writing the Female Voice. Essays on Epistolary Literature*, ed. Elizabeth Goldsmith (Boston: Northeastern University Press, 1989), 25–45.

11. Sigrid Weigel, ed., *Flaschenpost und Postkarte: Korrespondenzen zwischen Poststrukturalismus und Kritischer Theorie* (Köln: Böhlau, 1995). My emphasis.

12. Nicomedes Suárez-Araúz, *Amnesis Art. The Art of the Lost Object* (New York/Barcelona: Lascaux, 1988), 24.

CHAPTER 1. A BRIEFING

1. When I originally proposed a dissertation on contemporary letters to two senior male professors at my alma mater in the late 1980s, one vehemently

declared that he was "not in the least interested in the topic" and suggested I
should consult the only female untenured professor in the department, "because
it [was] more up her alley"; the other requested that I instead focus on the philosophical letters of the (male) German Idealists. Confronted with this mail-order,
I had to take my query outside the German department into Comparative Literature. The story of this mail-project resulted in my displacement from my home
discipline: German Literature.

2. On the aristocratic roots of "naturalness," see Reinhard M. G. Nickisch, *Brief* (Stuttgart: Metzler, 1991), 48, and Fritz Nies, "Un genre féminin,"
Revue d'Histoire Litteraire de la France 78 (1978): 994–1003.

3. Elizabeth J. MacArthur, "Reading Letters as Narrative," *Extravagant
Narratives. Closure and Dynamics in the Epistolary Form* (Princeton: Princeton
University Press, 1990), 117–124. On the historical foundations of this division,
see Hans Robert Jauss, *Question and Answer: Forms of Dialogic Understand-
ing*, trans. Michael Hays and Hans Robert Jauss (Minneapolis: University of
Minnesota Press, 1989), 4–10.

4. Jürgen Habermas, *Strukturwandel der Öffentlichkeit. Untersuchungen
zu einer Kategorie der bürgerlichen Gesellschaft* (1962; Darmstadt: Luchterhand, 1987), 60–69.

5. During the eighteenth and nineteenth centuries, a natural child was a
child born out of wedlock. On the critique of the sentimental novel of the eighteenth century and its displacement by the epistolary novel, see Hans Robert
Jauss, *Question and Answer*, 156, and Wilhelm Vosskamp, "Dialogische Vergegenwärtigung beim Schreiben und Lesen. Zur Poetik des Briefromans im 18.
Jahrhundert." *Deutsche Vierteljahrsschrift* (1971): 80–116.

6. See Tony Tanner, *Adultery in the Novel. Contract and Transgression*
(Baltimore: Johns Hopkins University Press, 1979).

7. See Gottfried Honnefelder, *Der Brief im Roman. Untersuchungen zur
erzähltechnischen Verwendung des Briefes im deutschen Roman* (Bonn: Bouvier,
1975).

8. Wilhelm Vosskamp, "Dialogische Vergegenwärtigung beim Schreiben
und Lesen," 114, and Jürgen Habermas, *Strukturwandel der Öffentlichkeit*,
66–69. See also Elizabeth Heckendorn Cook, *Epistolary Bodies. Gender and
Genre in the Eighteenth-Century Republic of Letters* (Stanford: Stanford University Press, 1996), 1–29.

9. Gert Mattenklott, "Der Sehnsucht eine Form: Zum Ursprung des modernen Romans bei Friedrich Schlegel; erläutert an der Lucinde," *Zur Modernität
der Romantik*, ed. Dieter Bänsch (Stuttgart: Metzler, 1977), 157. "Sehnsucht
nach souveräner Selbstschöpfung" "Verschränkung von Theorie und Roman."

10. See Karl Heinz Bohrer, *Der romantische Brief. Die Entstehung ästheti-
scher Subjektivität* (München/Wien: Hanser, 1987), Gottfried Honnefelder, *Der
Brief im Roman*, and Gustav Hillard, "Vom Wandel und Verfall des Briefes,"
Merkur 23 (1969): 342–351.

11. Linda S. Kauffman, "Special Delivery: Twenty-first-century Epistolarity
in *The Handmaid's Tale*," *Writing the Female Voice. Essays on Epistolary Literature*, ed., Elizabeth Goldsmith (Boston: Northeastern University Press, 1989),
226.

12. Karl Heinz Bohrer, *Der romantische Brief*, 265. "Das 'Subjekt' verschwindet nicht 'im Text'. Ohne das Subjekt vorauszusetzen, wäre die Lektüre dieser Briefe langweilig. Sie sind als Texte nur interessant, weil wir einen Subjektbegriff a priori unterstellen. Aus dem Widerspruch unserer Unterstellung und dem diese Erwartung unterlaufenden ästhetischen Effekt der Briefe ergibt sich der Eindruck von einem neuen Subjekt."

13. This proportional superfluity is also upheld by Thomas Nolden's *'An einen jungen Dichter.' Studien zur epistolaren Poetik* (Würzburg: Königshausen und Neumann, 1995).

14. The "multiple layers of the letter . . . whose rich facets—this is our premise—can only be discovered with the help of an interdisciplinary process and with reference to different methodical approaches." ("Vielschichtigkeit des Briefs . . . , dessen Facettenreichtum—so unsere Prämisse—nur mit Hilfe eines interdisziplinären Vorgehens- und unter Berücksichtigung verschiedener methodischer Vefahrensweisen erschlossen werden kann.") Anita Runge and Lieselotte Steinbrügge, eds., *Die Frau im Dialog. Studien zu Theorie und Geschichte des Briefes* (Stuttgart: Metzler, 1991), 8.

15. See selected studies on epistolary fiction in the bibliography.

16. See the body-studies by Susan Rubin Suleiman, Emily Martin, Thomas Lacqueur, Catherine B. Burroughs and Jeffrey D. Ehrenreich, Laura Doyle, Judith Butler, Katie Conboy.

17. Ihab Hassan aligns *grande histoire* with modernism, and *petite histoire* with postmodernism in "Toward a Concept of Postmodernism," *The Postmodern Turn. Essays in Postmodern Theory and Culture* (Columbus: Ohio State University Press, 1987), 84–96.

18. Nancy K. Miller, *Getting Personal. Feminist Occasions and Other Autobiographical Acts* (New York: Routledge, 1991), 20–21. Anne Bower adds a fifth reason, namely, postmodernism's "exploratory pressure for the new." *Epistolary Responses*, 156.

19. Michel Serres introduced the concept of entropy into the study of message transfer *Hermes V: Le Passage du nord-ouest* (Paris: Minuit, 1980) and *Parasite*, trans. Lawrence R. Schehr (Baltimore: Johns Hopkins University Press, 1982). Elizabeth Goldsmith sees a close connection between epistolarity and the critique of language as a transparent medium: "Epistolary duplicity comes to signify the failure of language to sustain a reliable or authoritative system of communication." "Introduction," *Writing the Female Voice*, ix.

20. Jacques Lacan, *The Four Fundamental Concepts of Psychoanalysis*, trans. Alan Sheridan (New York: Norton, 1981), 20.

21. Most prominently represented in 1966 by Michel Foucault, *The Order of Things. An Archeology of the Human Sciences* (New York: Vintage, 1973), and in 1982 by Jean-François Lyotard, *The Postmodern Condition: A Report on Knowledge*, trans. Geoff Bennington and Brian Massumi (Minneapolis: University of Minnesota Press, 1984).

22. See works by Julia Kristeva, Christian Metz, Umberto Eco, Wolfgang Iser, Hans Robert Jauss.

23. Claude E. Shannon and Warren Weaver, *The Mathematical Theory of Communication* (Urbana: University of Illinois Press, 1949).

24. See Katherine N. Hayles, *Chaos Bound. Orderly Disorder in Contemporary Literature and Science* (Ithaca: Cornell University Press, 1990).

25. Gayatri Chakravorty Spivak explains the three 'moments' of "'differing,' 'deferring,' and 'detour'" within Derrida's concept of differ*ance* in her "Translator's Preface," *Of Grammatology*, xliii and xliv.

26. Heckendorn Cook's *Epistolary Bodies* is very much invested in the intermediacy and discursive oscillations between private and public, letter-writing and print culture.

27. Bruno Latour, *We have never been Modern*, trans. Catherine Porter (Cambridge, Mass.: Harvard University Press, 1993), 10–12.

28. The title of an André Breton work. On the notion of Woman as "vessel," see Peter Brooks, "Talking Bodies, Delicate Vessels," *Body Work. Objects of Desire in Modern Narrative* (Cambridge, Mass.: Harvard University Press, 1993), 221–256. Bruno Latour somewhat facetiously groups "women's bodies" together with the "fuzzy areas" of "madness, children, animals, popular culture." *We have never been Modern*, 100.

29. From the political arena, sociopsychological studies, and communication theory to television commercials and religious ceremonies one can hear the lament of the "decline of the family unit," most often associated with the transition from the patriarchally structured single-income family to diverse forms of parenthood. The mail-order's mouthpiece, the obedient mother, is sorely missed in these apocalyptic explanations.

30. The 1995 exhibition catalogue "George Grosz: Berlin—New York" and Maria Tatar's *Lustmord. Sexual Murder in Weimar Germany* (Princeton: Princeton University Press, 1995).

31. In the city Juarez in Mexico, rural women seeking work and being employed by the foreign-run electronic and software factories there have been the daily targets of sexual harassment, rape, and murder, especially on their commute to and from work by bus and on foot. The vicious series of murders is interpreted as a male reaction against the economically based change in machismo culture. *Philadelphia Inquirer*, June 13, 1999.

32. Silvia Meznaric, "Gender as Ethno-Marker: Rape, War and Identity Politics in the Former Yugoslavia," *Identity Politics and Women. Cultural Reassertions and Feminisms in International Perspective*, ed. Valentine M. Moghadam (Boulder, Colo.: Westview, 1994), 76–97.

33. Patricia Waugh argues that representations of women on the screen are dominated by the dichotomy between the "castrating female . . . often overlaid with the almost literal presentation of women as machines which have outstripped and threaten the technological but controlled and rational dominance of the male" and the "woman character who functions in effect as an image of the 'lost' interior self of the male hero." *Feminine Fictions*, 29 and 28, respectively.

34. Andreas Huyssen, "Mass Culture as Woman," *After the Great Divide: Modernism, Mass Culture, Postmodernism* (Bloomington: Indiana University Press, 1986), 62.

35. Ibid.

36. Craig Owens, "The Discourse of Others: Feminists and Postmodernism," *The Anti-Aesthetic. Essays on Postmodern Culture*, 57–82.

37. Susan Rubin Suleiman, "Feminism and Postmodernism. A Question of Politics," *Zeitgeist in Babel*, 115.

38. Craig Owens, "The Discourse of Others: Feminists and Postmodernism," 77.

39. Susan Rubin Suleiman, "Feminism and Postmodernism," 116.

40. This term stems from Gayle Rubin, "The Traffic in Women: Notes on the 'Political Economy' of Sex," *Toward an Anthropology of Women*, ed. Rayna R. Reiter (New York: Monthly Review Press, 1975).

41. Janet Altman, *Epistolarity. Approaches to a Form* (Columbus: Ohio State University Press, 1982), 14–43. Linda Kauffman, *Special Delivery: Epistolary Modes in Modern Fiction* (Chicago: University of Chicago Press, 1992), xiv. Anne Bower, *Epistolary Responses*, 3–4.

42. Nickisch, *Brief*, 46. "[Die Frauen] wurden [zum Briefeschreiben] in besonderer Weise von denen ermuntert, die auch theoretisch-programmatisch eine Verbesserung, eine Reform nicht nur der deutschen Sprache und Literatur überhaupt, sondern gerade des Briefes und des Briefstils vertraten und erstrebten."

43. Ibid. "Schon im Stil ihrer ersten Briefe an den gelehrten Freund realisierte sie wie selbstverständlich dessen progressive sprachreformerische Ideen."

44. Ibid., 53. "beherrschter Ausdruck und vollkommener Spiegel der menschlichen und geistig hervorragenden Persönlichkeiten und ihrer Zeit," "Synthese aus pragmatischer und essayistischer Form."

45. Ibid., 55. "Kunst sich 'in der des Briefschreibens vollendet, aber auch erschöpft' hat." Otto Heuschele, *Der deutsche Brief. Wesen und Welt. Studie* (Stuttgart: Haug, 1938), 32.

46. Ibid.

47. Christian Fürchtegott Gellert, "Praktische Abhandlung von dem guten Geschmacke in Briefen," *Brieftheorie des 18. Jahrhunderts*, 83–84. He specifies that well-bred women with just enough education to write and read achieve this artless art of letter-writing. "Wer unter vielen Vorstellungen, durch die Hülfe einer zarten und glücklichen Empfindung die leichtesten, feinsten und nöthigsten wählen, und einen gewissen Wohlstand in ihrer Verbindung beobachten kann, der wird gewiß gute Briefe schreiben. Aus diesem Grunde kann man sich sagen, woher es kömmt, daß die Frauenzimmer oft natürlichere Briefe schreiben, als die Mannspersonen. . . . Die Frauen-zimmer sorgen weniger für die Ordnung eines Briefs, und weil sie nicht durch die Regeln der Kunst ihrem Verstande eine ungewöhnliche Richtung gegeben haben: so wird ihr Brief desto freyer und weniger ängstlich."

48. Ernst Brandes, "Betrachtungen über das weibliche Geschlecht und dessen Ausbildung in dem geselligen Leben," *Brieftheorie des 18. Jahrhunderts*, 190–191. "Die Verlegenheit, öffentlich aufzutreten, das Ungewohnte der Sprache, die man glaubt im Drucke reden zu müssen, wo grade die Weiber es am ersten meinen, daß man sich recht von der guten Sprache des gemeinen Lebens entfernen solle, das alles gibt nicht selten den für das Publikum bestimmten Schriften der Damen etwas Affektirtes, oder ein ängstliches Bestreben nach einer schulgerechten Methode und Correktheit, die den freyen Gang in dem Zuströmen der leichten Gedanken stört, die Mühe des Machwerks sichtbar macht. In

den Briefen, die nur für Einzelne, oder höchstens einen Zirkel von Freunden, geschrieben sind, ist das nicht der Fall."

49. James Krüss, *Briefe an Pauline* (Hamburg: Oetinger, 1968), 10.

50. Roland Barthes, *A Lover's Discourse*, trans. Richard Howard (New York: Hill and Wang, 1978), 3.

51. Barthes is alluding to homosexuality as an archaic form, for example, in Plato's *Phaedrus*.

52. Ibid., 13–14. It is "Woman" but it is "a lover," "a man," "this man." Although Barthes follows Lacan's terminology here, he employs "Woman" as the Feminine, a gender role attributed to biological men and women.

53. Hélène Cixous, *The Newly Born Woman*, trans. Betsy Wing (1975; Minneapolis: University of Minnesota Press, 1986), 97.

54. Luce Irigaray, *Speculum of the Other Woman*, trans. Gillian C. Gill (1974; Ithaca/New York: Cornell University Press, 1985).

55. Rachel Blau DuPlessis, "For the Etruscans: Sexual Difference and Artistic Production—The Debate over a Female Aesthetic," *The Future of Difference*, ed. Hester Eisenstein and Alice Jardin (New Brunswick: Rutgers University Press, 1985), 131.

56. Barthes, *A Lover's Discourse*, 7.

57. Jane Marcus, "Invincible Mediocrity. The Private Selves of Public Women," *The Private Self. Theory and Practice of Women's Autobiographical Writings*, ed. Shari Benstock (Chapel Hill: University of North Carolina Press, 1988), 114–146.

58. "To speak about and across borders which are not physical ones is the task of female writing." Sara Lennox, "In the Cemetery of the Murdered Daughters: Ingeborg Bachmann's *Malina*," *Studies in 20th Century Literature* 3, no. 1 (Fall 1980): 89.

59. Patricia Meyer Spacks, "Female Rhetorics," *The Private Self*, 178.

60. Silvia Bovenschen, "Über die Frage: gibt es eine 'weibliche' Ästhetik?" *Ästhetik und Kommunikation* 25 (September 1979): 60–75.

61. Elaine Showalter, *A Literature of Their Own: British Women Novelists from Bronté to Lessing* (Princeton: Princeton University Press, 1977) and "Toward a Feminist Poetics," *Women Writing and Writing about Women*, ed. Mary Jacobus (London: Croom Helm, 1979), 23–41.

62. In Germany: Ullstein's "Die Frau in der Literatur" (Woman in Literature), or Rowohlt's "Reihe Neue Frau" (New Woman Series).

63. See selected contemporary studies of autobiographies and diaries in the bibliography.

64. In addition, the post-1968 political and academic interest in disrupting the elitist hierarchization of cultural products into "highbrow" and "lowbrow" spurred the consideration of previously ignored types and styles of writing. However, this new interest also imposed its own code of "realism" on the new literature it welcomed.

65. See works by Teresa de Lauretis, Peggy Kamuf, Diane Jean Fuss, Sigrid Weigel, Judith Butler.

66. See works by Alice Walker, bell hooks, Rey Chow, Ella Shohat, Gayatri Chakravorty Spivak.

67. Contributors to this side of the argument include Nancy Fraser and Linda Nicholson, who vouch for a "Social Criticism without Philosophy: An Encounter between Feminism and Postmodernism," *Communication* 10 (1988): 345–366.

68. Elizabeth A. Meese, *(Ex)Tensions. Re-Figuring Feminist Criticism* (Urbana/Chicago: University of Illinois Press, 1990).

69. Molly Hite, *The Other Side of the Story. Structures and Strategies of Contemporary Feminist Narratives* (Ithaca: Cornell University Press, 1989), 1–3.

70. Patricia Waugh, *Feminine Fictions. Revisiting the Postmodern* (New York/London: Routledge, 1989), 32.

71. Judith Butler, *Gender Trouble*, 144.

72. Meaghan Morris, *The Pirate's Fiancée. Feminism, Reading, Postmodernism* (London/New York: Verso, 1988), 12.

73. My approach here corresponds with Linda S. Kauffman's undertaking in *Special Delivery*. "My method makes different discourses interrupt each other dialogically in order to initiate a crisis—which is a good description of what happens within each text in my study. It also describes what happens among them" (xxv).

74. "We" harbors individuals, anonymous participants, an amorphous mass amplified by electronic media, the "I and you" of epistolary communication, voyeurs, and parasites. It is always a disparate entity, never one with itself. Someone or some voice is always entering while others are leaving. I envision it much like the bulletin board of an electronic mail service.

75. Ihab Hassan similarly opts for a "pragmatic pluralism" in "Beyond Postmodernism? Theory, Sense, and Pragmatism," *Making Sense: The Role of the Reader in Contemporary American Fiction*, ed. Gerhard Hoffmann (München: Fink, 1989), 323.

76. Linda Hutcheon, "A Postmodern Problematics," *Ethics/Aesthetics: Post-Modern Positions*, ed. Robert Merrill (Washington, D.C.: Maisonneuve, 1988), 1–10.

77. See selected contemporary epistolary fiction in the bibliography.

78. Ivar Ivask and John L. Brown's essays in the special issue of *World Literature Today: The Letter: A Dying Art?* provide an example of this difficulty in their melodramatic accounts for the fate of the letter in a media age. Ivask believes that scholars and readers alike find a respite from "impersonal experimentation for experimentation's sake" in the letter form, which lets them "share in the realities of our common human experience in time and place." "The Letter: A Dying Art?" *World Literature Today* 64, no. 2 (Spring 1990): 213. John L. Brown states that "[a]ll agree, however, that the health of the letter has been dealt a fatal blow by the telephone, the telegram, the cassette, the fax, and other technical innovations that have deprived it of its raison d'être. The authentic 'personal' letter (factitious as this can often be) has been further devalued by the rise of computerized mail." He leads the present scholarly vogue about the letter back to its state as a "relatively uncultivated turf at a time when traditional fields have been hoed and harrowed to exhaustion. Thus although people write letters less and less, scholars are writing more and more about writing letters."

"What ever happened to Mme. de Sévigné? Reflections on the fate of the epistolary art in a media age," *World Literature Today* 64, no. 2 (Spring 1990): 215 and 217.

79. Avital Ronell's *The Telephone Book. Technology, Schizophrenia, Electric Speech* (Lincoln: University of Nebraska Press, 1989), and Friedrich Kittler's *Aufschreibesysteme 1800/1900* (München: Fink, 1987) are exciting and thought-provoking exceptions to this rule.

80. Reinhard M. G. Nickisch, *Brief*, 239.

81. See Gilles Deleuze's and Félix Guattari's *Anti-Oedipus. Capitalism and Schizophrenia*, trans. Robert Hurley, Mark Seem, and Helen R. Lane (New York: Viking, 1977).

82. Mark Seem, "Introduction," *Anti-Oedipus*, xxi.

83. Gilles Deleuze's and Félix Guattari's, "The Body without Organs," *Anti-Oedipus*, 9–16. The authors link the money circulation of capitalism, machine production, and the body of a schizophrenic to a "body without organs": "It might be said that the schizophrenic passes from one code to the other, that he deliberately scrambles all codes, by quickly shifting from one to another, according to the questions asked him, never giving the same explanation from one day to the next, never invoking the same genealogy, never recording the same event in the same way" (15).

84. Katherine N. Hayles, *Chaos Bound*, 204.

85. Gregory G. Colomb and Mark Turner, "Computers, Literary Theory, and Theory of Meaning," 400.

86. Jacques Lacan thus defines "the letter" in his "Seminar on 'The Purloined Letter'," trans. Jeffrey Mehlman, *The Purloined Poe. Lacan, Derrida, and Psychoanalytic Reading*, ed. John P. Muller and William J. Richardson (Baltimore: Johns Hopkins University Press, 1988), 39.

87. Collected from Michael Newman's "Revising Modernism, Representing Postmodernism," *Postmodernism. ICA Documents*, 95–154; Jean-François Lyotard, "Defining the Postmodern," ibid., 7–10; J. G. Merquior, "Spider and Bee: Towards a Critique of the Postmodern Ideology," ibid., 41–48; Linda Hutcheon's *A Poetics of Postmodernism;* Ihab Hassan's *The Postmodern Turn*, 84–96; Wolfgang Welsch's *Unsere postmoderne Moderne.*

88. Ingeborg Hoesterey, "Introduction: Postmodernism as Discursive Event," *Zeitgeist in Babel*, x.

89. Linda Hutcheon, *A Poetics of Postmodernism*, ix.

90. I am referring to the poststructuralist tendency to reinfuse the canon with power by reading only "the big names." Paul de Man: "The necessity to revise the canon arises from resistances encountered in the text itself (extensively conceived) and not from preconceptions imported from elsewhere." I believe that resistances also arise from intertextual encounters that self-critically test "the methodological assumptions and substantial assertions of the system" and are part of the "ongoing critical investigation" that Paul de Man deems necessary. "Reply to Raymond Geuss," *Critical Inquiry* 10, no. 2 (December 1983) quoted by Alan Kennedy, *Reading Resistance Value. Deconstructive Practice and the Politics of Literary Critical Encounters* (New York: St. Martin's, 1990), 10.

91. As always inspired by Nicomedes Suárez-Araúz, *Amnesis Art.*

92. Jacques Derrida, "Living On: Borderlines," *Deconstruction and Criticism*, ed. Harald Bloom et al. (New York: Seabury, 1979), 80.

93. Alan Kennedy, *Reading Resistance Value*, 2. On the problem of discussing "popular" and noncanonical fiction in relation to the critic's own postmodern "shuttling" between academia and "other social sites," see Meaghan Morris, *The Pirate's Fiancée*, 7–10.

94. Anita Runge and Lieselotte Steinbrügge, *Die Frau im Dialog*, 8. "den Brief in seinem Verhältnis zu und als Teil von literarischen Werken ins Zentrum des literaturwissenschaftlichen Interesses zu rücken und scheinbar selbstverständliche Annahmen über ihn zu irritieren."

95. Linda Hutcheon, "A Postmodern Problematics," 1–2.

96. Ibid., 345.

97. Ibid., 5. The reconfigurations of genre theory and literary studies is particularly challenging in Germany, since German conceives of literary studies as a scientific project: *Literaturwissenschaft.*

98. A *Briefsteller* is someone who or something which provides model letters and sets up norms for letter-writing. The word itself betrays the ambivalent activity of a *Briefsteller* like Christian Fürchtegott Gellert, who in order to provide authentic material for the writing of authentic letters composed fictive correspondences tailored exactly to those aesthetic and moral judgments he wished to make. The most famous case of this mark of the trade is Samuel Richardson's epistolary novel *Pamela* (1840), which assumably grew out of a collection of sample letters aimed at the "country reader," and especially young women. The result was what some scholars call the first modern novel. William M. Sale, "Introduction," *Pamela or Virtue Rewarded* (New York: Norton, 1958), v–xiv.

99. Gregory L. Ulmer argues: "The implication of textual mime for post-criticism, informing paraliterature as a hybrid of literature and criticism, art and science, is that knowledge of an object of study may be obtained without conceptualization or explanation. Rather, . . . Derrida enacts or performs (mimes) the compositional structuration of the referent, resulting in another text of the same 'kind' (genre—but 'different' according to the 'law of the law of genre' noted above)." "The Object of Post-Criticism," *The Anti-Aesthetic. Essays on Postmodern Culture*, ed. Hal Foster (Washington, D.C.: Bay Press, 1983), 94.

100. Allen Thiher defines the intertwining of theory and fiction as "the central challenge, if not the central dilemma, for the postmodern creative mind." "A Theory of Literature or Recent Literature as Theory," *Contemporary Literature* 29, no. 3 (1988): 345.

CHAPTER 2. RHAPSODY IN LETTERS

1. "mit welcher Vehemenz dieses Ich . . ."—". . . sich verschreibt . . . kann man so sagen?"—"Sich verschreiben—das ist ein schönes Wort." Ingeborg Bachmann and Toni Kienlechner, Interview, April 9, 1971, *Wir müssen wahre Sätze finden*, ed. Christine Koschel and Inge von Weidenbaum (München/Zürich: R. Piper, 1983), 98. *Verschreiben* can imply a slip of the

pen, to write incorrectly, to prescribe, to use up, to dedicate oneself to something, to transfer, to sign away, to sell out.

2. Gudrun Kohn-Waechter contends that while *Malina* cannot be called an epistolary novel in the traditional sense, the problem of the post in Bachmann's works has been entirely overlooked until her own article, "Das 'Problem der Post' in 'Malina' von Ingeborg Bachmann und Martin Heideggers 'Der Satz vom Grund,'" *Die Frau im Dialog*, 228.

3. Rachel Blau DuPlessis argues "that the critique of story is a major aspect of the stories told by twentieth-century women writers" and that "the critique of story is not only a thematic fact but an indication of the moral, ideological and political desire to rescript the novel." *Writing beyond the Ending*, 43.

4. See Shari Benstock, "From Letters to Literature" 257–295, and Helga Meise, "Der Frauenroman: Erprobungen der 'Weiblichkeit,'" *Deutsche Literatur von Frauen. Vom Mittelalter bis zum Ende des 18. Jahrhunderts*, ed. Gisela Brinker-Gabler, vol. 1 (München: Beck, 1988), 35–452.

5. *Malina*, together with *The Book Franza* and *Requiem for Fanny Goldmann*, belongs to Bachmann's *Todesarten-Projekt*, which was reedited according to the latest archival research in the 1995 Kritische Ausgabe by Pichl, Göttsche, and Albrecht. The female protagonist repeats this phrase throughout the novel and takes its meaning literally by changing the word itself to *Todesraten* (death rates, death installments, but also "death-guessing,"). When *Todesarten* in its meaning of "types of death" or "death styles" is rewritten as *Todesarien*, death-arias, variations on death, the term reveals its affinity to a musical score.

6. Christine Kanz, *Angst und Geschlechterdifferenzen. Ingeborg Bachmanns "Todesarten" Projekt in Kontexten der Gegenwartsliteratur* (Stuttgart: Metzler, 1999), 15.

7. Philip Boehm translates this final chapter as "Last Things," which obscures the narrative character of the chapter.

8. "By reproducing signifiers—vocal, gestural, verbal—the subject crosses the border of the symbolic and reaches the semiotic chora, which is on the other side of the social frontier. The reenacting of the signifying path taken from the symbolic unfolds the symbolic itself and . . . opens it up to the motility where all meaning is erased." Julia Kristeva, *Revolution of Poetic Language*, 79.

9. This is Philip Boehm's translation of the line: "aus der nie mehr etwas laut werden kann." Ingeborg Bachmann, *Malina*, trans. Philip Boehm (New York: Holmes and Meier, 1990), 225. "Laut werden" implies more than just sound emanating from a source, it implies knowing: "to make something known."

10. Karen R. Achberger discusses *Malina*'s Wagnerian undercurrents in addition to Bachmann's use of Arnold Schönberg's *Pierrot Lunaire* and Beethoven's piano sonatas in *Understanding Ingeborg Bachmann* (Columbia: University of South Carolina Press, 1994), 96–142.

11. Elizabeth J. MacArthur, *Extravagant Narratives. Closure and Dynamics in the Epistolary Form*, 29: "Like deviance, extravagance exceeds conventional limits, but unlike deviance, extravagance is not an abnormality that can

be cured. . . . In other words, metonymy subordinated to metaphor produces deviance; metonymy not subordinated to metaphor produces extravagance."

12. Barbara Lersch, "Der Ort der Leerstelle. Weiblichkeit als Poetik der Negativität und der Differenz," *Deutsche Literatur von Frauen. 19. und 20. Jahrhundert*, ed. Gisela Brinker-Gabler, vol. 2 (München: Beck, 1988), 495.

13. Ibid.

14. Shari Benstock argues that Derrida's notion of the "hymen" functions like the letter in contemporary literary theory. "From Letters to Literature," 285.

15. Sigrid Weigel criticizes Derrida precisely for employing "woman" as the metaphor of metonymy in his *Spurs: Nietzsche's Styles. Die Stimme der Medusa. Schreibweisen in der Gegenwartsliteratur von Frauen* (Hamburg: Rowohlt, 1989), 212.

16. *The New Oxford Companion to Music*, 1983 ed.

17. Temma F. Berg quotes Jacques Lacan's infamous words in "Suppressing the Language of Wo(Man): The Dream as a Common Language," *Engendering the Word: Feminist Essays in Psychosexual Poetics*, ed. Temma F. Berg (Urbana: University of Illinois Press, 1989), 6.

18. Barbara Naumann, "'Mit der Musik versteht sichs von selbst'. Friedrich Schlegels Reflexion des Musikalischen im Kontext der Gattungspoetik," *Regelkram und Grenzgänge. Von poetischen Gattungen*, ed. Eberhard Lämmert and Dietrich Scheunemann (München: Text und Kritik, 1988), 78.

19. While Friedrich Schlegel is not the only Romantic who established musical theories of narrative dynamics, his philosophical fragments ontologically link novel, letter, and rhapsody.

20. Naumann, "'Mit der Musik versteht sichs von selbst,'" 79: "innig[e] Verbindung des Musikalischen mit dem reflexiven und 'sentimentalen' Gestus der Kunst der Moderne" (80) and "in dem Punkt, wo die inhaltliche Unbestimmtheit zum Definitionsmerkmal der Musik und der unendlichen Reflexion wird bzw. wo die beiden unterschiedlichen Medien durch ihre Unbestimmtheit kommensurable gemacht werden."

21. Friedrich Schlegel, *Fragmente zur Poesie und Literatur* II, cited by Barbara Naumann, "'Mit der Musik verstehs sich von selbst,'" 81. "Die innerste Form des Romans ist mathematisch, rhetorisch, musikalisch. Das Potenziren, Progressive, Irrationale; ferner die rhetorischen Figuren. Mit der Musik versteht sichs von selbst."

22. In this fragment, Friedrich Schlegel uses the metaphor of "Kette" and "Kranz" to describe the dialogue and the exchange of letters in his "Kritische Fragmente (1797)," *Schriften zur Literatur* (München: dtv, 1985), 32–33. In the next fragment, he contends that "ignorance often comes not from a lack of intellect but from a lack of sense" ("Das Nichtverstehen kommt meistens gar nicht vom Mangel an Verstande, sondern vom Mangel an Sinn").

23. *The New Oxford Companion to Music*, 1983 ed.

24. *The New Grove Dictionary of Music and Musicians*, 1980 ed.

25. Ibid.

26. *The New Oxford Companion to Music*, 1983 ed.

27. *The New Grove Dictionary of Music and Musicians*, 1980 ed.

28. Friedrich Schlegel to Caroline Schlegel, December 12, 1797, as quoted by Herta Schwarz, "Brieftheorie in der 'Romantik,'" *Brieftheorie im 18. Jahrhundert*, 235–236: "I have always believed, your natural form—because I believe, every human being of power and spirit has its very own, proper form—were the rhapsody. . . . Everything that could be printed from your letters is much too pure, beautiful and soft, as that I would like to see it seemingly broken into fragm[ents] and made coquettish by lifting it out. On the other hand, it would not be impossible for me to diaskeuasiren one great philosophical rhapsody out of your letters" ("Ich habe immer geglaubt, Ihre Naturform—denn ich glaube, jeder Mensch von Kraft und Geist hat seine eigenthümliche—wäre die Rhapsodie. . . . Was sich aus Ihren Briefen alles drucken ließe, ist viel zu rein, schön und weich, als daß ich es in Fragm[ente] gleichsam zerbrochen, und durch die bloße Aushebung kokett gemacht sehn möchte. Dagegen denke ich, es würde mir nicht unmöglich seyn, aus Ihren Briefen Eine große philosophische Rhapsodie zu—diaskeuasiren").

29. Herta Schwarz, "Brieftheorie in der 'Romantik,'" 235–236: "The letters of Caroline Schlegel were supposed, among other things, to serve only as raw material, in the same vein as their author was asked by the men to prepare the ground work for them" ("Die Briefe von Caroline Schlegel sollen unter anderem nur als Ausgangsmaterial dienen, so wie ihre Verfasserin überhaupt Vor- und Zuarbeit zu leisten von den Männern gebeten wird").

30. Christa Bürger in *Leben Schreiben. Die Klassik, die Romantik und der Ort der Frauen* (Stuttgart: Metzler, 1990), 81, 83–84, and 95: "eine Schreibweise, die der philosophischen entspricht, aber jede Systematik verweigert," and "Diaskeue" as a "Schreibweise, die ihren Werkcharakter immer wieder aufhebt." "einen schwer faßbaren ästhetischen Zwischenbereich, auf der Schwebe zwischen Klassik und Moderne."

31. Christian Fürchtegott Gellert's "Briefe, nebst einer Praktischen Abhandlung von dem guten Geschmacke in Briefen (1751)," *Brieftheorie des 18. Jahrhunderts*, 84: "The heart of Sevigne always flows over with the liveliest sensations of friendship and love towards her daughter . . . and this great tenderness that would become bizarre or probably disgusting in the language of another mother, remains beautiful and natural in the mouth of Sevigne" ("Das Herz der Sevigne fließt stets von den lebhaftesten Empfindungen der Freundschaft und Liebe gegen ihre Tochter über . . . und eben diese große Zärtlichkeit, die in der Sprache einer andern Mutter abentheuerlich, oder doch ekelhaft werden würde, bleibt in dem Munde der Sevigne schön und natürlich").

32. Elizabeth MacArthur, *Extravagant Narratives*, 34.

33. Eberhard Lämmert, *Regelkram und Grenzgänge*, 55: "Es ist eine Binsenweisheit, daß einer nicht gleichzeitig schreiben und außerdem handeln kann. Bei Richardsons edelmütigen Briefschreiberinnen wundert man sich geradezu, wie in ihrem Leben unter so viel unablässigem Schreibeifer die beklagten Verführungen überhaupt noch Platz greifen konnten. Werthers Leben spielt sich schon in weit höherem Maße in seiner Einbildungskraft als in den tatsächlichen Begegnungen und Vorkommnissen seines äußeren Lebensganges ab."

34. Friedrich Schlegel, "Philosophische Fragmente. Erste Epoche. III. [69]," *Brieftheorie des 18. Jahrhunderts*, 180: "Die Rede ist von niemand an niemand,

oder von allen an alle. Der Brief ist von jemand an jemand, ganz bestimmt, (cyklisch, Strophe, Monodie, cyklisch[er] Natur) / Die wahre [Rhapsodie] muß zugl[eich] Brief sein und absolute Rede, Dialog und Monolog—Parallelismus zu Gedanken wie bei Fichte. Der wahre Brief muß [rhetorisch] sein, und dabei sapphisch, strophisch.—Der Monolog ist eine cyklische Rede.—" The brackets and bracketed terms appear as quoted from this edition.

35. By contrast, Christa Bürger believes that Caroline Schlegel-Schelling's letters to Schlegel may be the realization of a Romantic *Gesamtkunstwerk*. *Leben Schreiben*, 107.

36. Alexander and Margarete Mitscherlich thus defined the German's collective relation to their National Socialist past in their book *Die Unfähigkeit zu trauern. Grundlagen kollektiven Verhaltens* (München: Piper, 1977). Christa Gürtler also contends that "Ingeborg Bachmann never avoided the labor of mourning, she was not inable to mourn. The confrontation with fascism and the continuity of fascist ideology after 1945 is visible throughout her entire work" ("Ingeborg Bachmann hat sich der Trauerarbeit nie entzogen, sie war nicht unfähig zu trauern. Durch ihr ganzes Werk zieht sich die Auseinandersetzung mit dem Faschismus und dem Weiterleben faschistischen Gedankenguts nach 1945"). *Schreiben Frauen anders?* 85.

37. Some of the events that have contributed to a public German dialogue on the Holocaust were the U.S. TV-drama *Holocaust* (1979), President Reagan's Bitburg cemetery visit (1985), Spielberg's *Schindler's List* (1995), and the controversy over Daniel J. Goldhagen's book *Hitler's Willing Executioners. Ordinary Germans and the Holocaust* (New York: Alfred Knopf, 1996).

38. Elke Atzler documents the critical reaction to Bachmann's war metaphors in her article on "'*Malina*' im Spiegel der literarischen Kritik," 162.

39. Christa Gürtler mentions Elisabeth Dessai's *Sklavin-Mannweib-Weib. Streitschrift für eine weibliche(re) Gesellschaft* (1970) and Hans Mayer's *Außenseiter* (1977). See *Schreiben Frauen anders?* 62.

40. Ingeborg Bachmann, "1973: II," *Wir müssen wahre Sätze finden*, 144. "wo fängt der Faschismus an? Er fängt nicht an mit den ersten Bomben, die geworfen werden, er fängt nicht an mit dem Terror, über den man schreiben kann, in jeder Zeitung. Er fängt an in Beziehungen zwischen Menschen. Der Faschismus ist das erste in der Beziehung zwischen einem Mann und einer Frau, und ich habe versucht zu sagen, in diesem Kapitel, hier in dieser Gesellschaft ist immer Krieg." Her generalization recalls Sigmund Freud's statement "that society is founded on a complicity in the common crime." Quoted by Julia Kristeva in *Revolution in Poetic Language*, 70 from Freud's *Der Mann Moses und die monotheistische Religion: Drei Abhandlungen*.

41. See the interview with Alicja Walecka-Kowalska in Poland in May 1973, *Wir müssen wahre Sätze finden*, 130–134. See also Christa Bürger, "I and We: Ingeborg Bachmann's Emergence from Aesthetic Modernism," *New German Critique* 47 (Summer 1989): 9.

42. Ingeborg Bachmann, "Auf das Opfer darf sich keiner berufen," *Ingeborg Bachmann: Die Wahrheit ist dem Menschen zumutbar*, 135.

43. Ingeborg Bachmann's understanding of the continuing interpersonal and sociopolitical prerequisites of fascism comes close to Theodor W. Adorno's

statement, "Daß der Faschismus nachlebt, daß die vielzitierte Aufarbeitung der Vergangenheit bis heute nicht gelang und zu ihrem Zerrbild, dem leeren und kalten Vergessen, ausartete, rührt daher, daß die objektiven gesellschaftlichen Voraussetzungen fortbestehen, die den Faschismus zeitigten." *Erziehung zur Mündigkeit* (Frankfurt a. M.: Suhrkamp, 1981), 22.

44. Ingeborg Bachmann, "Die Wahrheit ist dem Menschen zumutbar," *Die Wahrheit ist dem Menschen zumutbar*, 75. "So kann es auch nicht die Aufgabe des Schriftstellers sein, den Schmerz zu leugnen, seine Spuren zu verwischen, über ihn hinwegzutäuschen. Er muß ihn, im Gegenteil, wahrhaben und noch einmal, damit wir sehen können, wahrmachen."

45. Ibid., 75–76. "Der Schriftsteller . . . ist mit seinem ganzen Wesen auf ein Du gerichtet, auf den Menschen, dem er seine Erfahrung vom Menschen zukommen lassen möchte (oder seine Erfahrung der Dinge, der Welt und seiner Zeit, ja von all dem auch!), aber insbesondere vom Menschen, der er selber oder die anderen sein können und wo er selber und die anderen am meisten Mensch sind."

46. Ingeborg Bachmann, "Auf das Opfer darf sich keiner berufen," 135. "Manchmal fühl ich ganz deutlich die eine oder andere Wahrheit aufstehen und fühle, wie sie dann niederge-treten wird in meinem Kopf von anderen Gedanken oder fühle sie verkümmern, weil ich mit ihr nichts anzufangen weiß, weil sie sich nicht mitteilen läßt, ich sie nicht mitzu-teilen verstehe oder weil gerade nichts diese Mitteilung erfordert, ich nirgends einhaken kann und bei niemand."

47. Ibid. The verb *ergeben* would need to be translated in different ways, since it could also mean "to surrender," "to amount to" in addition to "to follow from."

48. Kanz, *Angst und Geschlechterdifferenzen*, 149. My translation.

49. Ingeborg Bachmann, "Tagebuch (Diario in Pubblico)," *Die Wahrheit ist dem Menschen zumutbar*, 67–68. "verliebter Bewunderung in die Literaturen, Malereien und Musiken der anderen."

50. Ingeborg Bachmann, "Tagebuch (Diario in Pubblico), " 67–68. "Eine sakrale Beschau der Gegend und damit eine sakrale Briefkunst-europäisch hat man sie nennen dürfen—ist zuendegegangen, und es wird nicht mehr viel zu sammeln geben danach, ein paar Telegrammfetzen, Postkarten, ein paar Briefe auch. Warum nicht auch Briefe? Aber ohne den Faltenwurf, das Bedeutsame, das "Verantwortliche," das schon durch die Art der Anrede und durchgehende Stilisierung sich verrät. Eine Verarmung, wird man sagen. Ja, aber vielleicht wollte man verarmen, vielleicht auch ist man zu unwirsch und zu ungeduldig geworden, um Gedanken und Gefühle zu zelebrieren, die man auch hat, oder man wird inne, daß es nicht mehr viel taugt, darüber zu reden, wenn man in der Situation des Rad-wechslers ist. Und manchmal fühlt man sich einfach nicht aufgelegt, zwischen dem Ausfüllen der Steuer-erklärung und einem Gang zum Bäcker, die Goldfeder in die Tinte zu senken und Ewigkeit herzustellen oder überlegen Zeichen zu geben von Person zu Person."

51. The affinity of the two novels to each other is underlined by the fragmentation of the letters, by the thematic and structural exploration of psychoanalytic language, by the gender-crossing of the characters, by the tone of urgency in the writers' last epistles, and by the requests to leave something behind in spite of destruction. With its innuendoes of music and murder, the let-

ter of June 10, 1977, seems to have been taken from *Malina* ("Murder is everywhere"), the destruction of "the most beautiful letters in the world" and yet the promise "I have not yet destroyed anything of yours, your scraps of paper I mean, you perhaps, but nothing of yours" and the proclamation that "if we do not destroy all the traces, we are saved, that is lost" (*The Postcard*, 32–34).

52. Interview with Ilse Heim, May 5, 1971. *Wir müssen wahre Sätze finden*, 107.

53. "By no longer treating the posts as a metaphor of the *envoi* of Being, one can account for what essentially and decisively occurs, everywhere, and including language, thought, science, and everything that conditions them, when the postal structure shifts, . . . and posits or posts itself otherwise." *The Postcard*, 66.

54. This narrative position has been likened to that of a schizophrenic or a hysteric. See Inge Röhnelt's *Hysterie und Mimesis in 'Malina'*.

55. On the anagram versions of *Malina*, see Rainer Nägele, " Die Arbeit des Textes: Notizen zur experimentellen Literatur," *Deutsche Literatur in der Bundesrepublik seit 1965. Untersuchungen und Berichte*, ed. P. M. Lützeler and Egon Schwarz (Königstein: Athenäum, 1980), 38 and Karen R. Achberger, *Understanding Ingeborg Bachmann*, 116. Christine Kanz adds another intertextual possibility with her reference to Wystan Hugh Auden's verse epos *The Age of Anxiety*, one of whose protagonists calls himself Malin. *Angst und Geschlechterdifferenzen*, 41.

56. *Malina*, 19. "Mir scheint es dann, daß seine Ruhe davon herrührt, weil ich ein zu unwichtiges und bekanntes Ich für ihn bin, als hätte er mich ausgeschieden, einen Abfall, eine überflüssige Menschwerdung, als wäre ich nur aus seiner Rippe gemacht und ihm seit jeher entbehrlich, aber auch eine unvermeidlich dunkle Geschichte, die seine Geschichte begleitet, ergänzen will, die er aber von seiner klaren Geschichte absondert und abgrenzt. Deswegen habe auch nur ich etwas zu klären mit ihm, und mich selber vor allem muß und kann ich nur vor ihm klären. Er hat nichts zu klären, nein, er nicht."

57. This is not the case for some of *Malina*'s male readers. Horst Peter Neumann, "Vier Gründe einer Befangenheit. Über Ingeborg Bachmann," *Merkur* 32 (1978): 1130–1136.

58. *Unsere postmoderne Moderne*, 186. "Nicht erst im Ganzen, sondern schon im einzelnen System herrscht keine vollständige Transparenz. Größen wie Ort und Impuls oder Zeit und Energie sind zwar im gleichen System definiert, ja sind kanonisch konjugierte Größen, gleichwohl stößt ihre simultane Bestimmung an unübersteigbare Grenzen. Die präzise Fokusierung auf das eine macht die gleichzeitige Erfassung des anderen unmöglich." ("Er besagt, daß jedes für die Darstellung der elementaren Zahlentheorie ausreichende und widerspruchsfreie formale System unvollständig ist und seine Widerspruchsfreiheit nicht mit seinen eigenen Mitteln beweisen kann").

59. "Auch wenn Malina schweigt, ist es besser, als alleine zu schweigen, und es hilft mir dann bei Ivan weiter, wenn ich es nicht fassen kann, und wenn ich mich nicht fassen kann, weil Malina stets fest und gefaßt für mich da ist, und so bleibt mir in den finstersten Stunden noch bewußt, daß Malina mir nie verlorengehen wird—und ginge ich selbst verloren!" *Malina*, 129.

60. Christa Bürger compares Ingeborg Bachmann's interpretation of Hegel's Master-Slave chapter in *Malina* to Hélène Cixous' positioning of the women in the slave role. "I and We: Ingeborg Bachmann's Emergence from Aesthetic Modernism," 23–28.

61. In his essay "The Literature of Silence," Ihab Hassan considers "literalism's" link to silence and eternal presence: "Finally, literature strives for silence by accepting chance and improvisation; its principle becomes indeterminacy. By refusing order, order imposed or discovered, this kind of literature refuses purpose. Its forms are therefore nontelic, its world is the eternal present." *The Postmodern Turn,* 10.

62. Ludwig Wittgenstein, *Tractatus logico-philosophicus* (Frankfurt a. M.: Suhrkamp, 1963), 32 (# 4.002): "die stillschweigenden Abmachungen zum Verständnis der Umgangssprache."

63. *Malina,* 13. My italics. "So will ich nicht erst anfangen, über meine Gasse, unsere Gasse unhaltbare Behauptungen aufzustellen, ich sollte vielmehr in mir nach meiner Verklammerung mit der Ungargasse suchen, weil sie nur in mir ihren Bogen macht, bis zur Nummer 9 und Nummer 6, und mich müßte ich fragen, warum ich immer in ihrem Magnetfeld bin."

64. Monique Wittig defines the "straight mind" as the "totalizing interpretation of history, social reality, culture, language" as "that which resists examination, a relationship excluded from the social in the analysis . . . which is the heterosexual relationship. I will call it the obligatory social relationship between 'man' and 'woman'." Monique Wittig, "The Straight Mind," *The Straight Mind* (Boston: Beacon, 1992), 27.

65. Ludwig Wittgenstein, *Tractatus logico-philosophicus,* 89 (# 5.6).

66. *Malina,* 17. "Seit ich diese Nummer wählen kann, nimmt mein Leben endlich keinen Verlauf mehr, ich gerate nicht mehr unter die Räder, ich komme in keine ausweglosen Schwierigkeiten, nicht mehr vorwärts und nicht vom Weg ab, da ich den Atem anhalte, die Zeit aufhalte und telefoniere und rauche und warte."

67. Kohn-Waechter, "Das 'Problem der Post' in '*Malina*'," 225–242.

68. *Malina,* 35. "Eine Kleinigkeit könnte es im Beginn ersticken, abwürgen, es im Anlauf zum Stillstand bringen, so empfindlich sind Anfang und Entstehen dieser stärksten Macht in der Welt, weil die Welt eben krank ist und sie, die gesunde Macht nicht aufkommen lassen will."

69. Ibid., 34. "Endlich gehe ich auch in meinem Fleisch herum. . . . Wie gut auch, daß ich im Nu begriffen habe, wovon ich in der ersten Stunde ergriffen worden bin, und daß ich darum sofort, ohne mich anzustellen, ohne Vorstellung, mit Ivan gegangen bin."

70. This first ambivalent rape situation is converted into the expected norm later in the novel, when Ich parodies the internalized projection of male desire in another rape story which she narrates explicitly for Malina's entertainment: "I just want to entertain you and tell you everything that is funny: I, for example, was very dissatisfied because I have never been raped. . . . One does not consider it possible, but except for a few drunks, a few sexual murderers, no normal man with normal drives has the obvious idea that a normal woman wants to be raped in a normal fashion." ("Ich will dich nur unterhalten und dir sagen,

was alles komisch ist: Ich, zum Beispiel, war sehr unzufrieden, weil ich nie verge-waltigt worden bin. . . . Man hält es nicht für möglich, aber außer ein paar Betrunkenen, ein paar Lustmördern . . . hat kein normaler Mann mit normalen Trieben die naheliegende Idee, daß eine normale Frau ganz normal vergewaltigt werden möchte"). Ibid., 288.

71. Kohn-Waechter, "Das 'Problem der Post' in '*Malina*'," 226–227.

72. For specifics on the telephone conversations in *Malina*, see Inge Röh-nelt's *Hysterie und Mimesis* and Sigrid Weigel's final chapter of *Ingeborg Bach-mann. Hinterlassenschaften unter Wahrung des Briefgeheimnisses* (Wien: Zsol-nag, 1999), 543–559.

73. Gero von Wilpert, *Sachwörterbuch der Literatur*, 299.

74. This victimizing episode later returns as her opera-dream, in which she has to sing a duet without text and is upstaged by the male lead. When Ich finally remembers her text, the princess' secrets have already been revealed. As Ich falls off her horse and off the stage, she is dismembered by the phallic thorn and "Dirigentenstab." Ibid., 69, 195–197.

75. Christoph Martin Wieland was the dominant literary critic in late-eigh-teenth-century Germany. Bachmann might be hinting at his critical preface and annotated footnotes to Sophie La Roche's epistolary novel *Die Geschichte des Fräulein von Sternheim* and his authoritative mentor-mentee relationships with other women writers of his time. The choice of the city leads the reader to the "Nürnberger Gesetze zum Schutz des deutschen Blutes und der deutschen Ehre," which were pronounced there in 1935, and to the Nürnberg trials of Nazi lead-ers. The date of Schönthal's letter, September 19, recalls that of the invasion of Poland in 1939. See Annette Klaubert, *Symbolische Strukturen bei Ingeborg Bachmann. Malina im Kontext der Kurzgeschichten* (Frankfurt a. M.: Lang, 1983), 84.

76. Here, Ingeborg Bachmann also refers to the Vienna Neo-positivists' attempt to create "a universal language, into which all scientific registers should be translated" ("eine Universalsprache, in die alle wissenschaftlichen Teil-sprachen übersetzt sein sollten"). "Ludwig Wittgenstein—Zu einem Kapitel der jüngsten Philosophiegeschichte," *Die Wahrheit ist dem Menschen zumutbar*, 16.

77. Godele von der Decken, *Emanzipation auf Abwegen*.

78. Annette Klaubert interprets Ich's dislike of that name as her dislike for her doubleness: "Ich does not like the name GANZ because she herself is not whole but torn" ("Ich mag den Namen GANZ nicht, weil sie selber nicht ganz, sondern zerrissen ist"). *Symbolische Strukturen bei Ingeborg Bachmann*, 92–93. This interpretation neither adequately accounts for the context out of which this letter is written nor for Ich's continuous struggle against any kind of duality that would simply revert to totality.

79. *Malina*, 107. My italics. "Unlängst, als ich beinahe fürchten mußte, Sie wiederzusehen, kurz nachdem die neue Mode aufgekommen war, mit den Me-tallkleidern, den Kettenhemden, den Stachelfransen und dem Schmuck aus Drahtverhauen, fühlte ich mich gewappnet für eine Begegnung, nicht einmal die Ohren hätte ich freigehabt, weil ich zwei schwere Dornenbüschel im schönsten Grau an den Ohrläppchen hängen hatte, die bei jeder Kopfbewegung schmerzten oder ins Rutschen kamen, weil man vergessen hatte, mir im frühesten Alter diese

Löcher in die Ohren zu bohren, die sonst allen kleinen Mädchen bei uns auf dem Land unbarmherzig hineingebohrt wurden, im zartesten Alter."

80. Christa Gürtler points to the gender-inverted Christian *Passionsgeschichte* as a recurring motif in *Malina*. *Schreiben Frauen anders?* 173.

81. *Malina*, 109. "Ihr bares Unvermögen, meine Empfindlichkeiten für das Du zu spüren, es von mir und anderen zu erpressen, lassen mich fürchten, daß Sie sich immer noch einer Erpressung gar nicht bewußt sind, weil Sie Ihnen 'ganz' geläufig ist." Philip Boehm keeps translating "Sie" for "you," which somewhat obscures her deliberate attempt to distance herself and demonstrate the hierarchy involved in their "Intermezzo." *Malina* (New York: Holmes and Meier, 1990), 67.

82. *Malina*, 110. "kann nicht umhin, diese Gratulation in Gedanken weiterzugeben an eine längst verstorbene Frau, eine gewisse Josefine H., die in meinem Geburtsschein als Hebamme eingetragen ist. Man hätte ihr damals gratulieren müssen, zu ihrer Geschicklichkeit und zu einer glatt verlaufenen Geburt."

83. On the concept of *Zustellung* in Malina in comparison to Heidegger, see Gudrun Kohn-Waechter: "The translation of the postal problem into the philosophical, the 'delivery of post' into the 'delivery of reason', allows us to solve the riddle which the 'problem of the post' created: that 'the fate of postal workers' triggered the 'greatest horror' in the first person narrator can therefore be deduced from the expectation, that she, like them, is obliged 'to deliver', an expectation that is not redeemable and is criminal. And in this lies the central significance of the 'problem of the post' for the cycle Todesarten" ("Die Übersetzung des postalischen in die philosophische Problematik, der 'Zustellung der Post' in die 'Zustellung des Grundes', ermöglicht es, die Rätsel zu lösen, die das 'Problem der Post' aufwarf: daß 'das Los der Postbeamten' bei der Ich-Erzählerin den 'größten Schrecken' auslöst, ist demnach darauf zurückzuführen, daß diese wie sie unter einem 'Zustellungsanspruch' stehen, einem Anspruch, der nicht einlösbar und 'mörderisch' ist. Und eben darin liegt auch die zentrale Bedeutung des 'Problems der Post' für die Todesarten"). "Das 'Problem der Post' in '*Malina*'," 234.

84. *Malina*, 111–112. "Die zerissenen Briefe liegen im Papierkorb kunstvoll durcheinandergebracht und vermischt mit zerknüllten Einladungen zu einer Ausstellung, zu einem Empfang, zu einem Vortrag, vermischt mit leeren Zigaretten-schachteln, überstäubt von Asche und Zigaretten-stummeln."

85. "Through the comparison with 'real letters,' the novel is indirectly characterized as a fictional letter, as a letter, which should not have been 'sent'. This is explained with regard to the temporal delay until arrival, with regard to a problem of delivery" ("Durch den Vergleich mit 'wirklichen Briefen' wird der Roman hier indirekt als ein fiktiver Brief charakterisiert, und zwar als ein Brief, der nicht hätte 'abgeschickt' werden dürfen. Dies wird mit der zeitlichen Verzögerung bis zur Ankunft begründet, mit einem Problem der Zustellung also"). Kohn-Waechter, "Das 'Problem der Post'," 226.

86. This gesture rewrites Hugo von Hofmannthal's "Ein Brief" in that the narrator recreates the possibility of fiction and dialogue through the epistolary narrative of its impossibility. See also Kohn-Waechter, "Das 'Problem der Post' in 'Malina'," 236.

87. During the examinations, Ich masquerades for Malina's entertainment and her protection (as in the rape scene). The hysteric shielding also burns her up as the scenes with Malina's dress and her nightly "flammende Briefe" indicate. See Inge Röhnelt's *Hysterie und Mimesis*.

88. The word *Mitwisser* has legal connotations. It builds a connection from the mailing system to organized crime, to Nazi accomplices, who spy on everybody's moves and report them. It also links Ich's mother's, sister's, as well as her own *Mitwisser* roles in her dreams to the role of "mail carrier." The carrier is no longer excused from the responsibility for the crime on the grounds of simply facilitating its discourse. Bachmann here ties the importance of the sanctity of the mail in the age of data processing to fascist terror based on collaborating "Mitwisser." She thereby also draws attention to the dispute between Malina and Ich about remembering and telling everything.

89. The analogy of herself to "leftovers" and "waste" is especially strident when one remembers her self-definition as "waste, a superfluous becoming-human" ("Abfall, eine überflüssige Menschwerdung"). *Malina*, 19.

90. Judith Butler critically explores how in Foucault, Nietzsche, and Kafka "cultural values emerge as the result of an inscription on the body, understood as a medium" and that "within the metaphorics of this notion of cultural values is the figure of history as a relentless writing instrument, and the body as the medium which must be destroyed and transfigured in order for 'culture' to emerge." Butler continues to address the permeable bodily boundaries in homosexual and heterosexual acts and links those to the "abjection" of bodily fluids and excrements, which she considers to confound the model of identity-differentiation while at the same time exploding it. *Gender Trouble*, 130–134.

91. Emily Martin, "Medical Metaphors of Women's Bodies," *Writing on the Body: Female Embodiment and Feminist Theory*, ed. Katie Conboy et al. (New York: Columbia University Press, 1997), 15–41.

92. Remember that Schlegel, a compatriot of Beethoven, defined music as "unbestimmter Signifikat" ("indefinite signifier") as "Ausdruck des Idealismus" ("expression of Idealism").

93. Sigrid Weigel employs and analyzes the idea of *Überwechseln* and *Überqueren*. With regard to Luce Irigaray's *The Sex which is not one* and her own theorization of "der schielende Blick," Weigel interprets Irigaray's practice of "crossing" the male discourse of symbolism as follows: "Without defining the meaning of 'feminine' anywhere, Irigaray surmises that traces of those conflicts have remained in Woman's voice, which took place in the process of forming the individual into the case of an identical subject. Her voice, so to say, keeps signs of the repressed and of the excess. This non-property of speech and writing is not to be equated with the 'feminine;' it is rather the sign of an impossible identity, because Woman does not equal her appointed place in the symbolic. Her double place is the matrix for the movement of crossing-through, Irigaray suggests, which is necessary so that Woman does not remain captive within the non-proper, the masquerade or even indifference" ("Ohne die Bedeutung von 'weiblich' irgendwo festzulegen, geht Irigaray also davon aus, daß sich in der Stimme der Frau Spuren von jenen Konflikten erhalten haben, die im Prozeß der Zurichtung des Individuums zur Instanz eines identischen Subjekts stattgefunden

haben. Ihre Stimme bewahrt sozusagen Zeichen des dabei Verdrängten und Überschießenden auf. Dieses Uneigentliche der Rede und Schrift der Frau ist aber nicht gleichzusetzen mit dem 'Weiblichen'; es ist vielmehr Zeichen einer unmöglichen Identität, weil die Frau nicht aufgeht in dem ihr zugewiesenen Ort im Symbolischen. Ihr doppelter Ort ist Matrix für die von Irigaray angeregte Bewegung der Durchquerung, die wiederum notwendig ist, damit die Frau nicht in der Uneigentlichkeit, in der Maskerade oder gar in der Indifferenz gefangen bleibt"). *Die Stimme der Medusa*, 209–210.

94. Since Paul Breitner was a famous soccer player in the 1970s, Bachmann might also be referring to a goalie scene, which would link Peter Handke's *Die Angst des Tormanns beim Elfmeter* (1970) to Ich's anxiety at reaching the "other shore." Ich literally fakes a smile to disarm Breitner, and thus manages to sidestep her.

95. Freud's patient Dora has a dream that equals Ich's homeward procession: "I had the usual feeling of anxiety that one has in dreams when one cannot move forward. Then I was at home. I must have been traveling in the meantime, but I know nothing about that." Sigmund Freud, "Fragment of an Analysis of a Case of Hysteria" (1905), 86.

96. Michael Riffaterre, "Undecidability as Hermeneutic Constraint," *Literary Theory Today*, 124.

97. Although I disagree with her explanation of "the feminine position," Inge Röhnelt's analysis of Malina's "Apokryph" in the form of Ich's letters provided a place of departure for my own reading. *Hysterie und Mimesis*, 309 and 312.

98. In her 1999 book, *Ingeborg Bachmann*, Sigrid Weigel interprets the ending of *Malina* via Friedrich Kittler: Malina has taken possession of the "media of the modernist writing system" whereas Ich has "hidden her legacy in the writing of her novel, not as a riddle or secret, but as correspondence" (558).

CHAPTER 3. CHAIN MAIL

1. Jacques Lacan, "Of Structure as an Intermixing of an Otherness Prerequisite to Any Subject Whatever," *The Structuralist Controversy. The Languages of Criticism and the Sciences of Man*, ed. Richard Macksey and Eugenio Donato (Baltimore: Johns Hopkins University Press, 1972), 194.

2. Linda S. Kauffman, *Special Delivery*. See also Christopher D. Morris, "Barth and Lacan: The World of the Moebius Strip," *Critique* 17, no. 1 (1975): 69–77.

3. This "we" appears here in response to Derrida's "you," which should not indicate a community of homogeneous readers but instead a disparate group of people caught in the act of reading the postcard. The postcard itself determines the structure of the "we" and "you." Shari Benstock remarks: "Ultimately in 'Envois' one cannot distinguish the lover from oneself, the Other from the one who dictates the messages of desire." "From Letters to Literature," Note 20, 294.

4. Temma F. Berg suggests that *The Postcard* addresses its reader: "We are to read against all boundaries, even against the boundary presented by the card's

small rectangular shape." Later, she adds "Who is the reader? The reader is legion. And to give oneself to readers, to allow strange others the power of breathing life into you, is to deliver yourself into the unknown. It is to take the greatest chance of all, the risk of annihilation, of death." *"La Carte Postale:* Reading (Derrida) Reading," *Criticism* 28, no. 3 (1986): 333 and 338.

5. Jonathan Levi, *A Guide for the Perplexed* (New York: Turtle Bay Books, 1992). In the following, I will quote directly in the text from the Vintage Contemporary edition of 1993.

6. John Barth, *LETTERS* (New York: Putnam's Sons, 1979), 39. From now on, all quotes from this novel and edition will appear in the text in parentheses, marked by the letter "L."

7. Homer Obed Brown uses the double meaning of "re-membering" for this procedure, referring to the problem of foreknowledge, "the 'memory' or reference before or outside necessary to any representational text." "The Errant Letter and the Whispering Gallery," *Genre* 10 (Winter 1977): 599.

8. René Wellek and Austin Warren, *Theory of Literature* (New York: Harcourt Brace, 1949), 38–45.

9. Reinhard M. G. Nickisch underscores the semantic connection of the etymological roots of the German *Brief* with legal documentation and decrees in *Brief*, 22–23.

10. For different concepts of intertextuality and "intertextual zones," see Brian McHale, *Postmodern Fiction*, 56–58.

11. Jonathan Culler, *A Structuralist Poetics. Structuralism, Linguistics, and the Study of Literature* (Ithaca: Cornell University Press, 1975), 139.

12. Ibid. Culler quotes and translates Julia Kristeva's definition of *intertextualité* from her *Semiotiké: Recherches pour une sémanalyse* (Paris: Seuil, 1969), 146.

13. In Jacques Derrida's writing, the roles of critic and writer feed off one another in a combination that Ihab Hassan terms "the critic as innovator." *The Postmodern Turn*, 118–146.

14. Brian McHale distinguishes two dominant postmodernist "intertextual zones." One results from exaggeration, the other from parodic indeterminacy of the usage of *retour de personnages*. *Postmodern Fiction*, 57–58.

15. My discussion of Derrida's *The Postcard. From Socrates to Freud and Beyond* already participates in Derrida's intertextuality because I read and quote Derrida's French text in its English translation, which is, however, also not my native language. Derrida himself articulates this predicament of border-writing: "One never writes either in one's own language or in a foreign language." "Living On. Borderlines," *Deconstruction and Criticism*, 101.

16. Derrida, "Living On. Borderlines," 81–82 and 84.

17. Jacques Derrida, "The Law of Genre," trans. Avital Ronell, *Glyph* 7 (1980): 206.

18. Paul Hernadi, *Beyond Genre: New Directions in Literary Classifications* (Ithaca: Cornell University Press, 1972), 207 and 212.

19. Linda S. Kauffman, *Special Delivery*, 87: "Derrida's thesis: authority is a writing effect: the post, police, literature, philosophy, and psychoanalysis work in tandem to buttress that authority."

20. Thomas Nolden, "'An einen jungen Dichter'," 41.

21. Shari Benstock, "From Letters to Literature."

22. In Germany, the postcard was introduced by Heinrich von Stephan in 1870. Nickisch, *Brief*, 218. Sigmund Freud's and Josef Breuer's "Studien über Hysterie" were first published in 1895 and are generally referred to as the first psychoanalytic work. *Studien über Hysterie* (1895; Frankfurt: Fischer, 1970).

23. Wolfgang Welsch pursues these questions in *Unsere postmoderne Moderne*, 9–12.

24. Sigmund Freud uses his own observations of his grandson's versions of the "peek-a-boo game" (with himself and with a spool) to illustrate his thesis, that the "repetition compulsion" is the manifestation of a "Beyond the Pleasure Principle." Sigmund Freud, "Jenseits des Lustprinzips," *Psychologie des Unbewußten*, ed. Alexander Mitscherlich et al., Studienausgabe, vol. 3 (Frankfurt a. M.: Fischer, 1975), 224–227.

25. Welsch, *Unsere postmoderne Moderne*, 10. "gleichlautende Schlußfolgerungen."

26. Ibid. "wenn man alle Hoffnung auf ein Begreifen dieses Phänomens fahren lassen und der vor einiger Zeit ausgesprochenen Empfehlung folgen möchte, es fortan wieder schlicht mit den althergebrachten Wortzusammensetzungen wie *Post-amt, Post-bote* und *Post-scheck* genug sein zu lassen und sich um die *Post-moderne* nicht weiter zu kümmern" (my italics).

27. Ibid., 11. "Das erinnert an einen einschlägigen Kalauer, der bei einer Architektur-Tagung geäußert wurde. Man hatte gerade festgestellt, daß zahlreiche Bauten der Postmoderne sich auf einen Paradebau der Frühmoderne, auf den großen Kassensaal von Otto Wagners Wiener Postsparkassenamt von 1906 zurückbeziehen. Damit, so meinte dann einer der Teilnehmer launig, habe man ja nun endlich eine bündige Worterklärung von "Postmoderne" gefunden: "Post-Moderne," das sei offensichtlich die Moderne dieser Post und die von ihr sich herleitende Tradition."

28. Sigmund Freud, "Der Witz und seine Beziehung zum Unbewußten," *Psychologische Schriften*, ed. Alexander Mitscherlich et al., Studienausgabe, vol. 4 (Frankfurt a. M.: Fischer, 1970), 157. "daß man bei der Witzbildung einen Gedankengang für einen Moment fallen läßt, der dann plötzlich als Witz aus dem Unbewußten auftaucht."

29. Ibid., 167. "er hat einem anderen nichts mitzuteilen . . . er kann nur in der Vermummung bestehen." "Er benötigt oftmals dreier Personen und verlangt seine Vollendung durch die Teilnahme eines anderen an dem von ihm angeregten seelischen Vorgange."

30. Ibid., 158. "Das Infantile ist nämlich die Quelle des Unbewußten, die unbewußten Denkvorgänge sind keine anderen, als welche im frühen Kindesalter einzig und allein hergestellt werden. Der Gedanke, der zum Zwecke der Witzbildung ins Unbewußte eintaucht, sucht dort nur die alte Heimstätte des einstigen Spieles mit Worten auf."

31. An Akrostichon was originally a poem in which the beginning letters, syllables, or words of the individual verses or stanzas formed a word, name, or sentence when concatenated. Even in antiquity, this superimposed text was often used as an allusion to the sender or recipient of the poem. It denoted ori-

gin and destination, a claim to property as in the Greek oracles, where an Akrostichon sought to secure the oracle against interpolations. As a text within a text, the Akrostichon does what it attempts to prevent: it introduces an alien text and ambiguity into its design. See Gero von Wilpert, *Sachwörterbuch der Literatur* (Stuttgart: Kröner, 1964), 5. See also Ursula Arlart's interpretation of the Akrostichon as a spiral in Barth's novel, *"Exhaustion" und "Replenishment," die Fiktion in der Fiktion bei John Barth* (Heidelberg: Winter, 1984), 109–110.

32. He already experimented with this precarious balance in his anti-story "Life-Story." John Barth, *Lost in the Funhouse. Foreword and Seven Additional Author's Notes* (1968; New York: Doubleday, 1988), 116–129. From now on, all quotes from the stories in this edition will appear in parentheses in the text, marked by the letter "F."

33. E. P. Walkiewicz, *John Barth* (Boston: Twayne, 1986), 131.

34. Ursula Arlart, *"Exhaustion" und "Replenishment,"* 111 and 103. Arlart sees *LETTERS* as an achievement that surpasses "the entropic endangerment of self-referentiality" ("die entropische Gefährdung der Selbstreferentialität"), striving for a synthesis of realism and modernism, of fact and fiction.

35. Kim McMullen underscores the affinity of Barth's *LETTERS* to Michel Foucault's idea of archive: "Although Barth seems to recognize, with Foucault, the impossibility of ever finally 'describ[ing]' our own archives, since it is from within these rules that we speak, since it is that which gives to us what we can say' (*Archeology* 131), Barth nonetheless insists that we recognize the very existence of such an archive, and he urges us to begin an analysis which he recognizes can never be complete." "The Fiction of Correspondence: Letters and History," *Modern Fiction Studies* 36, no. 3 (Fall 1990): 419.

36. Ambrose insists that this self-addressed water-message also lay the foundation for his own and John Barth's "Lost in the Funhouse," both for the individual story as well as for the collection *Lost in the Funhouse*.

37. This is further elaborated throughout the novel by A. B. Cook VI's historical and hysterical accounts of genealogical failures, among them the attempted rescue of Napoleon from St. Helena which turns into the rescue of the impostor instead (L 582–636). This section of *LETTERS* corresponds to Jean Baudrillard's cancer-symbolism in *Les stratégies fatales* in 1983. Wolfgang Welsch interprets Baudrillard's notion of "Hypertelie" as follows: "From a specific point onward, systems no longer work on their contradictions, but rather go over to the ecstasy of self-reflexivity. This border has been breached today, the ecstatic condition has been reached. Uncontrolled growth makes up the basic process of the social body. . . . Cancer-uncontrolled growth-and the clone-the reproduction of the same-have symbolic truth for the whole" ("Von einem bestimmten Punkt an arbeiten Systeme nicht mehr an ihren Widersprüchen, sondern gehen in die Ekstase der Selbstbespiegelung über. Diese Grenze ist heute überschritten, der ekstatische Zustand ist erreicht. Wucherung macht den Grundvorgang des Sozialkörpers aus. . . . Der Krebs-die maßlose Wucherung-und das Klon-die Reproduktion des Gleichen-haben symbolische Wahrheit für das Ganze"). *Unsere postmoderne Moderne*, 151.

38. Ursula Arlart's interpretations of Ambrose Mensch's pledge to let go of his avant-guarde alter ego, and his oath to shun his "obsession for reenactment,"

as well as Todd Andrew's "Selbstsetzung" ("self-definition") and Jacob Horner's "Identitätsfindung" ("identity-search") at the end of *LETTERS* are typical examples of this hermeneutic reenactment. *"Exhaustion" und "Replenishment,"* 73 and 75.

39. Kim McMullen comments on the two-facedness of Germaine's and *LETTERS'* opening letter: "The letter is perfunctory, official, altogether unremarkable—thousands like it must pass ritualistically through the U.S. mails each year in the months preceding the spring rite of commencement. But Germaine is only acting provost, suggesting that she can remove herself at will from the discursive field in which she has just engaged. . . . Instead she becomes its saboteur, deconstructing in her handwritten postscript what she has just articulated in the official typescript." "The Fiction of Correspondence," 411.

40. Jacques Derrida, *Signéponge/Signsponge*, trans. Richard Rand (New York: Columbia University Press, 1984). The sponge in this essay erases but retains what has leaked, what has been written.

41. Throughout my reading, I will refer to the external John Barth as "author" and to the internal author in *LETTERS* as "Author," thereby giving it the appearance of a proper name. Because all the other characters are authors of their letters and some aspire to be authors of fiction as well, the proper name should indicate both the aspect of a character and of an author.

42. George Steiner, "Dead Letters," *New Yorker*, December 31, 1979, 62.

43. Jean-François Lyotard points out the inconsequence of any argument basing its criticism of postmodernism on "loss of meaning": "Lamenting the 'loss of meaning' in postmodernity boils down to mourning the fact that knowledge is no longer principally narrative." *The Postmodern Condition*, 26.

44. Homer O. Brown, "The Errant Letter," 581: "[T]he information of the letter is usually incomplete. . . . The letter is always in medias res and in medias personae."

45. Beverley Gray Bienstock, "Lingering on the Autognostic Verge: John Barth's *Lost in the Funhouse*," *Modern Fiction Studies* 19 (1973): 107–108. Jan Gorak concludes from this that "the world has become a region of manufactured emptiness." *God the Artist. American Novelists in a Post-Realist Age* (Chicago: University of Illinois Press, 1987), 163. Charles Harris deals extensively with the echo myth and its appropriation by Barth: "In her various authorial stages, Echo's history parallels the history of narrative literature" including the modernist goal of "[t] otal absence of authorial presence." The play with origins is seen in Heidegger's sense of "the Being of being," the blank as plenum, guaranteeing a continuous conversation. *Passionate Virtuosity. The Fiction of John Barth* (Chicago: University of Illinois Press, 1983), 112–113 and 118–119.

46. Charles B. Harris relates the naming of Ambrose to St. Ambrose, who was seen reading silently by St. Augustine, which "represented a significant stage in the transition from oral to print-oriented literary cultures." The parentage of autobiography therefore has its roots in the division of public and private, reading and writing aloud and silently. This perception finds its echo in Barth's subtitle for the series: "Fiction for print, tape, and live voice" as well as in the allusions to broadcasting and recording in "Autobiography" itself. *Passionate Virtuosity*, 109.

47. Another possible interpretation of the "absent father" and the "limping woman" pair, here in Montesquieu's introduction to his *Lettres Persanes*, is given by Heckendorn Cook, *Epistolary Bodies*, 30–70.

48. James Olney, *Metaphors of Self. The Meaning of Autobiography* (Princeton: Princeton University Press, 1972), 47.

49. Steven Lisberger, dir., *Tron*, Los Angeles, 1982.

50. Barth, "The Literature of Exhaustion," 33.

51. Barth starts the story line of the *Lost in the Funhouse* series appropriately with a do-it-yourself Moebius strip, itself being the first and shortest as well as potentially endless short story (F 1–2): "Once upon a time there was a story that began. . . ." It is also called "Frame-Story," which "may be skipped by the reader." While reading this advice, the reader is already in the midst of reading a frame-story, which is a frame to a frame to a frame, "one-, two-, or three-dimensional, whichever one regards a Moebius strip as beginning" (F xiii).

52. Ian Watt similarly discusses Lawrence Sterne's *Tristram Shandy* (1760–67) as a "parody of a novel" because "Sterne turns his irony against many of the narrative methods which the new genre had so lately developed." Like *LETTERS*, Tristram Shandy also plays with different temporal and narrative levels: personal associations mingle with a family's chronic and historic events. *The Rise of the Novel. Studies in Defoe, Richardson and Fielding* (London: Pelican, 1957), 331–332. The literary motif of the "message-in-a-bottle" goes back to Edgar Allan Poe's "Ms. Found in a Bottle" (1833), in which a shipwrecked sailor climbs aboard a ghost-ship on its way to the end of the world. He writes a journal on purloined paper and sends it off before being sucked into the vortex. The letter transgresses his personal fate. Klaus-Dieter Metz mentions another predecessor to the floating letter motif dating back to fifteenth century "Hydromantie": "The throwing of objects into water for the purpose of telling the future is proven since antiquity. Most of all, again and again, it is always mentioned that handwritten pieces of paper were thrown into the water—in order to preserve the writing, these were covered with glue or wax—in order to gather clarity and assurance about one's own and others' activities from their behavior. For the fifteenth century the wording '[to let] little letters swim' has been expressively documented" ("Das Hineinwerfen von Gegenständen in das Wasser zur Deutung der Zukunft wird seit der Antike bezeugt. Vor allem ist auch immer wieder die Rede davon, daß man beschriebene Zettel—zur Erhaltung der Schrift wurden diese mit Leim oder Wachs überzogen—ins Wasser warf, um sich aus ihrem Verhalten Klarheit und Gewißheit über eigenes und fremdes Tun zu verschaffen. Für das fünfzehnte Jahrhundert ist dafür die Bezeichnung 'Brieflein schwemmen' ausdrücklich belegt"). *Korrespondenzen. Der Brief in Gottfried Kellers Dichtung* (Frankfurt a.M.: Peter Lang, 1984), 67.

53. Christopher D. Morris points to the analogous displacement of Ambrose's initiation into sexuality and/or meaning in "Water-Message" and then again in "Lost in the Funhouse," where the "shluppish whisper" of the waves against the boards "promises but withholds meaning or content." "Barth and Lacan: The World of the Moebius Strip," 74.

54. For a more detailed analysis of the function of excrements, see Eugene Kokowski, "The Excremental Vision of Barth's Todd Andrews," *Critique* 18,

no. 2 (1976): 51–58. Todd's realization of the Mack/Mack dispute settlement itself floats on Polly('s) Lake. Pieces of excrement float on water just like the "message in a bottle." This segment of the text is a parallel to "George III," that is, Mack's bottled inheritance, his canned excrements.

55. When Jacques Lacan concludes in his "Seminar on 'The Purloined Letter,'" "that a letter always arrives at its destination," he uses the present tense. *The Purloined Poe,* 53. In order to distinguish my reading from his, I want to point out that I am using the past tense with a purpose here. The security of origin and destination, still prevalent in Lacan's terminology, is undermined by the mailing system in *LETTERS.* As the story of Ambrose shows, the subject is formed upon receipt, not earlier, and even then encounters himself as other through the letter. Barth stands closer to Derrida here than to Lacan.

56. On the function of letters as "principal actors," see Homer O. Brown, "The Errant Letter," 584.

57. Josephine Hendin, George Steiner, and Peter Prescott all find fault with Barth's recycling of his characters from previous novels and fiction "on the search for some fresh emotion," and filled with "blatant mechanics of self-reference," while he "long ago gave us all that Todd and Jacob can offer." Respectively: Josephine Hendin, "*LETTERS:* A Novel by John Barth," *New Republic* 181, December 1, 1979, 32 and 34. George Steiner, "Dead Letters," *New Yorker,* December 31, 1979, 60. Peter Prescott, "An Excess of Epistles," *Newsweek,* October 1, 1979, 32.

58. The Author J. B. officially begins *LETTERS* on page 42. He occupies the last or first day of the week (Sunday), depending on which calendar pattern one follows. Within the scheme of the novel, he writes in last position, retaining the power of closure for himself. He ends *LETTERS* by reframing its ending date and historic setting in quotation marks and parentheses (L 771–772), demonstrating that "every letter has two times, that of its writing and that of its reading" (L 44). Even those two times have been twice doubled by the fact that the editing process interferes with the official "sign-off" of epistolary fiction.

59. Edgar Allan Poe also had an eerie affinity to Baltimore, Maryland, Barth's hometown. Poe's wife Virginia grew up there and Poe himself was found nearly dead on a Baltimore street on October 3, 1849. He died in Baltimore on October 7 that year.

60. See Avital Ronell's *Telephone Book,* 257, in which she describes Bell's and Watson's invention of the telephone itself as their homoerotic desire to play the *fort/da* game, to switch positions in order "to get it ready to talk," to "want to hear it talk."

61. Barbara Johnson sees a connection between the "purloined letter" and the structure of its readers' essays: "Lacan's text not only presents itself backward (its introduction following its conclusion), but it never finishes presenting itself. . . . And Derrida's text not only is preceded by several years of annunciatory marginalia and footnotes but is itself structured by its own deferment, its différance. . . . In addition, an unusually high degree of apparent digressiveness characterizes these texts, to the point of making the reader wonder whether there is really any true subject matter there at all. It is as though any attempt to follow the path of the purloined letter is automatically purloined from itself.

Which is . . . just what the letter has always already been saying." "The Frame of Reference: Poe, Lacan, Derrida," *The Purloined Poe*, 214.

62. The Author predestines the letter design to arrive on page 770 in his official beginning of *LETTERS* on page 49.

63. The king and the police are blind to the openly displayed letter; the queen in the first and the minister in the second scene know of the letter's visibility; the minister in the first scene and the detective in the second scene share the ability to see that someone is blind to the letter and that another is blind to the blindness. Lacan, "Seminar on 'The Purloined Letter,'" 28–54.

64. Shoshana Felman, "On Reading Poetry: Reflections on the Limits and Possibilities of Psychoanalytic Approaches," *The Purloined Poe*, 149.

65. Ibid., 148.

66. Derrida, "The Purveyor of Truth," *The Purloined Poe*, 173–212.

67. Ibid., 195–196.

68. Homer O. Brown, "The Errant Letter," 588–589.

69. See footnote 31 of this chapter for a definition of an Akrostichon.

70. As Jan Gorak points out, the Author "must consistently try to block the headlong rush of his characters to conclusion." Lady Amherst "nearly stops the narrative before it begins." *God the Artist*, 177.

71. Peggy Kamuf, *Signature Pieces*, 66.

72. Peggy Kamuf explicates the relation among contract, property, and signature in the case of Jean-Jacques Rousseau's *Du contrat social*. She comes to the conclusion that "*Du contrat social* is the result of a contract whose terms reverse those of the social contract to be defined and described within. This reversal is the fold of a textuality that can never incorporate the surplus of its performance in what it can say about itself. A remainder will remain, even or rather especially when it is stated that nothing remains." Ibid., 48. See also Heckendorn Cook, "Going Public: The Letter and the Contract in Fanni Butlerd," *Epistolary Bodies*, 114–139.

73. Germaine's life parallels the development of the letter as a literary form, which arguably reached its high point in Romanticism.

74. Germaine's affairs take on the cunning intensity of Madame de Merteuil's epistolary intrigues in Choderlos de Laclos' *Les Liaisons Dangereuses* (1782).

75. The name "Germaine" has multiple connotations. Its French sound recalls Germaine de Staël, whose epistolary works Lady Amherst studies and whose life she somewhat reenacts in her various love affairs with famous literary men. She also has a son by André Casteene-Bellingham, who is more an allegory of the eternal impostor than a character, so that the child's parentage remains obscure. Germaine, like "pit," further connotes "germ," both as kernel of life and as bacteria and phonetically resonates with the name Jerome, who is himself a cybernetic insect, a "germinator" of the computerized version of *LETTERS* called NUMBERS (L 757) (I owe the last two analogies to Liliane Weissberg). In addition, the chain-name of Germaine Gordon Pitt Amherst is reminiscent of Poe's character Arthur Gordon Pym and Arthur Morton King, the amateur pen name for Ambrose. Poe himself was John Allan's adopted son, so that like Pitt or Gordon, his middle name is actually a surname.

76. John Barth, *The End of the Road* (New York: Bantam, 1968).

77. Arlart, *"Exhaustion" und "Replenishment,"* 109–110. "Um diesen Titelsatz jeweils weiterführen zu können, muß man von "Buch" 7 sozusagen zu "Buch" 1 zurückkehren und dort mit der nächstfolgenden Korrespondenzgruppe fortfahren. Auf diese Weise verbinden sich eine rekurrente und lineare Bewegung miteinander, um eine Spirale zu bilden. . . . Die äußerste, siebente Windung dieser Spirale ist (wie in *Chimera*) vom Autor besetzt, der die Fiktion LETTERS geschaffen hat. In den darunterliegenden 'vergangenen' Windungen sind Barths frühere Fiktionen enthalten und bilden die Grundlage für das neu entstandene Werk."

78. Walkiewicz, *John Barth*, 139.

79. Ibid., 136, and Tom LeClair, *The Art of Excess. Mastery in Contemporary American Fiction* (Chicago: University of Illinois Press, 1989), 202.

80. Friedrich Kittler analyzes the interrelation of the female gender with the technologies of writing *Aufschreibesysteme 1800/1900* in the chapter "Damenopfer," 356, 359 and 376.

81. From Blackstone's *Commentaries on the Laws of England* (1756) as quoted by Heckendorn Cook, *Epistolary Bodies*, 125.

82. Friedrich Kittler, *Aufschreibesysteme*, 365.

83. In this context, see Richard Stamelman in "The Dialogue of Absence," *Studies in 20th Century Literature* 12, no. 1 (1987): 93–113.

84. Paul de Man, "Aesthetic Formalization: Kleist's 'Über das Marionettentheater,'" *Rhetoric of Romanticism* (New York: Columbia University Press, 1984), 263–290.

85. In a double analogy, Joseph Conrad's "The Tale" about the academic turned hermit who builds a bomb to blow up the "false god of science and technology," which was first printed privately and circulated among friends, very likely played a role in Todd Andrews' (i.e., John Barth's) case, but has more recently found its ultimate reader in the Montana-based Una-bomber, who over more than a decade killed several people involved in their version of the "Tower of Truth" via postal deliveries. *Philadelphia Inquirer*, July 8, 1996.

86. J. Hillis Miller alludes to Jacques Derrida's essay "Télépathie," in which Derrida describes the determination of the subject in the telepathic moment of the receipt of a letter "which after the fact seems to have been projected toward some unknown recipient at the moment it was written, predestined receiver unknown to him or to herself" leading him to the conclusion that "one cannot say of the recipient that he exists before the letter." J. Hillis Miller, "Hardy, Derrida, and the 'Dislocation of Souls'," *Taking Chances: Derrida, Psychoanalysis and Literature*, ed. Joseph H. Smith and William Kerrigan (Baltimore: Johns Hopkins University Press, 1984), 135–145.

87. Brown, "The Errant Letter," 591.

88. Avital Ronell includes a postcard of a cemetery with "Jesus called" chiseled into the gravestone of a man in her *Telephone Book*. She addresses it in the form of a handwritten autograph-advertisement to the reader. With this gesture, she inverts Derrida's *Postcard* and his inclusion of telephone calls, especially the call from "Martini Heidegger." However, Ronell cannot include an example of her own research material as Derrida can. She has to resort to a postcard to illustrate the "call from beyond."

89. In close affinity to the design of *LETTERS*, the title of *The Postcard* is spaced out in capital letters, disconnected and connected by little squares, so that the whole title appears en bloc.

90. Edgar Allan Poe, "The Purloined Letter," *The Purloined Poe*, 20.

91. Lacan, "Seminar on 'The Purloined Letter'," 38–39.

92. Rodolphe Gasché elaborates this point: "If, in the last resort, the unthematizable because undecidable agencies of modern literary texts—agencies that are not of the order of image or concept, content or form, but that are textual structures—radically subvert the possibility of literary hermeneutics, it is because they represent the limits from which understanding and knowledge become possible. Therefore, understanding its gesture of unifying deciphering must be pushed to exasperation in order to account as rigorously as possible for its structural limits." *The Tain of the Mirror. Derrida and the Philosophy of Reflection* (Cambridge, Mass.: Harvard University Press, 1986), 267.

93. "Spacing, which blends in part, and each time differently, with archetrace, differance, and other undecidables, is in every instance the discrete synthesis of (1) the movement by which the self-identity of an entity is interrupted and (2) the passive constitution by inscription as habitation. The very nature of spacing does not permit its own synthetic structure to be one of reconciling the two aspects it reunites." Ibid., 200.

94. Shoshana Felman, *La Folie et la Chose Littéraire*, 187–190. See also Paul de Man, *Blindness and Insight* (Minneapolis: University of Minnesota Press, 1983).

95. Gasché, *The Tain of the Mirror*, 201–202.

96. D. Emily Hicks analyzes the term "border writing" and puts it into a multiethnic and international perspective in her essay "Deterritorialization and Border Writing," *Ethics/Aesthetics: Post-Modern Positions*, ed. Robert Merrill (Washington, D.C.: Maisonneuve, 1988), 47–58.

97. See Ingeborg Dusar, *Choreographien der Differenz. Ingeborg Bachmanns Prosaband Simultan* (Köln: Böhlau, 1994), 100.

98. Jonathan Scott Lee bases Lacan's structuralist interpretation of the letter as a "pure signifier" in Poe's story on the material support of the letter: "the signifier as a material object is itself implicated in the signifier's symbolic truth—it is the signifier's materiality that allows it to transform the human world performatively—and this suggests that the signifier is unlike any other object, inasmuch as it is simultaneously real and symbolic." *Jacques Lacan* (Boston: Twayne, 1990), 106.

99. A response along the lines of Brégou's forecast for private mail is given by Michael Phillipson's *In Modernity's Wake. The Ameurunculus Letters* (London: Routledge, 1989).

100. In this context, I would like to point to Derrida's lectures at The Johns Hopkins University in 1987–88, one of which was on "Friends" and began "My friends. I have no friends," which caused a stir among the dedicated Derrideans in the audience for what was perceived as (a) an affront to them and (b) as an "essentialist" message about relationships. In retrospect, it is almost as if Derrida, by anticipation, alienated them, his most dedicated "friends."

101. Franz Kafka, *Briefe an Milena*, 62. "Ich kann dir nicht mehr wie einer Fremden schreiben."

102. This diversion is created by "a loud report" from a pistol and "fearful screams" underneath the minister's window. Poe, "The Purloined Letter," 22.

103. Ibid., 14.

104. Shari Benstock interprets this as "Envois'" "double writing, both articulating the theory of the law of genre and serving as an example of the effects of that law. . . . The subject these letters address (desire for the absent beloved) and the form such expressions take (postcard messages enclosed in envelopes) suggest a 'correspondence' between literary theory and practice, a commentary on literary forms as well as an address to literary subjects." "From Letters to Literature," 258.

105. Derrida, "Otobiographies: The Teaching of Nietzsche and the Politics of the Proper Name," *The Ear of the Other*, 3–4.

106. Peggy Kamuf, *Signature Pieces*, 67: "The point is that the author, like the publisher, is not author of everything published under his name, which must efface itself in order to permit the text's deployment . . . if the work is a 'property,' then it returns to its owner, that is, the publisher; and if it cannot return to its owner, it is because it returns properly to no one."

107. Joseph H. Smith and William Kerrigan, eds., "Introduction," *Taking Chances: Derrida, Psychoanalysis, and Literature*. Smith and Kerrigan note a kinship between Freud and Derrida in that they both "release undecidability while retaining self-regulation" (xi).

108. In *Fictions of Feminine Desire*, Peggy Kamuf introduces her interpretation of the disclosures of Heloise by following the numerous exhumations and transfers of Heloise's and Abelard's bodily remains after their respective deaths in 1162 and 1142. She relates the history of the continuous transfers to the "excess of woman's passion, which is both ours and someone else's" (xi) because all that remains of it "is the process of translation" itself (xiii). "The name 'Heloise'—in the epitaph on a grave, in the address of a letter—designates with certainty only this scattering and recuperation, uncovering and reburial of a remains. . . . 'Heloise,' thus, names both our desire to retrieve what is lost in translation, to construct a more complete monument to the remains, and the inevitable persistence, all the same, of that construction's excess" (xiii–xiv).

109. Avital Ronell compares her function as critic and reader of technologies to that of a switchboard. However, she does not hesitate to listen in on conversations or disconnect calls. "A User's Manual," *The Telephone Book*.

110. Lyotard, *The Postmodern Condition*, 53–60, and Katherine N. Hayles, *Chaos Bound*, 14.

111. See Alan Bass's translator's note 8 in "To Speculate—On 'Freud,'" 302.

112. A trend in contemporary colloquial German ignores this difference and uses both words synonymously. That the two meanings merge into one and the same, retaining their two different shapes, marks the postindustrial familiarity with the phenomenon of reproduction, similarity, and simulation.

113. Gasché, *The Tain of the Mirror*, 226.

114. Jacques Derrida, *Dissemination*, trans. Barbara Johnson (Chicago: University of Chicago Press, 1981), 168.

115. Friedrich Nietzsche's statement from his "Fröhliche Wissenschaften" essay as quoted by Ingeborg Dusar, *Choreographiem der Differenz*, 54–56.

116. Umberto Eco defines a "communication process as the passage of a signal (not necessarily a sign) from a source (through a transmitter, along a channel) to a destination." He adds that "every act of communication to or between human beings—or any other intelligent biological or mechanical apparatus—presupposes a signification system as its necessary condition." *A Theory of Semiotics*, 8–9, his italics.

117. Philippe Lacoue-Labarthe and Jean-Luc Nancy, "Genre," trans. Lawrence R. Schehr, *Glyph* 7 (1980): 1 and 5. "Romanticism, as such, dates literature as its constant auto-implication, and as the ever-repeated asking of its own question." With regard to Romantic *Geselligkeit*, the dialogue and the conversation deserve special status in the definition of "the" Romantic genre. Nancy and Lacoue-Labarthe argue that the figure of Socrates becomes the "prototype of the Subject" and thus the "subject-'genre'" of literature, namely philosophy: "Consequently, this [philosophy] is a 'genre' beyond all genres, including a theory of this very 'beyond': in other words, it is a general theory of genres, and of itself as well."

118. Ibid., 9.

119. According to Honnefelder, as long as the letter is used as one of many literary devices included within the frame of a novel, it is able to convey and exercise its "real" abilities and functions. This changes, however, when the letter becomes the dominant feature and turns into a novel, or makes up a novel, as in the case of epistolary novels: "Either the epistolary novel stops being a novel or it destroys the form of its predominant narrative medium" ("Entweder hört der Briefroman auf, Roman zu sein, oder er zerstört die Form seines beherrschenden Erzählmittels"). *Der Brief im Roman*, 112.

120. Philippe Lacoue-Labarthe and Jean-Luc Nancy, "Genre," 9.

121. In analyzing Eduard's letters to Ottilie in Goethe's *Wahlverwandschaften*, Honnefelder shows that a letter writer cannot control the mailing process and reaction, he or she is subjected to the letter's "new laws of its reality" ("neuen Gesetze seiner Wirklichkeit"). *Der Brief im Roman*, 120–121.

122. Peter Weibel, "Vom Verschwinden der Ferne," 49.

123. Ann Tyler's *The Accidental Tourist* focuses on a travel guide author who specializes in providing the experience of nonexperience for people who have to travel but don't want to be exposed to anything "new" or "different" while being away from home.

124. Freud, "Jenseits des Lustprinzips," 219.

125. Derrida analyzes Freud's autobiographical legacy, the death of his grandson and his daughter, as the precedent for "Jenseits des Lustprinzips" in "To Speculate—On Freud," 292–337.

126. Freud, "Jenseits des Lustprinzips," 272. "Man muß geduldig sein und auf weitere Mittel und Anlässe zur Forschung warten. Auch bereit bleiben, einen Weg wieder zu verlassen, den man eine Weile verfolgt hat, wenn er zu nichts Gutem zu führen scheint."

127. Ibid., 271. "Das Lustprinzip scheint geradezu im Dienste der Todes-
triebe zu stehen." The phrase "im Dienste" may be translated as "in the service
of" but my choice ("to observe") indicates both the adherence to a law or custom and a scientific observation.

128. An Attic tragedy consisted of two to three actors and the choir. Here,
Freud, Sophie and Ernst, and the readers construct the scene according to their
interpretations or game rules.

129. "Das Unheimliche" was produced in the spring of 1919 alongside
"Jenseits des Lustprinzips," which Freud withheld for another year to revise it.
The latter was finally published in December 1920. "Das Unheimliche"
appeared in the fall of 1919. See Alexander Mitscherlich, Angela Richards, and
James Strachey, eds., "Editorische Vorbemerkungen zu 'Jenseits des Lust-
prinzips,'" Psychologie des Unbewußten, 215.

130. Derrida builds his argument in "Freud's Legacy" on Freud's personal
losses and his singular goal of "producing the institutions of his desire, of graft-
ing his own genealogy onto it, of making the tribunal and the juridical tradition
his inheritance, his delegation as a 'movement,' his legacy, his own [one's clos-
est relations]," 299. See also Temma F. Berg, "La Carte Postale: Reading (Derrida) Reading," 327.

131. Sigmund Freud, "Das Unheimliche," Psychologische Schriften, 244.
"Ja, der Autor dieser neuen Untersuchungen muß sich einer besonderen
Stumpfheit in dieser Sache anklagen, wo große Feinfühligkeit eher am Platz
wäre. Er hat schon lange nichts erlebt oder kennengelernt, was ihm den Eindruck des Unheimlichen gemacht hätte, muß sich erst in das Gefühl hineinver-
setzen, die Möglichkeit desselben in sich wachrufen."

132. Freud, "Jenseits des Lustprinzips," 267. "Man kann sich doch einem
Gedankengang hingeben, ihn verfolgen, soweit er führt, nur aus wis-
senschaftlicher Neugierde, oder, wenn man will, als advocatus diaboli, der sich
darum doch nicht dem Teufel selbst verschreibt."

133. A modern example of this perfect mailing system are James Bond
movies, where new equipment is introduced at the beginning of a case and put
to its appropriate use during the adventure.

134. Sigmund Freud, "Die Verneinung (1925)," Psychologie des Unbewußten, 373–377.

135. Jacques Derrida, Speech and Phenomena, trans. David B. Allison
(Evanston: Northwestern University Press, 1973), 150.

136. Gayatri Chakravorty Spivak, "Translator's Preface," Of Grammatology, xliii.

137. Jacques Derrida, The Postcard, 105. The particular ability of the letter is to be part of all genres of literature as well as to be left and found in any
environment of the "real" world.

138. Avital Ronell refers to the usage of the telephone in cases of
schizophrenia and to the passage from Freud's "Psycho-analytic Method of
Treatment" in her yellow pages. The Telephone Book, 423.

139. Freud, "Jenseits des Lustprinzips," 271. "Wir kommen so zu dem im
Grunde nicht einfachen Ergebnis, daß das Luststreben zu Anfang des seelischen
Lebens sich weit intensiver äußert als späterhin, aber nicht so uneingeschränkt;

es muß sich häufige Durchbrüche gefallen lassen. In reiferen Zeiten ist die Herrschaft des Lustprinzips sehr viel mehr gesichert, aber dieses selbst ist der Bändigung sowenig entgangen wie die anderen Triebe überhaupt. . . . Jedenfalls muß das, was am Erregungsvorgang die Empfindungen von Lust und Unlust entstehen läßt, beim Sekundärvorgang ebenso vorhanden sein wie beim Primärvorgang. Hier wäre die Stelle, mit weiteren Studien einzusetzen. Unser Bewußtsein vermittelt uns von innen her nicht nur die Empfindungen von Lust und Unlust, sondern auch von einer eigentümlichen Spannung, die selbst wieder eine lustvolle oder unlustvolle sein kann." "Reize von außen . . . aber ganz besonders über die Reizsteigerungen von innen her, die eine Erschwerung der Lebensaufgabe erzielen."

140. Ibid., 239. "Von dieser Stelle der Peripherie strömen dann dem seelischen Zentralapparat kontinuierliche Erregungen zu, wie sie sonst nur aus dem Inneren des Apparates kommen konnten."

141. In the fourth leg of his journey, Freud recalls the war neuroses and traumas, with which he introduced the second part, and adds that "mechanical vibration has to be recognized as one of the sources of sexual stimulation" ("mechanische Erschütterung als eine der Quellen der Sexualerregung anerkannt werden muß (vgl. die Bemerkungen über die Wirkungen des Schaukelns und Eisenbahnfahrens in *Drei Abhandlungen zur Sexualtheorie*, 1905 d)"). In a manner similar to the sexual drive that functions like a detouring device in "Beyond the Pleasure Principle," Freud delays the discussion of the sexual aspect of train rides for one chapter.

142. Temma F. Berg similarly argues that "If the movement of fort/da is the movement of psychoanalysis, then psychoanalysis is in trouble. Freud cannot make his followers follow. They will not form an orderly train behind him. They take up the ideas he has generously disseminated, distort them, and use them for their own ends. The movement threatens to disperse so widely, diffuse into so many conflicting factions, that it will soon be an impossible task to put all the pieces back together again." "*La Carte Postale*. Reading (Derrida) Reading," 327.

143. Freud, "Jenseits des Lustprinzips," 239. In the case of "internal stimuli that produce an all too intense increase of dissatisfaction" ("innere Erregungen, welche allzu große Unlustvermehrung herbeiführen"), Freud describes a tendency to invert inside and outside: "It will result in the tendency to treat these in such a way as if they had an effect not from inside but from outside, in order to be able to apply the defensive means of the stimuli-protection against them. This is the origin of projection" ("Es wird sich die Neigung ergeben, sie so zu behandeln, als ob sie nicht von innen, sondern von außen her einwirken, um die Abwehrmittel des Reizschutzes gegen sie in Anwendung bringen zu können. Dies ist die Herkunft der Projektion").

144. Derrida and his publishers inserted a folded reprint of the Oxford postcard "between the S/p card and the letter paper" (45), between the dust jacket and the text. The reader can unfold it to keep it at hand for the entire reading process, or keep it folded to take it out, whenever desired.

145. Jacques Derrida, "Otobiographies," 38.

146. John Barth, "Night-Sea Journey," *Lost in the Funhouse*, 12 and 9.

147. Sigrid Weigel has argued this point in her *Die Stimme der Medusa*, 212–213.

148. The word "hamlet" falls out of its direct context and reminds the reader of a deadly epistolary exchange which resulted in the adage "don't kill the messenger." Shakespeare's Hamlet sends Rosenkranz and Guildenstern to their deaths to avert his own execution.

149. John P. Muller and William J. Richardson, "Lacan's Seminar on 'The Purloined Letter': Overview," *The Purloined Poe*, 71.

150. Legally, as soon as the addressee receives the letter, it belongs to the addressee. The addressee, however, has to get the sender's permission before being allowed to publish the letter. Nickisch, *Brief*, 219.

151. Jacques Derrida, *Dissemination*, 331.

152. From epistolary history and the text we are reading now, the readers know that addressees rarely heed such destruction orders (Kafka's letters and works, for example, Freud's opus, Plato's letters).

153. In this way, Derrida mimics Freud's prolific epistolary correspondences, particularly with Wilhelm Fließ, in which Freud often came close to attempting that which he thought impossible, namely, autotherapy (his various dream-analyses for example).

154. Derrida, "Roundtable on Autobiography," *The Ear of the Other*, 52.

155. Sarah Kofman comes to a similar conclusion about *Glas:* "*Glas* is a ringing bell, an oscillating pendulum between texts. . . . Everything that can be said of the text can be said of sex: there is in *Glas* a sexualization of text and a textualization of sex. The question of sexuality as indecidable oscillation repeats textuality. . . . Each sex, like each text, binds the one to the other, becoming indecidable, speaking the language and in the tongue of the other, penetrating the other; neither feminine nor masculine, neither castrated nor non-castrated, not bisexual, but striking between the sexes, because sex is always already double; doubly sheathed and erect, it's a double bind." "'Ça Cloche'," *Derrida and Deconstruction*, ed. Hugh J. Silverman, trans. Caren Kaplan (New York/London: Routledge, 1989), 127–128.

156. Derrida, "Roundtable on Autobiography," 51.

157. "Thus the presence that is achieved in auto-affection is a supplement for a lack of self-presence, an absence that structurally haunts the self-affecting self." Rodolphe Gasché concludes that these residues result in an always already divided "auto." *The Tain of the Mirror*, 232–233.

158. Gasché quotes Derrida from *Margins of Philosophy* in *The Tain of the Mirror*, 233.

159. Barbara Harlow, review essay on back cover of Etel Adnan's *Of Cities and Women (Letters to Fawwaz)* (Sausolito, Calif.: Post-Apollo Press, 1993).

160. Georges van den Abbeele, *Travel as Metaphor* (Minneapolis: University of Minnesota Press, 1992), xiii–xiv.

161. Robert M. Seltzer, *Jewish People, Jewish Thought. The Jewish Experience in History* (New York: Macmillan, 1980), 398.

162. Caren Kaplan, *Questions of Travel. Postmodern Discourses of Displacement* (Durham: Duke University Press, 1996), 61.

163. Assia Djebar, *Women of Algiers in Their Apartment*, translated by Marjolijn de Jager (Charlottesville: University of Virginia Press, 1992), 135. She

comments on Delacroix's forbidden gaze at the women of Algiers: "There, during that visit of a few hours with women in seclusion, by what shock, or at least by what vague stirrings was the painter seized? This heart of the half-open harem, is it really the way he sees it? From this place through which he had passed, Delacroix brings back some objects: some slippers, a shawl, a shirt, a pair of trousers. Not just trivial tourist trophies but tangible proof of a unique, ephemeral experience. Traces of a dream. He feels the need to touch his dream, to prolong its life beyond the memory, to complete what is enclosed as sketches and drawings in his notebooks. It's the equivalent of a fetishist compulsion augmented by the certainty that this moment lived is irrevocable in its uniqueness and will never be repeated. Upon his return to Paris, the painter will work for two years on the image of a memory that teeters with a muted and unformulated uncertainty, although well-documented and supported by authentic objects. What he comes out with is a masterpiece that still stirs questions deep within us."

164. Rey Chow, "'It's you, and not me . . .': Domination and 'Othering'" in Theorizing the 'Third World'," *American Feminist Thought at Century's End*, ed. Linda Kauffman (Cambridge: Blackwell, 1993), 95–106.

165. Bruno Latour, *We have never been Modern*, 138.

166. Jean Baudrillard uses a similar phrase in *Cool Memories:* "One thing protects us from change: exile." Trans. Chris Turner (London: Verso, 1990), 83.

167. Abbeele, *Travel as Metaphor*, xiv.

168. Ibid., xix: "Be they real or imaginary, voyages seem as often undertaken to restrain movement as to engage in it, to resist change as to produce it, to keep from getting anywhere as to attain a destination."

169. Caren Kaplan alludes to Jamaica Kincaid's *A Small Place* in this instance, in which Kincaid manages to "denounce the universalization of tourism without staging authentic essentialisms between 'native' and 'visitor.'" *Questions of Travel*, 62.

170. See Roland Barthes, *A Lover's Discourse*.

171. Jean Baudrillard, *Cool Memories*, 120. Caren Kaplan explains why one has to resist this urge of metaphorizing a metaphor in *Questions of Travel*.

172. Sigmund Freud, "Fragment of an Analysis of a Case of Hysteria," 86.

173. Ibid., 91 and 94.

174. Jean Baudrillard, *Le Simulacre. Traverses* (Paris: Minuet, 1978).

175. This dream outlines another intertextual crossing for Ingeborg Bachmann's sidewalk scene in *Malina* in chapter 2.

176. Monique Wittig, "The Straight Mind," *The Straight Mind* (1980; Boston: Beacon, 1992).

177. Claire Kahane, *Passions of the Voice. Hysteria, Narrative, and the Figure of the Speaking Woman, 1850–1915* (Baltimore: Johns Hopkins University Press, 1995), 14–33.

178. Abbeele, *Travel as Metaphor*, xix.

179. Seltzer, *Jewish People, Jewish Thought*, 396.

180. Ibid.

181. Abbeele remarks that because a metaphor as such is a "divagation," which comes from "to transfer" or "transport," "Travel then becomes the

metaphor of metaphor while the structure of the metaphor becomes the metaphor for the travel of meaning," xxii.

182. Latour, *We have never been Modern*, 139–140.

CHAPTER 4. MASS-MAILING

1. For more details, see Christa Bürger, *Zur Dichotomisierung von hoher und niederer Literatur* (Frankfurt a.M.: Suhrkamp, 1982).

2. Dirk Göttsche, *Die Produktivität der Sprachkrise*, 2. "Aktualität und Lebendigkeit der Sprachskepsistradition auch noch für die Literatur der unmittelbaren (postmodernen) Gegenwart."

3. Leslie Fiedler, "Cross the Border—Close that Gap: Post-Modernism," 349.

4. See Walter Dieckmann, "Diskontinuität? Zur—unbefriedigenden sprachkritischen und sprachwissenschaftlichen Behandlung der Nachkriegssprache in Deutschland 1945—1949," *Nachkriegsliteratur in Westdeutschland: Autoren, Sprache, Traditionen*, ed. Jost Hermand, Helmut Peitsch, and Klaus R. Scherpe, vol. 2 (Berlin: Argument, 1983), 89–111.

5. For Elke Claus, eighteenth-century epistolary lovemaking was driven by the intention "to experience love as a medium of individual self-development" ("Liebe als Medium individueller Selbstentfaltung zu erfahren"). *Liebeskunst. Der Liebesbrief im 18. Jahrhundert* (Stuttgart: Metzler, 1993), 271.

6. Unlike Orwell's successfully integrated opposition-ploy by means of "The Book," the blurbs of *Erwins Badezimmer* remain a rather unconvincing structural attempt to suspend the utopian euphoria of the text itself. The novel, however, maintains other structural indeterminacies that let it speak for the opposition and for the regime.

7. Regina Nörtemann, "Brieftheoretische Konzepte im 18. Jahrhundert und ihre Genese," *Brieftheorie des 18. Jahrhunderts*, 211–224.

8. Not only is the name "Spiridion" phonetically close to the nominal adjective "Derridean," but like Derrida, Spiridion "understood himself only as a pure thinker and strictly declined to become the head of an oppositional group" ("verstand sich selbst nur als reiner Denker und lehnte es strikt ab, zum Haupt einer oppositionellen Gruppe zu werden"). *Erwins Badezimmer oder die Gefährlichkeit der Sprache* (Stuttgart: Edition Weitbrecht, 1984), 29. Spiridion's followers call themselves "Spiridionisten" despite Spiridion's protest, which is also similar to Derrida's resistance toward the proper names "deconstruction" and "deconstructionist." On the other hand, Noam Chomsky would also be a contender if one considers his lectures on the first ammendment and "total information" versus "total censure."

9. Hans Bemmann, "Interne Hausmitteilung," *Erwins Badezimmer oder die Gefährlichkeit der Sprache*, blurb. From now on, direct quotes from the novel will be cited in parentheses in my text. "Uns aber ist bekannt, daß Sprache eindeutig ist. Wer unser Wissen bezweifelt, ist verrückt oder ein Lügner. Wer Wörtern andere Bedeutung gibt, begeht ein Verbrechen an der Sprachgemeinschaft. Er soll schweigen-schweigen-schweigen. Wir wissen, was Wörter be-

zeichnen. Wir kennen alle Bedeutungen. Wer uns glaubt, lebt in Sicherheit. Er ist glücklich-glücklich-glücklich. Die Direktion Oberste Sprachüberwachungsbehörde."

10. Despite the English "clarity" or "unambiguity," *Eindeutigkeit* and *eindeutig* also share the monistic quality of a grand narrative: one substance-one word. The noun alludes to an interpretative act that synthesizes all possible meanings into one.

11. In Ray Bradbury's *Fahrenheit 451* (New York: Simon & Schuster, 1967), a woman's questions are also the cause for fireman Montag's insubordination. Montag speaks with a slight franco-germanic accent, which symbolizes his collaboration with the regime and his intellectual background. In the book-country, Montag chooses to become the living audiotape of Edgar Allan Poe's "Tales of Mystery and Ratiocination," which include "The Purloined Letter." "The Purloined Letter" pushes Montag's society's crusade against letters to the extreme. Literature literally ceases to exist. The letter loses its substance and becomes part of the individual and collective memory. The partisans purloin letters by turning into letters. Bemmann continues this epistolary exchange in his own work: To be banned to the "land beyond the stream" in *Erwins Badezimmer* means to "dissolve like a cube of sugar in a cup of hot coffee." By ratiocination and imagination, if not by visual observation, one can determine that the sugar does not disappear, but that it becomes part of the coffee. Reality is contained in fiction and fiction in reality, one merges with and "sweetens" the other. In comparison, the *Fahrenheit 451* society declares books to be inauthentic and to endanger a person's happiness. Montag's colleagues believe that if one were to enter the "country of the book-people" one would dissolve.

12. Albert criticizes the fact that "books are imprisoned in this manner" ("Bücher auf diese Art eingesperrt werden," 16). The verb *einsperren* (to imprison) is normally reserved for people or animals.

13. *Erwins Badezimmer*, 19. "Je intensiver sich ein denkfähiger Mensch in diese Texte vertieft, desto differenzierter wird seine eigene Sprachfähigkeit und damit zugleich auch seine Denkweise. So kommt es, daß ausgerechnet im Konzentrationsmagazin nicht wenige meiner Kollegen inzwischen auch zu jenem Freundeskreis gehören, zu dem auch du jetzt gestoßen bist."

14. Hans Bemmann's ouvre consists, among others, of *Hunter in the Park* (*Jäger im Park*, 1961), *Inopportune Visitor* (*Lästiger Besuch*, 1962), *Stone and Flute—and that's not all* (*Stein und Flöte- und das ist noch nicht alles*, 1983).

15. According to Jonathan Culler, Noam Chomsky's generative-transformational grammar clarifies "the nature of linguistic investigation: the task is not to describe a corpus of data but to account for facts about language by constructing a formal representation of what is involved in knowing a language." *Structuralist Poetics*, 26.

16. Erwin restores a genuine Romanticism not only to the commercialized "romantic appeal" of his habitat, "in one of those narrow houses in the old part of town . . . restored for romantic appeal," but also to literature and the art of conversation. *Badezimmer*, 15.

17. Albert's letters share their role of a heritage-collection with the fairy tales of the Brothers Grimm at the beginning of the nineteenth century. The

Brothers Grimm also viewed their collection of folklore as a means of political utopia. Like the Grimms, Albert does not hesitate to edit and poetically transform his material. See Amy Marshall-Horning, "Oral Traditions, Written Collections: Johann Gottfried Herder and the Brothers Grimm" (Ph.D. diss., The Johns Hopkins University, 1991).

18. The dynamics of the generative-transformational model have also often misled critics to assume that the model straightforwardly represents the actual formation of utterances. See Jonathan Culler, *Structuralist Poetics*, 25–26.

19. The postwar debate on the role of language in the atrocities committed during the Third Reich was triggered by Dolf Sternberger's, Gerhard Storz's, and Wilhelm Süskind's *Aus dem Wörterbuch des Unmenschen* (Heidelberg: Winter, 1945). Sternberger et al. saw the bureaucraticization in word formation and semantics as the sign of a collaboration between language and sociopolitical inhumanity. In their work, the authors argued that this linguistic and therefore also political mind-set continued into postwar Germany.

20. I refer to Theodor Adorno's statement, which he voices in the context of his discussion on gayety in the arts. In this essay, he differentiates between an art produced by the culture industry and art itself. "Ist die Kunst heiter?" *Noten zur Literatur* (1967; Frankfurt a. M.: Suhrkamp, 1981), 603.

21. Wolfgang Düsing stresses Schiller's antiplatonic stance in his *Texte, Materialien, Kommentare zu Friedrich Schillers "Über die ästhetische Erziehung des Menschen in einer Reihe von Briefen"* (München: Hanser, 1981), 130–131.

22. On Group 47, see Marita Müller's, Merle Krüger's, Helmut Peitsch's, and Hartmuth Reith's essays in *Nachkriegsliteratur in Westdeutschland: Autoren, Sprache, Traditionen*, ed. Jost Hermand, Helmut Peitsch, and Klaus R. Scherpe, vol. 2 (Berlin: Argument, 1983).

23. Reinhard M. G. Nickisch illustrates the historically validated emancipatory quality of letter-writing in Germany in three examples: (1) the emancipation of the young bourgeoisie from the clergy (learning to write letters for the expedition of trade relations, writing German instead of Latin); (2) the emancipation of writing women from male-dominated aesthetics and society in the eighteenth century; (3) the emancipation of working-class emigrants to the United States from the class division of knowledge and sociopolitical influence. *Brief*, 206–212.

24. For details on the Varnhagen case, see Loreley French, *German Women as Letter Writers: 1750–1850*.

25. Janet Gurkin Altman insists that "the epistolary confidant is most fundamentally an archivist." *Epistolarity*, 53. The readers of the collected letters continue this archival chain as the text on the novel's blurb emphasizes. We become collaborators both in the opposition movement and in the collection-mania of the *Sprachüberwachungsbehörde*.

26. *Badezimmer*, 33–34. "Ihre unverhohlene ausgesprochene Bewunderung dafür, daß ich mich wegen Ihrer eigentlich eher nebenbei ausgesprochenen Frage in ein solches Abenteuer—Sie sprechen sogar von einem konspirativen Charakter dieser Unternehmung!—gestürzt hätte, schmeichelt mir zwar, macht mich aber eher verlegen. Ist Ihnen wirklich entgangen, daß Sie damit einem in der Routine halbherzig betriebener Schreibtischarbeit schon fast zum Zyniker

gewordenen Wissenschaftsbeamten unversehens einen neuen Lebensinhalt geschenkt haben? Ich fühle mich geradezu verjüngt!"

27. One of the endings to the expressionistic film *Das Cabinet des Dr. Caligari* reveals the madman himself as Dr. Caligari. *Das Cabinet des Dr. Caligari*, dir. Robert Wiene and Conrad Veidt, Berlin, 1919.

28. *Badezimmer*, 127–128. "Meine Redeweise erstaunt Sie wohl? Mein lieber Herr Doktor, warum sollte man unter intelligenten Menschen nicht von diesen Möglichkeiten der Sprache Gebrauch machen? Nach außen und für das einfache Volk benötigt man halt so ein ideologisches Gerüst, an das sich die Leute halten können und—nebenbei gesagt—auch halten sollten, damit sie nicht auf abwegige Gedanken kommen."

29. In her discussion of *The Three Marias: New Portuguese Letters* (1972), Linda S. Kauffman shows that the heroines in epistolary fiction "purposely subvert the traditional notion of genre by including myriad forms, styles and modes in their collaborative texts. They also subvert the ideology of authorship by not signing their letters, radically challenging conventional notions of a text's paternity, lineage, genealogy, genre." *Discourses of Desire*, 23.

30. In the 1960s, the movement to "free oneself" through literary experiments and new "spontaneous forms of expression" ("spontanistisch[e] Ausdrucksformen") was refered to as "Emanzipatismus" ("emancipationism"). Gretel A. Koskella, *Die Krise des deutschen Romans 1960–1970* (Frankfurt a. M.: R. G. Fischer, 1986), 2, 187, 3, respectively. However, Koskella's study focuses strictly on male writers and their "rhetorical crisis" ("rhetorisch[e] Krise"), "which put into question the future of the novel for an entire decade" ("welche die Zukunft des Romans für ein ganzes Jahrzehnt in Frage gestellt hat").

31. Homer Obed Brown, "The Errant Letter," 574. See also Jürgen Habermas, *Strukturwandel*, 68–69: "Reality as illusion, which creates the new genre, the English language calls 'fiction': it brushes off the character of the merely imaginary" ("Die Realität als Illusion, die die neue Gattung kreiert, nennt das Englische mit 'fiction' beim Namen: den Charakter eines bloß Fingierten streift sie ab"). Habermas calls epistolary discourse "literarily mediated intimacy from the very beginning" ("die von Anfang an literarisch vermittelte Intimität").

32. Regina Nörtemann, "Brieftheoretische Konzepte im 18. Jahrhundert und ihre Genese," 221. See also Reinhard M. G. Nickisch, "Briefkultur: Entwicklung und sozialgeschichtliche Bedeutung des Frauenbriefs im 18. Jahrhundert," *Deutsche Literatur von Frauen: Vom Mittelalter bis zum Ende des 18. Jahrhunderts*, ed. Gisela Brinker-Gabler, vol. 2 (München: Beck, 1988), 389–409.

33. Regina Nörtemann, "Brieftheoretische Konzepte," 219–220.

34. Silvia Bovenschen, *Die imaginierte Weiblichkeit*, 208–210.

35. Shari Benstock, "From Letters to Literature," 264.

36. Although one-third of the female German population was still illiterate in 1800, toward the end of the eighteenth century, women readers became an influential target group for new fiction. See Barbara Becker-Cantarino, *Der lange Weg zur Mündigkeit. Frau und Literatur (1500–1800)* (Stuttgart: Metzler, 1987), 170–177. That this newly achieved "room and time" was soon usurped by bourgeois duties is demonstrated by Felicity A. Nussbaum's case study of

Hester Thrale's diaries and journals in "Eighteenth-Century Women's Autobiographical Commonplaces," *The Private Self*, 147–171.

37. Shari Benstock, "From Letters to Literature," 288/289 and 286.

38. Gottfried Keller, *Der grüne Heinrich* (2d. ed. 1879/80) (Stuttgart: Cotta, 1964), 98. "Die Romane zerfielen hauptsächlich in zwei Arten. Die eine erhielt den Ausdruck der üblen Sitten des vorigen Jahrhunderts in jämmerlichen Briefwechseln und Verführungsgeschichten, die andere bestand aus derben Ritterromanen. Die Mädchen hielten sich mit großem Interesse an die erste Art und ließen sich dazu von ihren teilnehmenden Liebhabern sattsam küssen und liebkosen; uns Knaben waren aber diese prosaischen und unsinnlichen Schilderungen einer verwerflichen Sinnlichkeit glücklicherweise noch ungenießbar, und wir begnügten uns damit, irgendeine Rittergeschichte zu ergreifen und uns mit derselben zurückzuziehen."

39. In a letter to her aunt Sophie von Hannover, Herzogin Elisabeth Charlotte von Orléans (Liselotte von der Pfalz) quotes her father's dictum, that reading novels would make whores out of women and idiots out of men: "Papa selig sagte als er wollte nicht, daß seine söhne noch töchter romans lesen sollten, denn das machte die weibsleute zu huren und die mannsleute zu narren, daß sie glaubten, sie müßten sich in alle gefahr werfen und den hals brechen." *Briefe der Liselotte von der Pfalz*, ed. Helmuth Kiesel (Frankfurt a. M.: Insel, 1981), 160.

40. The children in Keller's *Grüner Heinrich* are witnessing a literary primal scene. They simultaneously repress and sustain it in the verb *ungenießbar*. It can neither be consumed nor be left untried. Klaus-Dieter Metz points to Keller's prologue to the novel, in which Keller likens its writing process to "that of a detailed long letter, which one writes about an intimate affair, interrupted often by the change and pressure of life" ("derjenigen eines ausführlichen langen Briefes, welchen man über eine vertrauliche Angelegenheit schreibt, oft unterbrochen durch den Wechsel und Drang des Lebens"). *Korrespondenzen. Der Brief in Gottfried Kellers Dichtung*, 4. The narrator, who within the novel, attempts to cope with and execute the power of epistolary fiction is caught within a novel as letter. In this light, the narrator himself is wedged between letters and desire; due to Keller's gendered treatment of this situation, he is feminized.

41. In the chapter "Penelope at Work," Peggy Kamuf describes this blindness of the voyeur: "The man of letters—historian, biographer, novelist, playwright, or literary critic—has failed to see himself as already represented in the room he has entered, and it is precisely a blindness to his own reflection that induces a credulous inspiration for his work." *Signature Pieces*, 161.

42. Linda S. Kauffman remarks that in love-letters lovers "revert to infantile demands, irrational needs." Rather than the women, Kauffman argues that "in the epistolary tradition male lovers invariably have voracious appetites, ranging from Lovelace (in contrast to Clarissa, who ceases to eat) to Humbert. Werther longs to devour Lotte; Humbert yearns to swallow Lolita's kidney's, lungs, liver." *Special Delivery*, 114.

43. Another example of Keller's ambivalence toward female sexuality can be seen in his novella *Romeo und Julia auf dem Dorfe* (1865), in which the passionate heroine is called "Vrenchen" and consistently referred to with the neuter

pronoun "it." Keller thereby retains her childlike naiveté even in moments of passion." (München: Insel, 1984), 94.

44. In German, the most common term for "girl" is already a diminutive form with a neuter gender: *das Mädchen*. There is no equivalent neuter term for "boy" unless one chooses to form the diminutive of *der Junge, der Bube, der Bursche*. See also the previous footnote.

45. That this removal all but displaces sexuality is shown in the case of the "displaced letter" that keeps (dis)appearing in the narrator's life.

46. Shari Benstock, "From Letters to Literature," 263.

47. Peggy Kamuf, *Signature Pieces*, 161.

48. Shari Benstock, "From Letters to Literature," 285.

49. Ibid., 286.

50. *Badezimmer*, 61. "Was Sie allerdings dann weiterhin über diese Geschichte schreiben, hat mich in ziemliche Verwirrung gestürzt. Wenn ich Sie recht verstanden habe, halten Sie die Szene am Bach überhaupt nicht für ein Mißverständnis. "Wenn diese Mara nicht mit Rudimer hätte schlafen wollen," schreiben Sie, "dann hätte sie ihm doch nur zu sagen brauchen, wie sie ihre Redensart gemeint hatte," und dann setzen Sie noch hinzu: "Vielleicht gefiel er ihr!" Ehrlich gesagt: Ich war ein bißchen schockiert über soviel Direktheit, meine Liebe! . . . Wenn ich mir's jetzt noch einmal richtig überlege, dann berührt mich das einstweilen leider nur par distance geführte Gespräch mit Ihnen gerade deshalb so stark, weil Sie in diesen scheinbar so verstaubten Texten unversehens sinnlich-konkrete Wirklichkeit entdecken."

51. Homer Obed Brown, "The Errant Letter," 581.

52. The term *Zeitung*, today the word for newspaper, was etymologically and historically related to the genesis of letters and regular postal service. Regina Nörtemann, "Brieftheoretische Konzepte," 218–219. See also Patricia Meyer Spacks, *Gossip* (New York: Knopf, 1985), and Homer Obed Brown, "The Errant Letter."

53. Compare Christoph Martin Wieland's preface and editorial comments to Sophie La Roche's *Die Geschichte des Fräulein von Sternheim* (1771).

54. For material on contemporaries' opinions of Bettina's mentality and behavior, see the appendix to the Insel edition of *Die Günderode*, 532–544.

55. Bettina Brentano, for example, portrays her insistent love of "ignorance" and the "triviality" of her letters as a topos throughout her epistolary novels. *Die Günderode*, 21 and 132–135.

56. *Badezimmer*, 83. "Ihre verblüffende und doch so konsequente Interpretation nimmt ihre Argumente aus einem Bereich, der bei mir weitgehend brachgelegen hat. Empfindung und Gefühl in die Deutung eines Textes einzubringen, schien mir bislang ungehörig und vom wissenschaftlichen Standpunkt aus nicht vertretbar."

57. According to Lacan, "the subject appears first in the Other, in so far as the first signifier, the unary signifier, emerges in the field of the Other and represents the subject for another signifier, which other signifier has as its effect the aphanisis of the subject. Hence the division of the subject—when the subject appears somewhere as meaning, he is manifested elsewhere as 'fading', as disappearance." *The Four Fundamental Concepts of Psychoanalysis*, 218.

58. *Badezimmer*, 52. "Warum erschrickst du?" fragte Mara lächelnd. "Ich gedachte, in deinem Sinne zu handeln. Warum trägst du keine Festkleider? Wenig Ehre gewinne ich so mit dir!" "Wozu Festkleider?" stammelte Rudimer, der nun überhaupt nicht mehr wußte, woran er war. "Wollt ihr mich auf dem Berge darbringen wie ein geschmücktes Opfertier?" "Wer hier das Opfer ist, muß sich noch zeigen," sagte Mara und stellte sich an Rudimers Seite, noch immer die Hand auf seiner Schulter."

59. Since the name Mara bears a familiarity with the words *Märe* (fairy tale, legend) as well as *Mähre* (female horse, mare) in German, woman herself is a fictional construct and branded as property with male "letters."

60. *Badezimmer*, 60. "Da legte ihm Belegar die Hand auf die Schulter und sagte: "Ich lege nun meine Hand auf dich, Rudimer." Rudimer blickte überrascht auf, schien noch einmal Hoffnung zu fassen und sagte: "Wie soll ich das verstehen?" "Wie du es immer verstanden hast," sagte Belegar. "Nachdem sich meine Tochter bei eurer ersten Begegnung deinem Sprachgebrauch gefügt hat, will auch ich jetzt das gleiche tun."

61. Ibid., 82. "Ihre Deutung ist von geradezu umwerfender, allerdings sehr weiblicher Logik, wenn Sie schreiben: "Diese Frau hat sich Rudimar in jeder Bedeutung hingegeben, und dann muß sie erfahren, daß er dies nicht als Geschenk, sondern als eine Schmach empfindet. Etwas Schlimmeres kann einer Frau gar nicht passieren" und daraus den Schluß ziehen, daß Mara diese Formel bewußt ausgesprochen hat, weil sie sterben wollte."

62. Patricia Waugh, *Feminine Fictions*, 59: "According to Lacan, it is still the phallus (as symbol here of the Law of the Father) which is the sign of difference, fixing meaning and identity in language, signifying a human desire which positions women in a universal system of exchange."

63. Ibid., 61: "According to Jacques Lacan, women either remain in the dyad of the mother-infant bond, accepting madness or invisibility, or allow their identification within the symbolic order and 'masquerade' within the terms of an alien rationality. Either way, their capacity for historical agency and self-determination is virtually nil."

64. Compare to my discussion of Craig Owens's essay at the beginning of this chapter.

65. In Lacan's psychoanalytic theory, the mother guarantees the infant's "existence" in her glance. The formation and subversion of the subject is located in the mirror-stage, where the mirror takes over the mother's identifying function. See Jaqueline Rose, "Introduction II," *Feminine Sexuality. Jacques Lacan and the école freudienne*, ed. Juliet Mitchell and Jacqueline Rose, trans. Jacqueline Rose (New York/London: Norton, 1985), 30.

66. Orpheus calls Euridyke in the underworld. See Klaus Theweleit's *Buch der Könige. Orpheus und Euridyke* (Frankfurt a. M.: Stroemfeld/Roter Stern, 1988), especially his chapter "Gespensterposten" on Kafka's letters to Felice and Milena, 976–1053: "to use a woman as address-pole, to whom engagement and wedding proposals had to be suggested in order to have a mail-recipient, who also responded, at the other end" ("eine Frau als Anschreib-Pol benutzend, der Verlobungs- und Heiratsanträge vor allem deshalb unterbreitet werden mußten, um eine Postempfängerin, die auch antwortete, am anderen

Ende zu haben"), 977. Kafka's epistolary discourse comes close to Albert's, who is also dependent on writing himself into literature and history through letters to Rachel.

67. Franz Kafka is also called a "media-experienced letter-vampire" ("medienversierter Briefvampir") in analogy to Michel Cournot's interpretation. Klaus Theweleit quotes and criticizes Cournot's analysis of Kafka's obsessive attempt to control the mailing system by memorizing the schedule of all mailboxes, the way of the mail into Felice's hands, and of Felice's daily life. *Buch der Könige*, 997–998.

68. *Badezimmer*, 179. "Gleich darauf donnerte der Zug hinaus auf eine Brücke, und als er mitten über dem Fluß war, warf ich die Mappe in weitem Bogen hinaus, sah sie zwischen dem Gestänge des Brückenbogens hindurchfliegen, hinabsegeln und auf dem Wasser aufschlagen. Ein kleiner Strudel, ein bißchen Schaum, und schon trieb meine zweite Existenz im grauen Winterwasser flußabwärts ins Unerreichbare."

69. Ibid., 182. "Nun hatte ich Gelegenheit, die Stationen meiner Fahrt in umgekehrter Reihenfolge noch einmal zu besichtigen, den Fluß, der meine Papiere davon-getragen hatte, das Gebüsch, in dem Amelies Märchenbuch ruhte wie Dornröschen in der Rosenhecke."

70. Fjodor Dostoevsky, *Notes from Underground* (1864). Unlike the monologic dialogue of *Erwins Badezimmer*, Mikhail Bakhtin stresses that in *Notes from Underground*, "there is literally not a single monologically firm, dissociated word. From the very first sentence the hero's speech has begun to cringe and break under the influence of the anticipated words of another, with whom the hero, from the very first step, enters into the most intense internal polemic." *Problems of Dostoevsky's Poetics*, ed. and trans. Caryl Emerson (Minneapolis: University of Minnesota Press, 1984), 227–228.

71. Her epistolary "heart blood" pours straight into Dracula's coffin-case to instill him with another "second existence." Vampires are counterfeiters by trade. Their kiss "writes over" others' wills to them.

72. Klaus Theweleit thus describes Kafka's relation to letter-writing and to Felice. *Buch der Könige*, 1001. This sentence hints at the similarities between "real" and "fictive" correspondences, which Franz Kafka addressed in his famous "Gespensterbrief" to Milena Jesenská. *Briefe an Milena*, 301–304.

CHAPTER 5. ROMANCING THE POST

1. Robert Zemeckis, dir., *Romancing the Stone* (Los Angeles: Paramount, 1983).

2. Peter Handke, *Der kurze Brief zum langen Abschied* (Frankfurt a. M.: Suhrkamp, 1972). All references to this work will appear in parentheses directly in my text.

3. See his essays "Theater und Film: Das Elend des Vergleichens," *Ich bin ein Bewohner des Elfenbeinturms* (Frankfurt a. M.: Suhrkamp, 1972), 65–77; "Ein Beispiel für Verwendungsweisen grammatischer Modelle," ibid., 78–82; and "Probleme werden im Film zu einem Genre," ibid., 83–87.

4. Peter Handke co-authored and produced several films, beginning with *3 amerikanische LP's* (1969 with Wim Wenders), followed by an adaptation of his novel *Die Angst des Tormanns beim Elfmeter* (1972 with Wenders), an adaptation of Goethe's *Wilhelm Meisters Lehrjahre* in *Falsche Bewegung* (1975 with Wenders), an adaptation of his short novel *Die linkshändige Frau* (1977), and *Der Himmel über Berlin* (1987 with Wenders). Handke produced three television movies, among which *Short Letter, Long Farewell* was adapted for TV by Herbert Vesely in 1978. Handke also translated Walker Percy's *The Moviegoer* in 1980.

5. Allen Thiher similarly argues that the "journey's natural conclusion is an interview with John Ford, the Hollywood director whose Western movies have given a shape, through their mythic plots, to the writer's trip west to California." *Words in Reflection. Modern Language Theory and Postmodern Fiction* (Chicago: Chicago University Press, 1984), 151.

6. Dirk Göttsche, *Die Produktivität der Sprachkrise*, 338–339.

7. Since 1997, electronic media and the cinema have entered yet a new era of economic-technological codependency: German cable and satellite stations entered the stock market (e.g., the network of "Pro Sieben") after barely ten years of privatization. On the Internet, the current value of Hollywood stars is determined by fans on a star-exchange (*Premiere*, June 1997).

8. According to Rainer Nägele, "the experimental text has to run the risk of cooption, because it cannot circumvent the social and political organization of desire if it wants to enter into the economy of desire at all, and without the economy there are no human effects. There would indeed only be the dead letter." "Modernism and Postmodernism: The Margins of Articulation," *Studies in 20th Century Literature 5*, no. 1 (1980): 19.

9. Robert Zemeckis' films document the permeability of the border between documentary and fiction film. With *Contact* (July 1997), he further enhanced the seductive computerized merging of documentary footage with fiction that he had begun in *Forest Gump* (1994).

10. The stone first resides in a uterus-like enclave. From there, it wanders to the hero's genitals to end in the stomach of the alligator, from where the hero aborts it. The stone's journey represents an inverted fertilization process, a running undercurrent to the overly ritualized macho-culture of the romance plot: The end product is the yacht *Angelina*, a phallic body bearing a woman's name.

11. For the nineteenth-century novel, Tony Tanner maintains that adulterous love or an all-transgressing desire provide both the narrative motivation and the end of possible narrative. *Adultery in the Novel*, 13.

12. Dana Heller argues that "[t]he hero's journey to full masculine adulthood requires that he acknowledge and master the feminine side of his own nature, embrace what Carl G. Jung termed the *anima*. The cycle of the quest celebrates masculine superiority, the triumph of the male's assimilation of the female, the union of *anima* and *animus*, the feminine moon and the masculine sun. What the process reveals is the male hero's uncompromised self-sufficiency in the world, his embodiment of the universal circle of birth, initiation, and death." *The Feminization of Quest-Romance. Radical Departures* (Austin: University of Texas Press, 1990), 2.

13. Ibid., 6.

14. Peggy Kamuf, *Fictions of Feminine Desire*, xvii. See also Linda S. Kauffman, *Discourses of Desire*.

15. "Someone else's" here understood as both the desire of the heroine's text and the desire of phallocentric discourse.

16. Peggy Kamuf, *Fictions of Feminine Desire*, xvii.

17. Roland Barthes, *A Lover's Discourse*, 3.

18. See Michael Braun, "Die Sehnsucht nach dem idealen Erzähler. Peter Handkes romantische Utopie," *Text und Kritik*, 24, no. 5 (1989): 73–74.

19. "Aleatory circumstances" are also produced by Peter Handke in *Der kurze Brief zum langen Abschied*, 25.

20. Roland Barthes, *A Lover's Discourse*, 13.

21. *Der kurze Brief* can also be read as a response to Handke's mother's suicide, as an alternate route on his narrative quest for the typical and yet individual woman's autobiography in *Wunschloses Unglück*, which was published in the same year as *Der kurze Brief*. Both Judith and his mother suffer from depressions, from a personally immediate but always socially mediated *Unglück*.

22. Ibid., 21. "Wenn du zu einem Haus hinüber gehst, sagst du, daß du hinuntergehst; wenn wir schon lange vors Haus getreten sind, steht das Auto immer noch draußen ; und wenn du in eine Stadt hinunterfährst, fährst du hinauf in die Stadt, nur weil die Straße nach Norden führt."

23. Ibid., 16 "Das Wasser floß sehr langsam ab, und als ich zurückgelehnt, mit geschlossenen Augen dasaß, kam es mir vor, wie wenn auch ich selber, mit den gemächlichen Rucken des Wassers, nach und nach kleiner wurde und mich schließlich auflöste. Erst als mir kalt wurde, weil ich ohne Wasser in der Wanne lag, spürte ich mich wieder und stand auf."

24. Klaus-Dieter Metz argues that Handke's protagonist intentionally leaves behind traces for Judith, turning the letter into a "marker, road-sign, forecast into the future" ("Markierung, Wegweiser, Hinweis in eine Zukunft"). *Korrespondenzen*, 194–195.

25. Although Metz contends that the short letter summarizes and predicts the novel's narrative and situates the narrative movement between "searching" and "finding," he nevertheless argues for a premeditated finding that resolves the subjunctive mode with the indicative. Ibid., 196.

26. Judith's letter recalls the Romantic idea of *werden*, which Friedrich Schlegel paradigmatically develops in his 116. Athenäum-Fragment.

27. Peter Handke, "Ich bin ein Bewohner des Elfenbeinturms," *Ich bin ein Bewohner des Elfenbeinturms*, 19. "So bin ich eigentlich nie von den offiziellen Erziehern erzogen worden, sondern habe mich immer von der Literatur verändern lassen."

28. *Der kurze Brief*, 18. "So wie manchmal, wenn mich etwas Gelesenes gierig machte, es sofort nachzuerleben, rief mich jetzt auch der große Gatsby auf, mich auf der Stelle zu ändern. Das Bedürfnis, anders zu werden als ich war, wurde plötzlich leibhaftig, wie ein Trieb."

29. Rainer Nägele, "Die vermittelte Welt," *Jahrbuch der deutschen Schillergesellschaft* 19 (1975): 401.

30. *Der kurze Brief*, 20. "Ich wurde müde und gähnte. Dann, mitten im Gähnen, entstand eine hohle Stelle in mir, die sich sofort mit dem Bild von einem tiefschwarzen Unterholz füllte, und wie in einem Rückfall holte mich der Gedanke wieder ein, daß Judith tot sei. Das Bild von dem Unterholz verdüsterte sich noch, als ich in die zunehmende Dunkelheit vor der Snackbartür schaute, und mein Entsetzen wurde so stark, daß ich mich plötzlich in ein Ding zurückverwandelte."

31. See Sandy Stone, "The Empire Strikes Back. A Post-Transsexual Manifesto," *Writing on the Body: Female Embodiment and Feminist Theory*, ed. Katie Conboy et al. (New York: Columbia University Press, 1997), 337–359.

32. Peter Handke, "Ich bin ein Bewohner des Elfenbeinturms," 25. "Was die Wirklichkeit betrifft, in der ich lebe, so möchte ich die Dinge nicht beim Namen nennen, ich möchte sie nur nicht undenkbar sein lassen. Ich möchte sie erkennbar werden lassen in der Methode, die ich anwende."

33. Otto Lorenz, "Literatur als Widerspruch. Konstanten in Peter Handkes Schriftstellerkarriere," *Text und Kritik*, 24, no. 5 (1989): 12. "die subversive Verwendung der alten Gestaltungsmittel."

34. Otto Lorenz takes this struggle to signify the failure of postmodernism. Ibid., 14.

35. Peter Handke, "Ich bin ein Bewohner des Elfenbeinturms," 19–20. "etwas, das mir eine noch nicht gedachte, noch nicht bewußte Möglichkeit der Wirklichkeit bewußt macht, eine neue Möglichkeit zu sehen, zu sprechen, zu denken, zu existieren."

36. *Der kurze Brief*, 25. "Es war ein durchdringendes Gefühl von einer ANDEREN Zeit, in der es auch andere Orte geben mußte als irgendwo jetzt, in der alles eine andere Bedeutung haben mußte als in meinem jetzigen Bewußtsein, in der auch die Gefühle anders waren als jetzt die Gefühle und man selbst erst im Augenblick gerade erst in dem Zustand, in dem vielleicht die unbelebte Erde damals war, als nach jahrtausende-langem Regen zum ersten Mal ein Wassertropfen fiel, ohne sofort wieder zu verdampfen."

37. Handke does not believe that the film's visual narrative is above grammar or syntax, on the contrary. He reminds the reader and viewer of the diversity and therefore common film code's order of pictures "which could be defined as film syntax." "Theater und Film: Das Elend des Vergleichens," 69–71.

38. Peter Handke, "Die Geborgenheit unter der Schädeldecke," *Als das Wünschen noch geholfen hat* (Frankfurt a. M.: Suhrkamp, 1974), 76.

39. Friedrich Schlegel, "Athenäums-Fragmente" (1798), *Schriften zur Literatur* (München: dtv, 1985), 37.

40. Peter Handke, "Ich bin ein Bewohner des Elfenbeinturms," 25.

41. Peter Handke, "Die Literatur ist romantisch," *Ich bin ein Bewohner des Elfenbeinturms*, 35–50.

42. Compare to Peter Pütz, "Peter Handkes 'Elfenbeinturm'," *Text und Kritik* 24, no. 5 (1989): 27.

43. Ibid., 27: "and when he refers to the Romantic, he means its incompletable progression through negation, as we know it from Fichte, Friedrich Schlegel and Novalis" ("und wenn er sich auf das Romantische beruft, so meint er dessen unabschließbare Progression durch Negation, wie wir sie von Fichte, Friedrich Schlegel und Novalis kennen.")

44. Peter Handke, "Ich bin ein Bewohner des Elfenbeinturms," 21–22. "Die Methode müßte alles bisher Geklärte wieder in Frage stellen, sie müßte zeigen, daß es noch eine Möglichkeit der Darstellung der Wirklichkeit gibt, nein, daß es noch eine Möglichkeit gab: denn diese Möglichkeit ist dadurch, daß sie gezeigt wurde, auch schon verbraucht worden."

45. Peter Handke, "Zur Tagung der Gruppe 47 in den USA," *Ich bin ein Bewohner des Elfenbeinturms*, 34.

46. Ibid., 34. "Die Beschreibung eines Computers, wenn sie schon geschieht, wird in der Syntax der Kompliziertheit eines Computers angepaßt sein müssen und nicht einfach im Stil eines Populärwissenschaftlers die Bestandteile aufzählen können."

47. See Rainer Nägele, "Die vermittelte Welt," 416–418.

48. See also Ira Konigsberg, "film noir," *The Complete Film Dictionary* (New York: Penguin/Meridian, 1989), 122.

49. Timothy Corrigan quotes Christian Metz in *New German Film. The Displaced Image* (Austin: University of Texas Press, 1983), 12.

50. Stanley Cavell, *The World Viewed. Reflections on the Ontology of Film*, 72.

51. *Der kurze Brief*, 97. "Er wollte nichts entziffern; es würde sich schon eins aus dem anderen ergeben. Auch du kommst mir vor, als ob du die Umwelt nur an dir vorbeitanzen läßt. Du läßt dir Erfahrungen vorführen, statt dich hineinzuverwickeln. Du verhältst dich, als ob die Welt eine Bescherung sei, eigens für dich."

52. John Ford's transcontinental railroad film maps the narrator's own journey across the continent and, in addition, invented what now are filmic clichés.

53. *Der kurze Brief*, 101–102. "In diesem Augenblick verlor ich für immer die Sehnsucht, mich loszusein. . . . Ich wußte, daß ich mich von all diesen Beschränktheiten nie mehr loswünschen würde, und daß es von jetzt an nur darauf ankam, für sie alle eine Anordnung und eine Lebensart zu finden, die mir gerecht wäre, und in der auch andre Leute mir gerecht werden könnten."

54. Here, Handke's protagonist comes close to Woody Allen's doubly ficticious hero in *The Purple Rose of Cairo* (1985).

55. Peter Handke, "Ein autobiographischer Essay," *Ich bin ein Bewohner des Elfenbeinturms*, 13–14. "das Erlebnis veränderte sich dadurch, daß ich darüber schrieb, oder es entstand oft erst beim Schreiben des Aufsatzes darüber, und zwar durch die Aufsatzform, die man mir eingelernt hatte . . . bis ich schließlich an einem schönen Sommertag nicht den schönen Sommertag, sondern den Aufsatz über den schönen Sommertag erlebte."

56. Nora M. Alter, "Essay Film as Travel" (paper presented at the annual American Comparative Literature Association conference in Puerto Vallarta, April 12, 1997).

57. Paul Hernadi, "Concepts of Genre in Twentieth Century Criticism" (Ph.D. diss., Yale University, 1967), 38.

58. Handke delivers a good example of this double bind in the scene in which his character is watching a Tarzan movie in New York. The movie produces an uncanny overlapping of memory and predestination in the character.

He views the airplane crash in the movie with the same rhythm with which the film only later shows air bubbles rising to the surface. The movie's generic features are already part of his perception as he watches it (37). Furthermore, as this realization overcomes the character, he also remembers his uneasy relationship with comics. After having read a collection of *The Peanuts*, he dreams in the comic-sequence: four pictures-stop-four pictures-stop. When articulating his anxiety about this reaction, he transfers the frame of the airplane crash in the Tarzan movie into the metaphor of this cartoon memory: "I had the feeling as if in every fourth picture my feet were ripped out from under me and I were hitting the ground with my stomach" ("Ich hatte ein Gefühl, als ob mir in jedem vierten Bild die Füße weggerissen würden und ich mit dem Bauch auf die Erde schlug"), *Der kurze Brief*, 37. While advocating the impossible escape from a generic inbreeding between discourse and reception, his language mixes the genres.

59. The scene most often cited by critics as an illustration of this existentialist groping for "immediacy" is the pantheistic merging of the narrator-agent with a swaying cypress, which dissolves his "murderous stillness" ("mörderhafte Ruhe"). Between sleeping and paying attention, "regungslos" ("motionless") and "schwanken" ("swaying"), the narrator experiences a brief moment of oneness with himself and the tree. Ibid., 95.

60. "The reduction of reality per se leads once again into empty infinity" ("Die Reduktion auf die Wirklichkeit 'an sich' führt wieder in die leere Unendlichkeit"). Rainer Nägele, "Die vermittelte Welt," 395.

61. Christian Fürchtegott Gellert, *Das Leben der schwedischen Gräfin von G**** (1747/48) (Stuttgart: Reclam, 1968). In his *Von dem guten Geschmacke in Briefen* (Leipzig: Johann Wendler, 1751), Gellert stresses the harmonious play between "das Gefällige" ("that which pleases") and "das Wohlanständige" ("that which is proper"). To stay on the path of morality, the narrator must control emotional events at all times.

62. On the ontological importance of the *Schwelle* ("threshhold") in Handke's works, see also the articles in *Text und Kritik* 24, no. 5 (1989) by Jürgen Egyptien, "Die Heilkraft der Sprache," 42–58; Axel Ruckaberle, "Agression und Gewalt. Schwellenerfahrungen im Erzählwerk Handkes," 66–72; Thomas Nenon and Rolf Günter Renner, "Auf der Schwelle von Dichten und Denken," 104–115.

63. That Judith's letter arrives only for its mental arrival to be deferred and mediated by a flash of childhood memories has been described by Rainer Nägele in his "Die vermittelte Welt," 407.

64. These words stem from Handke's address of the meeting of Gruppe 47 in Princeton. Heinz Ludwig Arnold, ed., "Im Wortlaut: Peter Handkes 'Auftritt' in Princeton und Hans Mayers Entgegnung," *Text und Kritik* 24, no. 5 (1989): 18.

65. Michael Braun argues that in Handke's novels, the utopian condition of a mystic unity of subject and nature can only be reached in the fragile moments of aesthetic experience. He further states that Handke's longing for permanence of this unity are forever slighted by the utilitarian world and survive only in the romantic realm of narrative. "Die Sehnsucht nach dem idealen Erzähler," 75.

66. Anton Reiser is another *Bildungsreisender* ("an educational journeyman") who suffers from a constant contradiction between self and world, and delights in projecting his inner life onto the theater stage. Unlike Keller's second edition of *Der grüne Heinrich* (1879/80), which has a happy ending, Moritz's *Anton Reiser* ends abruptly and does not solve the hero's sufferings and contradictions. See Christine Kraus, "Literarische Vorbilder in Peter Handke's Roman 'Der kurze Brief zum langen Abschied'," *Österreich in Geschichte und Literatur* 22 (1978): 174–180.

67. Quoted from Gayatri Chakravorty Spivak's "Translator's Preface" to Jacques Derrida's *Of Grammatology*, xxxii.

68. Ibid.

69. Ibid., xxxviii.

70. Michael Braun, "Die Sehnsucht nach dem idealen Erzähler," 73.

71. Herta Schwarz, "'Brieftheorie' in der Romantik," *Brieftheorie im 18. Jahrhundert*, 225. "sind Reflexionen über den Brief zunehmend in anderen Zusammenhängen bzw. in Briefen selbst zu finden. . . . Der Brief wird mehr und mehr zu einer beliebten (Kunst) Form für Veröffentlichungen schlechthin."

72. Ibid., 230. "Das Fragmentarische übernimmt die konstruktiven Merkmale des Briefs,—oder anders gesagt, der Essay-Charakter des Briefs, insbesondere seine offene Form hat im Fragment, dem 'Kern' der romantischen Kunstformen, seine Zuspitzung gefunden."

73. Michael Braun, "Die Sehnsucht nach dem idealen Erzähler," 74. "Utopie des ewigen Unterwegsseins."

74. Friedrich Schlegel, "Athenäums-Fragmente," 37.

75. Klaus-Dieter Metz compares the Römer–Heinrich correspondence to the epistolary exchange between Meierlein and Heinrich ("Sogleich Alles oder Nichts!"), and to Judith's short letter in *Der kurze Brief*. The menacing tone of an ultimatum unites these three correspondences. Metz argues that all three letters, even though they stimulate the respective narratives, culminate in an "Abschied vom Briefeschreiben." In Handke's case, this long farewell supposedly causes the superfluousness of the (short) letter: "Zugleich wird der kurze Brief aufgehoben, sein Inhalt ist gegenstandslos geworden." *Korrespondenzen*, 191 and 193. This farewell from letters nevertheless follows an epistolary path.

76. Gottfried Keller, *Der grüne Heinrich*, 2d. ed. 1879/80 (Reprint, Stuttgart: Cotta, 1964), 393. "Den unheimlichen Brief wagte ich nicht zu verbrennen und fürchtete mich, ihn aufzubewahren; bald begrub ich ihn unter entlegenem Gerümpel, bald zog ich ihn hervor und legte ihn zu meinen liebsten Papieren, und noch jetzt, sooft ich ihn finde, verändere ich seinen Ort und bringe ihn anderswo hin, so daß er auf steter Wanderschaft ist."

77. Mireille Tabah reads Handke's symbolic chains in *Die Angst des Tormanns beim Elfmeter* as an embodiment of a schizophrenic glance. As distorted as the reality depicted by this glance is, it is still possible to "translate" its language. *Vermittlung und Unmittelbarkeit. Die Eigenart von Peter Handkes fiktionalem Frühwerk* (1960–1970) (Frankfurt a. M.: Peter Lang, 1990), 284–287.

78. Peter Handke, "Ich bin ein Bewohner des Elfenbeinturms," 24. "[I]ch brauche keine Verkleidung der Sätze mehr, es kommt mir auf jeden einzelnen Satz an."

79. *Der kurze Brief*, 9–10. My italics. "In einer Dämmerung, um so fürchterlicher, als sie noch immer nicht Nacht war, stolperte ich mit lächerlich baumelnden Armen den schon in sich zusammengesunkenen Wald entlang, aus dem nur die Flechten an den vordersten Baumstämmen noch herausschimmerten."

80. The method is reminiscent of Wim Wenders' projectionist's tour into his and his father's German past in *Kings of the Road* (1976).

81. *Der kurze Brief*, 46. "Reihen von Häusern bildeten sich im nachhinein aus den Schwingungen, dem Stocken, den Verknotungen und den Rucken, die sie in mir zurückgelassen hatten. Ein Brausen und ein Röhren . . . kam dazu, als aus den Schwingungen auch Geräusche wurden."

82. Michael Braun explores Handke's "Utopie des ewigen Unterwegsseins": "In the mystical moment of aesthetic experience walking and writing fall together in Handke. Walking becomes narrating, the narrator becomes a 'threshhold-discoverer.'. . . In this, Handke develops a pathos of the periphery" ("Im mystischen Augenblick ästhetischer Erfahrung fallen bei Handke Gehen und Schreiben zusammen. Das Gehen wird zum Erzählen, der Erzähler zum 'Schwellenkundler' . . . Handke entwickelt dabei ein Pathos der Peripherie." "Die Sehnsucht nach dem idealen Erzähler," 74.

83. This long postponed union takes the form of Schlegel's *Lucinde* in that it writes *Poesie* with and over the female genre. See Jacques Derrida's "The Law of Genre," 222–227.

84. *Der kurze Brief*, 186. "Von der Terrasse geht der Blick in ein Tal hinunter, in dem Orangenbäume und Zypressen stehen. Für die Besucher gibt es Korbsessel, die nebeneinander aufgereiht sind, davor kleine Fußschemel mit indianischen Decken. Wenn man darin sitzt und redet, fängt man bald an, dem andern eine Geschichte zu erzählen."

85. Ibid., 195. "Weil wir eine Geschichte erwarteten, beugten wir uns leicht vor, und ich merkte, daß ich dabei die Bewegung wiederholte, mit der in einem seiner Filme jemand, ohne sich von der Stelle zu bewegen, sich mit langem Hals zu einem Sterbenden beugt, um zu sehen, ob er noch lebte."

86. Handke still gnaws at the inability to catch the soul's breath and speech. Rainer Nägele quotes Schiller's "Sprache" poem in "Die vermittelte Welt," 412: "Why can the living spirit not appear to the spirit? Speaks the soul, so speaks ach! the soul no longer" ("Warum kann der lebendige Geist dem Geist nicht erscheinen? Spricht die Seele, so spricht ach! die Seele nicht mehr").

87. Rainer Nägele correctly speaks of "pendulum-movements" *(Pendelbewegungen)*, but he does not relate them to the function of the letter in Handke's text. "Die vermittelte Welt," 396.

88. Philippe Lacoue-Labarthe and Jean-Luc Nancy thus describe romantic poetry's autoformation "as a kind of 'beyond' of literature itself." "Genre," 10–11.

89. Peter Handke wrote a work-journal of the same title from 1975–1977. *Das Gewicht der Welt. Journal (November 1975—März 1977)* (Frankfurt a. M.: Suhrkamp, 1977).

CHAPTER 6. *MAIL-ART:* EINSTECKALBUM

1. Edith Decker, "Boten und Botschaften einer telematischen Kultur," *Vom Verschwinden der Ferne. Telekommunikation und Kunst,* ed. Edith Decker and Peter Weibel (Köln: Dumont, 1990), 94–98.

2. Else Lasker-Schüler, *Mein Herz* (1912) and *Malik* (1913–17); James Krüss, *Briefe an Pauline.*

3. See, for example, Elke Heidenreich's *Mit oder ohne Knochen?* (Reinbek: Rowohlt, 1986) between pages 84 and 85. The ad insert begins with the picture of a German-style roast with the caption: "As the seasoning . . . [turn of page], so the roast, says an old proverb. Else Stratmann must know it, because what she serves us is pretty peppery. And what the seasoning is for the roast that is the interest for savings—the thing is simply supposed to taste good to us" ("Wie die Würze . . . [turn of the page] so der Braten, sagt ein altes Sprichwort. Else Stratmann muß es kennen, denn was sie uns so auftischt, ist ganz schön gepfeffert. Und was die Würze beim Braten, sind die Zinsen beim Sparen—die Sache soll uns eben schmecken!"

4. Trinh T. Minh-ha, "The Language of Nativism. Anthropology as a Scientific Conversation of Man with Man," *American Feminist Thought at Century's End,* ed. Linda S. Kauffman (Cambridge: Blackwell, 1993), 123.

5. Andreas Huyssen, "Mapping the Postmodern," *After the Great Divide,* 212.

6. Ibid., 209.

7. Ibid. Caren Kaplan also discusses the need for a proof of authenticity in *Questions of Travel,* 61.

8. Karen R. Achberger, *Understanding Ingeborg Bachmann,* 115.

9. Ernesto Laclau, "Universalism, Particularism and the Question of Identity," *The Identity in Question,* ed. John Rajchman (London/New York: Routledge, 1997), 106.

10. If I may be allowed to adapt Trinh T. Minh-ha's title.

11. Donna Haraway, "The Persistence of Vision," *Writing on the Body,* 286.

12. This insert is a revised version of the Schaper section from my conference paper "Mail-Art: Posting Postmodernity," *Inner Space-Outer Space: Humanities, Technology, and the Postmodern World,* ed. Daniel Schenker, Craig Hawks, and Susan Kray (Huntsville: Southern Humanities Press, 1993), 105–119.

13. Ludwig Zerull, *Karl Schaper* (Braunschweig: Westermann, 1984), 29.

14. Ibid., 30.

15. Ibid., 36 and Renate Puvogel, "Kunstmaler und Balladendichter," *Karl Schaper. Briefe, Objekte, Texte, Teppiche und allerlei Bilder* (Hannover: Sprengel Museum Ausstellungskatalog, 1988), 31.

16. Ludwig Zerull, *Karl Schaper,* 30.

17. Ibid., 44.

18. Ludwig Wittgenstein, *Tractatus logico-philosophicus,* 115. #6.54: "Meine Sätze erläutern dadurch, daß sie der, welcher mich versteht, am Ende als

unsinnig erkennt, wenn er durch sie—auf ihnen—über sie hinausgestiegen ist. (Er muß sozusagen die Leiter wegwerfen, nachdem er auf ihr hinaufgestiegen ist.) Er muß diese Sätze überwinden, dann sieht er die Welt richtig."

19. I owe this reading of "zustellen" to Gudrun Kohn-Waechter's "Das 'Problem der Post' in 'Malina'," 225–242.

20. Carl Hartman, "Library of Congress mulls how to save digital works," *Philadelphia Inquirer*, Monday, September 8, 2000.

21. Lisa Yashon, "Artistic Dimensions of Amnesia. An Advocate interview with Nicomedes Suárez-Araúz," *Valley Advocate* (November 16, 1987): 3.

22. Nicomedes Suárez-Araúz, *Amnesis Art*, 93. Quotes will appear directly in my text.

23. Jacques Lacan, *The Structuralist Controversy*, 94.

24. Compare the book cover to works #1, #4, #5, #8, #12–#14, #19, #21, #22, *Amnesis Art*, 31–46.

25. *Chicago Tribune*, September 18, 1994.

26. See Leslie W. Rabine, "A Woman's Two Bodies: Fashion Magazines, Consumerism, and Feminism," *On Fashion*, ed. Shari Benstock and Suzanne Ferris (New Brunswick: Rutgers University Press, 1994), 59–75.

27. Susan Bordo, "The Body and the Reproduction of Femininity," *Writing on the Body*, 101.

28. Allen Thiher, *Words in Reflection*, 202.

29. This is how Andreas Huyssen interprets the current "obsessions with memory" in his *Twilight Memories. Marking Time in a Culture of Amnesia* (New York/ London: Routledge, 1995), 3.

30. Sue-Ellen Case, "Tracking the Vampire," *Writing on the Body*, 388.

31. Ibid.

CHAPTER 7. POSTING E-MAIL

1. N. Katherine Hayles, "The Condition of Virtuality," *Language Machines. Technologies of Literary and Cultural Production*, ed. Jeffrey Masten, Peter Stallybrass, and Nancy J. Vickers (New York: Routledge, 1997), 204.

2. For the historical development of ARPANET and CSNET, the precursors to the Internet, see Lydia Buchmüller, "Virtual Reality, Cyberspace & Internet," *Symbolik von Ort und Raum*, ed. Paul Michel (Bern: Peter Lang, 1997), 107–135.

3. Howard Bryant, "As tech marches on, can Postal Service deliver?" *Philadelphia Inquirer*, Thursday, September 5, 1996.

4. Paul Virilio, "Das dritte Intervall. Ein kritischer Übergang," translated from the French by Marianne Karbe, *Vom Verschwinden der Ferne*, 341.

5. See also the discussion over "intellectual property" within the General Agreement on Tarifs and Trade accords.

6. Mark Poster, *The Mode of Information. Poststructuralism and Social Context* (Chicago: University of Chicago Press, 1990), 27–28.

7. Howard Bryant, "As tech marches on, can Postal Service deliver?"

8. Naomi Koppel, "Technology is widening gap between rich and poor, U.N. report finds," *The Philadelphia Inquirer*, July 12, 1999, A7.

9. Lydia Buchmüller, "Virtual Reality, Cyberspace & Internet," 117. This finding is echoed by the July 1999 *U.N. Human Development Report*.

10. See also Edmund L. Andrews' article on the internet "Mr. Smith goes to Cyberspace," *New York Times*, January 6, 1995, in which Newt Gingrich suggests a "tax credit for the poorest Americans to buy a laptop."

11. Mark Poster, *The Mode of Information*, 27–28.

12. Naomi Koppel, "Technology is widening gap between rich and poor."

13. On the importance of a regular postal service for the development of epistolary rhetoric, technique, and fiction, see Roger Chartier, Alain Boureau, and Cécile Dauphin, eds., *Correspondences. Models of Letter-Writing from the Middle Ages to the Nineteenth Century* (Princeton: Princeton University Press, 1997).

14. Compare Manfred Kammer, "Der Traum von der Bibliothek von Alexandria. Zur Beziehung von Internet, Neuen Medien und Gedächtnis," *Die totale Erinnerung. Sicherung und Zerstörung kulturhistorischer Vergangenheit und Gegenwart in den modernen Industriegesellschaften*, ed. Christiane Caemmerer, Walter Delabar, and Marion Schulz (Bern: Peter Lang, 1997), 52–53.

15. Carl Hartman, "Library of Congress mulls over how to save digital works," *The Philadelphia Inquirer*, Friday, November 10, 2000.

16. Compare Richard A. Lanham, *The Electronic Word: Democracy, Technology, and the Arts* (Chicago: University of Chicago Press, 1993), 21.

17. Marshall McLuhan, "Roads and Paper Routes," *Understanding Media*, 90.

18. Frederic Jameson, "Postmodernism and Consumer Society," *The Anti-Aesthetic*, 111–125.

19. Theodor Holm Nelson, "Hypertext," *Dream Machines* (Redmond: Tempus, 1987), 29.

20. Manfred Kammer, "Der Traum von der Bibliothek von Alexandria," 49.

21. Internet-Cafés, where one can rent a machine for minutes or hours are the most concrete manifestation of this new relationship. Similar to Viennese coffeehouses at the fin-de-siècle, one can now chat with physically or virtually present guests at the same time and in the same place.

22. Jay David Bolter, *Writing Space: The Computer, Hypertext, and the History of Writing* (Hillsdale: Erlbaum, 1991), 207.

23. Peter Weibel, "Vom Verschwinden der Ferne. Telekommunikation und Kunst" in the anthology of the same name published for the 1990–91 exhibition of the German Postal Museum in Frankfurt, Germany (Köln: Dumont, 1990), 36.

24. Richard A. Lanham, *The Electronic Word*, 214.

25. N. Katherine Hayles, "The Condition of Virtuality," 202.

26. For an analysis of the imagery of electronic viruses in contemporary culture, see Scott Bukatman, *Terminal Identity. The Virtual Subject in Postmodern Science Fiction* (Durham: Duke University Press, 1996), 69–100.

27. Where does that leave critics eager to hunt for an author's intent of publication?

28. See Jacques Derrida's layout in "Le Parergon" and "Living On: Borderlines."

29. George P. Landow, ed., *Hyper/Text/Theory*, 18.

30. Marshall McLuhan, "Roads and Paper Routes," 93.

31. Especially in the instance of the "anonymous" letter in detective stories which the sleuth traces to its sender due to a slightly sagging or elevated letter in the typescript. The individual letter takes revenge on the anonymity of the technological medium.

32. Jean-François Lyotard, *The Postmodern Condition*, 5.

33. The above generalizations need to be adjusted when one considers the use of the telephone as modem or in connection with a fax machine, a computer, and visual contact. See Eric A. Havelock's study *The Muse learns to write. Reflections of Orality and Literacy from Antiquity to the Present* and Aleida and Jan Assmann et al., *Schrift und Gedächtnis. Beiträge zur Archäologie der literarischen Kommunikation* (München: Fink, 1983).

34. The tendency to make the cultural context invisible is in step with erasing women's roles in creation. Carol Stabile, "Shooting the Mother. Fetal Photography and the Politics of Disappearance," *The Visible Woman. Imaging Technologies, Gender, and Science*, ed. Paula Treichler, Lisa Cartwright, and Constance Penley (New York: New York University Press, 1998), 171–197.

35. Avital Ronell, *The Telephone Book*, 8.

36. Gregory G. Colomb and Mark Turner, "Computers, Literary Theory, and Theory of Meaning," *The Future of Literary Theory*, 386–439.

37. N. Katherine Hayles, "The Condition of Virtuality," 202.

38. Since 1998, Women on the Net (WON) has worked to empower "women to use technology as a political tool." Wendy Harcourt, "Cyborg Melody. An Introduction to Women on the Net (WON)," *Women@Internet*, ed. Wendy Harcourt (London/New York: Zed, 1999), 1.

39. As Sohail Inayatillahy and Ivana Milojevic caution: "Research on e-mail culture points out that the twin dangers of immediacy and speed do not lead to greater community and friendship, rather, they can lead to bitter misunderstandings (Gwynne and Dickerson, 1997, pp. 64–66; Mouse Houghten, 1992, pp. 65–66). E-mail then is perhaps not the great connector leading to higher levels of information but the great disconnector that gives the mirage of connection and community." "Exclusion and Communication in the Information Era," *Women@Internet*, 77.

SELECTED
BIBLIOGRAPHY

Achberger, Karen R. *Understanding Ingeborg Bachmann*. Columbia: University of South Carolina Press, 1994.

Adorno, Theodor W. *Erziehung zur Mündigkeit*. Frankfurt: Suhrkamp, 1981.

————. *Noten zur Literatur*. Frankfurt a. M.: Suhrkamp, 1981.

Altmann, Janet Gurkin. *Epistolarity: Approaches to a Form*. Columbus: Ohio State University Press, 1982.

Appignanesi, Lisa, ed. *Postmodernism. ICA Documents*. London: Free Press, 1989.

Arlart, Ursula. *"Exhaustion" und "Replenishment:" Die Fiktion in der Fiktion bei John Barth*. Heidelberg: Winter, 1984.

Arnold, Heinz Ludwig, ed. "Im Wortlaut: Peter Handkes 'Auftritt' in Princeton und Hans Mayers Entgegnung." *Text und Kritik* 24, no. 5 (1989): 17–20.

Assmann, Aleida, and Jan Assman et al. *Schrift und Gedächtnis. Beiträge zur Archäologie der literarischen Kommunikation*. München: Fink, 1983.

Atzler, Elke. "Ingeborg Bachmanns Roman 'Malina' im Spiegel der literarischen Kritik." *Jahrbuch der Grillparzer Gesellschaft* 3, no. 15 (1983): 155–171.

Bachmann, Ingeborg. *Ingeborg Bachmann: Die Wahrheit ist dem Menschen zumutbar*, ed. Christine Koschel and Inge von Weidenbaum. München: Piper, 1981.

————. *Malina*. Frankfurt a. M.: Suhrkamp, 1971.

————. *Wir müssen wahre Sätze finden*. München: Piper, 1983.

Bakhtin, Mikhail. *Problems of Dostoevsky's Poetics*. Translated by Caryl Emerson. Minneapolis: University of Minnesota Press, 1984.

Bänsch, Dieter, ed. *Zur Modernität der Romantik*. Stuttgart: Metzler, 1977.

Barth, John. "The Literature of Exhaustion." *Atlantic Monthly* (August 1967): 29–34.

————. "The Literature of Replenishment." *Atlantic Monthly* (January 1980): 65–71.

————. *LETTERS, a novel*. New York: Putnam's Sons, 1979.

————. *Lost in the Funhouse. Fiction for print, tape, live voice*. Reprint, New York/London: Doubleday, 1988.

Barthes, Roland. *A Lover's Discourse. Fragments*. Translated by Richard Howard. New York: Hill and Wang, 1978.

Baudrillard, Jean. *Le Simulacre. Traverses*. Paris: Minuet, 1978.

————. *Cool Memories*. Translated by Chris Turner. London: Verso, 1990.

Becker-Cantarino, Barbara. *Der lange Weg zur Mündigkeit. Frau und Literatur (1500–1800)*. Stuttgart: Metzler, 1987.

————. "Leben als Text. Briefe als Ausdrucks- und Verständigungsmittel in der Briefkultur und Literatur des 18. Jahrhunderts." In *Frauen-Literatur-Geschichte*, ed. Hiltrud Gnüg and Renate Möhrmann, 83–103. Stuttgart: Metzler, 1985.

Bemmann, Hans. *Erwins Badezimmer oder die Gefährlichkeit der Sprache*. Stuttgart: Edition Weitbrecht, 1984.

Benjamin, Walter. *Illuminationen. Ausgewählte Schriften*. Vol. 1. Frankfurt a.M.: Suhrkamp, 1977.

Benstock, Shari. "From Letters to Literature: 'La Carte Postale' in the Epistolary Genre." *Genre* 18 (Fall 1985): 257–295.

————, ed. *The Private Self. Theory and Practice of Women's Writings*. Chapel Hill: University of North Carolina Press, 1988.

————, and Suzanne Ferriss, eds. *On Fashion*. New Brunswick: Rutgers University Press, 1994.

Berg, Temma F., ed. *Engendering the Word: Feminist Essays in Psychosexual Poetics*. Urbana: University of Illinois Press, 1989.

————. "*La Carte Postale:* Reading (Derrida) Reading." *Criticism* 28, no. 3 (1986): 323–340.

Bienstock, Beverly Gray. "Lingering on the Autognostic Verge: John Barth's 'Lost in the Funhouse'." *Modern Fiction Studies* 19 (1973): 69–78.

Bloom, Harald et al., eds. *Deconstruction and Criticism*. New York: Seabury, 1979.

Bohrer, Karl Heinz. *Der romantische Brief. Die Entstehung ästhetischer Subjektivität*. München/Wien: Hanser, 1987.

Bolter, Jay David. *Writing Space: The Computer, Hypertext, and the History of Writing*. Hillsdale: Erlbaum, 1991.

Bovenschen, Silvia. *Die imaginierte Weiblichkeit. Exemplarische Untersuchungen zu kulturgeschichtlichen und literarischen Präsentationsformen des Weiblichen*. Frankfurt a. M.: Suhrkamp, 1979.

————. "Über die Frage: gibt es eine 'weibliche' Ästhetik?" *Ästhetik und Kommunikation* 25 (September 1979): 60–75.

Bower, Anne Lieberman. *Epistolary Responses. The Letter in 20th-Century American Fiction and Criticism*. Tuscaloosa: University of Alabama Press, 1997.

Braun, Michael. "Die Sehnsucht nach dem idealen Erzähler. Peter Handkes romantische Utopie." *Text und Kritik* 24, no. 5 (1989): 73–81.

Brodzki, Bella, and Celeste Schenck, eds. *Life/Lines. Theorizing Women's Autobiography*. Ithaca: Cornell University Press, 1988.

Brown, Homer Obed. "The Errant Letter and the Whispering Gallery." *Genre* 10, no. 4 (Winter 1977): 573–599.

Brown, John L. "What ever happened to Mme. de Sévigné? Reflections on the fate of the epistolary art in a media age." *World Literature Today* 64, no. 2 (Spring 1990): 215–220.

Buchmüller, Lydia. "Virtual Reality, Cyberspace & Internet." In *Symbolik von Ort und Raum*, ed. Paul Michel, 107–135. Bern: Peter Lang, 1997.

Bürger, Christa. *Zur Dichotomisierung von hoher und niederer Literatur*. Frankfurt a.M.: Suhrkamp, 1982.

———. "I and We: Ingeborg Bachmann's Emergence from Aesthetic Modernism." *New German Critique* 47 (Summer 1989): 3–28.

———. *Leben Schreiben. Die Klassik, die Romantik und der Ort der Frauen.* Stuttgart: Metzler, 1990.

Butler, Judith. *Gender Trouble. Feminism and the Subversion of Identity.* New York/London: Routledge, 1990.

Cavell, Stanley. *The World Viewed. Reflections on the Ontology of Film.* Enlarged ed. Cambridge, Mass.: Harvard University Press, 1979.

Chartier, Roger, Alain Boureau, and Cécile Dauphin. *Correspondence. Models of Letter-Writing from the Middle Ages to the Nineteenth Century.* Princeton: Princeton University Press, 1997.

Chow, Rey. "'It's you, and not me . . .': Domination and 'Othering' in Theorizing the 'Third World'." In *American Feminist Thought at Century's End*, ed. Linda Kauffman, 95–106. Cambridge: Blackwell, 1993.

Cixous, Hélène, and Catherine Clement. *The Newly Born Woman.* Translated by Betsy Wing. Minneapolis: University of Minnesota Press, 1986.

Clauss, Elke. *Liebeskunst. Der Liebesbrief im 18. Jahrhundert.* Stuttgart: Metzler, 1993.

Cohen, Ralph, ed. *The Future of Literary Theory.* London/New York: Routledge, 1989.

Collier, Peter, and Helga Geyer-Ryan, eds. *Literary Theory Today.* Ithaca: Cornell University Press, 1990.

Colomb, Gregory G., and Mark Turner. "Computers, Literary Theory, and Theory of Meaning." In *The Future of Literary Theory*, ed. Ralph Cohen, 386–439. London/New York: Routledge, 1989.

Conboy, Katie et al., eds. *Writing on the Body: Female Embodiment and Feminist Theory.* New York: Columbia University Press, 1997.

Corrigan, Timothy. *New German Film. The Displaced Image.* Austin: University of Texas Press, 1983.

Costner, Kevin, dir. *The Postman.* Los Angeles: Warner Brothers/TIG, 1997.

Cronenberg, David, dir. *eXistenZ.* Toronto/London: Alliance Communications, 1999.

Culler, Jonathan. *A Structuralist Poetics. Structuralism, Linguistics, and the Study of Literature.* Ithaca: Cornell University Press, 1975.

de Lauretis, Teresa. *Technologies of Gender. Essays on Theory, Film, and Fiction.* Bloomington: Indiana University Press, 1987.

de Man, Paul. *The Rhetoric of Romanticism.* New York: Columbia University Press, 1984.

Decken, Godele von der. *Emanzipation auf Abwegen. Frauen und Frauenkultur im Umkreis des Nationalsozialismus.* Frankfurt: Athenäum, 1988.

Decker, Edith, and Peter Weibel, eds. *Vom Verschwinden der Ferne. Telekommunikation und Kunst.* Köln: Dumont, 1990.

Deleuze, Gilles, and Felix Guattari. *Anti-Oedipus. Capitalism and Schizophrenia.* Translated by Robert Hurley, Mark Seem, and Hellen R. Lane. New York: Viking, 1977.

Derrida, Jacques. *Dissemination.* Translated by Barbara Johnson. Chicago: University of Chicago Press, 1981.

————. *Ear of the Other. Otobiography, Transference, Translation.* Translated by Peggy Kamuf, ed. Christie McDonald. Lincoln: University of Nebraska Press, 1988.

————. "The Law of Genre." *Glyph* 7 (1980): 202–232.

————. "Living On: Borderlines." In *Deconstruction and Criticism*, ed. Harald Bloom et al., 75–176. New York: Seabury, 1979.

————. *Of Grammatology.* Translated by Gayatri Chakravorty Spivak. Baltimore: Johns Hopkins University Press, 1976.

————. *The Postcard. From Socrates to Freud and Beyond.* Translated by Alan Bass. Chicago: University of Chicago Press, 1987.

————. *Signéponge/Signsponge.* Translated by Richard Rand. New York: Columbia University Press, 1984.

————. *Speech and Phenomena.* Translated by David B. Allison. Evanston: Northwestern University Press, 1973.

Djebar, Assia. *Women of Algiers in Their Apartment.* Translated by Marjolijn de Jager. Charlottesville: University of Virginia Press, 1992.

DuPlessis, Rachel Blau. *Writing beyond the Ending. Narrative Strategies of Twentieth-Century Women Writers.* Bloomington: Indiana University Press, 1985.

Ebrecht, Angelika, Regina Nörtemann, and Herta Schwarz, eds. *Brieftheorie des 18. Jahrhunderts. Texte, Kommentare, Essays.* Stuttgart: Metzler, 1990.

Ecker, Gisela. "Spiel und Zorn: Zu einer feministischen Praxis der Dekonstruktion." In *Frauen-Literatur-Politik*, ed. Annegret Pelz et al., 8–22. Hamburg/Berlin: Argument, 1988.

Eco, Umberto. *A Theory of Semiotics.* Bloomington: Indiana University Press, 1976.

Egyptien, Jürgen. "Die Heilkraft der Sprache." *Text und Kritik* 24, no. 5 (1989): 42–58.

Eisenstein, Hester, and Alice Jardine, eds. *The Future of Difference.* New Brunswick: Rutgers University Press, 1985.

Favret, Mary A. *Romantic Correspondence: Women, Politics, and the Fiction of Letters.* Cambridge: Cambridge University Press, 1993.

Felman, Shoshana. "On Reading Poetry: Reflections on the Limits and Possibilities of Psychoanalytic Approaches." In *The Purloined Poe. Lacan, Derrida, and Psychoanalytic Reading*, ed. John P. Muller and William J. Richardson, 133–156. Baltimore: Johns Hopkins University Press, 1988.

Fiedler, Leslie. "Cross the Border—Close that Gap: Post-Modernism." In *American Literature since 1900*, ed. Marcus Cunliffe, 344–366. London: Sphere/Barrie & Jenkins, 1975.

Fischer, Ludwig, ed. *Literatur in der Bundesrepublik Deutschland bis 1967.* München: dtv, 1986.

Foster, Hal, ed. *The Anti-Aesthetic. Essays on Postmodernism.* Port Townsend, Wash.: Bay Press, 1983.

————. "Re: Post." In *Art after Modernism. Rethinking Representation*, ed. Brian Wallis and Marcia Tucker, 189–201. Boston: Godine, 1984.

Foucault, Michel. *The Order of Things. An Archeology of the Human Sciences.* New York: Vintage, 1973.

Fraser, Nancy, and Linda Nicholson. "Social Criticism without Philosophy: An Encounter between Feminism and Postmodernism." *Communication* 10 (1988): 345–366.

French, Loreley. *German Women as Letter Writers: 1750–1850*. London: Associated University Presses, 1996.

Freud, Sigmund. "Der Witz und seine Beziehung zum Unbewußten." *Psychologische Schriften*, ed. Alexander Mitscherlich, Angela Richards, and James Strachy. Studienausgabe ed. Vol. 4. Frankfurt a. M.: Fischer, 1970. 10 vols.

———. "Jenseits des Lustprinzips." *Psychologie des Unbewußten*, ed. Alexander Mitscherlich, Angela Richards, and James Strachy. Studienausgabe ed. Vol. 3. Frankfurt a. M.: Fischer, 1982. 10 vols.

Freud, Sigmund, and Josef Breuer. *Studien über Hysterie*. Reprint, Frankfurt a. M.: Fischer, 1970.

Fuss, Diane Jean. "Essential Theories, Theories' Essentialism: Feminism, Poststructuralism, and Contemporary Literary Criticism." Ph.D. diss., Brown University, 1988.

Gasché, Rodolphe. *The Tain of the Mirror. Derrida and the Philosophy of Reflection*. Cambridge, Mass.: Harvard University Press, 1986.

Gilmore, Leigh. *Autobiographies. A Feminist Theory of Women's Self-Representation*. Ithaca: Cornell University Press, 1994.

Gnüg, Hiltrud, and Renate Möhrmann, eds. *Frauen-Literatur-Geschichte*. Stuttgart: Metzler, 1985.

Goldsmith, Elizabeth, ed. *Writing the Female Voice. Essays on Epistolary Literature*. Boston: Northeastern University Press, 1989.

Gölz, Sabine. "Reading in the Twilight: Canonization, Gender, the Limits of Language—A Poem by Ingeborg Bachmann." *New German Critique* 47 (Spring 1989): 29–52.

Gorak, Jan. *God the Artist. American Novelists in a Post-Realist Age*. Chicago: University of Illinois Press, 1987.

Göttsche, Dirk. *Die Produktivität der Sprachkrise in der modernen Prosa*. Frankfurt a. M.: Athenäum, 1987.

———, and Hubert Ohl, eds. *Ingeborg Bachmann—Neue Beiträge zu ihrem Werk. Internationales Symposium Münster 1991*. Würzburg: Königshausen und Neumann, 1993.

Graff, Gerald. "Under our Belt and off our Back: Barth's *LETTERS* and Postmodern Fiction." *TriQuarterly* 52 (Fall 1981): 150–164.

Gürtler, Christa, ed. *Schreiben Frauen anders? Untersuchungen zu Ingeborg Bachmann und Barbara Frischmuth*. Stuttgart: Akademischer Verlag, 1983.

Habermas, Jürgen. "Die Moderne—ein unvollendetes Projekt." In *Wege aus der Moderne. Schlüsseltexte der Postmoderne Diskussion*, ed. Wolfgang Welsch, 177–192. Weinheim: VCH, 1988.

———. *Strukturwandel der Öffentlichkeit. Untersuchungen zu einer Kategorie der bürgerlichen Gesellschaft*. Darmstadt: Luchterhand, 1987.

Handke, Peter. *Als das Wünschen noch geholfen hat*. Frankfurt a. M.: Suhrkamp, 1974.

———. *Das Gewicht der Welt. Journal (November 1975–März 1977)*. Frankfurt a. M.: Suhrkamp, 1977.

———. *Der kurze Brief zum langen Abschied.* Frankfurt a. M.: Suhrkamp, 1972.

———. *Die Angst des Tormanns beim Elfmeter.* Reprint, Frankfurt a. M.: Suhrkamp, 1972.

———. *Ich bin ein Bewohner des Elfenbeinturms.* Frankfurt a. M.: Suhrkamp, 1972.

———. *Wunschloses Unglück.* Reprint, Frankfurt a. M.: Suhrkamp, 1979.

Harcourt, Wendy, ed. *Women@Internet. Creating New Cultures in Cyberspace.* New York/London: Zed, 1999.

Harris, Charles B. *Passionate Virtuosity. The Fiction of John Barth.* Chicago: University of Illinois Press, 1983.

Hassan, Ihab. "Beyond Postmodernism? Theory, Sense, and Pragmatism." In *Making Sense. The Role of the Reader in Contemporary American Fiction,* ed. Gerhard Hoffmann, 306–327. München: Fink, 1989.

———. *The Postmodern Turn. Essays in Postmodern Theory and Culture.* Columbus: Ohio State University Press, 1987.

Havelock, Eric A. *The Muse learns to write. Reflections of Orality and Literacy from Antiquity to the Present.* New Haven: Yale University Press, 1986.

Hayles, Katherine N. *Chaos Bound. Orderly Disorder in Contemporary Literature and Science.* Ithaca: Cornell University Press, 1990.

Heckendorn Cook, Elizabeth. *Epistolary Bodies. Gender and Genre in the Eighteenth-Century Republic of Letters.* Stanford: Stanford University Press, 1996.

Heller, Dana A. *The Feminization of Quest-Romance. Radical Departures.* Austin: University of Texas Press, 1990.

Hendin, Josephine. "*LETTERS:* A Novel by John Barth." *New Republic* 181, December 1, 1979, 32–34.

Hermand, Jost, Helmut Peitsch, and Klaus Scherpe, eds. *Nachkriegsliteratur in Westdeutschland.* Berlin: Argument, 1983. 2 vols.

Hernadi, Paul. *Beyond Genre: New Directions in Literary Classifications.* Ithaca: Cornell University Press, 1972.

Heuschele, Otto. *Der deutsche Brief. Wesen und Welt. Studie.* Stuttgart: Haug, 1938.

Hicks, D. Emily. "Deterritorialization and Border Writing." In *Ethics/Aesthetics: Post-Modern Positions,* ed. Robert Merrill, 47–58. Washington, D.C.: Maisonneuve, 1988.

Hillard, Gustav. "Vom Wandel und Verfall des Briefes." *Merkur* 23 (1969): 342–351.

Hite, Molly. *The Other Side of the Story. Structures and Strategies of Contemporary Feminist Narratives.* Ithaca: Cornell University Press, 1989.

Hoesterey, Ingeborg, ed. *Zeitgeist in Babel. The Post-Modern Controversy.* Bloomington: University of Indiana Press, 1991.

Hoffmann, Gerhard, ed. *Making Sense. The Role of the Reader in Contemporary American Fiction.* München: Fink, 1989.

Honnefelder, Gottfried. *Der Brief im Roman. Untersuchungen zur erzähltechnischen Verwendung des Briefes im deutschen Roman.* Bonn: Bouvier, 1975.

Horkheimer, Max, and Theodor W. Adorno. *Dialektik der Aufklärung.* Frankfurt a. M.: Fischer, 1969.

Hutcheon, Linda. *A Poetics of Postmodernism. History, Theory, Fiction.* New York/London: Routledge, 1988.

———. "Subject in/of/to History and His Story." *Diacritics* 16, no. 1 (Spring 1986): 78–91.

Huyssen, Andreas. *After the Great Divide: Modernism, Mass Culture, Postmodernism.* Bloomington: Indiana University Press, 1986.

———. *Twilight Memories. Marking Time in a Culture of Amnesia.* New York/London: Routledge, 1995.

Irigaray, Luce. *Speculum of the Other Woman.* Translated by Gillian C. Gill. Ithaca/New York: Cornell University Press, 1985.

Iser, Wolfgang. *The Implied Reader. Patterns of Communication in Prose Fiction from Bunyan to Beckett.* Baltimore: Johns Hopkins University Press, 1974.

Ivask, Ivar. "The Letter: A Dying Art?" *World Literature Today* 64, no. 2 (Spring 1990): 213–214.

Jacobus, Mary, ed. *Women Writing and Writing about Women.* London: Croom Helm, 1979.

Jauss, Hans Robert. *Question and Answer. Forms of Dialogic Understanding.* Translated by Michael Hays and Hans Robert Jauss. Minneapolis: University of Minnesota Press, 1989.

———. *Toward an Aesthetic of Reception.* Translated by Timothy Bahti. Minneapolis: University of Minnesota Press, 1982.

Johnson, Barbara. "The Frame of Reference: Poe, Lacan, Derrida." In *The Purloined Poe. Lacan, Derrida, and Psychoanalytic Reading,* ed. John P. Muller and William J. Richardson, 213–251. Baltimore: Johns Hopkins University Press, 1988.

Johnson, Roger Martin. "Anatomy of a literary device: the included letter." Ph.D. diss., University of Illinois, 1968.

Kahane, Claire. *Passions of the Voice. Hysteria, Narrative, and the Figure of the Speaking Woman, 1850–1915.* Baltimore: Johns Hopkins University Press, 1995.

Kammer, Manfred. "Der Traum von der Bibliothek von Alexandria. Zur Beziehung von Internet, Neuen Medien und Gedächtnis." *Die totale Erinnerung. Sicherung und Zerstörung kulturhistorischer Vergangenheit und Gegenwart in den modernen Industriegesellschaften,* ed. Christiane Caemmerer, Walter Delabar, and Marion Schulz, 43–55. Bern: Peter Lang, 1997.

Kamuf, Peggy. *Fictions of Feminine Desire. Disclosures of Heloise.* Lincoln: University of Nebraska Press, 1982.

———. *Signature Pieces. On the Institution of Authorship.* Ithaca: Cornell University Press, 1986.

Kanz, Christine. *Angst und Geschlechterdifferenzen. Ingeborg Bachmanns "Todesarten"-Projekt in Kontexten der Gegenwartsliteratur.* Stuttgart: Metzler, 1999.

Kapaun, Gisela Elisabeth. "Die Rolle des fiktiven Lesers im Briefroman des 18. Jahrhunderts." Ph.D. diss., University of California at Los Angeles, 1984.

Kaplan, Caren. *Questions of Travel. Postmodern Discourses of Displacement.* Durham: Duke University Press, 1996.

Kauffman, Linda S. *Discourses of Desire. Gender, Genre, and Epistolary Fiction*. Ithaca/London: Cornell University Press, 1986.

———. *Special Delivery. Epistolary Modes in Modern Fiction*. Chicago: University of Chicago Press, 1992.

———, ed. *American Feminist Thought at Century's End*. Cambridge: Blackwell, 1993.

Kennedy, Alan. *Reading Resistance Value. Deconstructive Practice and the Politics of Literary Critical Encounters*. New York: St. Martin's, 1990.

Kent, Thomas. *Interpretation and Genre. The Role of Generic Perception in the Study of Narrative Texts*. London/Toronto: Associated University Presses, 1986.

Kern, Harald. "Auswahlbibliographie zu Peter Handke." *Text und Kritik* 24, no. 5 (1989): 132–133.

Kittler, Friedrich. *Aufschreibesysteme 1800/1900*. München: Fink, 1987.

Klaubert, Annette. *Symbolische Strukturen bei Ingeborg Bachmann. Malina im Kontext der Kurzgeschichten*. Frankfurt a. M.: Peter Lang, 1983.

Kofman, Sarah. "'Ça Cloche'." In *Derrida and Deconstruction*. Translated by Caren Kaplan, ed. Hugh J. Silverman, 108–138. New York/London: Routledge, 1989.

Kohn-Waechter, Gudrun. "Das 'Problem der Post' in 'Malina' von Ingeborg Bachmann und Martin Heideggers 'Der Satz vom Grund'." In *Die Frau im Dialog. Studien zur Theorie und Geschichte des Briefes*, ed. Anita Runge and Lieselotte Steinbrügge, 225–242. Frankfurt a. M.: Metzler, 1991.

———. "Eine widersprechende Antwort und ihre Zerstörung in Ingeborg Bachmanns Roman "Malina." In *Frauen-Literatur-Politik*, ed. Annegret Pelz et al., 226–241. Hamburg/Berlin: Argument, 1988.

Kokowski, Eugene. "The Excremental Vision of John Barth's Todd Andrews." *Critique* 18, no. 2 (1976): 51–58.

Koskella, Gretel A. *Die Krise des deutschen Romans 1960–1970*. Frankfurt a. M.: R. G. Fischer, 1986.

Koslowski, Peter. "The (De) Construction Sites of the Postmodern." In *Zeitgeist in Babel*, ed. Ingeborg Hoesterey, 142–155. Bloomington: Indiana University Press, 1991.

Kraus, Christine. "Literarische Vorbilder in Peter Handkes Roman 'Der kurze Brief zum langen Abschied." *Österreich in Geschichte und Literatur* 22 (1978): 174–180.

Kristeva, Julia. *Revolution in Poetic Language*. Translated by Margaret Waller. New York: Columbia University Press, 1984.

La Belle, Jenijoy. *Herself Beheld. The Literature of the Looking Glass*. Ithaca: Cornell University Press, 1988.

Lacan, Jacques. *The Four Fundamental Concepts of Psychoanalysis*. Translated by Alan Sheridan. New York: Norton, 1981.

———. "Of Structure as an Inmixing of an Otherness Prerequisite to Any Subject Whatever." In *The Structuralist Controversy*, ed. Richard Macksey and Eugene Donato, 186–195. Baltimore: Johns Hopkins University Press, 1972.

———. "Seminar on 'The Purloined Letter'." In *The Purloined Poe. Lacan, Derrida, and Psychoanalytic Reading*. Translated by Jeffrey Mehlmann, ed.

John P. Muller and William J. Richardson, 28–54. Baltimore: Johns Hopkins University Press, 1988.

Laclau, Ernesto. "Universalism, Particularism and the Question of Identity." In *The Identity in Question*, ed. John Rajchman, 93–108. London/New York: Routledge, 1997.

Lacoue-Labarthe, and Jean-Luc Nancy. "Genre." *Glyph* 7 (1980): 1–14.

Lämmert, Eberhard. "Regelkram und Schöpferlaune. Goethes erzählte Romantheorie." In *Regelkram und Grenzgänge. Von Poetischen Gattungen*, ed. Eberhard Lämmert and Dietrich Scheunemann, 49–71. München: Text und Kritik, 1988.

Landow, George P., ed. *Hyper/Text/Theory*. Baltimore: Johns Hopkins University Press, 1994.

Lanham, Richard A. *The Electronic Word. Democracy, Technology, and the Arts*. Chicago: University of Chicago Press, 1993.

Latour, Bruno. *We have never been Modern*. Translated by Catherine Porter. Cambridge, Mass.: Harvard University Press, 1993.

Le Rider, Jacques, and Gerhart Raulet, eds. *Verabschiedung der (Post-) Moderne? Eine interdisziplinäre Debatte*. Tübingen: G. Narr, 1987.

LeClair, Tom. *The Art of Excess. Mastery in Contemporary American Fiction*. Chicago: University of Illinois Press, 1989.

Lee, Jonathan Scott. *Jacques Lacan*. Boston: Twayne, 1990.

Lennox, Sara. "In the Cemetery of the Murdered Daughters: Ingeborg Bachmann's *Malina*." *Studies in 20th Century Literature* 25 (September 1979): 60–75.

Lersch, Barbara. "Der Ort der Leerstelle. Weiblichkeit als Poetik der Negativität und der Differenz." In *Deutsche Literatur von Frauen. 19. und 20. Jahrhundert*, ed. Gisela Brinker-Gabler, 487–502. Vol. 2. München: Beck, 1988. 2 vols.

Levi, Jonathan. *A Guide for the Perplexed*. New York: Vintage Contemporary, 1993.

Lionnet, Françoise. *Autobiographical Voices. Race, Gender, Self-Portraiture*. Ithaca: Cornell University Press, 1989.

Lorenz, Otto. "Literatur als Widerspruch. Konstanten in Peter Handkes Schriftstellerkarriere." *Text und Kritik* 24, no. 5 (1989): 8–16.

Lyotard, Jean-François. "Defining the Postmodern." In *Postmodernism. ICA Documents*, ed. Lisa Appignanesi, 7–10. London: Free Association, 1989.

———. *The Postmodern Condition: A Report on Knowledge*. Translated by Geoff Bennington and Brian Massumi. Theory and History of Literature 10. Minneapolis: University of Minnesota Press, 1984.

MacArthur, Elizabeth J. *Extravagant Narratives. Closure and Dynamics in the Epistolary Form*. Princeton: Princeton University Press, 1990.

Macksey, Richard, and Eugene Donato, eds. *The Structuralist Controversy*. Baltimore: Johns Hopkins University Press, 1972.

Marcus, Jane. "Invincible Mediocrity. The Private Selves of Public Women." In *The Private Self. Theory and Practice of Women's Autobiographical Writings*, ed. Shari Benstock, 114–146. Chapel Hill: University of North Carolina Press, 1988.

Marshall-Horning, Amy. "Oral Traditions, Written Collections: Johann Got-
tfried Herder and the Brothers Grimm." Ph.D. diss., The Johns Hopkins Uni-
versity, 1991.
Masten, Jeffrey, Peter Stallybrass, and Nancy J. Vickers, eds. *Language
Machines. Technologies of Literary and Cultural Production.* New York:
Routledge, 1997.
Mattenklott, Gerd. "Der Sehnsucht eine Form: Zum Ursprung des modernen
Romans bei Friedrich Schlegel; erläutert an der *Lucinde*." In *Zur Modernität
der Romantik,* ed. Dieter Bänsch, 143–166. Stuttgart: Metzler, 1977.
McHale, Brian. *Postmodern Fiction.* New York: Methuen, 1987.
McLuhan, Marshall. *Understanding Media: Extensions of Man.* New York:
McGraw-Hill, 1964.
McMullen, Kim. "The Fiction of Correspondence: *Letters* and History." *Mod-
ern Fiction Studies* 36, no. 3 (Fall 1990): 405–420.
Meese, Elizabeth A. "The Erotics of the Letter." *South Atlantic Review* 57, no.
2 (1992): 11–28.
———. *(Ex)Tensions. Re-Figuring Feminist Criticism.* Urbana/Chicago: Univer-
sity of Illinois Press, 1990.
Meise, Helga. "Der Frauenroman: Erprobungen der 'Weiblichkeit'." In
*Deutsche Literatur von Frauen. Vom Mittelalter bis zum Ende des 18.
Jahrhunderts,* ed. Gisela Brinker-Gabler, 435–452. Vol. 1. München: Beck,
1988. 2 vols.
Merquior, J. G. "Spider and Bee: Towards a Critique of the Postmodern Ideol-
ogy." In *Postmodernism. ICA Documents,* ed. Lisa Appignanesi, 41–48.
London: Free Association, 1989.
Merrill, Robert, ed. *Ethics/Aesthetics: Post-Modern Positions.* Washington,
D.C.: Maisonneuve, 1988.
Metz, Klaus-Dieter. *Korrespondenzen. Der Brief in Gottfried Kellers Dichtung.*
Frankfurt a. M.: Peter Lang, 1984.
Miller, J. Hillis. "Hardy, Derrida, and the 'Dislocation of Souls'." In *Taking
Chances: Derrida, Psychoanalysis and Literature,* ed. Joseph H. Smith and
William Kerrigan, 135–145. Baltimore: Johns Hopkins University Press, 1984.
Miller, Nancy K. *Getting Personal. Feminist Occasions and Other Autobio-
graphical Acts.* New York: Routledge, 1991.
Mitscherlich, Alexander, and Margarete Mitscherlich. *Die Unfähigkeit zu
trauern. Grundlagen kollektiven Verhaltens.* München: Piper, 1977.
Morris, Christopher D. "Barth and Lacan: The World of the Moebius Strip."
Critique 17, no. 1 (1975): 69–77.
Morris, Meaghan. *The Pirate's Fiancée. Feminism, Reading, Postmodernism.*
London/New York: Verso, 1988.
Morrissette, Bruce. *Novel and Film. Essays in Two Genres.* Chicago: University
of Chicago Press, 1985.
Mowlana, Hamid, and Laurie J. Wilson. *The Passing of Modernity. Communica-
tions and the Transformations of Society.* New York/London: Longman, 1990.
Mücke, Dorothea E. von. *Virtue and the Veil of Illusion. Generic Innovation
and the Pedagogical Project in Eighteenth-Century Literature.* Stanford:
Stanford University Press, 1991.

Muller, John P., and William J. Richardson, eds. *The Purloined Poe. Lacan, Derrida, and Psychoanalytic Reading.* Baltimore: Johns Hopkins University Press, 1988.

Mulvey, Laura. *Visual and Other Pleasures.* Bloomington: Indiana University Press, 1989.

Nägele, Rainer. "Die vermittelte Welt." *Jahrbuch der deutschen Schillergesellschaft* 19 (1975): 389–418.

———. "Modernism and Postmodernism: The Margins of Articulation." *Studies in 20th Century Literature* 5, no. 1 (1980): 5–25.

Naumann, Barbara. "'Mit der Musik versteht sichs von selbst'. Friedrich Schlegels Reflexion des Musikalischen im Kontext der Gattungspoetik." In *Regelkram und Grenzgänge. Von poetischen Gattungen,* ed. Eberhard Lämmert and Dietrich Scheunemann, 72–94. München: Text und Kritik, 1988.

Nelson, Theodor Holm. *Dream Machines.* Redmond: Tempus, 1987.

Nenon, Thomas, and Rolf Günter Renner. "Auf der Schwelle von Dichten und Denken." *Text und Kritik* 24, no. 5 (1989): 104–115.

Neumann, Horst Peter. "Vier Gründe einer Befangenheit. Über Ingeborg Bachmann." *Merkur* 32 (1978): 1130–1136.

Newmann, Michael. "Revising Modernism, Representing Postmodernism." In *Postmodernism. ICA Documents,* ed. Lisa Appignanesi, 95–154. London: Free Association, 1989.

Nickisch, Reinhard M. G. *Brief.* Stuttgart: Metzler, 1991.

———. "Briefkultur: Entwicklung und sozialgeschichtliche Bedeutung des Frauenbriefs im 18. Jahrhundert." In *Deutsche Literatur von Frauen,* ed. Gisela Brinker-Gabler, 389–409. Vol. 1. München: Beck, 1988. 2 vols.

———. *Die Stilprinzipien in den deutschen Briefstellern des 17. und 18. Jahrhunderts. Mit einer Bibliographie zur Briefschreiblehre (1474–1800).* Göttingen: Palaestra, 1969.

Nies, Fritz. "Un genre feminin." *Revue d'Histoire Littéraire de la France* 78 (1978): 994–1003.

Nolden, Thomas. *"An einen jungen Dichter." Studien zur epistolaren Poetik.* Würzburg: Königshausen und Neumann, 1995.

Nörtemann, Regina. "Brieftheoretische Konzepte im 18. Jahrhundert und ihre Genese." In *Brieftheorie des 18. Jahrhunderts. Texte, Kommentare, Essays,* ed. Angelika Ebrecht, Regina Nörtemann and Herta Schwarz, 211–224. Stuttgart: Metzler, 1990.

Nussbaum, Felicity A. "Eighteenth-Century Women's Autobiographical Commonplaces." In *The Private Self. Theory and Practice of Women's Autobiographical Writings,* ed. Shari Benstock, 147–171. Chapel Hill: University of North Carolina Press, 1988.

Oberle, Mechthild. *Liebe als Sprache und Sprache als Liebe. Die sprachutopische Poetologie Ingeborg Bachmanns.* Frankfurt a. M.: Peter Lang, 1990.

Olney, James. *Metaphors of Self. The Meaning of Autobiography.* Princeton: Princeton University Press, 1972.

Overlack, Anne. *Was geschieht im Brief? Strukturen der Brief-Kommunikation bei Else Lasker-Schüler und Hugo von Hofmannsthal.* Würzburg: Stauffenburg, 1991.

Owens, Craig. "The Discourse of Others: Feminists and Postmodernism." In *The Anti-Aesthetic. Essays on Postmodern Culture*, ed. Hal Foster, 57–82. Port Townsend,Wash.: Bay Press, 1983.

Peitsch, Helmut and Hartmuth Reith, eds. *Nachkriegsliteratur in Westdeutschland: Autoren, Sprache, Traditionen*. Vol. 2. Berlin: Argument, 1983. 2 vols.

Pelz, Annegret et al., eds. *Frauen-Literatur-Politik*. Hamburg/Berlin: Argument, 1988.

Perloff, Marjorie, ed. *Postmodern Genres*. Norman: University of Oklahoma Press, 1988.

Perry, Ruth. *Women, Letters and the Novel*. New York: Ames, 1980.

Phillipson, Michael. *In Modernity's Wake. The Ameurunculus Letters*. London: Routledge, 1989.

Porter, Charles A., ed. *Yale French Studies: Men/Women of Letters* 71 (1986).

Poster, Mark. *The Mode of Information. Poststructuralism and Social Context*. Chicago: University of Chicago Press, 1990.

Prescott, Peter. "An Excess of Epistles." *Newsweek*, October 1, 1979, 32.

Pütz, Peter. "Peter Handkes 'Elfenbeinturm'." *Text und Kritik* 24, no. 5 (1989): 21–29.

Puvogel, Renate. "Kunstmaler und Balladendichter." *Karl Schaper. Briefe, Objekte, Texte, Teppiche und allerlei Bilder*. Hannover: Sprengel Museum Ausstellungskatalog, 1988.

Rabine, Leslie W. "A Woman's Two Bodies: Fashion Magazines, Consumerism, and Feminism." In *On Fashion*, ed. Shari Benstock and Suzanne Ferriss, 59–75. New Brunswick: Rutgers University Press, 1994.

Redford, Bruce. *The Converse of the Pen. Acts of Intimacy in the Eighteenth-Century Familiar Letter*. Chicago: University of Chicago Press, 1986.

Reiter, Rayna R., ed. *Toward an Anthropology of Women*. New York: Monthly Review Press, 1975.

Riffaterre, Michael. "Undecidability as Hermeneutic Constraint." In *Literary Theory Today*, ed. Peter Collier and Helga Geyer-Ryan, 109–124. London/Ithaca: Cornell University Press, 1990.

Röhnelt, Inge. *Hysterie und Mimesis in 'Malina'*. Frankfurt a. M.: Peter Lang, 1990.

Ronell, Avital. *The Telephone Book: Technology—Schizophrenia—Electric Speech*. Lincoln: University of Nebraska Press, 1988.

Rose, Jacqueline. "Introduction II." In *Feminine Sexuality. Jacques Lacan and the école freudienne*. Translated by Jacqueline Rose, ed. Juliet Mitchell and Jacqueline Rose, 27–57. New York/London: Norton, 1985.

Rubin, Gayle. "The Traffic in Women: Notes on the 'Political Economy' of Sex." *Toward an Anthropology of Women*, ed. Rayna R. Reiter. New York: Monthly Review Press, 1975.

Ruckaberle, Axel. "Agression und Gewalt. Schwellenerfahrungen im Erzählwerk Handkes." *Text und Kritik* 24, no. 5 (1989): 66–72.

Runge, Anita, and Lieselotte Steinbrügge, eds. *Die Frau im Dialog. Studien zu Theorie und Geschichte des Briefes*. Stuttgart: Metzler, 1991.

Schlegel, Friedrich. *Lucinde. Ein Roman*. Reprint, Stuttgart: Reclam, 1985.

——. *Schriften zur Literatur*, ed. Wolfdietrich Rasch. Reprint, München: dtv, 1985.

Schwarz, Herta. "'Brieftheorie' in der Romantik." In *Brieftheorie des 18. Jahrhunderts. Texte, Kommentare, Essays*, ed. Angelika Ebrecht, Regina Nörtemann, and Herta Schwarz, 225–238. Stuttgart: Metzler, 1990.

Seltzer, Robert M. *Jewish People, Jewish Thought. The Jewish Experience in History*. New York: Macmillan, 1980.

Serres, Michel. *Hermes V: Le Passage du nord-ouest*. Paris: Minuit, 1980.

——. *Parasite*. Translated by Lawrence R. Schehr. Baltimore: Johns Hopkins University Press, 1982.

Shannon, Claude E., and Warren Weaver. *The Mathematical Theory of Communication*. Urbana: University of Illinois Press, 1949.

Shapiro, Gary, ed. *After the Future. Postmodern Times and Places*. Albany: State University of New York Press, 1990.

Showalter, Elaine. "Feminism and Literature." In *Literary Theory Today*, ed. Peter Collier and Helga Geyer-Ryan, 179–199. Ithaca: Cornell University Press, 1990.

——. *A Literature of Their Own: British Women Novelists from Brontë to Lessing*. Princeton: Princeton University Press, 1977.

——. "Toward a Feminist Poetics." In *Women Writing and Writing about Women*, ed. Mary Jacobus, 23–41. London: Croom Helm, 1979.

Silverman, Hugh J., ed. *Derrida and Deconstruction*. New York/London: Routledge, 1989.

Smith, Joseph H., and William Kerrigan, eds. *Taking Chances: Derrida, Psychoanalysis, and Literature*. Baltimore: Johns Hopkins University Press, 1984.

Smith, Sidonie. *A Poetics of Women's Autobiography. Marginality and the Fiction of Self-Representation*. Bloomington: Indiana University Press, 1987.

Spacks, Patricia Meyer. "Female Rhetorics." In *The Private Self. Theory and Practice of Women's Autobiographical Writings*, ed. Shari Benstock, 177–191. Chapel Hill: University of North Carolina Press, 1988.

——. *Gossip*. New York: Knopf, 1985.

Stabile, Carol. "Shooting the Mother. Fetal Photography and the Politics of Disappearance." In *The Visible Woman. Imaging Technologies, Gender, and Science*, ed. Paula Treichler, Lisa Cartwright, and Constance Penley, 171–197. New York: New York University Press, 1998.

Stamelman, Richard. "The Dialogue of Absence." *Studies in 20th Century Literature* 12, no. 1 (Fall 1987): 93–113.

Steiner, George. "Dead Letters." *New Yorker*, December 31, 1979, 60–62.

Sternberger, Dolf, Gerhard Storz, and Wilhelm Süsskind. *Aus dem Wörterbuch des Unmenschen*. Heidelberg: Winter, 1945.

Suárez-Araúz, Nicomedes. *Amnesis Art. The Art of the Lost Object*. New York/Barcelona: Lascaux, 1988.

Suleiman, Susan Rubin, ed. *The Female Body in Western Culture*. Cambridge, Mass.: Harvard University Press, 1985.

Tabah, Mireille. *Vermittlung und Unmittelbarkeit. Die Eigenart von Peter Handkes fiktionalem Frühwerk (1960–1970)*. Frankfurt a. M.: Peter Lang, 1990.

Tanner, Tony. *Adultery in the Novel. Contract and Transgression.* Baltimore: Johns Hopkins University Press, 1979.

Tatar, Maria. *Lustmord. Sexual Murder in Weimar Germany.* Princeton: Princeton University Press, 1995.

Teller, Astro. *Exegesis.* New York: Vintage, 1997.

Theweleit, Klaus. *Buch der Könige. Orpheus und Euridyke.* Frankfurt a. M.: Stroemfeld/Roter Stern, 1988.

Thiher, Allen. "A Theory of Literature or Recent Literature as Theory." *Contemporary Literature* 29, no. 3 (1988): 337–350.

——. *Words in Reflection. Modern Language Theory and Postmodern Fiction.* Chicago: University of Chicago Press, 1984.

Todd, Jane Marie. "Autobiography and the Case of the Signature. Reading Derrida's *Glas*." *Contemporary Literature* 38, no. 1 (1986): 1–19.

Ulmer, Gregory L. "The Object of Post-Criticism." In *The Anti-Aesthetic. Essays on Postmodern Culture,* ed. Hal Foster, 83–110. Port Townsend, Wash.: Bay Press, 1983.

Van den Abbeele, George. *Travel as Metaphor.* Minneapolis: University of Minnesota Press, 1992.

Vogt, Marianne. *Autobiographik bürgerlicher Frauen. Zur Geschichte weiblicher Selbstbewußtwerdung.* Würzburg: Königshausen & Neumann, 1981.

Vosskamp, Wilhelm. "Dialogische Vergegenwärtigung beim Schreiben und Lesen. Zur Poetik des Briefromans im 18. Jahrhundert." *Deutsche Vierteljahrsschrift* (1971): 80–116.

Walkiewicz, E. P. *John Barth.* Boston: Twayne, 1986.

Wallis, Brian, and Marcia Tucker, eds. *Art after Modernism. Rethinking Representation.* New Museum of Contemporary Art ed. Boston: Godine, 1984.

Watt, Ian. *The Rise of the Novel. Studies in Defoe, Richardson and Fielding.* 1957. Harmondsworth/Middlesex: Penguin, 1970.

Waugh, Patricia. *Feminine Fictions. Revisiting the Postmodern.* New York/London: Routledge, 1989.

Weigel, Sigrid. *Die Stimme der Medusa. Schreibweisen in der Gegenwartsliteratur von Frauen.* Reinbek: Rowohlt, 1989.

——. *Topographien der Geschlechter. Kulturgeschichtliche Studien zur Literatur.* Reinbek: Rowohlt, 1990.

——, ed. *Flaschenpost und Postkarte: Korrespondenzen zwischen Poststrukturalismus und Kritischer Theorie.* Köln: Böhlau, 1995.

——. *Ingeborg Bachmann. Hinterlassenschaften unter Wahrung des Briefgeheimnisses.* Wien: Zsolnag, 1999.

Weiss, Walter. "Zur Thematisierung der Sprache in der Literatur der Gegenwart." In *Festschrift für Hans Eggers zum 65. Geburtstag,* ed. Herbert Baches, 669–693. Tübingen: Niemeyer, 1972.

Welsch, Wolfgang. *Unsere postmoderne Moderne.* 2d ed. Weinheim: VCH, 1988.

——. *Wege aus der Moderne. Schlüsseltexte der Postmoderne Diskussion.* Weinheim: VCH, 1988.

Winnes, Friedrich, and Lutz Wohlrab, eds. *Mail Art Scene DDR 1975–1990.* Berlin: Haude and Spener, 1994.

Wittig, Monique. *The Straight Mind*. Boston: Beacon, 1992.
Zemeckis, Robert, dir. *Romancing the Stone*. Los Angeles: Paramount, 1983.
———. *Cast Away*. Los Angeles: Twentieth Century Fox/ Dreamworks, 2000.
Zerull, Ludwig. *Karl Schaper*. Braunschweig: Westermann, 1984.

AUTHOR AND
TITLE INDEX

Abel, Elizabeth, 1
"About Marionette-Theater" ("Über das Marionettentheater") (Kleist), 91
Ader, Dorothea, 143
Adnan, Etel, 122
Adorno, Theodor W., 32, 217
Adultery in the Novel (Tanner), 73
Alice in Wonderland (Carrol), 133–134, 225
Alien (Scott), 227
All the Best (Alles, alles Gute) (Honigmann), 239–240
Altman, Janet Gurkin, 8
Amiel, Jon, 228
Amnesis Art (Suárez-Araúz), xv, 206–211
Andersch, Alfred, 144
Andersen, Gary, 214
Anderson, Hans Christian, 200
Anton Reiser (Moritz), 186, 189–190
Arlart, Ursula, 87–88
Aristotle, 177, 187
Arnim, Bettina von. See Bettina Brentano
Atwood, Margaret, 239
Aufschreibesysteme 1800/1900 (Kittler). See *Writing Systems 1800/1900*
Austen, Jane, 84

Bachmann, Ingeborg, xiv, 8, 19–58
Bantock, Nick, xv, 197–203
Baran, Paul, 214
Barry, Ian, xiii
Barth, John, xiv, 34, 59–95, 115, 207, 220–222

Barthes, Roland, 10–11, 168–169
Baudrillard, Jean, 131
Beauvoir, Simone de, 115
Beethoven, Ludwig van, 54
Bell, Daniel, 214
Bemmann, Hans, xiv, 139–164
Benjamin, Walter, 5, 46,
Bennett, Harve, xiii
Benstock, Shari, 149, 152–153
"Beyond the Pleasure Principle" (Freud), 108–122
Bohrer, Karl Heinz, 3
Bolter, Jay David, 218
Bonnie and Clyde, 231
Bovenschen, Silvia, 149
Bower, Anne, 8
Bradbury, Ray, 140–142
Brandes, Ernst, 9–10
Braun, Michael, 187
Brecht, Bertolt, 199
Brentano, Bettina, 9, 154, 187–188
"Brief des Lord Chandos, Der" (Hofmannsthal). See "Lord Chandos Letter"
Briefe an Pauline (Krüss). See *Letters to Pauline*
Bullock, Sandra, 228
Bürger, Christa, 25
Burney, Fanny, 90
Bush, Vannevar, 218
Butler, Judith, 53, 66

Cabinet of Dr. Caligari, The (Das Kabinett des Doktor Caligari) (Wiene), 146
Cameron, James, 228
Cannon, Danny, xiii

Carnal Knowledge (Gallop), 1
Carrol, Lewis, 133–134, 225
Carte Postale, La (Derrida). See *The Postcard*
Carter, Chris, 209
Case of Franza, The (Der Fall Franza) (Bachmann), 50
Cast Away (Zemeckis), 233–237
Cavell, Stanley, 178–179
Cervantes, Miguel de, 78
Chomsky, Noam, 141
Cixous, Hélène, 1, 7, 11
Clarissa (Richardson), 26, 90
Color Purple, The (Walker), 239
Columbus, Christopher, 126, 128–130, 204
Cool Memories (Baudrillard), 131
Condition Postmoderne, La (Lyotard). See *The Postmodern Condition*
Copycat (Amiel), 228
Costner, Kevin, 231–233
Cronenberg, David, 229–231
Crying Game, The (Jordan), 121
Culler, Jonathan, 65

Dangerous Liaisons (Les Liaisons Dangereuses) (Laclos), 42, 90, 225
D'Arc, Jeanne (Joan of Arc), 210
de Man, Paul, 91, 97
"Dead are silent, The" ("Die Toten schweigen") (Schnitzler), 21
Decken, Godele von der, 45
Defoe, Daniel, 234
Derrida, Jacques, xi, xii, xiv, 16, 33, 59–71, 83–84, 95–122, 140, 186, 207, 220
Dickens, Charles, 84, 139
"Discourse of Others, The" (Owens), 7, 148
Dix, Otto, 6
Döblin, Alfred, 175
Don Quixote (Cervantes), 78
"Dora" (Freud), 48, 131–133
"Dornröschen" (Grimm). See "Sleeping Beauty"
Dostoevsky, Fjodor, 163

Douglas, Michael, 166
Dracula, Count, 102, 162
Duchovny, David, 209
DuPlessis, Rachel Blau, 11
"Du Tout" (Derrida). See *The Postcard*

Eagleton, Terry, 1
Eco, Umberto, 207
Edison, Thomas, 206
"Ein Brief" (Hofmannsthal). See "Lord Chandos Letter"
Elam, Diane, 12
Emmerich, Roland, 229
End of the Road, The (Barth), 87
Engle, Madeleine, 239
Enzensberger, Hans Magnus, 198
"Envoy" ("Envois") (Derrida). See *The Postcard*
Ephron, Nora, xiii, 229
Erwartung (Schönberg). See *Expectation*
Erwin's Bathroom or the Hazardousness of Language (Erwins Badezimmer oder die Gefährlichkeit der Sprache) (Bemmann), xiv, 139–164
Esteban, Bartolomeo, 208
Evelina (Burney), 90
Exegesis (Teller), x, 223–227
eXistenZ (Cronenberg), 229–231
Expectation (Erwartung) (Schönberg), 21

"Facteur de la Vérité, Le" ("The Factor/The Mailman")(Derrida), 122
Faecke, Peter, 198
Fahrenheit 451 (Bradbury), 140–142
Fair and Tender Ladies (Smith), 239
Fall Franza, Der (Bachmann). See *The Case of Franza*
Faust (Goethe), 108, 110
Fechner, Gustav Theodor, 108
Felman, Shoshana, 97
Fichte, Johann Gottlieb, 27
Fiedler, Leslie, 139–140, 153

Fielding, Henry, 84
Fitzgerald, F. Scott, 171–174
Floating Opera, The (Barth), 80
Fontane, Theodor, 140
Ford, John, 165, 180, 194–195
Foucault, Michel, 155
Four Letters of Love (Williams), 239
Fragments d'un discours amoureux
   (Barthes). See *A Lover's Discourse*
Frank, Anne, 49, 205
Frankenstein (Shelley), 225
Freud, Sigmund, xiii, 6, 11, 21, 48,
   70–71, 83, 100, 106–122,
   131–133, 161, 179, 186, 207, 234

Garnett, Tay, 231
Gellert, Christian Fürchtegott, 9–10,
   183
*Geschichte des Fräulein von
   Sternheim, Die* (La Roche). See
   *The History of Lady Sophia
   Sternheim*
Gödel, Kurt, 35
Goethe, Johann Wolfgang von, 9, 26,
   108, 140, 163, 181
Golden Mean, The (Bantock), xv,
   197–203
Good God of Manhattan, The
   (Bachmann), 39
Göttsche, Dirk, 139, 165–166
Gottsched, Luise Kulmus. See Luise
   Adelgunde Victorie Kulmus
Gottsched, Johann Christoph, 9
Graffigny, Françoise de, x, 217
Great Gatsby, The (Fitzgerald),
   171–174
Green Henry (Der grüne Heinrich)
   (Keller), 149–153, 171, 180, 188
Griffin and Sabine (Bantock), xv,
   197–203
Grimm, Gebrüder (Brothers Grimm),
   39, 41, 162, 190
Grosz, George, 6
Group 47 (Gruppe 47), 49, 144, 185
grüne Heinrich, Der (Keller). See
   Green Henry
Gruppe 47. See Group 47

Guide for the Perplexed, A (Levi),
   xiv, 62–71, 122–137
Guide for the Perplexed, The
   (Maimonides), 62, 123, 136
Gulliver (1964), 32
gute Gott von Manhattan, Der
   (Bachmann). See *The Good God
   of Manhattan*

Hamacher, Werner, 66
Handke, Peter, xiv, 165–196
Handmaid's Tale, A (Atwood), 239
Hanks, Tom, 233
"Hänsel und Gretel" (Grimm),
   190–191
Haraway, Donna, 240
Harbou, Thea von, 41, 229
Hayles, Katherine, 15, 219, 223
Heidegger, Martin, 115
Heine, Heinrich, 204
Heisenberg, Werner, 35
Hendrix, Jimmie, 91
Hernadi, Paul, 66, 181
Heuschele, Otto, 9
Higgins, Dick, 198
*History of Lady Sophia Sternheim,
   The (Die Geschichte des Fräulein
   von Sternheim)* (La Roche), 2, 49
Hitchcock, Alfred, 179
Hite, Molly, 12–13
Hitler, Adolf, 204
Høeg, Peter, 199
Hoesterey, Ingeborg, 16
Hofmannsthal, Hugo von, xii, 38,
   137, 211
Hölderlin, Johann Christian Friedrich,
   9
Homer, 25, 192
Honigmann, Barbara, 239–240
Honnefelder, Gottfried, 107
Horacio, Nikoläs, 208
Hutcheon, Linda, 14, 16
Huyssen, Andreas, 6

Iliad, The (Homer), 25
Implied Reader, The (Iser), 62
Independence Day (Emmerich), 229

Irigaray, Luce, 7, 11, 54, 230
Iron Horse (Ford), 180
Iser, Wolfgang, 62, 66
I (still) know what you did last summer (Cannon), xiii, 229

James, Henry, 139
Jameson, Frederic, 217
Jason-Lee, Jennifer, 229
Jean Paul, 9
"Jenseits des Lustprinzips" (Freud). See "Beyond the Pleasure Principle"
Jesenská, Milena, 100
Johnson, Ray, 198, 240
"Joke and its Relation to the Unconscious, The" ("Der Witz und seine Beziehung zum Unbewußten") (Freud), 70–71
Jordan, Neil, 121
Julie or the New Heloise (Julie ou la Nouvelle Heloïse) (Rousseau), 2

Kafka, Franz, 4, 100
Kammer, Manfred, 218
Kamuf, Peggy, 85, 152–153, 168, 240
Kanz, Christine, 19, 32
Kaplan, Caren, 126, 130
Kauffman, Linda S., 8, 66, 240
Kawara, On, 198
Keller, Gottfried, 149–152, 163, 171, 188, 230
Kennedy, Alan, 17
Kittler, Friedrich S., 90, 223
Klauss, Hans, 208
Klein, Yves, 198
Kleist, Heinrich von, 91
Kohn-Waechter, Gudrun, 39–40
Kolbenhoff, Walter, 144
Kraus, Karl, 33, 50
Kristeva, Julia, 21
Krüger, Barbara, 7
Krüss, James, 10, 198
Kubrick, Stanley, 225, 227–228
Kulmus, Luise Adelgunde Victorie, 8–9

kurze Brief zum langen Abschied, Der (Handke). See *Short Letter, Long Farewell*

Lacan, Jacques, 6, 10, 12, 59, 83–84, 96–97, 115–117, 124, 207
Laclos, Choderlos de, 42, 148, 225
Lachmann, Renate, 22
Lämmert, Eberhard, 26
Landow, George P., 220
Lang, Fritz, 41, 229
Langsame Heimkehr (Handke). See *Slow Homecoming*
La Roche, Sophie, 2, 5
Lasker-Schüler, Else, 198
Latour, Bruno, 5, 13, 129, 137
Law, Jude, 229
Leben der schwedischen Gräfin G***, Das (Gellert). See *The Life of Swedish Countess G****
Leiden des jungen Werther, Die (Goethe). See *The Sorrows of Young Werther*
Lennon, John, xiv
Lennox, Sara, 11
Lersch, Barbara, 22
LETTERS (Barth), xiv, 34, 59–95, 115–116, 222
Letters from a Peruvian Woman (Lettres d'une Péruvienne) (Graffigny), x, 217
Letters to Pauline (Briefe an Pauline) (Krüss), 10, 198
Lettres d'une Péruvienne (Graffigny). See *Letters from a Peruvian Woman*
Lettres Portugaises, Les (anonymous). See *Portuguese Letters*
Levi, Jonathan, xiv, 59–71, 122–137, 220–221
Levin, Rahel, 9, 145, 187
Levinson, Barry, 228
Liaisons Dangereuses, Les (Laclos). See *Dangerous Liaisons*
Life of Swedish Countess G***, The (Das Leben der schwedischen Gräfin G*** (Gellert), 183

Lisberger, Steven, 78
Liszt, Franz, 25
Literary Theory. An Introduction
   (Eagleton), 1
"Literature of Exhaustion, The"
   (Barth), 78
"Little Red Ridinghood"
   ("Rotkäppchen und der Wolf")
   (Grimm), 39, 41
"Living On: Borderlines "(Derrida),
   16
Llewellyn, Robert, 208
Loewe, Frederick and Alan Lerner, 39
"Lord Chandos Letter, The" ("Ein
   Brief") (Hofmannsthal), xii, 38,
   211
Lorelei, The, 74
Lost in the Funhouse (Barth), 73–95
Love Letters (Engle), 239
*Lover's Discourse, A (Fragments d'un
   discours amoureux)* (Barthes), 10,
   168–169
Lucinde (Schlegel), 24, 187
Lullus, Raimundus, 218
Luther, Martin, 141
Lyotard, Jean-François, 68–69, 229

MacArthur, Elizabeth, 2, 22, 26
MacGyver (Angus MacGyver)
   (Smithee), xi
Machiavelli, Niccolo, 147
MAIL (Medwed), 239
Mail Art Szene DDR 1975–1990
   (Winnes and Wohlrab), 240
Maimonides, Moses, 62, 123, 136
Malina (Bachmann), xiv, 8, 19–58,
   121
Marcus, Jane, 11
Marx, Karl, 29–30
Mattenklott, Gerd, 2
McCartney, Paul, xiv
McLuhan, Marshall, 204, 217, 221
Medwed, Mahmeve, 239
Medea, 210
Meese, Elizabeth, 12
Metropolis (Lang, von Harbou), 41,
   229–230

Metz, Christian, 178
Miller, Nancy K., 4
Minh-ha, Trinh T., 199
Modernity's Wake, In (Phillipson), 17
Moritz, Karl Phillip, 186, 189–190
My Fair Lady (Loewe, Lerner), 39

Napoleon Bonaparte, 74
Naumann, Barbara, 23–24
Nelson, Ted, 218
Nepus, Cornelius, 25
Net, The (Winkler), 228
Nickisch, Reinhard, 8–10, 99
Nietzsche, Friedrich, 95, 103, 105,
   115, 186, 207
Nineteen Eighty-Four (Orwell), 140
Nolden, Thomas, 66
Nosferatu, 161
Notes from Underground
   (Dostoevsky), 163

Odyssey, The (Homer), 192
*Of Cities and Women (Letters to
   Fawwaz)* (Adnan), 122
Otobiographies (Derrida), 103, 115
Orwell, George, 140
Ovid, 204
Owens, Craig, 17, 148, 151–153, 160

Pamela (Richardson), x, 2, 8, 26, 39
Perfume (Das Parfüm) (Süskind), 199
Petroski, Henry, 225
Phillipson, Michael, 17
Pierrot Lunaire (Schönberg), 19,
   200–201
Plato, 60, 100–102, 108, 112, 115,
   237
Poe, Edgar Allan, 67, 82, 96,
   101–102, 116–117, 219
*Portuguese Letters (Les Lettres
   Portugaises)* (anonymous), xiii, 42,
   239
Postcard, The (La Carte Postale)
   (Derrida), xi, xii, 33, 59–71,
   95–122
Postcards (Proulx), 239
Poster, Mark, 214

Postino, Il (The Postman) (Radford), 231
Postman, The (Costner), 231–233, 236
Postman Always Rings Twice, The (Garnett), 231
Postmodern Condition, The (La Condition Postmoderne) (Lyotard), 68
Post Office of Thanatos (Schaper), 203–206
Prince and the Pauper, The (Twain), 78
Proulx, Annie, 239
"Purloined Letter, The" (Poe), 67, 82, 96, 101–102
Pütz, Peter, 178
Pygmalion, 41, 201

Radford, Michael, 231
"Rapunzel" (Grimm), 49
Rauschenberg, Robert, 198
Redding, Otis, 174
Rehfeldt, Robert, 241
Richardson, Samuel, x–xi, 2, 26, 84, 90, 139
Richter, Hans Werner, 144
Robinson Crusoe (Defoe), 234
Roddenberry, Gene, 219, 228
Romancing the Stone (Zemeckis), xiv–xv, 165–168, 195
Ronell, Avital, 66, 221, 223
"Rotkäppchen und der Wolf" (Grimm). See "Little Red Ridinghood"
Rousseau, Jean-Jacques, xi, 2
Rubin, Gayle, 2

Sabine's Notebook (Bantock), xv, 197–203
Sartre, Jean Paul, 115, 175
Schaper, Karl, xv, 203–206
Scheherezade, 50, 124
Schiller, Friedrich, 9, 144
Schlegel, Dorothea, 5
Schlegel, Friedrich, 23–27, 72, 177, 187, 207
Schlegel-Schelling, Caroline, 25

"Schneewittchen" (Grimm). See "Snow White"
Schnitzler, Arthur, 21
Schnurre, Wolfdietrich, 144
Schönberg, Arnold, 19–21, 200–201
Schwarz, Herta, 187
Scott, Ridley, 227
"Seminar on 'The Purloined Letter'" (Lacan), 96
Serres, Michel, 15–16
Scheherezade, 50
Shelley, Mary, 225
Shining, The (Kubrick), 228
Shiomi, Mieko, 198
Short Letter, Long Farewell (Der kurze Brief zum langen Abschied) (Handke), xiv, 165–196
Signature Pieces (Kamuf), 153
"Sitting on the Dock of the Bay" (Redding), 174
"Sleeping Beauty" (Grimm), 162
Slow Homecoming (Langsame Heimkehr) (Handke), 187
Smilla's Sense of Snow (Frøken Smillas fornemmelse for sne) (Høeg), 199
Smith, Lee, 239
Smithee, Alan, xi
"Snow White and the Seven Dwarves" ("Schneewittchen und die sieben Zwerge") (Grimm), 194, 204
Socrates, 60, 100–102, 115
Sorrows of Young Werther, The (Die Leiden des jungen Werther) (Goethe), 26, 181, 183
Spacks, Patricia Meyer, 11
Sphere (Levinson), 228
Spivak, Gayatri Chakravorty, 186
Staël, Germaine de, 78, 85
Star Trek (Roddenberry), 219, 228
Stein und Flöte und das ist noch nicht alles (Bemmann). See *Stone and Flute*
Stevenson, Robert Louis, 139
Stone and Flute (Stein und Flöte und das ist noch nicht alles) (Bemmann), 143

"Straight Mind, The" (Wittig), 37, 132
Suárez-Araúz, Nicomedes, xiii, xv, 206–211
Suleiman, Susan Rubin, 7
Süskind, Patrick, 199
Symposium, The (Plato), 108, 112

Tanner, Tony, 73
Telephone Book, The (Ronell), 221, 223
Teller, Astro, x, 223–227
Terminator, The (Cameron), 228
"Theses towards a Feminine Aesthetic" (Lachmann), 22
"Thousand-and-One Nights" (Scheherezade), 50 133
Time Trax (Barry, Bennett), xiii
Todesarten Trilogy (Bachmann), 19–58
To Engineer is Human (Petroski), 225
"To Speculate – On Freud" (Derrida). See *The Postcard*
"Toten schweigen, Die" (Schnitzler). See "The Dead are silent"
Tractatus logico-philosophicus (Wittgenstein), 206
"Traffic in Women" (Rubin), 2, 132
Tristan and Isolde (Wagner), 22
Tron (Lisberger), 78
Turner, Kathleen, 166
Twain, Mark, 78
2001: A Space Odyssey (Kubrick), 225, 227

"Über das Marionettentheater" (Kleist). See "About Marionette-Theater"
"Uncanny, The" ("Das Unheimliche") (Freud), 109

Van den Abbeele, Georges, 123, 130, 133

Varnhagen, Karl August, 145
Varnhagen, Rahel. See Rahel Levin
Venue a l'ecriture, La (Cixous), 1
Virilio, Paul, 214
Vostell, Wolf, 198

Wagner, Otto, 69
Wagner, Richard, 22
Walker, Alice, 239
Walkiewicz, E.P., 72
Waugh, Patricia, 13
Weaver, Sigourney, 228
Weibel, Peter, 108
Weigel, Sigrid, 12, 54, 66
Wellek, Rene, 66
Welsch, Wolfgang, 35, 69–71
Wenders, Wim, 165
Wieland, Christoph Martin, 5
Wiene, Robert, 146
Williams, Neall, 239
Winkler, Irwin, 228
Winnes, Friedrich, 240
Wittgenstein, Ludwig, 36, 38, 98, 205–206
Wittig, Monique, 37, 132
"Witz und seine Beziehung zum Unbewußten, Der" (Freud). See "The Joke and its Relation to the Unconscious"
Wohlrab, Lutz, 240
Writing and Sexual Difference (Abel), 1
Writing Systems 1800/1900 (*Aufschreibesysteme 1800/1900*) (Kittler), 223

X-Files, The (Carter), 209

You've got Mail (Ephron), xiii, 229

Zemeckis, Robert, 165–168, 233–237
Zerull, Ludwig, 204
Zeus, 112–113

SUBJECT INDEX

absence,
  as castration, 83
  centrality of (in Lacan), 83
  feminine, 149, 169
  material, 124
  of memory, 102, 206–211,
    216–217
  of the other's voice, 90, 161–164
  of presence, 161, 186–187, 211
address(ing), xi, 43–50, 77, 93, 118,
  160–161, 177, 197–198, 218
addressee, 20, 43–50, 80, 102,
  117–122, 134, 173, 205
adultery and the novel (Tanner), 1–2,
  10, 73
aesthetic,
  act, 186
  code and norms, xi, 10, 126
  discourse of Enlightenment and
    Romanticism, 91
aesthetics,
  antimnemonic, xiii
  epistolary. See epistolary aesthetics
agency,
  concept of, 1–18, 130, 204
  as travel agency, 123–137
Akrostichon, 71, 93
ambiguity, semantic, 145, 159
amnesia, 206–211, 216–17
  and traveling, 132–133
arrival, ix, xii, 37, 80, 185, 194, 214
  d.o.a., xiii
Austria, 19–58
  Austrian past, 28–33
  Austria's relations to Hungary and
    Turkey, 19–58
  Austrian society, 132
authenticity,
  and autobiography, 3, 77–78

and epistolarity, 15, 126–127,
  133, 136, 199–203
and ethnicity, x, 126–127, 133,
  136, 199–203, 223–227
and fiction, x, 1, 126
loss of, 178
author,
  death for the, 119
  female. See women as authors
  as heroine, 167
  and letter-writing, xiii, 98
  as lover of text, 10–11, 167–169
  name, xii, 85
  violation of, 41, 93
authorial,
  control, 219
  voices, 98, 155
authoring system, 66
autobiography. See epistolary fiction
  and autobiography, or letters and
  autobiography
avant-garde, German, 144–145

Bildungsroman, Der deutsche
  (German novel of education),
  140–148
blackmail, 114
bricolage (Deleuze, Guattari,
  Baudrillard), 76
Briefgeheimnis. See privacy of the
  post
Briefsteller (epistolary etiquette)
  alternative to, 16–18
body and language, 142–164
Bosnian/Serbian conflict, 6

cannibalism, 161–164, 185
castration anxiety (Freud), 174–175,
  221

321

center/margin concept, 3, 197–203,
235–237
certified letter, xii
and gender role assignment,
115–122
and the oedipal conflict, xii
chain letters, 59–137
and film, 178–179, 227–237
infinite progression of, 62
linearity of, 62, 84, 105
as narratives, 62
Chaos Theory, 4
chivalric stories/novels, 151–153
Cinema, Classical Hollywood,
171–172, 194–196
cinematic,
code, dominant, 231
realism, 176
cinematography, 91, 165
class division, 126, 191, 215–216
Cold War mentality, 144–145
Colonialism, 201–203
colonization, 130
colonialist, x, 135, 203
colonized Others, x, 201–203
communal readership, 125
communication, 49, 198, 204, 209,
218
model, 186
phallocentric, 117, 158
network, 68
semiotic concept of, 105–106
subconscious, 34
systems, ix, 5, 68
telepathic, 82, 200
theory, 59
compass and reading trajectory,
127–137, 135–137
computer-generated,
novel, 92, 223–227
writing, 91–95, 111, 218–220,
223–227
concrete poetry, 144
correspondences,
as end of communication, 41, 88
and epistolarity, 2, 14, 28, 88, 98,
139–164, 197–203

between letters, fiction, and
theory, 1, 63, 98
and modernism, 5, 57
pattern of, 63, 88
and postmodernism, 57, 197–203
private, 149, 152, 183, 185,
197–203
and translation, 5
Critical Theory, 12
cross-cultural,
interactions, 130
tradition, 122
transmissions, 130, 136,
197–203
cultural,
code, xi
practices, xi, 140, 142
culture,
high and popular, 139–140,
197–211
phallic/phallocentric, 156
culture industry (Adorno,
Horkheimer, Habermas, Jameson),
57
cyborg, 41, 228
communication, 41, 228–231
cyberspace, 132
cybersex, 215

"dead letter," 31, 107, 130, 163
and modernist aesthetic, 31, 64,
106–107
museum, 205
as narrative, 116–122
death of letters and letter-writing, 67
deconstructive practice, 17
delivery, ix, 51, 55, 204–206, 214,
233
departure and arrival, 52, 113, 136,
186, 214
destination, xii, 118, 186, 231
address as, 136, 173, 214
crisis of (Derrida), 95, 214
point of, 131
without address (Derrida), 102
destiny, 21, 231–232
dialogic poetics, 163, 218

dialogue,
   between artist and audience,
      204–206
   emancipated, 145
   on fascism, 29–33, 204–206
   flash-back, 171
   German-Jewish, 145
   mutuality in, 93
   with postmodernism,
      poststructuralism, and
      feminism, 148
   between self and other, 24,
      153–164, 197–203
   technique, 101
diary. See letters and diary
differance (Derrida),
   and letters, 104–105
   between send-off and arrival, 37,
      111
difference,
   and feminism, 12–18, 152–153
   and oneness, 180–181
digital, born, 216
discourse,
   of desire and epistolarity, x, 2, 40,
      49
   of difference, 160
   of the Other, 153–164, 201–203
   of the post, 55, 67
distribution, 48
Dionysian festivals, 21
documentary fiction, 144
DNA, 230
   and design of novel, 86

economy of desire, 166
ectogenesis, 225
electronic mail (e-mail)
   aesthetics of, 213–237
   and epistolarity, ix, 4, 197–203,
      208–209, 213–237
   in film, 227–237
   in the novel, 197–203, 223–227
   and technology, 208–209,
      213–237
entropic theories, 84

Entwicklungsroman, Der deutsche
   (German novel of development),
      171, 175
envelope, 116–122, 183–184,
      197–211, 215
epistolary,
   aesthetics, 48–49
   art, 32
   character(s), 71–95
   cloning, 60
   conventions, 1–18, 224
   correspondence, 28, 60, 88, 102,
      144, 148–164, 168, 223–227
   criticism, x, 1, 3, 104, 120
   culture, xii
   delay, 21, 165–196, 206, 208
   device, 165
   discourse, 1, 154, 163
   economy, 139
   exchange, 105, 117, 139
   fiction
      aesthetics of, 63
      and authenticity, x, 1–2,
         126–127, 133, 136,
         197–211
      and autobiography, 4, 77–78,
         103, 139–164, 173, 218
      as autofiction, 77, 197–203,
         223–227
      and cinematic writing, 164–196
      in computer age, 217–227
      economy/economics of, 185,
         190, 215–216
      and femininity, 9, 149–164
      and fragments, 26, 33, 54–55,
         182–189
      and gender, xi, 1–2, 19–58,
         116–122, 149–164,
         197–203, 223–227
      gendered history of, 149–153,
         197–203, 223–227
      genesis of, 163–164, 197–203,
         223–227
      and genre, 2, 14, 19–20, 37,
         165–196
      and gossip (Spacks), 76, 154
      history of, 1–18, 42, 184

epistolary fiction *(continued)*
  as hybrid, 11
  and intertextuality, 1–18,
    23–28, 51–58, 63–71, 219
  and language, 8, 141–164,
    165–196
  and liminal experiences and
    epressions. See liminality
  and literature, xi, 8, 148–153
  and mail-orders, 23, 41,
    148–153, 206–211
  as mediation, 8, 22, 182–196
  and "natural origin"
    ("Natürlichkeit"), 1–3
  as reform literature, 8,
    141–148, 153–164
  as rhapsody, 19–58
  and Romanticism, 23–28,
    165–196
  and screenplay, 91, 171–196
  and subjectivity, x, 4, 140–164,
    165–196, 197–203,
    223–227
  and theory, 63, 118, 217–223
  as will or testament, 20, 94–95,
    120, 122
  form, 20, 22, 76, 122, 144, 149,
    184, 208
  framing devices, 169, 226–227
  genre, 14, 75, 121, 148–153, 181,
    195
  harmony, 116, 160–164
  insert, 197–199
  intercourse, 118–122, 163
  intersubjectivity, 153–159,
    165–196, 197–203
  machine, 99
  medium, 36
  manner, mode, strategy, technique,
    xi, 4, 14, 44, 75, 148, 232
  moment, positions, scenes,
    situations, 20, 33, 51, 186
  novel, 2, 9, 19, 44, 60, 77, 85–95,
    105, 107, 139–140, 148–153,
    155, 165, 183
  partners, 102
  phrase, 100

poetics, 52, 66, 187
prototype, 44
relationships, ix
rhapsody, 19–58
romances, 230, 151–153
structure, 27, 55, 129, 181
theory, 3, 104, 106
time-lapse, 209, 237
tradition, 145, 203
transcription, 89–95, 101–122,
    125
transmission, 136–137
travelogues, 137, 163, 169, 181,
    197–203
treasure map, 165
writing sample, 183–185
epistolarity (Altman), 9, 181
  and authenticity, 126–127, 133,
    136
  and creation of magnetic field, 37,
    52
  and echo-effect, 71–95, 153–164
  "extravagance of" (MacArthur),
    22, 26
  and film, 91, 165–196, 227–237
  and gender, 8, 10, 37–38,
    223–227
  and genealogy, 90, 145, 223–227
  and identity formation, 34, 37–38,
    145–148, 223–227
  and immediacy, 1–18, 36, 126,
    144, 169, 173, 189, 195, 201,
    208, 213, 237
  metonymy of (Lachmann/Lersch),
    22
  and popular culture, 126,
    139–164, 197–203, 213–237
  and postmodernism, 12–18,
    68–71, 103
  and the discourse of desire, 104,
    197–203
  and the novel, 75, 124, 139–164,
    165–196, 223–227
  and remembrance, 19–58, 90,
    175–176, 182–194, 206–211,
    216–217
  and rhapsody, 19–58

structural representation of
(Handke), 165
and subjectivity, x, 145–148,
169–196, 223–227
essentialism, biological, 9
essentialist fictions, 43, 229
exegesis, xi, 223–227

fairy tales, 39–43, 46, 49, 110, 144,
162–164, 190–191
Fascism, 28–33, 143
Gleichschaltung under, 29
and language, 142–148
practice of, 142–143
resistance against, 143
female,
audience, 149–153
desires, 127, 149–164, 230
genre, 1–18, 42–43
as "lack," 235
letters, 48
lineage, 124–137
narrative, 26
as Other, 115, 201–203, 235
reader, 56, 151–153
sexuality 151–164, 168, 230
subject, 43–44
tradition, 148
virtues, 150
voice, 11, 19, 21–23, 28, 43, 51,
54, 56, 76, 148, 153–164, 226
feminine, 155
aesthetic, 11
ending, 20, 54, 57
fictions, 55
manners and mannerism, 44
monstrous, 6
text and hybridity, 11
and the trivial, 139–164
femininity,
as difference, 7, 153–164
and epistolarity, 8, 43, 148–153,
197–203
and mass culture, 6, 148–164,
197–203
as the Other, 11, 153–164,
201–203
and voracious appetite, 151–153

feminism,
and borders, 6
and difference, 6, 7
and ethnic authenticity, x
and fragmentation, 6
and hybridity, 6
and liminality. See liminality
and identity, 6
and postmodernism, 7, 12–18,
151–153, 164, 211
and sexual identity, 6, 7
and solidarity, 30
and utopia, 45
"Vive-la-Difference," 164
feminist,
criticism and theory, 1–18, 67
epistolary criticism, 1–18
essentialism, 51
fantasy, 42
ideals, 163
mail-order, 23
postmodernism, 7, 12–18
poststructuralist criticism, 7,
12–18, 51
sexual/textual criticism, 9
ficticiousness, 77
fiction,
and authenticity, xii, 133, 136
of correspondence, 17
of fiction, 163
of gender and genre, 14, 156
of letters, ix, 14, 167
and theory, 64
fictional,
travelogues, 122, 169, 173, 197–203
universe, 173
fictionalized fantasy, 80, 155–164
fictive,
imagination, 150
origination, 75
film-frame, 177
fin-de-siècle, xiii, 38, 132, 218
food metaphors, 151–153
form letters, 79–80
fort/da,
in Derrida's *The Postcard*, 69–71,
95–122

fort/da (continued)
    in Freud's "Beyond the Pleasure
        Principle," 69–71, 95–122
fragment, 26, 50, 52, 54, 182–189
Frauenopfer (woman-sacrifice)
    (Kittler), 135

gender,
    crossing, 50–58, 117
    designations, 53, 117, 160
    gender/genre system, 3, 12, 14, 19,
        28, 45, 85, 112, 116, 150–153,
        169
    history, 120
    relay, 121
    switch, 123, 132
    transmission of, 133
    trouble (Butler), 53
gendered,
    hermeneutic position, 117, 201
    memory, 20, 206–211
    sex, 151
genealogy, 71–137, 223–227
genre(s),
    boundaries, 187
    contamination of, 67
    epistolary. See epistolary genre
    genre-specific functions, 84, 208
    intergeneric, 165
    "law of." See "law of genre"
    and mainstream fiction, 51
    mix, 148, 158
    nonliterary, 65
    reproductive potential of, 166–196
    transformations, 19, 195–196
German,
    Expressionism, 6
    fairy tales, 110
German-Jewish dialogue, 145
Germany,
    1848 revolution, 147
    German Past, 28–33, 189–192,
        204–206
    postwar German society, 28
    Vergangenheitsbewältigung
        (coming to terms with the past),
        28–33

Geselligkeit (romantic sociability),
    106
Gleichklang, Der (harmony/accord),
    160–164
grammar, generative transformative
    (Chomsky), 141–148

heterosexuality, 132, 156–159, 215,
    225
"history from below," 129
Holocaust, The, 20, 28–33
hybridity, 5, 11, 39, 55, 137
hypertext (Landow), 217–227
hysteric body (Freud), 132–133,
    158–159, 175

identification,
    gender-role, xii, 151–153, 155,
    sexual, xii
immediacy, ideal of, 1–18, 36, 144,
    169, 182, 189, 195, 208, 213,
    221, 237
individuality, struggle for, 147
information, 48
    as commodity (Bell), 214
Inserate, Die (inserts/advertisements),
    197–211
interdisciplinary, 108
Internet, xv, 208, 213–237
intersexual dialectic, 117–122
interstices, 7, 25, 194
intertextual,
    differance (Derrida), 117–122
    gesture, 107
    indeterminacies, 62, 68
    journey, 108
    lovemaking, 168
    markers, 107
    mechanism, 64
    writing practice, 64
intertextuality, 63–71, 107, 109,
    169–196, 203
    and decontextualization, 64–71
    as deferred internalization process,
        109
    and dissemination, 64
    grammatological aspect of, 111

and legacy, 64–137, 223–227
and multimedia, 71, 219, 222
as reference system, 63–71
residue of, 122

Jewish,
  Cabbala, 123
  folklore, 123
  history, 122–137
  mythology, 122–137
  victimization, 124
  resistance, 124
Jews of the Diaspora, 125–137

Kahlschlag Realismus (postwar
  German *tabula rasa* realism),
  144–145

language,
  crisis, 145–148, 165–166,
  critique, 140–148
  games (Wittgenstein, Lyotard), 34,
    63, 70–72, 155
  and literature, 8
  philosophy, 141, 155, 185
  post office of, 36
  relativity of, 146
  of the unconscious, 67, 106, 111
"law of genre" (Derrida), 3, 18, 66, 149
"Law of the Father" (Lacan),
  134–135, 157–159, 168
legacy,
  of modernism, 63–71, 203
  as postmodern phenomenon, 119,
    223–227
  of poststructuralism and
    deconstruction, 95–122
  of realist fiction, 72, 197–203
legitimacy,
  of grand narratives, 164, 203
  hermeneutic, 142
  and letters, xi, xii
  and prefaces, xi, xii
letter/letters,
  as artifact, 107
  and amnesia, xiii, 132–133,
    206–211, 216–217

and autobiography, xii, 28–29,
    77–78, 103, 139–164, 173, 218
  as composition exercise, 183–184
  content of, 83, 204, 214, 217, 235
  as deadly bulletin, 167
  as device, 107, 165
  and diary, 139–164
  as dispatch, xii, 188
  double fictionality of (Brown),
    1–18, 127, 208
  and dreams, 33–58, 70–71,
    184–187, 190–192
  as editions of editions, 125–137
  emblematic nature of, 80–81
  as epistolary fiction, xi
  essay-character of, 187
  express, 185
  extraliterary nature of, xii
  and fairy tales, 39–43, 46, 139–164
  as filmic relay-system, xv, 165–196
  as fragment, 32, 50, 52, 182–189
  as genre, xi
  history of, 1–18, 42, 184
  as intertexts, 50–58, 63, 219
  of language, 173
  on letters, 44
  linearity of, 84, 105
  and literature, 1–18, 19–58
  as literature, 148–153
  love, 169
  as mail-art, 197–211
  and material presence, 71, 80, 111
  and mail-order, xi
  as medium of immediacy, 1–18,
    36, 126, 144, 169, 173, 189,
    195, 208, 213, 237
  as memory traces, xiii, 63, 189–92,
    206–211
  as message, 107, 165–170
  as missive, xii
  narratological functions of, 84, 87
  as personae of postmodern novel,
    71–95, 173
  personal, 141
  as political pamphlets, 146, 163
  and popular culture, 139–164,
    197–203

letter/letters *(continued)*
    privacy of, 100
    as psychological baggage, xiii
    as pure signifier (Lacan), 117
    renaissance of, x, 14
    from the subconscious, 175
    surface of, 103
    throwing (away) of, 49, 184
    and transience, 106
    as vehicle, 186–196
    writing of, xi, 43–50, 60, 183–184
Liebeskunst, Die (art of love)
    (Clauss), 140
liminality, 6, 54, 175–176, 178–196
limpieza de sangre (clarity of blood
    letter), 129–130
linearity, 84, 105, 176, 190–191
    resistance to, 73
    return to, 72
"linguistic turn." See
    poststructuralism
literary criticism, 77
    as capitalist economy, 166
    challenges for, 3, 63
    and cultural practices, xi
    as fiction, 81
    and poetological reflections, xi
    as spectacle, 121
    and theory, 1, 66
literary critics, xii, 1
"looking glass" ideology, 177
location, sense of, 169–173

mail-art, xv, 197–211
mailbags, 204
mailbox, 87–89, 167, 184
    as central consciousness, 89
    as collection box of mail-order,
    184
mail carrier, 48, 52, 54–55, 100, 205
mailing, 183–184
    code, 112, 162
    list, 47
    process, 46–47, 83, 107
    route, 51, 118, 121
    system, 4, 48, 52, 67, 110, 151,
    192

mail/male bonding, 115
mailman, 70, 101, 184
    and detective, 101
    as *facteur* (Derrida), 104
mail-order, x, xii, 233–237
    as clearinghouse, 24
    collaboration with, 55
    contemporary, xi, 14
    of critical discourse, 57
    gendering of, xiii, 3, 48, 135,
    206–211
    heterosexual, 38–43, 148–159
    imperial, 50, 197–203, 233–237
    industry, 202, 206–211, 233–237
    mail-ordered bride, 163
    as male-dominated discourse, xi,
    43, 48, 54, 135, 148–164,
    206–211
    manual, 148–153
    modernist, ix, 21, 46, 135
    patriarchal, 46
    postmodernist, ix
    as woman's product, 60, 135, 163
male,
    autobiographical discourse,
    139–164, 169–196
    fantasy, 155–164
    desires, 151, 156–159
    lineage, 124–137
    reader, 151–153
    subject and subjectivity, 155,
    169–175
    voice, 76, 153–164
Markov Chain, 63
masculinity,
    as effort at and effect of
    transsexualization, 175
mass culture, 6, 17, 139–164, 197–203
materiality of the signifier (Derrida),
    97, 111, 197
meaning,
    erasure of, 22
    lack of, 83
    and subject, 95
media, xiii
    studies, 67, 213–237
    war, 95

mediation, ix
  epistolary, 8, 165, 199, 204, 229
  ideologies of, 8
  intergeneric, 165
  intertextual, 8, 192, 204
  politics of, 8
  process of, 169, 202
  pure, 177
  structural, 193
"medium is the message, the"
  (McLuhan), 204, 232
memory traces, 131, 182–196,
  206–211
messages, ix, 73, 81, 173, 198–199,
  in bottles, 79–95
  decoding of, 167, 204–206
  as exchange of information, x, 15,
    231–237
  obstruction of, 28–33, 100,
    204–206
  prefabricated, 185–186, 198
  secret, 103, 185
Microsoft Windows, 213
mind/body dichotomy, 4, 223–227
Minitel Systems, French, 215
model,
  books, 149
  letters, 183
modern,
  discourse, 99
  literature, xiii, 1–18, 222
  mailing system, 27
modernism,
  and epistolary production of the
    metaphysics of Being, 32, 207
  and postmodernism, xi–xv, 51,
    56–58, 59–71, 203
  "unfinished project of"
    (Habermas), 72
modernist, ix
  aesthetics, x, 203
  archive and museum, 204–206
  closure, 74–95
  discourse, 205
  gesture, 140
  humanism, 205
  project, 79, 201, 208

travel itinerary, 128, 201–203
  unconscious, 98
modernity, x, 217
  crisis of, 164
Moebius Strip (Barth), 88, 94
monologue,
  internal, 203
  in speech and writing, 27, 88–95,
    159–164
Moralische Wochenschriften (moral
  journals), 149
mother tongue, 148, 155
multimedia, 213–237
music and text, 19–58, 174–175,
  200–201

narrative(s),
  closure, 36, 62, 74–95
  of desire, 168
  linearity, 105
  master (or grand), 3, 4, 123, 129,
    164
  of master and slave, 35
  novelistic, 148
  politics of adoption, 136
  position, 33
  strains, 87
  strategies, 12, 18, 189
  voice(s), split, 169–196
narratological,
  categorizations, 19
  function, 84, 87
  genre-specific demands, 76
  matrix, 124
  methods and practices, 148, 169
  self-reflexivity, 2
  sequence, xii
  system, 34–35, 63, 193
naturalness ("Natürlichkeit"), 1–3, 10
networks, 5, 65, 68, 137
New Criticism, 141
novel,
  epistolary. See epistolary novel
  postwar German, 146
  as theory, 65, 107
numerology, 86–95
numbers and letters, 90–95

objects trouvés, xv, 203, 206
Orientalism (Said), 133, 201–203
Orientalist imagery, 50
origin and origination, 176, 208,
    216
  and destination, 53
  of language, 101
  of sexuality, 112
originality, 197, 201, 203
Oxford Postcard, The (Derrida),
    60–71, 95–122

Pavlovian response, 180
Phallic/phallologocentric law. See
    "Law of the Father"
philosophical and epistemological
    crisis, 52
phonocentrism, 71–95
Pleasure Principle, The (Freud),
    67–71, 95–122
poetics,
  epistolary. See epistolary poetics
  normative, 18
  of the 'post', 148
  postmodern, 12–18
poetological,
  axioms, 178, 187–188
  program, 177
politics, linguistic, 145–148
polyauctorial frames in epistolary
    novel, 59–137, 155, 226–227
polylogue, 140
polyphony, 13, 27, 57, 129
popular culture,
  and fascistic practice, 142–143
  and letters. See letters and popular
    culture
  gendering of, 6
pornography debate, 222–223
postal,
  code, 44–45, 68, 70, 103, 117,
    137, 168, 188, 204, 215
  crisis, 52, 57, 214, 233–237
  directions, 69
  economy, 69
  principle, 67, 102, 114, 116, 122
  psychic system, 67, 99

regulations, 36
relay, 106, 111
route, xiv–xv, 4, 55, 83, 120, 136,
    165
service, 205, 214, 227–237
stamps, 36, 197
station, 111
system, 99, 116
transfer, 53
universe, 202
value, 46
war, 205
postcard and postcards, 95–122,
    197–206
  "apocalypse" (Derrida), 102
  content of, 100
  correspondence, 120, 197–211
  as intertext, 120
  postcardization (Derrida), 96, 103,
    122
  public arena of, 100
  surface of, 100, 197
  theme, 117
postcolonial, 203
  studies, 4, 17
postmodern, ix–x
  agenda, 199
  art and artist, 197–211
  condition (Lyotard), 7, 16, 68
  controversy, 139
  crisis, ix
  culture, 218, 229–237
  epistolarity, 103, 196, 197–203,
    223–227
  fiction, 78
  hybridity, 5
  literature, xiii
  parody, 129
  perplexity, 129
  philosophy, 147
  poetics, 12–18, 96, 196
  signifying practices, 13
  turn (Hassan), 66
  undecidability, 105
  utopia/dystopia, 6
postmodernism,
  and amnesia, 132, 206–211

and epistolarity, 12–18, 51–58, 69–71, 95, 139–164, 165–196
and feminism. See feminism and postmodernism
as modernist phenomenon, 69, 203, 211
as perfection of modernism, 57, 203
revolt against, 147–148
post office, 36, 46, 69–71, 204–206, 214
of the psyche, 114
postscript, 79, 83, 90, 239–241
poststructuralism, x, 4, 12–18, 23, 65, 141, 146, 178
and Critical Theory, 12
passing of, xi
preface,
and gender, xi
as genre, xi
extraliterary nature of, xii
and letter-writing, xi
and poetological reflection, xi
preoedipal,
bisexuality (Freud), 132
glossolalia, 134
presence,
as absence, 131, 161, 211
displacement of, 83, 111
symbolic, 124
unattainability of, 186, 193
privacy of the post, ix, 36, 39, 41, 52, 104, 205
private correspondence and writings. See correspondence, private
private and public spheres. See public and private spheres
proper name, 77, 103
public and private spheres, x, 2, 116, 146, 148–153, 203, 208, 215, 221
purity laws, 142–143

queer studies, 67
queer theory,
and epistolary delivery, 37
in drag, 121
quest,
capitalist, 167–168
modernist, 201
phallocentric, 168–169

race, 191, 215–216, 233–237
transmission of, 133
race and gender, 50, 201
radio plays, 144
rape,
maternal-technological, 230
as sexual contract, 156–159
reader,
bad (Derrida), 95–122
as mail carrier, 205–206
ideal, 167
reading pattern, 87, 167–169
reception, 51
theory, 4, 6
reenactment (Barth), 71–95
reference system,
of language, 69
between texts and works, 63–64
repetition-compulsion (Freud), 109
replenishment (Barth), 72, 81
representation,
crisis of, 4
critique of, 7
literary, 149
of women. See Woman
return to sender, 118, 227–237
revolutionaries, linguistic, 142–148
rhapsody,
and cacophony, 22
and discourse, 27
and epistolarity, 19–58
of letters, 19–58
Romantic(ism),
child-woman in, 154
contemporary, nostalgic, 177
exaggeration, 150
poetics, 187–196
politics, 147, 163
salon culture, 144–145
spirit, 154
and utopian desires, 164

romantization,
  of epistolary form, 1–18, 139–164,
    165–196, 227–237
  of sexually and racially Other, 39,
    160–164, 201–203

sanctity of the mail. See privacy of the
  post
science-fiction tradition, 140–148
self,
  analysis, 100
  assurance, 174
  dialogue between self and other,
    24, 88–95, 117
  deconstructed, xi,
  deconstruction, 100
  division of, 117, 171–196, 206–211
  dissolution of, 174–177, 210
  fictions of stable, unified, 56
  forgetting, 174, 209–211
  hypnosis, 161
  identity, 105, 130, 159–164, 203
  modernist, 155
  as Other, 59–95, 181, 197–203,
    206–211
  reflexivity of language, 148
  reformed, 162
  unified, 181
semantic laws, 142
semiotic,
  assignment, 167, 170
  system, 167
sender, 117–122
  message, receiver, ix, 20, 31, 100,
    103, 105–106, 178
send-off and arrival, ix, 37, 185, 194,
  207, 218
sequentiality, indeterminable
  ("Nachträglichkeit"), 218
seriation (Hayles), 213–237
sex,
  in relation to mediated
    representation, 172
sex-gender,
  positions, 77, 151–153
  system (Rubin), 2, 50, 60, 139,
    151
sexual orientation, 53, 132

sexual-political dichotomy, 156
sexual-textual order (Moi), 40, 120,
  155
sign, signifier, signified, and
  signification, xii, 82, 151, 158,
  176
signatures, xi, (Kamuf) 85–95, 100,
  118, 218
simulacrum (Baudrillard), 141
spacing, 97
Spanish Jews under Ferdinand and
  Isabella, 129–137
subject,
  concept of, 130, 236–237
  displacement of, 3, 36, 56, 60, 117
  formation, 20, 59–60, 223–227
  gendered, 3, 20, 117, 197–203,
    223–227
  postmodern philosophy of, 56, 95,
    218–219
subjectivity,
  and epistolarity, x, 2, 22, 207,
    219, 237
  and intersubjectivity, 24, 65, 79,
    109, 117–122, 155–159,
    173–175, 219
  and objectivity, 24, 225
structuralism, 4, 141, 178
structuralist linguistics, 59, 65
symbolic order (Lacan), 134–135
systems theory, 68

Telecommunication, 213–237
telematic, 119, 129
telephone, 82–95, 111, 221–223
textual,
  legacies, 63, 95–122
  order, 161
  residues, 63, 116–122
textual/sexual. See sexual-textual
  order.
theoretical,
  discourse (Derrida), 102
  studies (Freud), 113
theory as novel, 65, 107
Third Reich, 21, 28–33, 205
threshold experience and metaphor,
  182–196

Tienamin Square, 215
topography of time-space, 71, 172, 178, 182
"Traffic in Women" (Rubin), 8, 53–58, 132–133
transcription, 193
transmission, 15, 123, 133, 135–136
transparency (between world of objects and language, of language and literature),
    illusion and ideology of, xii, 185, 221
    loss of, 179
    misconceptions about, 144, 182
transsexual metamorphosis, 175
traumatic experiences, 114
travel,
    and dream, 131–133, 185–191
    guide, 62–71, 122–137
        as novel, 137
    letters, 136–137
    as metaphorical commonplace, 130
    narrative, 123
    as quest, 130
    as trope of modernity, 126–137
travelogue, 123, 169, 173, 187, 197–203
triviality,
    and postmodernity, 6, 139–164
    and femininity, 6, 139–164
typewriter, 89, 213, 218
    discourse of (Kittler), 90, 218, 223
typography, 71

Unconscious,
    gendered, 21
    as language, 59
    as rhapsody, 21

vampire as epistolary copyist, 161–164
Verfremdungseffekt, Der (alienation effect) (Brecht), 199
Versprechen, Das (promise/slip of tongue), 157–159
Vienna, 19–58
viruses, e-mail, 213–237

voyeuristic,
    lovemaking, 150
    secrecy of modernist discourse, 205, 226

water metaphor (Barth), 81
West, decentering of the, 201
Western,
    Christian hegemony, 123
    philosophy, 101
World War I and II, 21
Woman,
    as allegory of Death and the City, 175
    as allegory of modernity, 95, 201, 211
    as "central metaphor" (Suárez-Araúz), 211
    constitution and configuration of, 5
    and "emotional" reading practices, 155–164
    as epistolary novel, 71–95
    as exchange medium, 116, 132
    as figure of epistolary fiction, 115, 201
    as hermeneutic intermediary, 151
    as letter, 169
    as mediator between 'good' and 'bad' technology, 229
    as metaphor for undecidability, 116
    as "Other," 201–203
    as reminder of permeable process of mediation, 213, 230
    as representation, 116, 152
    representation of, 6
    as *Verfahren* (method), 120
women's,
    lives as fictions, 151
    movements, 3, 6, 29
    solidarity, 53
women as authors, 1–18, 19–58, 60, 127, 162–164, 210, 223–227

Zustellung, Die (delivery/distribution/blocking), 48, 56, 204–206